Software Testing with Visual Studio Team System 2008

A comprehensive and concise guide to testing your software applications with Visual Studio Team System 2008

Subashni.S, PMP

N Satheesh Kumar

BIRMINGHAM - MUMBAI

SHROFF PUBLISHERS & DISTRIBUTORS PVT. LTD.

Mumbai Bangalore Chennai Kolkata New Delhi

Software Testing with Visual Studio Team System 2008

Originally published by Packt Publishing Ltd., 32 Lincoln Road, Olton, Birmingham, B27 6PA, UK.
Production Reference: 1121208 ISBN 978-1-847195-58-6 www.packtpub.com

Cover Image by Parag Kadam (paragvkadam@gmail.com)

Printing History:

First published: December 2008

First Indian Reprint: February 2009

ISBN 10: 81-8404-687-1

ISBN 13: 978-81-8404-687-8

Published by **Shroff Publishers and Distributors Pvt. Ltd.** C-103, MIDC, TTC Industrial Area, Pawane, Navi Mumbai 400 705, Tel: (91 22) 2763 4290, Fax: (91 22) 2768 3337, e-mail: spdorders@shroffpublishers.com. Printed at Decora Book Prints Pvt. Ltd., Mumbai.

Credits

Authors

Subashni S

N Satheesh Kumar

Reviewer

Stefan Turalski

Senior Acquisition Editor

Douglas Paterson

Development Editor

Ved Prakash Jha

Technical Editor

Bhupali Khule

Copy Editor

Sumathi Sridhar

Editorial Team Leader

Akshara Aware

Project Manager

Abhijeet Deobhakta

Project Coordinator

Rajashree Hamine

Indexer

Monica Ajmera

Proofreader

Camille Guy

Production Coordinator

Rajni R. Thorat

Cover Work

Rajni R. Thorat

About the Authors

Subashni.S, holds a Bachelors Degree in Computer Science Engineering and has around 10 years of experience in software development and testing life cycle, project, and program management. She is a certified PMP (Project Management Professional) and CSTM (Certified Software Test Manager). She started her career as DBA in Oracle 8i technology and later developed many software applications using Borland software products for a multinational company based in Chennai, India and then moved to Bangalore, India. She is presently working for a multinational company in the area of Project Management for developing and testing projects. Currently working for one of the top multinational companies headquartered at Dallas, Texas and placed at a MNC client in Austin, Texas.

I would like to thank my husband for helping me in co-authoring and supporting me in all the ways to complete this book. I also would like to thank my other family members and friends for their continuous support in my career and success.

N. Satheesh Kumar holds a Bachelor's degree in Computer Science Engineering and has around 12 years of experience in software development life cycle, project, and program management. He started his career developing software applications using Borland software products in a company based in India. He then moved to the UAE where he continued developing applications using Borland Delphi and customizing Great Plain Dynamics (now known as Microsoft Dynamics) for an automobile sales company. He later moved to India again, spending three years in designing and developing application software using Microsoft products for a top multinational company. A couple of years were also spent in Project Management and Program Management activities. Now he works as a Technical Architect for a top retail company based in the United States. He works with the latest Microsoft technologies and has published many articles on LINQ and other features of .NET. He has also authored *LINQ Quickly* for Packt Publishing.

I would like to thank my wife for helping me in co-authoring and supporting me in all the ways to complete this book. I also would like to thank my other family members and friends for their continuous support in my career and success.

Table of Content

Preface

The first time we looked at the Visual Studio Team System 2008, we realized that there were lot of features that used to be different individual products on their own, that were very well integrated, and readily available under a single IDE. Some of these were available with earlier versions of Visual Studio, but this version is tightly integrated with the Team Foundation Server.

Microsoft Visual Studio Team System 2008 suite contains several tools that satisfy the needs of developers, testers, managers, and architects. Not only are the tools available, but they are also well integrated to collect information at every stage of the project life cycle and to maintain this information under one roof. The Visual Studio Team System 2008 is supported by Team Foundation Server, which is the central repository system that provides version control, process guidance and templates, automated build, manual and automated testing, bug tracking, work item tracking, and reporting.

Visual Studio Team System 2008 Team Suite provides all of the integrated tools for different team members. There are different editions for specific team members, including Architecture Edition, Test Edition, Database Edition, and Development Edition. This book covers the tools for the test and development phase of a project and for reporting the project status.

This book will help developers to get to know how to use the tools for automated unit testing, code analysis, and profiling to test their own code and to find out the performance and quality of their code. Testers will learn more about creating the web test, load test, and manual test, to determine the quality of the product, and also to raise defects and assign them to the developers for fixing.

VSTS provides different tools, such as the Test List Editor, Test View, and Test Configuration user interfaces, to easily manage the multiple tests created during the project life cycle. This book covers in-depth details of creating and maintaining different test types using VSTS.

What This Book Covers

Chapter 1, Software Testing and Visual Studio Team System 2008—This chapter gives an overall introduction to software testing and the types of testing involved in the software development life cycle (SDLC). It also provides an introduction to the different tools available in Visual Studio Team System 2008 to support different testing types for the SDLC.

Chapter 2, Unit Testing—This chapter explains the testing tool used by developers to make sure that the code produces the expected result. Creating unit tests, generating code and different assert statements, and the types used for testing are explained in detail in this chapter. Various attributes used for differentiating classes from test classes and methods from test methods, along with the initializing and cleaning methods are also explained in detail in this chapter.

Chapter 3, Web Testing—This chapter walks us through the tool used for testing web applications developed using .NET. This tool is used for recording a test scenario and then testing it with sample data from different data sources. Applying validation and extraction rules, adding data sources, and adding transactions are explained in detail using a sample application in Visual Studio Team System 2008. Some of the features, such as adding Plug-ins, parameterizing the web server, and running and debugging the web tests, are covered in this chapter.

Chapter 4, Advanced Web Testing—Generating coded web tests from recorded web tests and creating coded web tests using the Visual Studio Team System 2008 tool are explained in detail and with examples. Some of the other advanced topics covered in this chapter include adding dynamic parameters, adding rules to the coded web test, creating custom rules, and running the coded web test.

Chapter 5, Load Testing—This chapter explains how to use unit testing or web testing, and how to simulate a realistic scenario such as the number of concurrent users that have different browsers and different network speed, and are accessing the system from multiple locations. This testing collects the application performance and stability data in different scenarios, and is used for analyzing this data in order to scale the application for better performance.

Chapter 6, Manual, Generic, and Ordered Test—This chapter explains different tools that support testing an application manually, without using an automated testing tool. In the case of multiple interdependent tests, we can easily define the tests to be run in a specific order so that the dependent tests don't fail. Visual studio supports all these including Generic and Smoke tests which are explained here.

Chapter 7, Managing and Configuring Tests—Even though we have a lot of testing types and tools, managing these tests is sometimes a very difficult task. This chapter explains the easy way to organize the tests into lists, to enable and disable tests, configure the tests and test runs, view the tests using the Test View window and the test list editor, and run the tests in Visual Studio Team System 2008.

Chapter 8, Deploying and Running the tests—Once we are ready with the required type of test for the application, we have to deploy it on the test machines, run the test application, and collect the results for analysis. There are multiple ways of deploying the application and running the application using some of the advanced features provided by Visual Studio Team system 2008, and these are explained in detail in this chapter.

Chapter 9, Command Line—There are different ways of running a test based on the environment and requirements. In some situations, we may need a test to be run from the command line without using the user interface. The test works in the same way, but it runs without any user interaction. This chapter explains the different command line options and parameters used for running a test using command line commands.

Chapter 10, Working with Test Results—The main objective of running the tests is to collect the results and analyze them to correct any application errors, to make sure that the test is producing the expected result, and to increase the performance and stability of the application. This chapter explains in detail how to look at the test results and code coverage, and publish the test results.

Chapter 11, Reporting—Reporting is one of the main areas of software development in which the software quality is reported and monitored. Visual Studio Team System 2008 provides lot of reporting templates and features that can be used to upload the test results and publish them to the management and the team, in order to monitor the project's quality and performance. This chapter explains the detailed steps involved in publishing the results and creating and customizing the report using the available reporting templates in Visual Studio Team System 2008 and Team Foundation Server.

What You Need for This Book

This book requires a basic knowledge of Visual Studio Team System 2008 and of integrating this with Team Foundation Server. The reader must be familiar with the Visual Studio IDE. Most testers might have used different testing tools, but they should be little bit familiar with coding in Visual Studio if they are intent on using the coded web test and their own unit testing. The following tools are required by testers and developers in order to make the most of all of the chapters of this book.

1. Visual Studio Team System 2008 Team Suite, Test Edition, or Developer edition
2. SQL Server Express
3. Team Foundation Server 2005 or later
4. Microsoft Office (Word is required for Manual testing)
5. SQL Server Analysis and Reporting Server (for customizing reports and publishing them)

Who is This Book For

This book is for Microsoft developers and testers who are working with Visual Studio 2008, and who need to create a structured testing environment for their applications. No prior knowledge of testing is required. The reader will need to be familiar with the standard Visual Studio 2008 environment, but anyone who has previously created and compiled code in this environment will easily follow this book.

Conventions

In this book, you will find a number of styles of text that distinguish between different kinds of information. Here are some examples of these styles, and an explanation of their meaning.

Code words in text are shown as follows: "We can include other contexts through the use of the `include` directive."

A block of code will be set as follows:

```
<Deployment>
  <DeploymentItem filename="Test.dll" />
  <DeploymentItem filename="ClassLibrary1.dll" />
  <DeploymentItem filename="CustomeRules.dll" />
</Deployment>
```

When we wish to draw your attention to a particular part of a code block, the relevant lines or items will be shown in bold:

```
    pdbFile="C:\Workspace\WebTestPluginSample\
                                     bin\Debug\WebTestPluginSample.pdb"
                           instrumentInPlace="true" />
        <CodeCoverageItem binaryFile="C:\Workspace\
                                         WebTestPluginSample\bin\Debug\
                                         WebTestPluginSampleTwo.dll"
                           pdbFile="C:\Workspace\WebTestPluginSample\
                                     bin\Debug\WebTestPluginSampleTwo.pdb"
                           instrumentInPlace="true" />

      </Regular>
```

Any command-line input and output is shown as follows:

```
mstest /testmetadata:[file name] /testlist:[test list name]
```

New terms and **important words** are shown in bold. Words that you see on the screen, for example in menus or dialog boxes, appear in the text like this: "Select the test project, right-click, and choose **Add**. Then select the option **Web test** from the context menu."

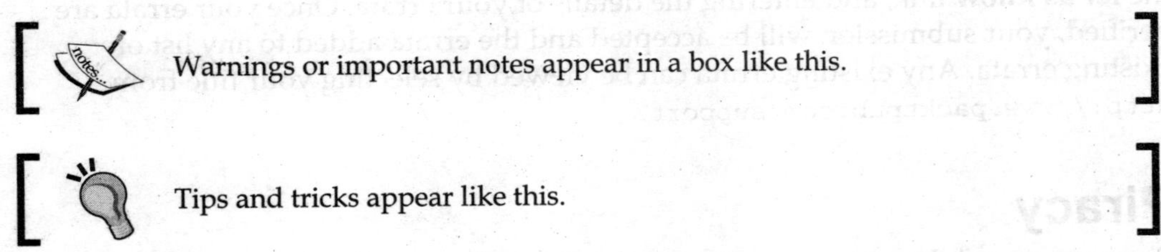

Warnings or important notes appear in a box like this.

Tips and tricks appear like this.

Reader Feedback

Feedback from our readers is always welcome. Let us know what you think about this book—what you liked or may have disliked. Reader feedback is important for us to develop titles that you really get the most out of.

To send us general feedback, simply send an email to `feedback@packtpub.com`, making sure that you mention the book title in the subject of your message.

If there is a book that you need and would like to see us publish, please send us a note via the **SUGGEST A TITLE** form on `www.packtpub.com`, or send an email to us at `suggest@packtpub.com`.

If there is a topic that you have expertise in and you are interested in either writing or contributing to a book on, see our author guide on `www.packtpub.com/authors`.

Customer Support

Now that you are the proud owner of a Packt book, we have a number of things to help you to get the most from your purchase.

Downloading the Example Code for the Book

Visit `http://www.packtpub.com/files/code/5586_Code.zip` to directly download the example code.

The downloadable files contain instructions on how to use them.

Errata

Although we have taken every care to ensure the accuracy of our contents, mistakes do happen. If you find a mistake in one of our books—maybe a mistake in the text or in the example code code—we would be grateful if you would report this to us. By doing this you can save other readers from frustration, and help to improve subsequent versions of this book. If you find any errata, please report them by visiting `http://www.packtpub.com/support`, selecting your book, clicking on the **let us know** link, and entering the details of your errata. Once your errata are verified, your submission will be accepted and the errata added to any list of existing errata. Any existing errata can be viewed by selecting your title from `http://www.packtpub.com/support`.

Piracy

Piracy of copyright material on the Internet is an ongoing problem across all media. At Packt, we take the protection of our copyright and licenses very seriously. If you come across any illegal copies of our works in any form on the Internet, please provide the location address or website name to us immediately, so that we can pursue a remedy.

Please contact us at `copyright@packtpub.com` with a link to the suspected pirated material.

We appreciate your help in protecting our authors, and supporting our ability to bring you valuable content.

Questions

You can contact us at `questions@packtpub.com` if you are having a problem with some aspect of the book, and we will do our best to address it.

1
Visual Studio Team System 2008 Test Types

Software testing is one of the most important phases of the **Software Development Life Cycle (SDLC)**. The end product is based on design, coding, testing, and meeting the specified requirements. The quality of the end product is measured by testing the product based on the requirement, using different testing tools and techniques. Even though we test the product with different tools, the real judgement of the product comes from the testing that simulates the real life situation, for example, by simulating the actual number of users, by simulating the load and simulating the actual production environment, and then by measuring the product. Microsoft Visual Studio 2008 provides not only the development environment and code maintenance for application but also different testing features such as Unit test, Load test, Web test, Coded tests, and Ordering tests list.

This chapter will give us an understanding of the tools in Visual Studio and an overview of the different types of testing supported by Visual Studio.

Software testing in Visual Studio Team System 2008

Before going into the details of the actual testing using Visual Studio 2008, we need to understand the different tools provided by **Visual Studio Team System (VSTS)** and their usage. Once we understand the tools usage, then we should be able to perform different types of testing using VSTS. As we go along creating a number of different tests, we will encounter difficulty in managing the test similar to the code and its different versions during application development. There are different features such as the Test List Editor and Test View and the **Team Foundation Server (TFS)** for managing and maintaining all the tests created using VSTS. Using this Test List Editor, we can group similar tests, create number of lists, add, or delete tests from the list.

The other aspect of this chapter is to see the different file types getting created in Visual Studio during testing. Most of these files are in XML format, which get created automatically whenever the corresponding test is created.

The tools such as the Team Explorer, Code Coverage, Test View and Test Results are not new to Visual Studio 2008 but actually available since Visual Studio 2005. For the new learners of Visual Studio, there is a brief overview on each one of those windows as we are going to deal with these windows throughout all or most of the chapters in this book. While we go through the windows and their purposes, we can check the IDE and the tools integration into Visual Studio 2008.

Testing as part of Software Development Life Cycle

The main objective of testing is to find the defects early in the SDLC. If the defect is found early, then the cost will be less, but if the defect is found during production or implementation stage, then the cost will be higher. Moreover, testing is carried out to assure the quality and reliability of the software. In order to find the defect earlier, the testing activities should start early, that is, in the **Requirement** phase of SDLC and continue till the end of SDLC.

In the **Coding** phase, various testing activities takes place. Based on the design, the developers start coding the modules. Static and dynamic testing is carried out by the developers. Code reviews and code walkthroughs are also conducted.

Once the coding is completed, then comes the **Validation** phase, where different phases or forms of testing are performed.

- **Unit Testing**: This is the first stage of testing in SDLC. This is performed by the developer to check whether the developed code meets the stated requirements. If there are any defects, the developer logs them against the code and fixes the code. The code is retested and then moved to the testers after confirming the code without any defects for the piece of functionality. This phase identifies a lot of defects and also reduces the cost and time involved in testing the application and fixing the code.

- **Integration Testing**: This testing is carried out between two or more modules or functions together with the intent of finding interface defects between them. This testing is completed as a part of unit or functional testing, and sometimes becomes its own standalone test phase. On a larger level, integration testing can involve putting together groups of modules and functions with the goal of completing and verifying that the system meets the system requirements. Defects found are logged and later fixed by the developers. There are different ways of integration testing such as top-down testing and bottom-up testing:
    - The **Top-Down** approach is followed to test the highest level of components and integrate first to test the high-level logic and the flow. The low-level components are tested later.
    - The **Bottom-Up** approach is the exact opposite of the top-down approach. In this case, the low-level functionalities are tested and integrated first and then the high-level functionalities are tested. The disadvantage in this approach is that the high-level or the most complex functionalities are tested later.
    - The **Umbrella** approach uses both the top-down and bottom-up patterns. The inputs for functions are integrated in the bottom-up approach and then the outputs for the functions are integrated in the top-down approach.

- **System Testing**: It compares the system specifications against the actual system. The system test design is derived from the system design documents and is used in this phase. Sometimes, system testing is automated using testing tools. Once all the modules are integrated, several errors may arise. Testing done at this stage is called system testing. Defects found in this testing are logged and fixed by the developers.
- **Regression Testing**: This is not mentioned in the testing phase, but is carried out once the defects are fixed by the developers. The main objective of this type of testing is to determine if bug fixes have been successful and have not created any new problems. Also, this type of testing is done to ensure that no degradation of baseline functionality has occurred and to check if any new functionality was introduced in the software.

Types of testing

Visual Studio provides a range of testing types and tools for software applications. Following are some of those types:

- Unit test
- Manual test
- Web test
- Load test
  - Stress test
  - Performance test
  - Capacity Planning test
- Generic test
- Ordered test

In addition to these types, there are additional tools provided to manage, order the listing, and execute tests created in Visual Studio. Some of these are the Test View, Test List Editor, and the Test Results window. We will look at these testing tools and the supporting tools for managing the testing in Visual Studio 2008 in detail later.

Unit test

As soon as the developer finishes the code, the developer wants to know if it is producing the expected result before getting into any more detailed testing or handing over the component to the tester. The type of testing performed by the developers to test their own code is called Unit testing. Visual Studio has great support for Unit testing.

The main goal of the unit testing is to isolate each piece of the code or individual functionality and test if the method is returning the expected result for different set of parameter values. It is extremely important to run unit tests to catch the defects in the early stage.

The methods generated by the automated unit testing tool call the methods in the classes from the source code and test the output of each of the methods by comparing them with the expected values. The unit test tool produces a separate set of test code for the source. Using the test code we can pass the parameter values to the method and test the value returned by the method, and then compare them with the expected result.

Unit testing code can be easily created by using the code generation feature, which creates the testing source code for the source application code. The generated unit testing code will contain several attributes to identify the Test Class, Test Method, and Test Project. These attributes are assigned when the unit test code gets generated from the original source code. Then using this code, the developer has to change the values and assert methods to compare the expected result from these methods.

The Unit test class is similar to the other classes in any other project. The good thing here is that we can create new test classes by inheriting the base test class. The base test class will contain the common or reusable testing methods. This is the new Unit testing feature which helps us reduce the code and reuse the existing test classes.

Whenever any code change occurs, it is easy to figure out the fault with the help of Unit tests, rerun those tests, and check whether the code is giving the intended output. This is to verify the code change the developer has made and to confirm that it is not affecting the other parts of the application.

All the methods and classes generated for the automated unit testing are inherited from the namespace `Microsoft.VisualStudio.TestTools.UnitTesting`.

Manual test

Manual testing is the oldest and the simplest type of testing, but yet very crucial for software testing. It requires a tester to run all the tests without any automation tool. It helps us to validate whether the application meets various standards defined for effective and efficient accessibility and usage.

Manual testing comes to play in the following scenarios:

1. There is not enough budget for automation.
2. The tests are more complicated, or are too difficult to be converted into automated tests.
3. The tests are going to be executed only once.
4. There is not enough time to automate the tests.
5. Automated tests would be time-consuming to create and run.

Manual tests can be created either using a Word document or Text format in Visual Studio 2008. This is a form of describing the test steps that should be performed by the tester. The step should also mention the expected result out of testing the step.

Web tests

Web tests are used for testing the functionality of the web page, web application, web site, web services, and a combination of all these. Web tests can be created by recording the interactions that are performed in the browser. These can be played back to test the web application. Web tests are normally a series of HTTP requests (GET/POST).

Web tests can be used for testing the application performance as well as for stress testing. During HTTP requests, the web test takes care of testing the web page redirects, validations, viewstate information, authentication, and JavaScript executions.

There are different validation rules and extraction rules used in web testing. The validation rules are used for validating the form field names, texts, and tags in the requested web page. We can validate the results or values against the expected result as per business needs. These validation rules are also used for checking the time taken for the HTTP request.

At some point in time, we need to extract the data returned by the web pages. We may need the data for future use, or we may have to collect the data for testing purposes. In this case, we have to use the extraction rules for extracting the data returned by the page requested. Using this process, we can extract the form fields, texts, or values in the web page and store it in the web test context or collection.

Web tests cannot be performed only with the existence of a web page. We need some data to be populated from the database or some other source to test the web page functionality and performance. There is a data binding mechanism used in Web test, which is used for providing the data required for the requested page. We can bind the data from a database or any other data source. For example, the web page would be a reporting page that might require some query string parameters as well as the data to be shown in the page according to the parameters passed. To provide data for all these data-driven testing, we have to use the concept of data binding with the data source.

Web tests can be classified into Simple Web tests and Coded Web tests. Both these are supported by VSTS.

- **Simple Web tests** are very simple to create and execute. It executes on its own as per the recording. Once the test is started, there won't be any intervention. The disadvantage is that it is not conditional. It's a series of valid flow of events.

- **Coded Web tests** are bit more complex, but provide a lot of flexibility. For example, if we need some conditional execution of tests based on some values then we have to depend on this coded web test. These tests are created using either C# or Visual Basic code. Using the generated code we can control the flow of test events. But the disadvantage is its high complexity and maintenance cost.

Load test

Load testing is a method of testing used in different types of testing. The important thing with Load testing is that it is about performance. This type of testing is conducted with other types of testing, which means that it can be performed along with either Web testing or Unit testing.

The main purpose of load testing is to identify the performance of application based on different scenarios. Most of the time, we can predict the performance of the application that we develop, if it is running on one machine or a desktop. But in the case of web applications such as online ordering systems, we know the estimated maximum number of users, but do not know the connection speeds and location from where the users will access the web site. For such scenarios, the web application should support all the end users with good performance irrespective of the system they use, their Internet connection, the place, and the tool they use to access the web site.

So before we release this web site to the customers or the end users, we should check the performance of the application so that it can support the mass end user group. This is where load testing will be very useful in testing the application along with Web test or Unit test.

When a Web test is added to a Load test, it will simulate multiple users opening simultaneous connections to the same web application and making multiple HTTP requests. Load testing in Visual Studio comes with lots of properties which can be set to test the web application with different browsers, different user profiles, light loads, and heavy loads. Results of different tests can be saved in a repository to compare the set of results and improve their performance.

In case of client server and multi-tier applications, we will be having a lot of components which will reside in the server and serve the client requests. To get the performance of these components, we have to make use of a Load test with a set of Unit tests. One good example would be to test the data access service component that calls a stored procedure in the backend database and returns the results to the application that is using this service.

Load tests can be run either from the local machine or by submitting to a **rig**, which is a group of computers used for simulating the tests remotely. A rig consists of a single **controller** and one or more **agents**.

Load tests can be used in different scenarios of testing:

1. **Stress testing**: This checks the functionality of the application under heavy load. The resource provided to the application could vary based on the input file size or the size of the data set, for example, uploading a file which is more than 50MB in size.
2. **Smoke testing**: This checks if the application performs well for a short duration with a light load.
3. **Performance testing**: This checks the responsiveness and throughput of the application with different loads.
4. **Capacity Planning test**: This checks the application performance with various capacities.

We will see more about setting the Load test properties, working with test rig and analysing the Load test results later in this book.

Ordered test

As we know, there are different types of testing required to build quality software. We take care of running all these tests for the applications we develop. But we also have an order in which to execute all these different tests. For example, we do the unit testing first, then the integration test, then the smoke test, and then we go for the functional test. We can order the execution of these tests using Visual Studio.

Another example would be to test the configurations for the application before actually testing the functionality of the application. If we don't order the test, we would never know whether the end result is correct or not. Sometimes, the tests will not go through successfully if the tests are not run in order.

Ordering of tests is done using the Test View window in Visual Studio. We can list all the available tests in the Test View and choose the tests in the same order using different options provided by Visual Studio and then run the tests. Visual Studio will take care of running the tests in the same order we have chosen in the list.

So once we are able to run the test successfully in an order, we can also expect the same ordering in getting the results. Visual Studio provides the results of all the tests in a single row in the Test Results window. Actually, this single row result will contain the results of all the tests run in the order. We can just double-click the single row result to get the details of each tests run in the ordered test.

Ordered test is the best way of controlling the tests and running the tests in an order.

Generic test

We have seen different types and ways of testing the applications using VSTS. There are situations where we might end up having other applications for testing, which are not developed using Visual Studio. We might have only the executables or binaries for those applications. But we may not have the supported testing tool for those applications. This is where we need the generic testing method. This is just a way of testing third-party applications using Visual Studio.

Generic tests are used to wrap the existing tests. Once the wrapping is done, then it is just another test in VSTS.

Using Visual Studio, we can collect the test results, and gather the code coverage data too. We can manage and run the generic tests in Visual Studio just like the others tests.

Test management and new testing features in VS 2008

Visual Studio Team 2008 has great features for working with the type of tests we've just described. These features are greatly improved from the previous versions of VSTS. The Team Explorer, Test View, and Test List Editor are some of those main IDE add-ins used for tests management.

Team explorer

Team Explorer is the add-on to the VSTS IDE. Using this explorer, the developer or a user of Visual Studio can browse through the Team Projects in the TFS to which the explorer is connected. TFS is the central repository for managing and controlling the team projects. To work with any of the team projects in the TFS, first we have to connect to it using VSTS. After connecting to the server, we can use Team Explorer to browse through the details of the particular Team Project.

Team Explorer is a client of TSF and is integrated with the VSTS. Team Explorer provides features to work with the team project details such as:

- Accessing project, process guidance documents that explain the process to be followed for the Team Project. This process guidance helps the team follow the process for the Team Project items such as work items, reports, queries, and work products.

- Managing work items such as tasks, defects, issues, and requirements.
- Importing and exporting the work items.
- Accessing the project files and source control management.
- Adding, removing, configuring, and managing the Team Projects.
- Creating, managing, and automating the project builds.
- Managing favorites which are shortcuts to the favorite nodes of the Team Project.
- Managing the reports. It could be defect reporting or any type of work items reporting.

Team system testing tools introduction

Visual Studio 2008 provides many tools to create, run, debug, and view results of the tests for the applications. It is very flexible for running a test and getting the results. Given below are an overview of the tools and windows provided by Visual Studio to view the test details and test output details. We will look into more details of the actual usage of these tools later in Chapter 10. But here, we will look into the overview of each of the tools available in Visual Studio 2008.

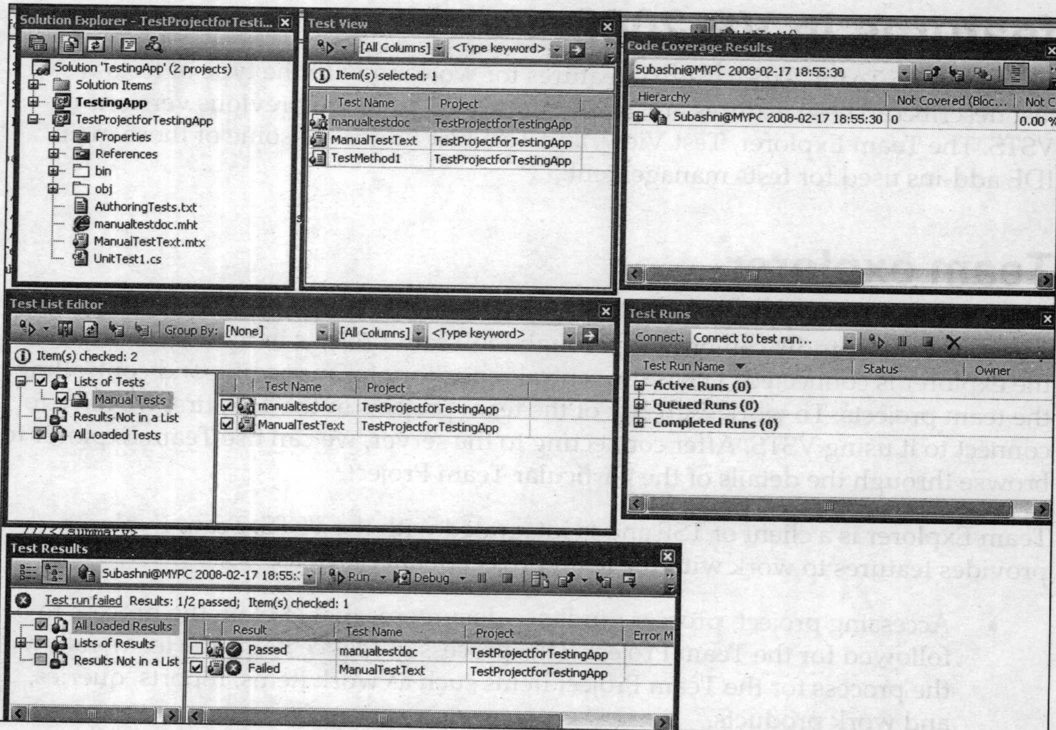

Let us see how we can create a new testing project using Visual Studio 2008, and then we will test a sample project to get to know about the tools and features.

Open Visual Studio 2008 and open the solution of the application which is developed using C# or VB.NET. We will not go into the details of the sample application **TestingApp** as shown in the preceding screenshot. We will just create a test project for the sample application and see the features of the tools and windows.

Now similar to adding the projects and code files to the solution, we have to create the test project and test files and add the test project to the solution. There are different ways of creating test projects under the solution.

1. Select the solution and add a project using the **Add | New Project....** Then select the project type as **Test** from the list of project types under the language, which we are going to use. Then select the template as **Test Project**.

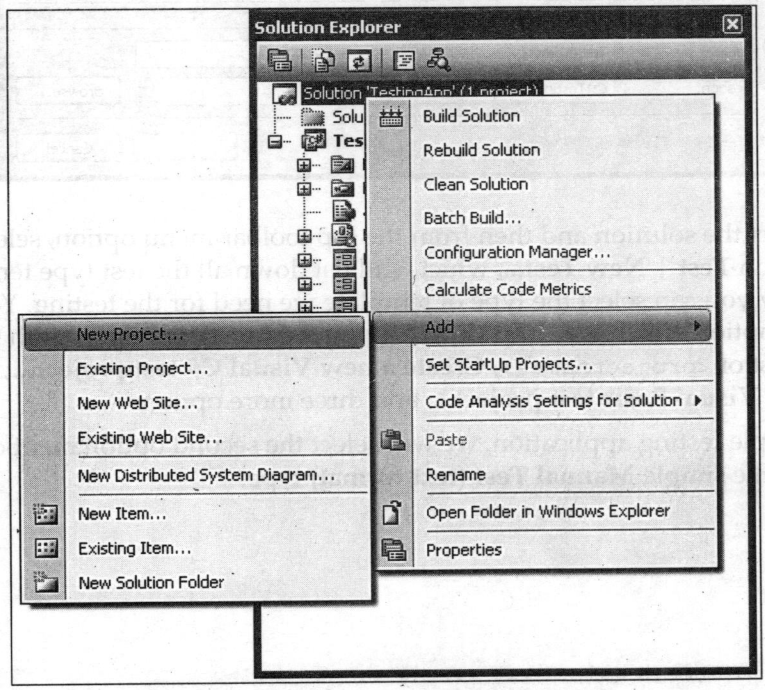

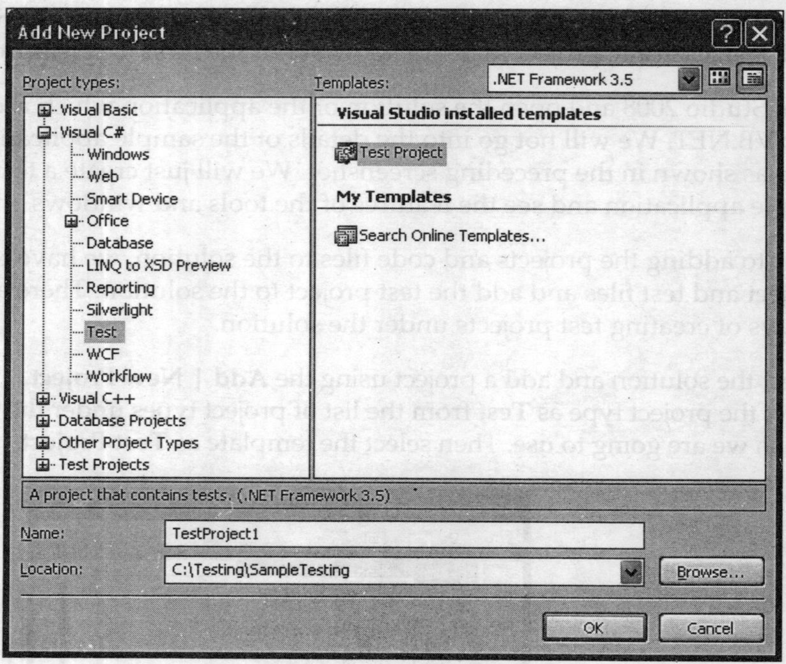

2. Select the solution and then from the top toolbar menu option, select the option **Test | New Test...,** which will list down all the test type templates. Now you can select the type of template we need for the testing. You can see the option which is a drop-down saying **Add to Test Project** with the options as list of <projectnames>, **Create a new Visual C# test project...**, **Create a new Visual Basic test project...**, and three more options.

For our sample testing application, we will select the second option mentioned above and choose the simple **Manual Test (text format)** type.

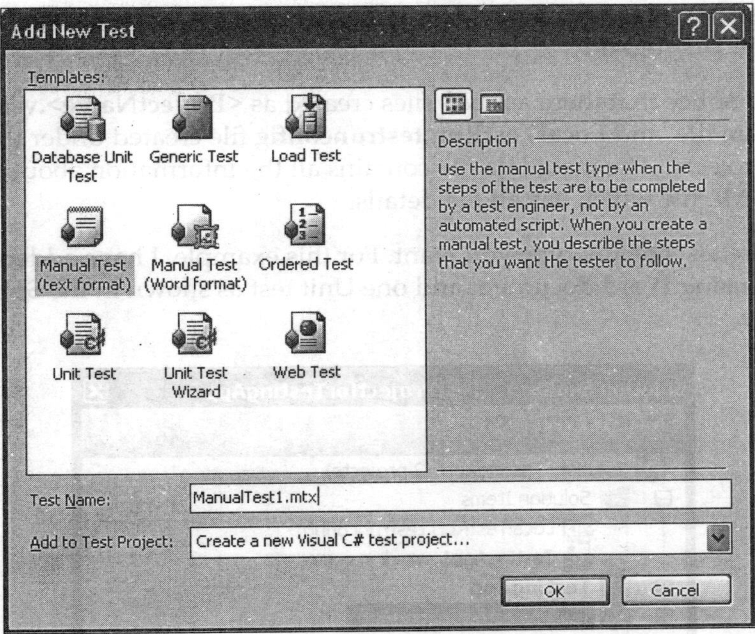

The **Add New Test** dialog contains nine different template options for creating the tests. There are two different templates for the **Manual Test** with one using Text file and the other using a Word document. The Unit testing template is of three types; one is for the Database Unit Test, the second one for the general Unit Test, and the third one for the Unit Test Wizard. Following are the file extensions for each of the VSTS test types as shown in the preceding in the image.

- `.vb`—is for the Database Unit test
- .generictest—for the Generic test type
- `.loadtest`—for test which is of type load test
- `.mtx`—for manual test using text file format
- `.mht`—for manual test using word document format
- `.orderedtest`—for ordered test types
- `.vb`—for unit test
- `.webtest`—for web testing

After selecting the test type, give a name for the test in the **Test Name** field. Select the **Create new Visual C# test Project...** in the **Add to Test Project** option. We will see more details about this later. For now, consider that we have added the testing project to the existing solution.

Now, the system will ask for a name for the new test project. Let us name it **TestProjectforTestingApp**.

Now, we can notice that there are two files created as **<ProjectName>.vsmdi**, which is the metadata file, and **LocalTestRun.testrunconfig** file created under the solution for the test projects. The metadata file contains all the information about the tests list. It is an XML file which has all the details.

Add two more tests of any type you want. For this example, I have added one more Manual Test using Word document and one Unit test as shown in the **Solution Explorer** here.

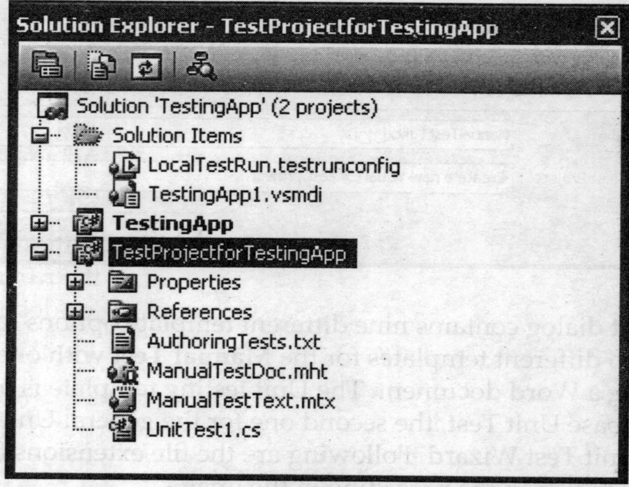

Now, let us see the different windows and tools available in support of all the tests that we can perform using Visual Studio. We will take the sample Manual testing example for getting to know about the tools.

Test view

The **Test View** window is used for viewing the available tests and also for selecting the test and run it. We can also see the properties of each test from here. It is similar to the solution explorer from where we can get the list of class files in the project. We can also group the available tests based on the type, or owner, or project, or solution, or priority, or any other property of the test. The **Test View** window can be opened using the Visual Studio IDE menu option **Test | Windows | Test View**. Now, you can see the following **Test View** screen which displays a list of all the tests created in the current Test Project.

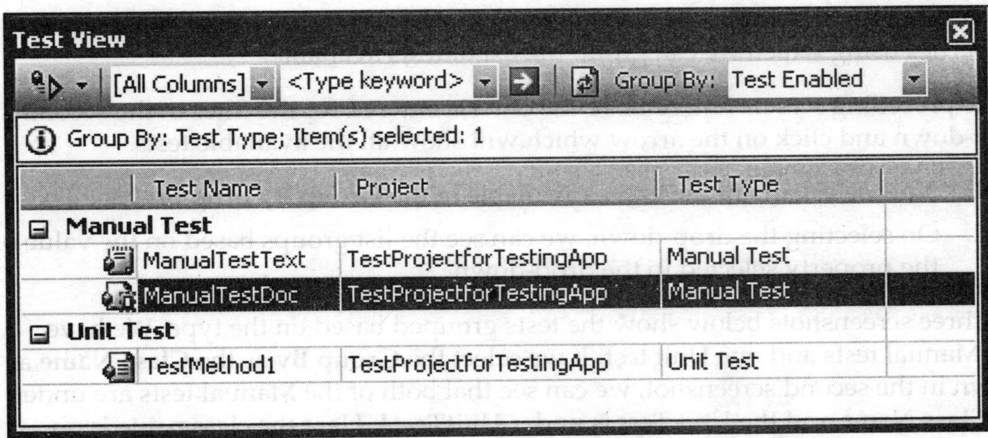

The screenshot shows the default test view with the list of tests based on the type. We can customize the test view using the filters, grouping and adding or removing the columns which we are going to see in the coming paragraphs.

The **Test View** window has its own toolbar for different operations that can be performed on the list. The left-most option in the toolbar is the run and debug option, by which we can start the VSTS process for running or debugging the selected tests.

The second is the Filter option in the toolbar, which contains a drop-down listing of all the columns related to the **Test View** and the test properties and a box which says <Type keyword> for entering the value that can be used against the field selected in the second drop-down for filtering the list of tests shown. When the button with the arrow next to these drop-downs is clicked, the actual filtering will take place, and the grid will show the filtered list of tests. For example, the following image shows a list of tests filtered with **Test Type** which are **Manual**.

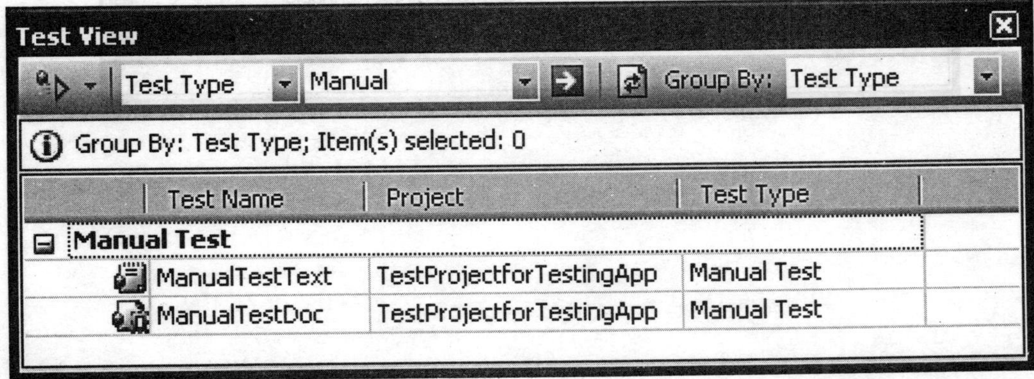

The third one is the **Group By** option which has a drop-down with a list of test properties using which we can group the list of tests available.

In the preceding screenshot, remove the criteria entered for the filter in the second drop-down and click on the arrow which will show all the available tests.

1. Now select any of the values available in the **Group By** drop-down.
2. On selecting the drop-down, we can see the list groups based on the value of the property selected in the drop-down.

The three screenshots below show the tests grouped based on the type. We have two Manual tests and one Unit test. If we select the **Group By** as the **Class Name** as shown in the second screenshot, we can see that both of the Manual tests are under **No Class Name** and the Unit Test is under **UnitTest1**. Here the class name is no name because the manual tests will not have any classes. Same is the case when we select **Description** as the **Group By** field as shown in the third screenshot below. The test which is of type Unit test, and the test which is of type **Manual Test** are shown together because both these tests do not have a description.

The screenshot below shows the tests grouped by Test type. There are two manual tests and one Unit test.

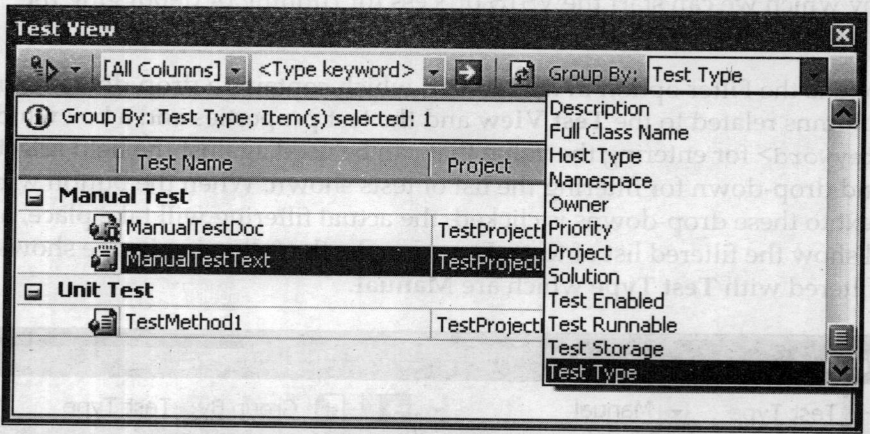

The screenshot below shows the tests grouped by Class Name. The Manual tests does not have class name as it is not derived from any class and does not have a class.

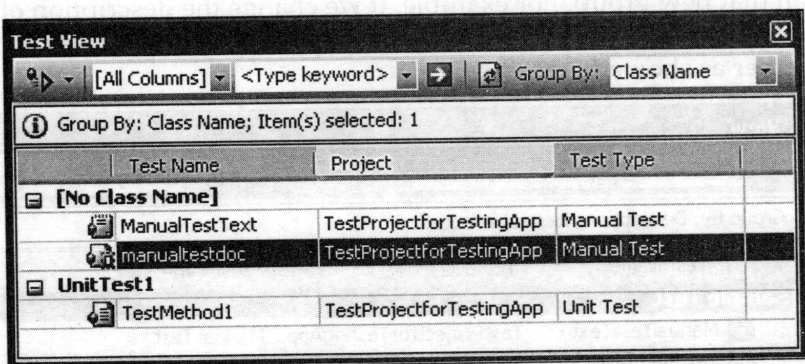

The below screenshot shows the grouping of tests based on the description. The unit test has a description but not the manual tests as there is no description for tests which is of type Manual

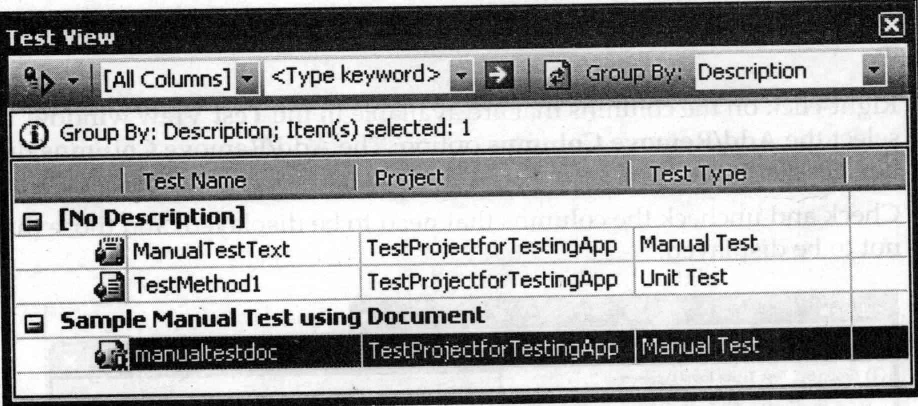

We can change the descriptions of the tests and group them together. Whenever we change the description or class name or an editable property of the test, it will be grouped under that property, if it exists. Otherwise, it will be shown as a new property with that new group. For example, if we change the description of all the tests to **Sample Test** and group the tests by description, then we can see all the tests grouped together as shown here:

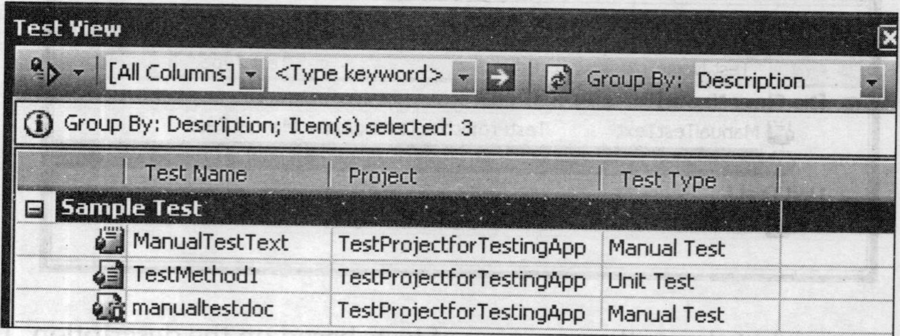

In the **Test View,** we can select the available columns to display in the view, and we can also sort them using the column header.

The following steps explain how to show a column in the view display and how to sort them:

1. Right-click on the columns that are available in the **Test View** window, and select the **Add/Remove Columns** option. The **Add/Remove Columns** dialog box get displayed.
2. Check and uncheck the columns that need to be displayed, and those that are not to be displayed.

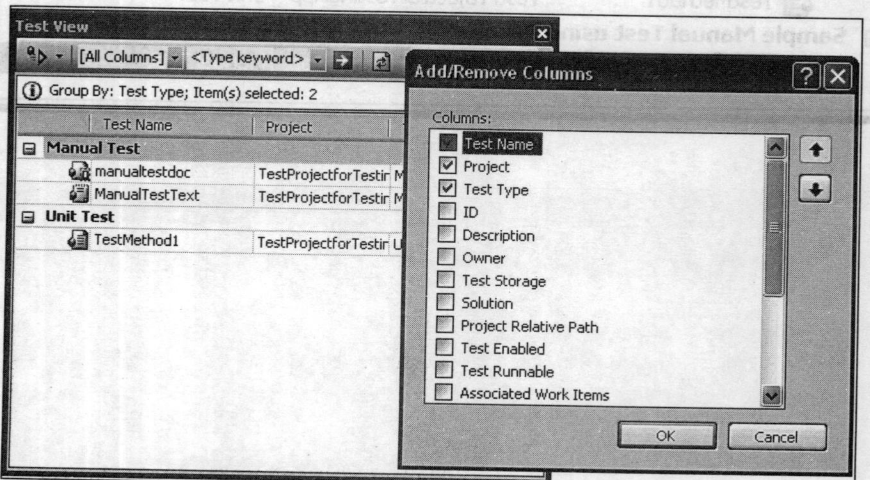

For sorting the columns, click on each column header to change the sorting order. If the same column is already sorted, then the sorting order will be changed.

Test list editor

All features available in **Test View** are also available in the **Test List Editor** with some additional features. Through this window, we can create the test lists by grouping the available tests. We can also select multiple tests from the list and run them using this window.

Whenever we open the **Test List Editor** using the menu option **Test | Windows | Test List Editor**, we can see the window as follows showing all the available tests:

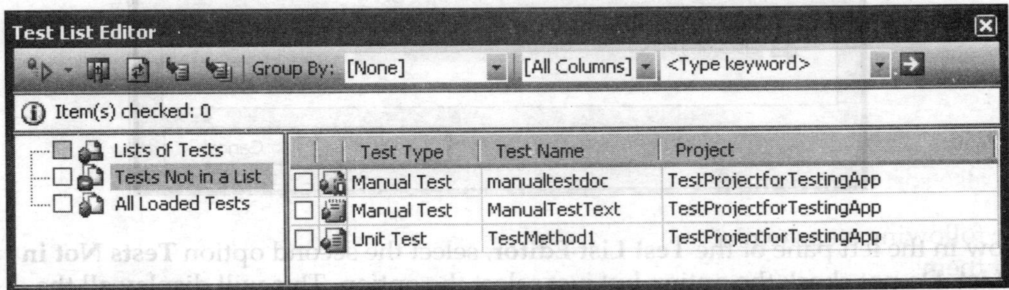

The toolbar in the **Test List Editor** window has the same features that we saw in the **Test View** window. But you can see that the details section of the list window is split into two panes. The left pane of the window has three nodes, and the right pane displays all the tests in the lists based on the selection in the left pane. The **Test List Editor** displays the following three options as nodes.

Lists of tests

This is the first node in the list which is initially empty. It also asks us to create the list and add the tests to the list

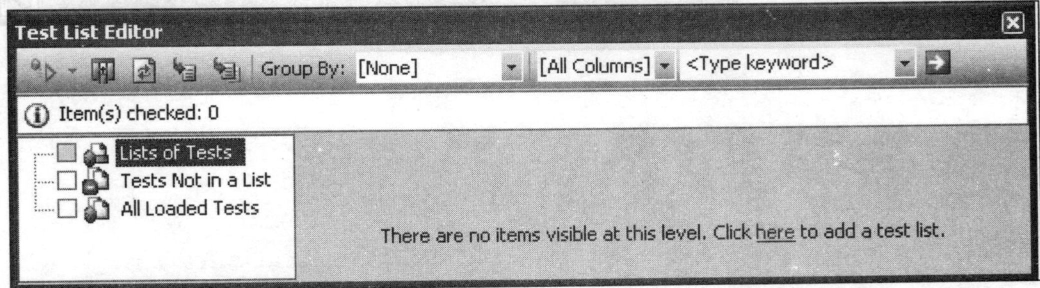

We can click on the **here** link and give the details for the new test list in the window that opens up as **Create New Test List**. Let's call that test list **Manual Tests** to group all the available manual tests.

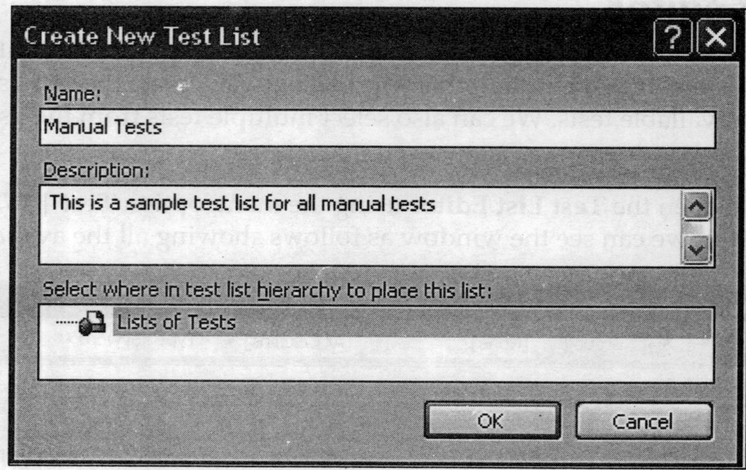

Now in the left pane of the **Test List Editor**, select the second option **Tests Not in a List**. Do not check the option but just select the option. This will display all the available tests in the project, which are not part of any other Test list as shown below:

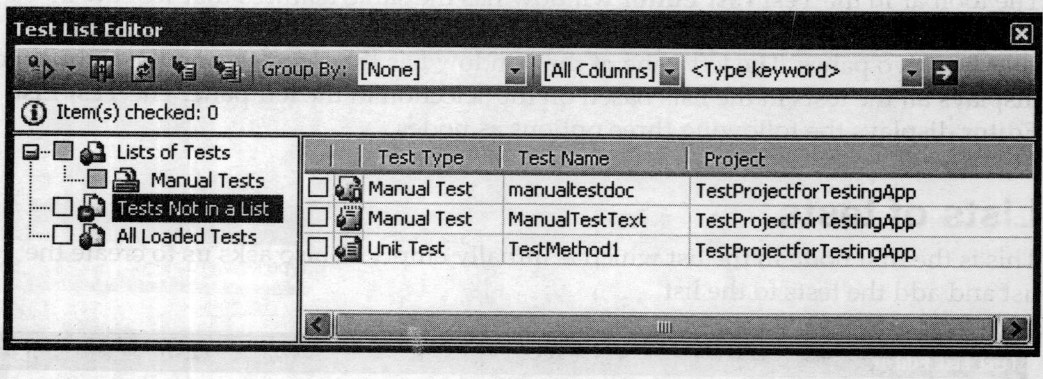

Now choose both the Manual tests on the right pane and just drag and drop them on the **Manual Tests** node on the left pane, which we created earlier. The other way of doing the same is, after selecting both manual tests, by right-clicking and choosing the **New Test List..** option. We will get a window similar to what we saw earlier in **Create New Test List**.

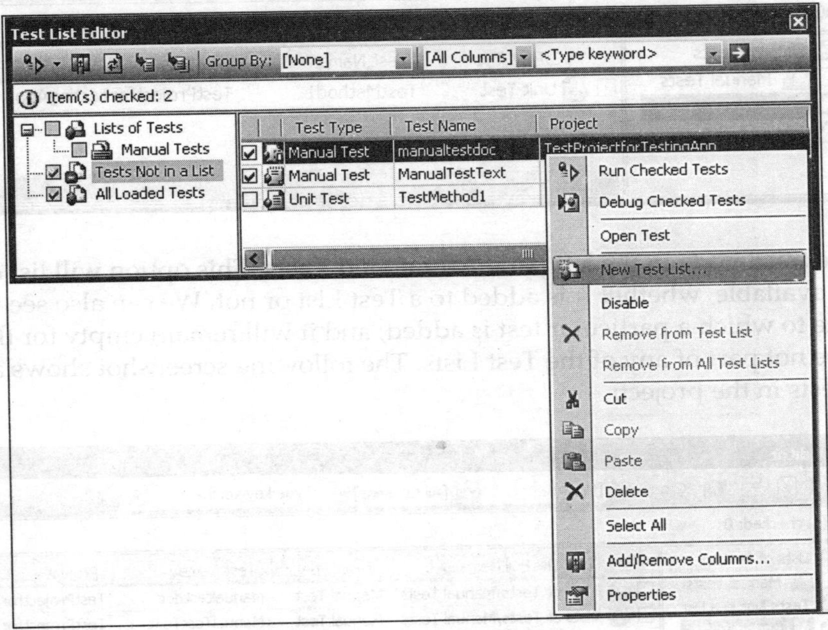

Since we have already created the Test list, we will just drag and drop the tests on the test list name. Now when we select the newly created **Manual Tests** list, we can both the manual tests listed on the right-side pane.

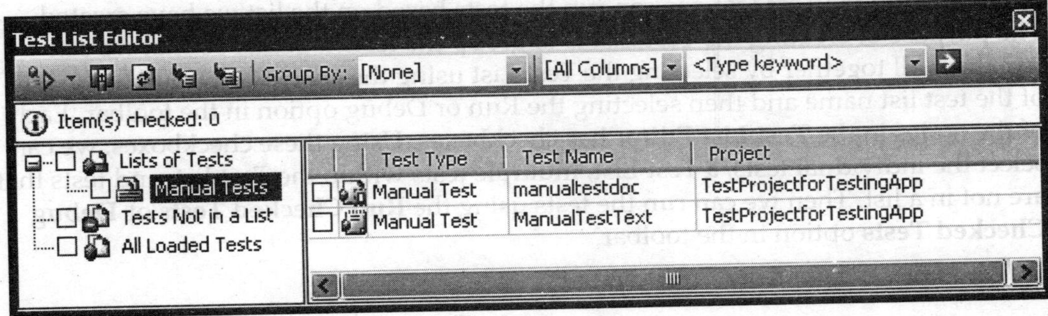

Now if we select the node **Tests Not in a List**, we can see only the other tests that we had not selected in our previous steps to add to the Manual Tests list.

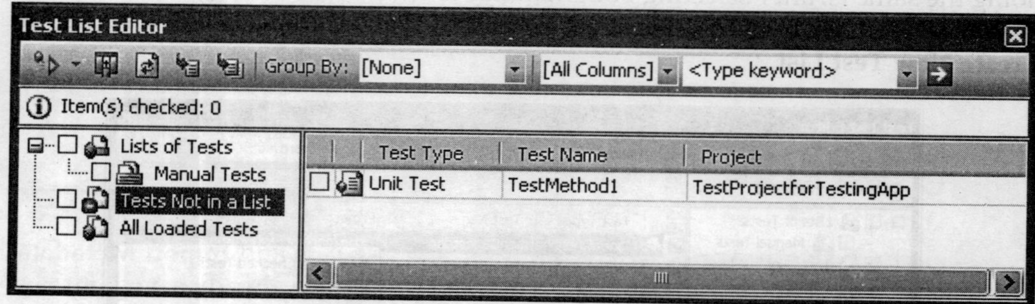

Select the third node in the left pane **All Loaded Tests**. This option will list down all the tests available, whether it is added to a Test List or not. We can also see the Test List name to which a particular test is added; and it will remain empty for the tests which are not part of any of the Test Lists. The following screenshot shows all the loaded tests in the project:

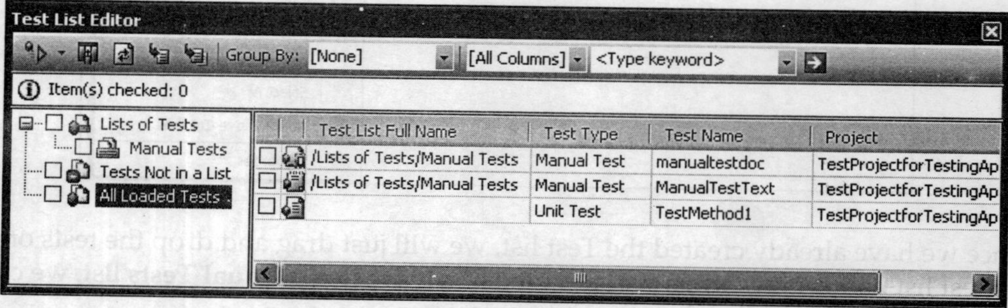

After creating the Test List, we can run the tests based on the list we have created. The purpose of creating the Test List is to group the tests together so that we can run them all together by selecting the Test List using the checkbox option to the left of the test list name and then selecting the Run or Debug option in the toolbar. Each of the nodes in the **Test List Editor** has checkboxes. Using these checkboxes, we can select the individual tests, a Test List, multiple tests within the Test list, and tests that are not in a list. Then we can run the tests using the **Run Checked Tests** or **Debug Checked Tests** option in the toolbar.

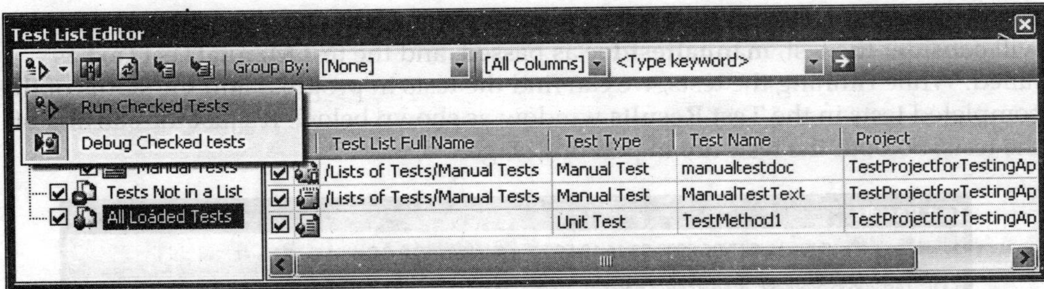

There are two more options in editor toolbar: **Load Metadata** and **Import Metadata**. These are helpful in loading the existing Test Lists, which are already saved but not available in the current list. This Import and Load refer to the metadata file that gets created for the Test Project under the solution. It's the file with the extension `vsmdi`, which contains all the information about the tests lists.

All other options in the toolbar are the same as the options available in the **Test View** window such as grouping, filtering, and adding or removing columns.

Test results

This window shows the results of the tests run. It shows the error messages or the statuses of the multiple tests run. We can also reselect the tests from the **Test Results** window and rerun the tests. Using this window, we can export the test results or import the results already exported. This is useful in viewing the result in the **Test Results** window and rerun the test.

Now, as we have seen in the previous section about the **Test List Editor**, select the **Manual Tests** list and run the tests.

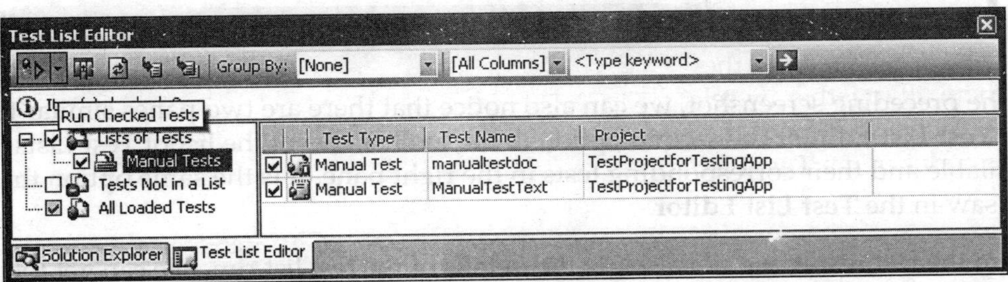

We will see more details about the Manual Tests in Chapter 5. But for now, we will consider the test, **manualtestdoc** as passed, and the test **ManualTestText** as failed. While running the tests, we can find the tests in progress and the status of the completed tests in the **Test Results** window as shown below. It's just the starting of the tests. So both the tests are in pending stage.

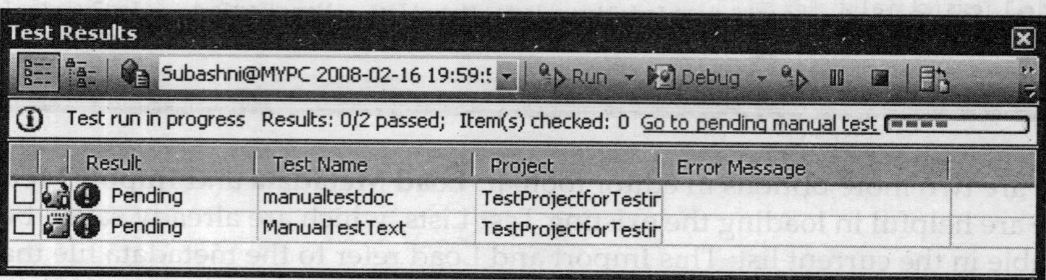

After completing both the tests, we can see the results as shown in the following screenshot. It will clearly indicate the status for each result. The window also shows the summary of the results, passed and failed. If we want to rerun the test, we don't need to go to the List Editor. From the results window, we can select the tests and rerun them. Using the checkbox before the test in the list window, we can select the test and then choose the **Run** or **Debug** option to rerun it.

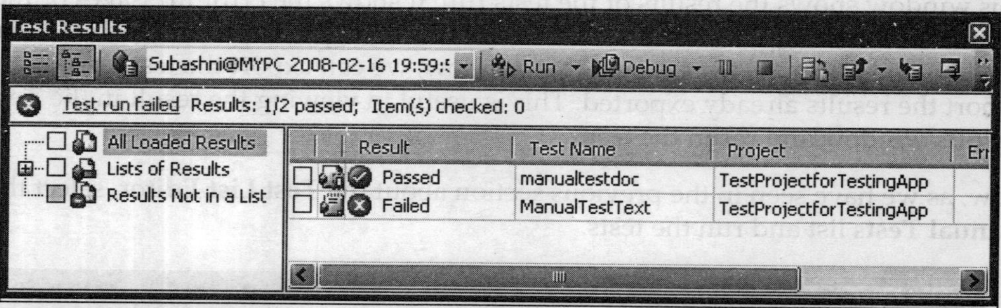

In the preceding screenshot, we can also notice that there are two panes similar to the **Test List Editor**. The second option in the toolbar shows the list of Test Lists available and their corresponding tests in the right pane. It is the same option that we saw in the **Test List Editor**.

From the test result, we can also get the details of the test list run. We can get the details such as start time, end time, test location, and the user who ran the test and also the summary of the test results as shown in the following screenshot:

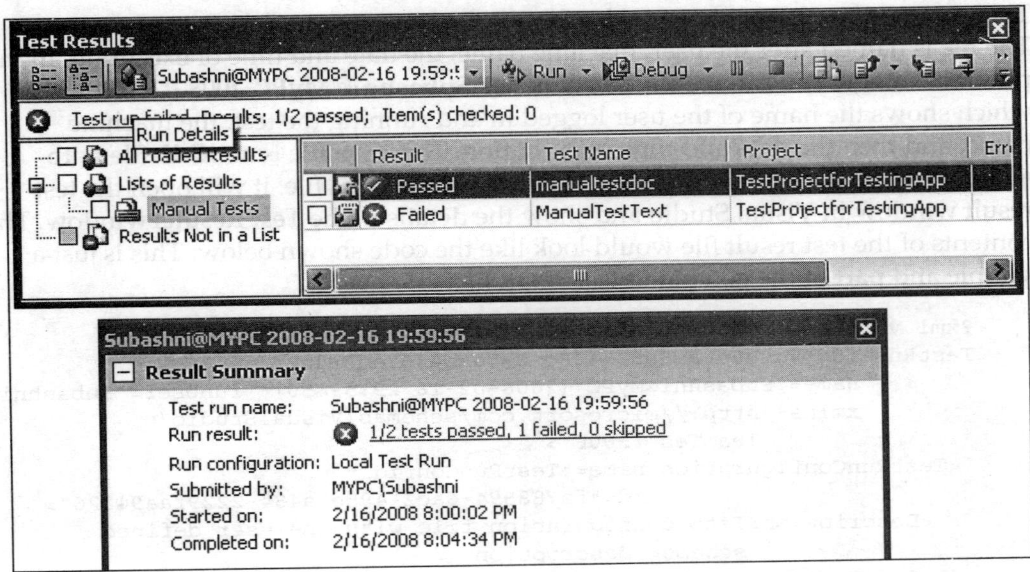

There is another option in the Test Results, which is the option to export the results. Whenever we finish our testing, we always would want to save the results of the tests for our further analysis. In the toolbar, we can see the option for exporting the test results. It provides two options, **Export Test Run Results...** to export all test results and **Export Selected Test Results...** to export only the selected test run result. We can also import the saved result using this window. Refer Chapter 10 for more details about the export and import functionality.

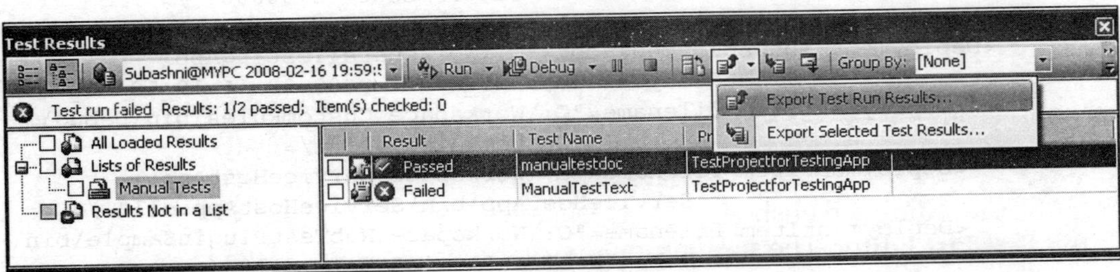

Once we choose any of these options, we can see the file dialog for saving the file. We can also notice that the file type is `*.trx`, which is the Visual Studio Test Results file for saving all the test results.

The `.trx` test result file is created by the VSTS on execution of the test every time. The file is named after the user, machine name, the date and time of execution. In the previous image, you can see the test name as **Subashni@MyPC 2008-02-16 19:59:50,** which shows the name of the user logged in and running the test, the machine name, and then the date and time of execution. The `.trx` file is an XML file with all information about the test result. If you open the `.trx` file, it will open the test result window in Visual Studio and show the details in the Test Results window. The contents of the test result file would look like the code shown below. This is just a sample and part of the generated test result file:

```
<?xml version="1.0" encoding="UTF-8"?>
<TestRun id="7c0e0d0a-5068-436c-887e-b4367ad893c2"
         name="Subashni@MyPC (2008-02-16 29:59:50)" runUser="Subashni"
         xmlns="http://microsoft.com/schemas/VisualStudio/
                TeamTest/2006">
  <TestRunConfiguration name="TestRunConfig1"
                        id="fa788594-6ac2-495e-a484-2229faa94326">
    <Description>Test configuration file with the user defined
                 scheme</Description>
    <CodeCoverage enabled="true">
      <Regular>
        <CodeCoverageItem binaryFile="C:\Workspace\CustomRules\bin\
                                      Debug\CustomRules.dll"
                          pdbFile="C:\Workspace\CustomRules\bin\
                                   Debug\CustomRules.instr.pdb"
                          instrumentInPlace="true" />
      </Regular>
    </CodeCoverage>
    <Timeouts runTimeout="1800000" testTimeout="2700000" />
    <Remote controllerName="&lt;Local - No controller&gt;" />
    <Deployment runDeploymentRoot="C:\Workspace\TestingApp\
                TestResults\Subashni_MyPC _2008-02-16 19_59_50_">
      <DeploymentItem filename="C:\Workspace\CustomRules\bin\Debug\
                                CustomRules.dll" />
      <DeploymentItem filename="C:\Workspace\ServiceHostApp\
                      ServiceHostApp\bin\ServiceHostApp.dll" />
      <DeploymentItem filename="C:\Workspace\WebTestPluginSample\bin\
                      Debug\WebTestPluginSample.dll" />
      <DeploymentItem filename="C:\Workspace\ProjectGenericsSample\
                      bin\Debug\ProjectGenericsSample.exe" />
      <DeploymentItem filename="Test.dll" />
      <DeploymentItem filename="C:\Workspace\TestLibrary\bin\Debug\
                                TestLibrary.dll" />
      <DeploymentItem filename="C:\Program Files\
                      Microsoft Visual Studio 9.0\Common7\IDE\
                      PrivateAssemblies\Microsoft.VisualStudio.
                      SmartDevice.TestHostAdapter.dll" />
      <DeploymentItem filename="ClassLibrary1.dll" />
```

```
    </Deployment>
    <NamingScheme baseName="Subashni@MyPerPC" useDefault="false" />
    <Scripts setupScript="C:\Workspace\TestingApp\

                               SetEnvironment.bat" />
```

Code coverage results

Code coverage provides information about codes and how many kinds of codes are covered during the test run. This is to view the statistical information about the test run. This result will show how many lines of code are executed and how many lines are not executed. We can also get the color coding for the lines run, and different color coding for the lines not run. This is also a kind of test result.

Before starting the code coverage we have to configure the code coverage. Select the **Test | Edit Test Run Configurations | Local Test Run** option. These configurations are stored in the configuration file, `localtestrun.testrunconfig`. In the configuration window, select the option **Code Coverage** in the left pane. On the right-side pane, we can see the list of all the available artifacts for code coverage. The artifacts could be an application, or a library, or any type of assembly. We can choose the artifacts from the list, or we can also import the artifacts using the **Add Assembly** option and then choose that for the code coverage. As shown in the following screenshot, let us select the test project library, `TestProjectforTestingApp.dll`

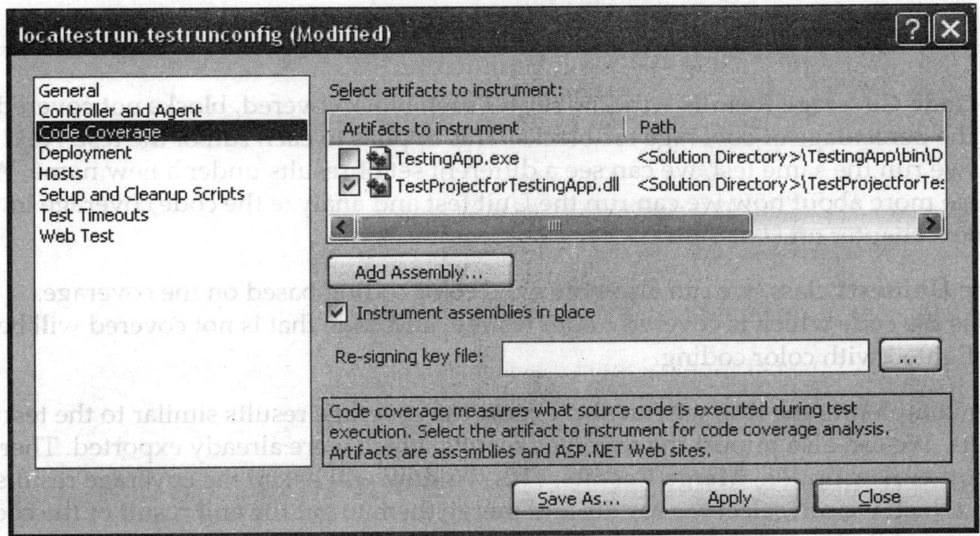

When we click on apply in the above window, the code coverage is enabled only for the assemblies selected. When the application is executed, we can see the code coverage window collecting information about the source code covered in testing as shown in the following screenshot. The code coverage window is available under the menu option **Test | Windows | Code Coverage Results**. Lets try running the unit test application available in the test list editor under the **Tests Not in a List** which has the Unit test. After running the test, we can see the code coverage results as shown in the following screenshot:

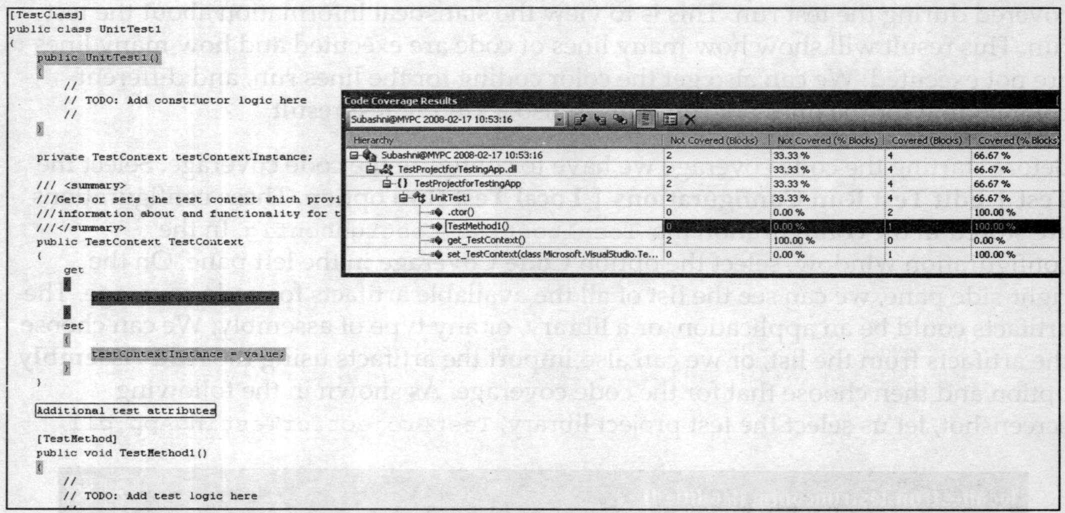

The **Code Coverage Results** window shows each block covered, blocks not covered, and the percentage of coverage for blocks. This applies to each run of the test. Next time we run the same test, we can see a different set of results under a new name. We can see more about how we can run the Unit test and analyze the code coverage in the next chapter on *Unit Tests*.

In the **Unittest1** class, we can also notice the color coding based on the coverage. This is the code which is covered under testing, and code that is not covered will be highlighted with color coding.

After completing the test, we can also export the coverage results similar to the test results. We can also import the coverage results which were already exported. There is another new option, **Merge Results**. This window will list all the coverage results from which we can select the results and merge them to get the end result of the code coverage collectively from various results.

Overview of XML files for testing tools in Visual Studio 2008

There are several XML files used by the VSTS Test Edition for storing the test information. All these documents should conform to the schema defined in the `TestTypes.xsd` file.

We have seen some of the XML document types in the previous examples, and here is the summary of all the XML documents for different test types supported by Visual Studio. Each of these is explained in detail in the individual chapter that explains the type of test.

1. **Test Metadata file**: This file stores information about all the tests in the solution. It has the extension `.vsmdi`.
2. **Test Results file**: This file contains the results of the tests that were run. This file will be created automatically by Visual Studio when any test is run. It has the extension `.trx`.
3. **Test Run Configuration file**: This file contains the settings that specify how the test runs should proceed further. It has the extension `.testrunconfig`.
4. There are other XML files for different test types with some specific extensions such as `.webtest`, `.loadtest`, `.orderedtest`, `.generictest`.

XML schema was changed from Visual Studio 2005 Team Edition to the release of Visual Studio Team System 2008 Test Edition. So the XML documents that were created using Visual Studio 2005 Team Edition for Testers need to be upgraded to VSTS 2008 Test Edition before starting to use those XML documents. These XML documents can be converted to the current format using the exe, `VSTST-FileConverter.exe`.

This file accepts one parameter which is the XML document for the test created using Visual Studio 2005. For example, if the test is an ordered test with the name SampleOrderedTest1, then it should be converted using the converter to

```
>VSTST-FileConverter.exe SampleOrderedTest1.orderedtest
```

To get help on the file converter, we can use the following command:

```
>VSTST-FileCOnverter.exe /help
```

Summary

This chapter gave an overview of the different types of testing that we can perform using Visual Studio 2008. We have also looked at how we can create the test project in Visual Studio, and how we make use of different tools that support testing in Visual Studio. Now, we should be able to create and execute a test project and create the test lists. We got an idea of how to view the test results using the **Test Results** window and look into the **Code Coverage Results** window. This chapter also explained about different types of XML and configuration documents that were created during the testing.

Now, we should be able to convert our existing testing application created using Visual Studio 2005 to the Visual Studio 2008 format using the converter tool, which we saw in this chapter, and continue our testing. The later chapters will discuss in detail about conducting different types of testing using Visual Studio 2008.

2
Unit Testing

Unit testing is the testing technique used for confirming if the piece of code is producing the result as expected. In project development, there may be many modules and each module comprises a set of code or functionalities. Identifying the piece of code in the module, which causes the defect is always a time-consuming task and the cost involved is also more. It is always better to test the code in units and confirm the functionality before integrating the code into module(s). Requiring all code to pass the unit tests before they can be integrated ensures that the functionality always works. Make sure each unit of code is written for one piece of functionality so that the result produced by each unit test is for a single functionality. Every time a defect is fixed or code is modified, we don't have to manually retest the unit, spending a lot of time and money. The automated unit test will help us make sure the functionality is unaffected.

VSTS is used for generating the unit test for the methods irrespective of whether they are public or private. Unit test is another class file similar to any other class and methods having additional attributes to define the Test class and the Test method. The unit tests can be created either by manually writing the code or by generating the unit test code using the **Create Unit Tests** option from the context-menu in VSTS.

The generated unit test class contains special attributes assigned to the class and methods in the class. Test classes are marked by the attribute [`TestClass()`] and each test method is marked with the attribute [`TestMethod()`]. Apart from these two, there are many other attributes used for unit testing. After generating the unit test class and methods, we can use the `Assert` method to verify the produced result with the expected value.

All of the unit test classes and methods are defined in the namespace `Microsoft.VisualStudio.TestTools.UnitTesting`. Whenever we create a new unit test in Visual Studio, we have to include this namespace to the class file. One of the main properties of the test classes in unit testing is the `TestContext` which holds all the information about tests.

Creating unit tests

There are two different ways of creating a unit test. One is the manual way of writing the code and the other is to generate the unit test code for the class using the option in Visual Studio. To see how a test class is generated, let us consider the class library below, following which is a very simple example of total price calculation.

For creating a new class library, open VSTS and select **New Project** under the **File** menu option and then select **Class Library** from the available templates.

```
using System;
using System.Collections.Generic;
using System.Linq;
using System.Text;

namespace TestLibrary
{
    public class Class1
    {
        public double CalculateTotalPrice(double quantity)
        {
            double totalPrice;
            double unitPrice;
            // Todo get unit price. For test let us hardcode it
            unitPrice = 16.0;

            totalPrice = unitPrice * quantity;
            return totalPrice;
        }

        public void GetTotalPrice()
        {
            int qty = 5;
            CalculateTotalPrice(qty);
        }
    }
}
```

Now within the class file, right-click on the method for which we want to create the unit test. In the above code, we have `CalculateTotalPrice` and `GetTotalPrice`. Right-click on the `CalculateTotalPrice` method, which will show up on the dialog for creating the unit testing.

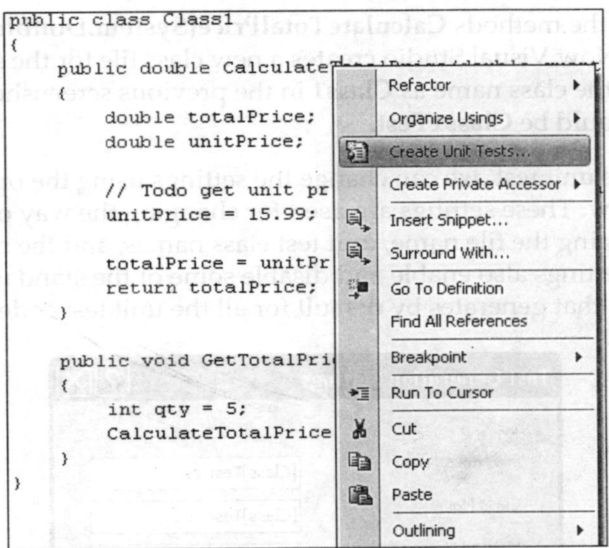

Once the **Create Unit Tests...** option is selected, we can see that the window that displays all the projects and all the methods within the class from where we selected the method. The selected method will be checked in the list leaving the other methods unchecked, which means that the unit test will be generated only for the selected method in the list. We can select and unselect any number of methods in the list based on the requirements. The output project's drop-down lists the option for creating a new test project in C# or Visual Basic or C++ and the list of existing test projects if the current solution already has some test projects. Choose the required option and provide a new name for the test project if the selected option is for a new project.

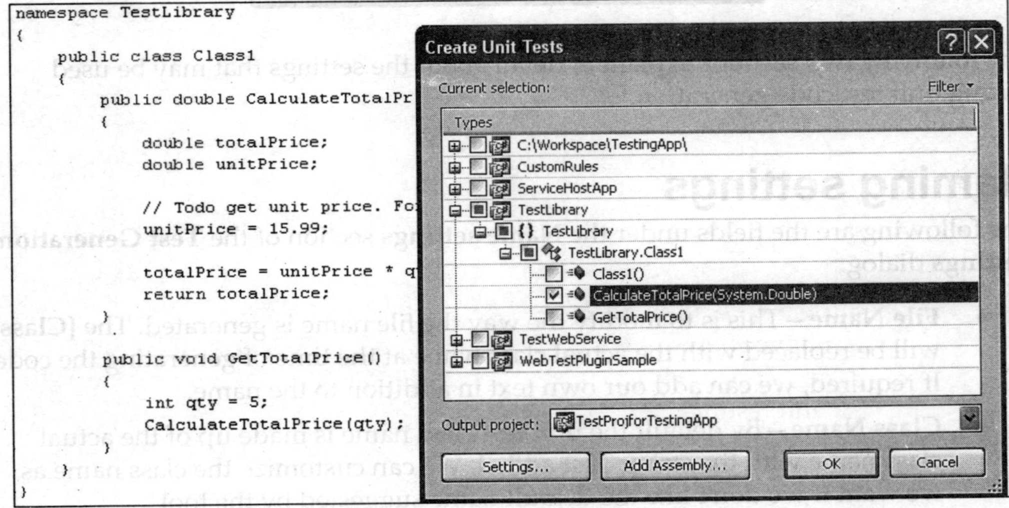

Let us select both the methods **CalculateTotalPrice(System.Double)** and **GetTotalPrice()**. Now Visual Studio creates a new class file for the selected method's class. We can see the class name as **Class1** in the previous screenshot. So the test class created for this would be **Class1Test**.

While creating the unit test, we can change the settings using the option in the **Create Unit Tests** window. These settings are used for changing the way of creating the unit tests by changing the file name, unit test class names, and the method name generation. The settings also enable and disable some of the standard code and method attributes that generates by default for all the unit test code.

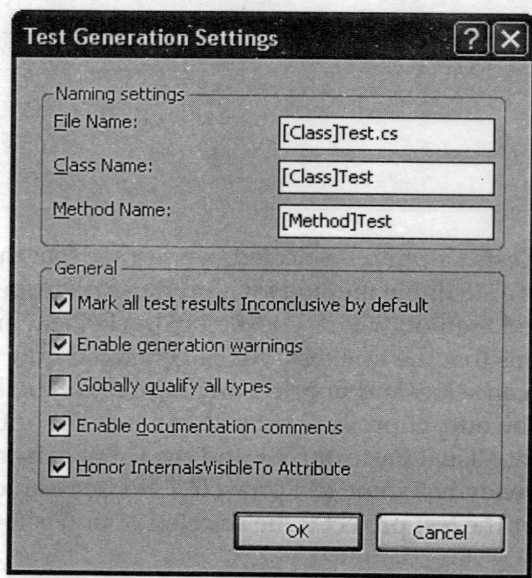

The following two sections explain in detail about the settings that may be used during unit test code generation.

Naming settings

The following are the fields under the **Name settings** section of the **Test Generation Settings** dialog:

- **File Name** – This is to modify the way the file name is generated. The **[Class]** will be replaced with the actual class name at the time of generating the code. If required, we can add our own text in addition to the name.
- **Class Name** – By default the unit test class name is made up of the actual class name with the string Test added. We can customize the class name as we want if we don't like the default name suggested by the tool.

- **Method Name**—This is similar to the **Class Name** and the **File Name**. By default VSTS assigns the actual method name followed by the text **Test**. The **[Method]** is replaced with the actual method name at the time of code generation.

General settings

These are the general settings applicable for the default basic code generated for each unit test. Using this we can enable or disable some of the common code generated for the classes.

- **Mark all test results Inconclusive by default**—When this option is enabled, the `Assert.Inconclusive` statement is added to all the methods in the unit test class. This is useful to specify the method is incomplete, as we have not added any test code yet. The method only contains the skeleton of the auto-generated test method. Later on, once we add the actual test code to the method we can safely remove this `Assert.Inconclusive` call.

```
Assert.Inconclusive("Verify the correctness of
                    this test method.");
```

- **Enable generation warnings**—If there are any unexpected errors during the test method generation, the code generator will add the error message as a comment within the test method body. This will help us resolve the issue and add the code later on.
- **Globally qualify all types**—This is to resolve the conflict between the same type name used in multiple classes. The unit test code may contain multiple class file test methods. Sometimes the same type may be used in different class files. So to make sure the types are unique across the test, the namespaces are added to all the types in the test.
- **Enable documentation comments**—This is to generate the comments for each method. The comments are in XML format by default. The default comments can be modified or added with more comments describing the test method. If this option is disabled, the comments won't be generated for the test methods.

```
/// <summary>
///A test for GetuserDetails
///</summary>
```

- **Honor InternalsVisiableTo Attribute** – This attribute will make all the internal attributes visible to the assembly and we will be able to call this just like any other public method.

  For example if we have an internal method like this,

```
  // Sample method for generating unit test for Internal
 // method
internal static bool MethodforInternalExample(string str)
{
     bool result = false;
     if (str == "return true") result = true;
     if (str == "return false") result = false;
     return result;
 }
```

  The unit test generated for this internal method would be just a public method like any other method.

```
/// <summary>
///A test for MethodforInternalExample
///</summary>
[TestMethod()]
public void MethodforInternalExampleTest()
{
     string str = string.Empty; // TODO: Initialize to an
                                // appropriate value
     bool expected = false; // TODO: Initialize to an
                            // appropriate value
     bool actual;
     actual = Class1.MethodforInternalExample(str);
     Assert.AreEqual(expected, actual);
     Assert.Inconclusive("Verify the correctness of this
                         test method.");
}
```

- **Add assembly** – This option in the **Create Unit Tests** dialog, is used for adding additional assemblies for generating the unit tests. The **Add assembly** option helps us select the assembly to be added and then displays the methods and classes from the assembly. We can select the methods from the tree view and then generate the unit test.

Generated unit test code

The following is the unit test code generated for the selected methods and the class with all the default attributes set for each method. You may also notice that the `Assert.Inconclusive` call is added to all the methods by default based on the settings. VSTS also adds the default start up and cleaning methods, which we can make use of for testing. The following are the list of attributes used for test class and test methods:

Attributes	Description
`TestClass()`	To identify the unit test class within the file.
`ClassInitialize()`	The method with this attribute is used for preparing the class for the test; for example, setting up the environment or collecting details which are required for testing are handled within this method; the method with this attribute is executed just before the first test in the class; each test class can have only one method as the class initializer.
`ClassCleanup()`	The method with this attribute is used for cleaning or destroying the objects used in the test; this method is executed after all the tests in the class are run; test class can contain only one method as the `ClassCleanup` method.
`TestInitialize()`	The method with this attribute is used for initializing or running the code before each test.
`TestCleanup()`	This method is run after each test in the class; this is similar to the `ClassCleanup` but the difference here is that the method is executed once after each test.
`TestMethod()`	This attribute identifies the method to be included as part of the test; this method has the unit test code for the method in the original class file.

In the following code, we can see many attributes and properties set to the class and methods. Visual Studio by default creates some methods with special attributes which are commented. If these methods are required for testing, we can uncomment it and make use of it.

```
using TestLibrary;
using Microsoft.VisualStudio.TestTools.UnitTesting;
namespace TestProjforTestingApp
{
    ///<summary>
    ///This is a test class for Class1Test and is intended
    ///to contain all Class1Test Unit Tests
    ///</summary>
    [TestClass()]
```

```
    public class Class1Test
    {
        private TestContext testContextInstance;
        /// <summary>
        ///Gets or sets the test context which provides
        ///information about and functionality for the current test
        ///run.
        ///</summary>
        public TestContext TestContext
        {
            get
            {
                return testContextInstance;
            }
            set
            {
                testContextInstance = value;
            }
        }
         #region Additional test attributes
         //
         //You can use the following additional attributes as you
        //write your tests:
         //
         //Use ClassInitialize to run code before running the first
        //test in the class
         //[ClassInitialize()]
         //public static void MyClassInitialize(TestContext
                                                   testContext)
         //{
         //}
         //
         //Use ClassCleanup to run code after all tests in a class
        //have run
         //[ClassCleanup()]
         //public static void MyClassCleanup()
         //{
         //}
         //
         //Use TestInitialize to run code before running each test
         //[TestInitialize()]
         //public void MyTestInitialize()
```

```
        //{
        //}
        //
        //Use TestCleanup to run code after each test has run
        //[TestCleanup()]
        //public void MyTestCleanup()
        //{
        //}
        //
        #endregion

        /// <summary>
        ///A test for GetTotalPrice
        ///</summary>
        [TestMethod()]
        public void GetTotalPriceTest()
        {
            Class1 target = new Class1(); // TODO: Initialize to an
                                          //appropriate value
            double expected = 0F; // TODO: Initialize to an
                                  //appropriate value
            double actual;
            actual = target.GetTotalPrice();
            Assert.AreEqual(expected, actual);
            Assert.Inconclusive("Verify the correctness of this test
                              method.");
        }

        /// <summary>
        ///A test for CalculateTotalPrice
        ///</summary>
        [TestMethod()]
        public void CalculateTotalPriceTest()
        {
            Class1 target = new Class1(); // TODO: Initialize to an
                                          //appropriate value
            double quantity = 0F; // TODO: Initialize to an
                                  //appropriate value
            double expected = 0F; // TODO: Initialize to an
                                  //appropriate value
            double actual;
            actual = target.CalculateTotalPrice(quantity);
            Assert.AreEqual(expected, actual);
            Assert.Inconclusive("Verify the correctness of this test
                              method.");
        }
    }
}
```

It is recommended to use the `TestCleanup` and `ClassCleanup` methods instead of the `Finalizer` method for all the test classes. The exceptions thrown from the `Finalizer` method will not be caught leading to unexpected result. The cleanup activity should be used for bringing the environment to its original state. For example, during testing we might have updated or inserted more records to the database tables or would have created lot of files and logs. This information should be removed once the testing is complete and the exceptions during this process should be caught and rectified.

Assert statements

The assert statement is used for comparing the result from the method with the expected result and then passing or failing the test based on the match. Whatever may be the result produced by the method, the end result of the test method depends on the return value of the assert method. The assert statement takes care of setting the result. There are different statements supported by the `Assert` class to set the return value to `Pass` or `Fail` or `Inconclusive`. If the assert statement is not present in the test method, the test method will always return a `Pass`. If there are many assert statements in the test method, the test will be in `Pass` state until one of the assert statements returns `Fail`.

In the previous example, the test method `CalculateTotalPriceTest` has two assert statements `Assert.AreEqual` and `Assert.Inconclusive`. The `Assert.AreEqual` has two parameters—one as `expected` which is the expected value that should be returned by the `CalculateTotalPrice` method and the other as `actual` indicating the actual value returned by the method. The `Assert.AreEqual` statement, which is explained in detail in the next section, compares these two values and returns the test result as `Pass` if both the value matches. Returns `Fail` if there is a mismatch between these two values.

```
[TestMethod()]
public void CalculateTotalPriceTest()
{
    Class1 target = new Class1(); // TODO: Initialize to an
                                  //appropriate value
    double quantity = 0F; // TODO: Initialize to an
                          //appropriate value
    double expected = 0F; // TODO: Initialize to an
                          //appropriate value
    double actual;
    actual = target.CalculateTotalPrice(quantity);
    Assert.AreEqual(expected, actual);
    Assert.Inconclusive("Verify the correctness of this test
                         method.");
}
```

The test method also has the `Assert.Inconclusive` statement to return the result as inconclusive if the test method is not complete. We can remove this line if the code is complete and we do not want the test result to be inconclusive. In the previous code, if we run the test without setting the value for `quantity` and `expected` the return would be `Inconclusive`. Now set the value for the `quantity` and `expected` as:

- `double quantity = 10F;`
- `double expected = 159F;`

The result returned would be a `Fail` because the actual value returned by the method would be 160, while our expected value is 159. If you change the expected value to 160 then the test would pass. We have seen only one type of assert statement. There are many other asserts, which we can use in test methods for passing or failing the test.

Types of asserts

The Assert classes in VSTS contain the comparison and conditional testing capabilities. The namespace `Microsoft.VisualStudio.TestTools.UnitTesting` in VSTS contains all these asserts. The actual and the expected values are compared based on the type of assert used and the result decides the test pass or failure.

The assert class

The assert class has many different overloaded methods for comparing the values. Each method is used for a specific type of comparison. For example, an assert can compare a string with a string or an object with another object, but not an integer with an object. Overloaded methods are like the additional or optional parameters to the method in case we want custom messages or the additional functionality to be added. For example, the assert method provides an overloaded method to compare the values within a specified accuracy, which we will see in detail when comparing double values.

Let us consider a simple `Item` class with three properties each with different data types.

```
public class Item {
    public int ItemID { get; set; }
    public string ItemType { get; set; }
    public double ItemPrice { get; set; }
}
```

The code shown here is a sample which creates a new `Item` object with values set for the properties:

```
public Item GetObjectToCompare() {
    Item objA = new Item();
    objA.ItemID = 100;
    objA.ItemType = "Electronics";
    objA.ItemPrice = 10.99;
    return objA;
}
```

Generate the unit test for the above method and set the properties for the local expected object similar to the one shown here:

```
[TestMethod()]
public void GetObjectToCompareTest()
{
    Class1 target = new Class1();
    Item expected = new Item();
    expected.ItemID = 100;
    expected.ItemType = "Electronics";
    expected.ItemPrice = 10.39;
    Item actual;
    actual = target.GetObjectToCompare();
    Assert.AreEqual(expected, actual);
}
```

With the above sample code and the unit test we will look at the results of each overloaded methods in the `Assert` class.

Assert.AreEqual

This is used for comparing and verifying actual and expected values. The following are the overloaded methods for the `Assert.AreEqual()` and the result for the above code samples.

Method	Description
`Assert.AreEqual(Object, Object);`	Verifies if both the objects are equal. The test fails because the actual and the expected are two different objects even though the properties are the same. Try setting `expected = actual` just before the assert statement and run the test again; the test would pass as both the objects are the same now.

Method	Description
`Assert.AreEqual(Object, Object, String)`	Used for verifying two objects and displays the string message if the test fails; for example, if the statement is like this `Assert.AreEqual(expected, actual, "Not equal")` The output if the test fails would be **Assert.AreEqual failed. Expected:<TestLibrary.Item>. Actual:<TestLibrary.Item>. Objects are not equal**
`Assert.AreEqual(Object, Object, String, Object[])`	Used for verifying two objects and displays the string message if the test fails; the formatting is applied to the displayed message; for example, if the assert statement is like this `Assert.AreEqual(expected, actual, "Objects {0} and {1} are not equal", "ObjA", "ObjB")` The displayed message if the test fails would be **Assert.AreEqual failed. Expected:<TestLibrary.Item>. Actual:<TestLibrary.Item>. Objects ObjA and ObjB are not equal**
`Assert.AreEqual(String, String, Boolean)`	Used for comparing and verifying two strings; the third parameter is to specify whether to ignore cases or not; if the assert statement is like this `Assert.AreEqual(expected.ItemType, actual.ItemType, false)` The test will pass only if both the values are the same including the cases.
`Assert.AreEqual(String, String. Boolean, CultureInfo)`	Used for comparing two strings specifying cases to include for comparison including the culture info specified; for example, if the assert is like this `Assert.AreEqual(expected.ItemType, actual.ItemType, false, System.Globalization.CultureInfo.CurrentCulture.EnglishName)` If the property value for `expected.ItemType="electronics"` then the result would be **Assert.AreEqual failed. Expected:<electronics>. Case is different for actual value:<Electronics>. English (United States)**

Method	Description
`Assert.AreEqual(String, String, Boolean, String)`	Used for comparing two strings specifying casing to include for comparison; display the specified message if the test fails; for example, if the statement is like this `Assert.AreEqual(expected.ItemType, actual.ItemType, false, "Both the strings are not equal")` The test result would be **Assert.AreEqual failed. Expected:<electronics>. Case is different for actual value:<Electronics>. Both the strings are not equal**
`Assert.AreEqual(String, String, Booelan, CultureInfo, String)`	Used for comparing two strings specifying casing and culture info to include for comparison; displays the specified message if the test fails the following is an example, `Assert.AreEqual(expected.ItemType, actual.ItemType, false, System.Globalization.CultureInfo.CurrentCulture.EnglishName, "Both the strings {0} and {1} are not equal", actual.ItemType, expected.ItemType)`
`Assert.AreEqual(String, String, Booelan, String, Object[])`	Used for comparing two strings specifying the casing; the specified message is displayed with the specified formatting applied to it; for example, if the statement is like this `Assert.AreEqual(expected.ItemType, actual.ItemType, false, "Both the strings '{0}' and '{1}' are not equal", actual.ItemType, expected.ItemType);` The test result if the test fails would be **Assert.AreEqual failed. Expected:<electronics>. Case is different for actual value:<Electronics>. Both the strings 'Electronics' and 'electronics' are not equal**

<table>
<tr><th>Method</th><th>Description</th></tr>
<tr><td><code>Assert.
AreEqual(String,
String, Booelan,
CultureInfo,
String,
Object[])</code></td><td>Used for comparing two strings specifying casing and culture information to include for comparison; display the specified message if the test fails; the specified formatters are applied to the message to replace it with the parameter values. The following is an example,

<code>Assert.AreEqual(expected.ItemType, actual.
ItemType, false, System.Globalization.
CultureInfo.CurrentCulture.EnglishName, "Both
the strings '{0}' and '{1}' are not equal",
actual.ItemType, expected.ItemType);</code>

If the test fails, it displays the message with the formatters <code>{0}</code> and <code>{1}</code> replaced with the values in <code>actual.Itemtype</code> and <code>expected.ItemType</code>.</td></tr>
<tr><td><code>Assert.
AreEqual(Double,
Double, Double)</code>

<code>Assert.
AreEqual(Double,
Double, Double,
String)</code>

<code>Assert.
AreEqual(Double,
Double, Double,
String,
Object[])</code></td><td>These are the three different overloaded assert methods for comparing and verifying the <code>Double</code> values; the first and second parameter values are the expected and actual values; the third parameter is to specify the accuracy within which the values should be compared. The fourth parameter is for the message and fifth is the formatter to be applied for the message; for example, if the assert is like this

<code>Assert.AreEqual(expected.ItemPrice, actual.
ItemPrice, 0.5, "The values {0} and {1} does
not match within the accuracy", expected.
ItemPrice, actual.ItemPrice);</code>

The test would produce a result as Assert.AreEqual failed. Expected a difference no greater than <0.5> between expected value <10.39> and actual value <10.99>. The value 10.39 and 10.99 does not match within the accuracy. Here the expected accuracy is 0.5 but the difference is 0.6.</td></tr>
<tr><td><code>Assert.
AreEqual(Single,
Single, Single)</code>

<code>Assert.
AreEqual(Single,
Single, Single,
String)</code>

<code>Assert.
AreEqual(Single,
Single, Single,
String,
Object[])</code></td><td>This is very similar to the <code>Double</code> value comparison as shown above but the values here are of type <code>Single</code>; this method also supports the message and the formatters to be displayed if the test fails.</td></tr>
</table>

Method	Description

`Assert.AreEqual<T>(T, T,)`
 	
`Assert.AreEqual<T>(T, T, String)`
 	
`Assert.AreEqual<T>(T, T, String, Object[])`
	These overloaded methods are used for comparing and verifying the generic type data; the assertion fails if they are not equal and displays the message by applying the specified formatters; for example, if the assert is like
	
	`Assert.AreEqual<Item>(actual, expected, "The objects '{0}' and '{1}' are not equal", "actual", "expected")`
	
	The test would produce the result if the test fails as **Assert.AreEqual failed. Expected:<TestLibrary.Item>. Actual:<TestLibrary.Item>. The objects 'actual' and 'expected' are not equal**

Assert.AreNotEqual

All the above said overloaded methods for `Assert.AreEqual` also applies to `Assert.AreNotEqual` but the only difference is that the comparison is the exact opposite of the `AreEqual` assert. For example, the following method verifies if the two strings are not equal by ignoring or not ignoring the casing as specified by Boolean. The test fails if they are equal and the message is displayed with the specified formatting applied to it.

```
Assert.AreNotEqual(String, String, Booelan, String, Object[])
```

The following code compares two strings and verifies whether they are equal or not:

```
Assert.AreNotEqual(expected.ItemType, actual.ItemType, false,
  "Both the strings '{0}' and '{1}' are equal", expected.ItemType,
  actual.ItemType);
```

If the string values are equal, the output of this would be:

Assert.AreNotEqual failed. Expected any value except:<Electronics>. Actual:<Electronics>. Both the strings 'Electronics' and 'Electronics' are equal

Assert.AreSame

Method	Description

`Assert.AreSame( Object, Object)`	This method compares and verifies whether both the object variables refer to the same object; even if the properties are the same the objects might be different; for example, the following test will pass because the objects are the same.
	`ArrayList A = new ArrayList(5);`
	`ArrayList B = A;`
	`Assert.AreSame(A, B);`
	Both the objects `A` and `B` refer to the same object and so they are the same.

`Assert.AreSame (Object,Object, String)`	This method compares and verifies whether both the object variables refer to the same object; if not, the message will be displayed; for example, the following code compares the two objects `A` and `B`:
	`ArrayList A = new ArrayList(5);`
	`ArrayList B = new ArrayList(10);`
	`Assert.AreSame(A, B, "The objects are not same");`
	The test fails with the output **Assert.AreSame failed.** The objects expected and actual are not same

Method	Description

`Assert.AreSame(Object, Object, String, Object[])`	This method compares and verifies whether both the object variables refers to the same object; if not, the message will be displayed with the specified formatting; for example, the following code compares the two objects A and B:
	`ArrayList A = new ArrayList(5);`
	`ArrayList B = new ArrayList(10);`
	`Assert.AreSame(A, B, "The objects {0} and {1} are not same", "A", "B");`
	The test fails with the output **Assert.AreSame failed.** The objects A and B are not same

Assert.AreNotSame

This assert is used for verifying whether the two objects are not the same. The test fails if the objects are the same. The same overloaded methods for `Assert.AreSame` applies here as well, but the comparison is the exact opposite. Following are the three overloaded methods applied to `Assert.AreNotSame`:

- `Assert.AreNotSame(Object,Object)`
- `Assert.AreNotSame(Object, Object,String)`
- `Assert.AreNotSame(Object,Object,String,Object[])`

For example, the following code verifies if objects A and B are not the same. If they are the same, the test fails with the specified error message with the specified formatting applied to it.

```
ArrayList A = new ArrayList(5);
ArrayList B = A;
Assert.AreNotSame(A, B, "The test fails because the
                  objects {0} and {1} are same", "A", "B");
```

The above test fails with the message **Assert.AreNotSame failed. The test fails because the objects A and B are same**.

Assert.Fail

This Assert is used for failing the test without checking any condition. `Assert.Fail` has three overloaded methods.

Method	Description
`Assert.Fail()`	Fails the test without checking any condition
`Assert.Fail(String)`	Fails the test without checking any condition and displays the message
`Assert.Fail(String, Object[])`	Fails the test without checking any condition and display the message with the specified formatting applied to the message; for example, the following code does not check for any condition but fails the test and displays the message `Assert.Fail("This method '{0}' is set to fail temporarily", "GetItemPrice");` The output for the above code would be **Assert.Fail failed.** This method **'GetItemPrice'** is set to fail temporarily

Assert.Inconclusive

This is useful in case the method is incomplete and we cannot determine whether the output is true or false. We can set the assertion to be inconclusive until we complete the method for testing. There are three overloaded methods for `Assert.Inconclusive`.

Method	Description
`Assert.Inconclusive()`	Assertion cannot be verified; set to inconclusive
`Assert. Inconclusive(String)`	Assertion cannot be verified; set to inconclusive and displays the message
`Assert. Inconclusive(String, Object[])`	Assertion cannot be verified; set to inconclusive and displays the message with the specified formatting applied to it; for example, the following code sets the assertion as inconclusive which means neither true nor false `Assert.Inconclusive("This method '{0}' is not yet ready for testing", "GetItemPrice");` The output for the above code would be **Assert.Inconclusive failed.** This method **'GetItemPrice'** is not yet ready for testing

Assert.IsTrue

This is used for verifying if the condition is true. The test fails if the condition is false. There are three overloaded methods for `Assert.IsTrue`.

Method	Description
`Assert.IsTrue()`	Used for verifying the condition; test fails if the condition is false
`Assert.IsTrue(String)`	Used for verifying the condition and display the message if the test fails with the condition false.

`Assert.IsTrue(String, Object[])`	Verifies the condition and display the message if the test fails with the condition false; apply the specified formatting to the message.
	
	For example, the following code fails the test as the conditions returns false.
	
	`ArrayList A = new ArrayList(5);`
	
	`ArrayList B = new ArrayList(10);`
	
	`Assert.IsTrue(A == B, "Both '{0}' and '{1}' are not equal", "A", "B");`
	
	The output message for the above test would be **Assert.IsTrue failed. Both 'A' and 'B' are not equal**

Assert.IsFalse

This is to verify if the condition is false. The test fails if the condition is true. Similar to `Assert.IsTrue`, this one has three overloaded methods.

Method	Description
`Assert.IsFalse()`	Used for verifying the condition; test fails if the condition is true.
`Assert.IsFalse(String)`	Used for verifying the condition; display the message if the test fails with the condition true.

Method	Description

`Assert.IsFalse(String, Object[])`	Verify the condition and display the message if the test fails with the condition true and apply the specified formatting to the message.
	
	For example, the following code fails the test as the conditions returns true.
	
	`ArrayList A = new ArrayList(5);`
	
	`ArrayList B = A;`
	
	`Assert.IsFalse(A == B, "Both '{0}' and '{1}' are equal", "A", "B");`
	
	The output message for the above test would be **Assert. IsFalse failed. Both 'A' and 'B' are equal**

Assert.IsNull

This is useful in verifying whether the object is null. The test fails if the object is not null. Given here are the three overloaded methods for `Assert.IsNull`.

Method	Description
`Assert.IsNull(Object)`	Verify if the object is null.
`Assert.IsNull(Object, String)`	Verify if the object is null and display the message if the object is not null and the test fails.

`Assert.IsNull(Object, String, Object[])`	Verify if the object is null and display the message if the object is not null; apply the formatting to the message
	
	For example, the following code verifies if the object is null and fails the test if it is not null and displays the formatted message:
	
	`ArrayList A = new ArrayList(5);`
	
	`ArrayList B = A;`
	
	`Assert.IsNull(B, "Object '{0}' is not null", "B");`
	
	The code above fails the test and displays the error message **Assert.IsNull failed. Object 'B' is not null.**

Assert.IsNotNull

This is to verify if the object is null or not. The test fails if the object is null. This is the exact opposite of the `Assert.IsNull` and has the same overloaded methods.

Method	Description
`Assert.IsNotNull(Object)`	Verifies if the object is not null
`Assert.IsNotNull(Object, String)`	Verifies if the object is not null and display the message if the object is null and test fails

`Assert.IsNotNull(Object, String, Object[])`	Verify if the object is not null and displays the message if the object is null; applies the formatting to the message
	
	For example, the following code verifies if the object is not null and fails the test if it is null and displays the formatted message:
	
	`ArrayList B = null;`
	
	`Assert.IsNotNull(B, "Object '{0}' is null", "B");`
	
	The code above fails the test and displays the error message **Assert.IsNotNull failed. Object 'B' is null**

Assert.IsInstanceOfType

This method verifies whether the object is of the specified `System.Type`. The test fails if the type does not match.

Method	Description

`Assert.IsInstanceOfType(Object,Type )`	This method is used for verifying whether the object is of specified `System.Type`
	
	For example, the following code verifies whether the object is of type `ArrayList`
	
	`Hashtable obj = new Hashtable();`
	
	`Assert.IsInstanceOfType(obj, typeof(ArrayList));`
	
	The test fails as the object `obj` is not of type `ArrayList`. The error message returned would be like **Assert.IsInstanceOfType failed. Expected type:<System.Collections.ArrayList>. Actual type:<System.Collections.Hashtable>**

Method	Description
`Assert.IsInstanceOfType (Object, Type, String)`	This is the overloaded method for the above method with an additional parameter; the third parameter is the message to be displayed in case the test fails
`Assert. IsInstanceOfType(Object, Type, String, Object[])`	The purpose of this method is the same as that of the above methods; but the additional parameter is the formatter to be applied on the error message displayed if the test fails

StringAsserts

This is another `Assert` class within the unit test namespace `Microsoft.VisualStudio.TestTools.UnitTesting` that contains methods for the common text-based assertions. `StringAssert` contains the following methods with additional overloaded methods. Overloaded methods are the additional or optional parameters to the method in case we want custom messages.

StringAssert.Contains

This method verifies if the second parameter string is present in the first parameter string. The test fails if the string is not present. There are two more overloaded methods for `StringAssert.Contains`. The third parameter specifies the message to be displayed if the assertion fails and the fourth parameter specifies the message formatter to be applied on the error message for the assertion failure. The formatters are the placeholders for the parameters values.

- `StringAssert.Contains(String, String)`
- `StringAssert.Contains(String, String, String)`
- `StringAssert.Contains(String, String, String, Object[])`

For example, the following code verifies if the string **Test** is present in the first string. If not, the message is displayed with the formatters applied to it.

```
string find = "Testing";
StringAssert.Contains("This is the Test for StringAsserts",
      find, "The string '{0}' is not found in the first
      parameter value", find);
```

The assertion fails with the specified error message added to its default message as **StringAssert.Contains** failed. String **'This is the Test for StringAsserts'** does not contain string **'Testing'**. The string **'Testing'** is not found in the first parameter value.

StringAssert.Matches

As the name suggests, this method verifies if the first string matches the regular expression specified as the second parameter. This assert method contains two additional overloaded methods to display the custom error message and apply formatters to the message if the assertion fails.

- `StringAssert.Matches(String, Regex)`
- `StringAssert.Matches(String, Regex, String)`
- `StringAssert.Matches(String, Regex, String, Object[])`

For example, the following code verifies if the string contains any numbers between 0 and 9. If not, the assertion fails with the message specified with the formatters.

```
Regex regEx = new Regex("[0-9]");
StringAssert.Matches("This is first test for StringAssert",
     regEx, "There are no numbers between {0} and {1} in the
     string", 0, 9);
```

The error message would be **StringAssert.Matches failed**. String **'This is first test for StringAssert'** does not match pattern **'[0-9]'**. There are no numbers between 0 and 9 in the string.

StringAssert.DoesNotMatch

This is the exact opposite of the `StringAssert.Matches`. This assert method verifies whether the first parameter string matches the regular expression specified as the second parameter. The assertion fails if it matches. This assert type also has two additional overloaded methods to display the error message and apply the message formatting to it which is the place holder for the parameter values in the message.

- `StringAssert.DoesNotMatch(String, Regex,)`
- `StringAssert.DoesNotMatch(String, Regex, String)`
- `StringAssert.DoesNotMatch(String, Regex, String, Object[])`

For example, the following code verifies if the first parameter string does not match with the regular expression specified in the second parameter. The assertion fails if it does match and displays the specified error message with the formatting applied to it.

```
Regex regEx = new Regex("[0-9]");
StringAssert.DoesNotMatch("This is 1st test for StringAssert",
     regEx, "There is a number in the string");
```

The assertion fails with the error message **StringAssert.DoesNotMatch failed. String 'This is 1st test for StringAssert' matches pattern '[0-9]'. There is a number in the string.**

StringAssert.StartsWith

This is to verify whether a string in the first parameter starts with the value in the second parameter. The assertion fails if the string does not start with the second string. There are two overloaded methods to specify the error message to be displayed and to specify the formatting to be applied to the error message.

- `StringAssert.StartsWith(String, String)`
- `StringAssert.StartsWith(String, String, String)`
- `StringAssert.StartsWith(String, String, String, Object[])`

For example, the following code verifies if the first string starts with the specified second parameter value. The assertion fails if it does not, and displays the specified error message with the specified formatting.

```
string startWith = "First";
StringAssert.StartsWith("This is 1st test for StringAssert",
      startWith, "The string does not start with '{0}'",
      startWith);
```

The assertion fails with the error message **StringAssert.StartsWith failed. String 'This is 1st test for StringAssert' does not start with string 'First'. The string does not start with 'First'**.

StringAssert.EndsWith

This is similar to the `StringAssert.StartsWith`, but here it verifies if the first string ends with the specified string in the second parameter. The assertion fails if it does not end with the specified string and displays the error message. There are two additional overloaded methods to specify the custom error message and the formatting.

- `StringAssert.EndsWith(String, String)`
- `StringAssert.EndsWith(String, String, String)`
- `StringAssert.EndsWith(String, String, String, Object[])`

For example, the following code verifies whether the first string ends with the specified string as the second parameter. The assertion will fail and display the message with the specified formatting.

```
string endsWith = "Testing";
StringAssert.EndsWith("This is 1st test for StringAssert",
    endsWith, "'{0}' is not the actual ending in the
    string", endsWith);
```

The error message displayed would be **StringAssert.EndsWith failed. String 'This is 1st test for StringAssert' does not end with string 'Testing'. 'Testing' is not the actual ending in the string.**

CollectionAssert

Visual Studio provides another type of assert through the namespace `Microsoft.VisualStudio.TestTools.UnitTesting` which helps us to verify the objects that implements the `ICollection` interface. The collections might be the system collection type or the custom collections. Using the `CollectionAssert` we can compare and verify whether the objects implementing the `ICollection` interface returns the contents as expected.

We will consider the following array lists and find out the usage of Collection Assert Statements. These array lists are used in all the collection assert samples given here in this section.

```
ArrayList firstArray = new ArrayList(3);
firstArray.Add("FirstName");
firstArray.Add("LastName");

ArrayList secondArray = new ArrayList(3);
secondArray = firstArray;
secondArray.Add("MiddleName");
ArrayList thirdArray = new ArrayList(3);
thirdArray.Add("FirstName");
thirdArray.Add("MiddleName");
thirdArray.Add("LastName");

ArrayList fourthArray = new ArrayList(3);
fourthArray.Add("FirstName");
fourthArray.Add("MiddleName");
```

The `firstArray` array list has a maximum index of three but it has only two elements added to it.

The `secondArray` array list has a maximum index of three and `firstArray` is assigned to it with an additional item `MiddleName` added to it.

The `thirdArray` array list has a maximum index of three and contains three items in the array.

The `fourthArray` array list also has three as maximum index but contains only two items.

CollectionAssert.AllItemsAreNotNull

This assert will verify if any of the items in the collection is not null. The assertion will pass as none of the items is null in `firstArray`.

```
CollectionAssert.AllItemsAreNotNull(firstArray)
```

The assertion will fail if we add the third item as:

```
firstArray.Add(null)
```

There are two additional overloaded methods to display the custom error message and to specify the formatting for the message if the assertion fails.

- `CollectionAssert.AllItemsAreNotNull(ICollection)`
- `CollectionAssert.AllItemsAreNotNull(ICollection, String)`
- `CollectionAssert.AllItemsAreNotNull(ICollection, String, Object[])`

CollectionAssert.AreEquivalent

The `CollectionAssert.AreEquivalent` verifies if both the collections are equivalent. It means that even if the items are in different order in the collections, the items should match.

```
CollectionAssert.AreEquivalent(thirdArray, secondArray);
```

In the example, we can see that the `MiddleName` is the last item in the `secondArray` but it is the second item in the `thirdArray`. But both the collection have the same items, so the assertion will pass. The following are the overloaded methods for the `Collectionassert.AreEquivalent:`

- `CollectionAssert.AreEquivalent (ICollection, ICollection)`
- `CollectionAssert.AreEquivalent (ICollection, ICollection, String)`
- `CollectionAssert.AreEquivalent (ICollection, ICollection, String, Object[])`

CollectionAssert.AreNotEquivalent

`CollectionAssert.AreNotEquivalent` statement verifies if both first and second parameter collections does not contain the same items. It means that the assert fails even if one item in the first collection is present in the second collection. In the example, if we remove or replace one of the items from any of the two collections `secondArray` or the `thirdArray`, the assertion will pass as the items will not match.

```
thirdArray.Remove("MiddleName");
thirdArray.Add("FullName");
CollectionAssert.AreNotEquivalent(thirdArray, secondArray);
```

The following are the method syntax and the overloaded methods for the `CollectionAssert.AreNotEquivalent` assert to specify the custom error message and the formatting for the message.

- `CollectionAssert.AreNotEquivalent (ICollection, ICollection)`
- `CollectionAssert.AreNotEquivalent (ICollection, ICollection, String)`
- `CollectionAssert.AreNotEquivalent (ICollection, ICollection, String, Object[])`

CollectionAssert.AllItemsAreInstancesOfType

This statement verifies if all the items in the collection are of specified/expected type specified in the second parameter. The following code verifies if all the elements of the collection `thirdArray` is of type string. The assertion will pass as the items are string.

```
CollectionAssert.AllItemsAreInstancesOfType(thirdArray,
  typeof(string))
```

The following are the syntax and the overloaded methods for the `CollectionAssert.AllItemsAreInstacesOfType` assert, with parameters for custom error message and to specify the formatters or the placeholders for the parameter values in the message:

- `CollectionAssert.AllItemsAreInstancesOfType(ICollection, Type)`
- `CollectionAssert.AllItemsAreInstancesOfType(ICollection, Type, String)`
- `CollectionAssert.AllItemsAreInstancesOfType(ICollection, Type, String, Object[])`

CollectionAssert.IsSubsetOf

This statement verifies whether the collection in the first parameter contains some or all the elements of the collection in the second parameter. But all the items of the first parameter collection should be part of the collection in the second parameter. As per the example, the following assertion will pass as the items in the `fourthArray` are the subset of the items in the `thirdArray`:

```
CollectionAssert.IsSubsetOf(fourthArray, thirdArray)
```

The following are the syntax and the overloaded methods for the `CollectionAssert.IsSubsetOf` assert:

- `CollectionAssert.IsSubsetOf(ICollection, ICollection)`
- `CollectionAssert.IsSubsetOf(ICollection, ICollection, String)`
- `CollectionAssert.IsSubsetOf(ICollection, ICollection, String, Object[])`

CollectionAssert.IsNotSubsetOf

This statement verifies whether the collection in the first parameter contains at least one element not present in the second parameter collection. As per the example, the following assertion will fail as the items in the `fourthArray` are the subset of the items in the `thirdArray`. It means that there are no items in `fourthArray` which is not present in `thirdArray`.

```
CollectionAssert.IsSubsetOf(fourthArray, thirdArray)
```

Try adding a new element to the `fourthArray` which is not present in `thirdArray` such as:

```
fourthArray.Add("FullName");
```

Now try the same above the `CollectionAssert` statement. The assertion will fail as the `fourthArray` is not a subset of `thirdArray` collection.

The following are the syntax and the overloaded methods for the `CollectionAssert.IsSubsetOf` assert to specify the custom error message and the formatter for the error message:

- `CollectionAssert.IsNotSubsetOf(ICollection, ICollection)`
- `CollectionAssert.IsNotSubsetOf(ICollection, ICollection, String)`
- `CollectionAssert.IsNotSubsetOf(ICollection, ICollection, String, Object[])`

CollectionAssert.AllItemsAreUnique

This verifies whether the items in the collection are unique. The following assertion will pass as per the same collection. The assertion fails if we add a third item as `LastName` which duplicates the existing item.

```
firstArray.Add("LastName")
```

The syntax for this method and its two overloaded methods are given here. The additional parameters are to specify the custom error message and the formatters for the error message.

- `CollectionAssert.AllItemsAreUnique(ICollection)`
- `CollectionAssert.AllItemsAreUnique(ICollection, String)`
- `CollectionAssert.AllItemsAreUnique(ICollection, String, Object[])`

CollectionAssert.Contains

This assert verifies if any of the elements of the collection specified as the first parameter contains the element specified as the second parameter. The following assert given below will pass as the `FirstName` is an element in the `fourthArray` collection.

```
CollectionAssert.Contains(fourthArray, "FirstName")
```

We can specify the custom error message and custom formatters for the assertion failure. This assert has two overloaded methods in addition to the default method.

- `CollectionAssert.Contains(ICollection, Object)`
- `CollectionAssert.Contains(ICollection, Object, String)`
- `CollectionAssert.Contains(ICollection, Object, String, Object[])`

CollectionAssert.DoesNotContain

This is exact opposite of the `CollectionAssert.Contains` statement. This assert verifies if any of the elements in the first parameter collection does not equal to the element specified as the second parameter.

```
CollectionAssert.Contains(fourthArray, "Phone Number")
```

We can specify the custom error message and custom formatters for the assertion failure. This assert has two overloaded methods in addition to the default method.

- `CollectionAssert.DoesNotContain(ICollection, Object)`
- `CollectionAssert.DoesNotContain(ICollection, Object, String)`
- `CollectionAssert.DoesNotContain(ICollection, Object, String, Object[])`

CollectionAssert.AreEqual

This method verifies if both the collections are equal. The following assertion fails as the number of items added to the `firstArray` is different from the `thirdArray`.

```
CollectionAssert.AreEqual(firstArray, thirdArray)
```

The assertion will pass if we add the same items as of `firstArray` to the `thirdArray` or assign the `firstArray` to `thirdArray` which makes both the arrays equal:

```
thirdArray = firstArray;
```

This assert type has five more additional overloaded methods

- `CollectionAssert.AreEqual(ICollection, ICollection)`
- `CollectionAssert.AreEqual(ICollection, ICollection, IComparer)`
- `CollectionAssert.AreEqual(ICollection, ICollection, IComparer, String)`
- `CollectionAssert.AreEqual(ICollection, ICollection, IComparer, String, Object[])`
- `CollectionAssert.AreEqual(ICollection, ICollection, String)`
- `CollectionAssert.AreEqual(ICollection, ICollection, String, Object[])`

The parameter `String` and `Object[]` can be used when we need a custom error message and formatters for the error message in case of assertion failure.

The `IComparer` can be used in case if we have the custom objects in the collection and if we want to use a particular property of the object for comparison. For example, if collection contains a list of Employee objects, which contains FirstName, LastName, and EmployeeID of each employee, we may want to sort the elements in the collection based on the `FirstName` of the employees. We may want to compare the two collections containing the employees list based on the `FirstName` of the employees. To do this we have to create the custom comparer.

Consider the `Employee` class below, which has a `EmployeeComparer` class which compares the `FirstName` in the `Employee` which implemented from `IComparable` interface.

```
public class Employee : IComparable
  {
        public string FirstName { get; set; }
        public string LastName { get; set; }
        public int ID { get; set; }

        public Employee (string firstName, string lastName,
                           int employeeID)
        {
            FirstName = firstName;
            LastName = lastName;
            ID = employeeID;
        }

        public int CompareTo(Object obj)
        {
             Employee emp = (Employee)obj;
             return FirstName.CompareTo(emp.FirstName);
        }

        public class EmployeeComparer : IComparer
        {
            public int Compare(Object one, Object two)
            {
                Employee emp1 = (Employee)one;
                Employee emp2 = (Employee)two;
                 return emp1.CompareTo(two);
            }
  }
```

Now create two collections of type `ArrayList` and add employees to the lists. The First name of the employees are same in both the lists but the last name and id varies.

```
ArrayList EmployeesListOne = new ArrayList();
EmployeesListOne.Add(new TestLibrary.Employee("Richard",
                                    "King", 1801));
EmployeesListOne.Add(new TestLibrary.Employee("James",
                                    "Miller", 1408));
EmployeesListOne.Add(new TestLibrary.Employee("Jim",
                                    "Tucker", 3234));
```

```
EmployeesListOne.Add(new TestLibrary.Employee("Murphy",
                        "Young", 3954));
EmployeesListOne.Add(new TestLibrary.Employee("Shelly",
                        "Watts", 7845));
ArrayList EmployeesListTwo = new ArrayList();
EmployeesListTwo.Add(new TestLibrary.Employee("Richard",
                        "Smith", 4763));
EmployeesListTwo.Add(new TestLibrary.Employee("James",
                        "Wright", 8732));
EmployeesListTwo.Add(new TestLibrary.Employee("Jim",
                        "White", 1829));
EmployeesListTwo.Add(new TestLibrary.Employee("Murphy",
                        "Adams", 2984));
EmployeesListTwo.Add(new TestLibrary.Employee("Shelly",
                        "Johnson", 1605));
```

Now in the test method, use the `CollectionAssert.AreEqual` to compare the above collections.

```
CollectionAssert.AreEqual(EmployeesListOne, EmployeesListTwo,
   "The collections '{0}' and '{1}' are not equal",
   "EmployeesListOne", "EmployeesListTwo");
```

This assertion will fail because the objects in the collection are not same. Even if you update the employee object properties to be the same in both the collections it will fail because the objects are not same. The error message would be the specified custom message with the specified formatters.

But we can use the custom comparer we created to compare the collection objects based on the `FirstName` element which is used in the comparer. We can create the custom comparer on any of the object properties.

```
TestLibrary.Employee.EmployeeComparer comparer = new
TestLibrary.Employee.EmployeeComparer();
CollectionAssert.AreEqual(EmployeesListOne, EmployeesListTwo,
     comparer, "The collections '{0}' and '{1}' are not
     equal", "EmployeesListOne", "EmployeesListTwo");
```

The assertion will pass now as the comparison is done on the first name of the elements in both the collection.

CollectionAssert.AreNotEqual

This is similar to the `CollectionAssert.AreEqual` but this will verify if the collections are not equal. This assert type also has multiple overloaded methods similar to the `CollectionAssert.AreEqual`.

- `CollectionAssert.AreNotEqual(ICollection, ICollection)`
- `CollectionAssert.AreNotEqual(ICollection, ICollection, IComparer)`
- `CollectionAssert.AreNotEqual(ICollection, ICollection, IComparer, String)`
- `CollectionAssert.AreNotEqual(ICollection, ICollection, IComparer, String, Object[])`
- `CollectionAssert.AreNotEqual(ICollection, ICollection, String)`
- `CollectionAssert.AreNotEqual(ICollection, ICollection, String, Object[])`

AssertFailedException

This is to catch the exception thrown when the test fails. This exception is thrown whenever there is a failure of the assert statement.

The code in the following screenshot verifies if the **fourthArray** contains the string **Phone Number**. The assertion fails and the exception **AssertFailedException** is caught using the **catch** block. For this example, we will add the exception message and a custom message to the test trace.

```
try
{
    CollectionAssert.Contains(fourthArray, "Phone Number");
}
catch (AssertFailedException e)
{
    Trace.WriteLine(e.Message);
    Trace.WriteLine("...e array list does not contain the string 'Phone Number' ");
}
    }
}
```

The test would be a pass as the expected exception is thrown by the test. The test results details would show the details of tracing. The following screenshot depicts the test result with the trace:

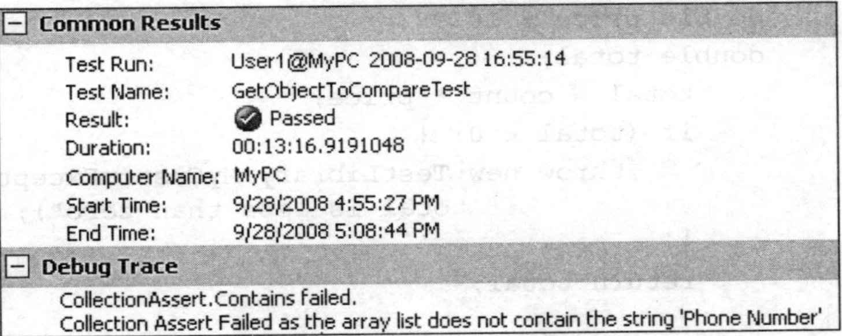

UnitTestAssertionException

This is the base class for all unit test exceptions. If we have to write our own custom `Assertion` class, we can inherit the class from `UnitTestAssertionException` class to identify the exceptions thrown from the test.

The code debug image with the exception shown in the previous section shows the `AssertFailedException` which is derived from `UnitTestAssertException`.

ExpectedExceptionAttribute

This attribute can be used to test if any particular exception is expected from the code. The attribute expects the exact exception that is expected to arise out of the code to be specified as the parameter. Let's discuss this step-by-step with the help of an example. The code below shows the custom exception which is derived from the application exception. This custom exception does nothing but just sets a message.

```
namespace TestLibrary
{
    class MyCustomException : ApplicationException
    {
        public string CustomMessage { get; set; }

        public MyCustomException(string message)
        {
            CustomMessage = message;
        }
    }
}
```

The class contains a method which returns the total price but throws the custom exception with a message, if the total price is less than zero.

```
public double GetTotalItemPrice(int count) {
    double price = 10.99;
    double total;
        total = count * price;
        if (total < 0) {
            throw new TestLibrary.MyCustomException("the
                        total is less than zero");
        }
        return total;
}
```

Create a unit test method for the above method by choosing the create unit test option from the context-menu. The following code shows the unit test method for the above code that returns the total item price;

```
[TestMethod()]
public void GetTotalItemPriceTest()
{
    Class1 target = new Class1();
    int count = 0;
    double expected = 0F;
    double actual;
    actual = target.GetTotalItemPrice(count);
    Assert.AreEqual(expected, actual);
}
```

To test the above method set the count to a value less than zero and run the test from the Test View window. The assertion would fail. For example, for a value -1 the assertion would fail with the below message which says the application thrown by an exception is of type **MyCustomException**.

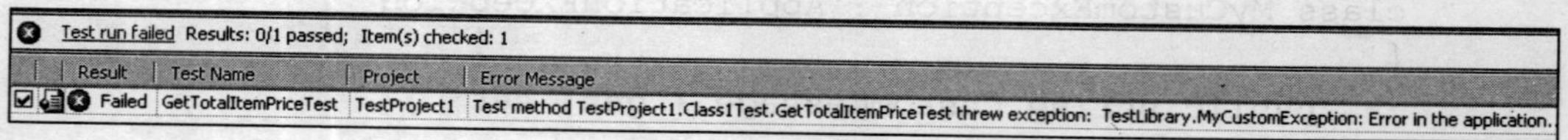

Test run failed Results: 0/1 passed; Item(s) checked: 1

Result	Test Name	Project	Error Message
Failed	GetTotalItemPriceTest	TestProject1	Test method TestProject1.Class1Test.GetTotalItemPriceTest threw exception: TestLibrary.MyCustomException: Error in the application.

This is not what we want here. This is the application we are going to use for testing the expected exception.

Now we have to test the method `GetTotalItemPrice` for `MyCustomException`. To do this, add the `ExpectedException` attribute to the test method as shown below and run the test by setting different values for the variable count.

```
[TestMethod()]
[ExpectedException(typeof(TestLibrary.MyCustomException))]
public void GetTotalItemPriceTest()
{
    Class1 target = new Class1();
    int count = -1;
    double expected = 0F;
    double actual;
    actual = target.GetTotalItemPrice(count);
    Assert.AreEqual(expected, actual);
}
```

The above test would pass as the method throws `MyCustomException`. which means the method resulted in exception because of the total value, which is less than zero.

We can include any exception as attribute to the test method and verify the actual method if it actually throws an exception. This is very useful in case very complex methods where there is a high possibility of getting exceptions like divide by zero or File IO or file/folder access permissions.

Unit tests and generics

Before going into the actual testing of generics, let us understand the use of generics. Generics in .NET Framework helps us to design the classes and methods without any specific parameter types but allows us to realize type safety at compile time. It means that we can still continue working with the class in a type-safe way but we don't have to force it to be of any specific type. Generics help us to reuse the code and increase the performance. Generics are mostly used with the collections such as ArrayList, Linked List, Stacks, Queues, and other collections. This is because the collections can hold any type of items, for example, an array list can be a list of integers or it can be a list of strings. Given below is an example of a generic method, which just accepts two generic values and copies the first one into the second one.

```
public static void CopyItems<T>(List<T> srcList, List<T>
                                        destList)
{
    foreach (T itm in srcList)
    {
        destList.Add(itm);
    }
}
```

Here you can notice that the type is not specified anywhere. It is generic, which is denoted by `<T>`. It can be integer or string or any type identified when the method is called. The code below shows the example for using the `CopyItems<T>` generic method. When first time the `CopyItems` is called, the `listSource` collection passed as first parameter contains `String` items. The second time the `CopyItems` method is called the `listSrc` collection passed as first parameter contains items of type `Employee` object.

```
static void Main(string[] args)
{
    List<string> listSource = new List<string>();
    listSource.Add("String1");
    listSource.Add("string2");
    List<string> listDestination = new List<string>();
    Console.WriteLine("Items count in listDestination
    before copying items: {0} ", listDestination.Count);
    CopyItems(listSource, listDestination);
    Console.WriteLine("Items count in listDestination
    after copying items: {0} ", listDestination.Count);
    Console.WriteLine("");
    List<Employee> listSrc = new List<Employee>();
    listSrc.Add(new Employee(1001, "Employee 1001"));
    listSrc.Add(new Employee(1002, "Employee 1002"));
    listSrc.Add(new Employee(1003, "Employee 1003"));
    List<Employee> listDest = new List<Employee>();
    Console.WriteLine("Items count in listDest before
    copying items: {0} ", listDest.Count);
    CopyItems(listSrc, listDest);
    Console.WriteLine("Items count in listDest after
    copying items: {0} ", listDest.Count);
}
```

The result would be the copy of the objects in the destination collection which is the second parameter to the generic method. The output of the method after calling the generic method would be as shown in the following screenshot:

```
file:///C:/Temp/GenericTest/GenericTest/GenericTest/bin/Debug/GenericTest.EXE
Items count in listDestination before copying items: 0
Items count in listDestination after copying items: 2

Items count in listDest before copying items: 0
Items count in listDest after copying items: 3
```

The unit testing for generic method can be generated similar to any other method. Now right-click on the **CopyItems** generic method and select **Create Unit Tests** option and select the option for the project. You can notice that the Visual Studio generates two methods for the selected generic method one as a helper method and the other one as the test method. The generics can contain one or more type constraints so that the type arguments satisfies the constraints. For example, the `GenericSample` shown below has a constraint where `T : Employee` which should be satisfied by the arguments.

```
public class GenericSample<T> where T : Employee
{
...
}
```

The test method calls this helper method with the constraint to make sure the method under test works as expected.

The unit test for the generic method `CopyItems` example would be:

```
public void CopyItemsTestHelper<T>()
{
    List<T> srcList = null; // TODO: Initialize to an
                            //appropriate value
    List<T> destList = null; // TODO: Initialize to an
                             //appropriate value
    Program.CopyItems<T>(srcList, destList);
    Assert.Inconclusive("A method that does not return a
                        value cannot be verified.");
}
[TestMethod()]
public void CopyItemsTest()
{
    CopyItemsTestHelper<GenericParameterHelper>();
}
```

Let us try customizing the above generated unit test code to pass the collection with employee type items and see the output.

```
public void CopyItemsTestHelper<T>()
{
    List<Employee> srcList = new List<Employee>();
    srcList.Add(new Employee(1001, "Employee 1001"));
    srcList.Add(new Employee(1002, "Employee 1002"));
    srcList.Add(new Employee(1003, "Employee 1003"));
    List<Employee> destList = new List<Employee>();
    Program.CopyItems<Employee>(srcList, destList);
```

```
        Assert.AreEqual(3, destList.Count);
    }

    [TestMethod()]
    public void CopyItemsTest()
    {
        CopyItemsTestHelper<GenericParameterHelper>();
    }
```

The assertion for the test method will pass because the `destList.Count` would contain three items after calling the `CopyItems` method which equals the expected value. We can create collections with any type of items and use the same generic method to copy the items.

Data-driven unit testing

This type of testing is useful in carrying out the same test multiple times with different input data from a data source. The data source can have any number of records or data row for which we wanted the test to be carried out.

Instead of passing each data row values to the test application and executing entire test for each data row, we can link the test method to the data source. So when the test is run, the test method will take the data row one by one from the data source and will carry out the test for that many numbers of times with different input values.

This is similar to the web testing or load testing with data source attaching to the web method parameters. This could be used in case of testing number of user scenarios with different user logins to check the access permission or to see the validation based on the user roles, if anything is applicable to the application.

There are two different ways of configuring the data source or attaching the source to the test method. Let us consider one simple example of a method which takes two parameters as quantity and unit price. The result of the method would be returning the multiplied value of these two values and applying a percentage of tax on it.

```
public double CalculateTotalPrice(double uPrice, int Qty)
{
    double totalPrice;
    double tax = 0.125;
    totalPrice = uPrice * Qty + (uPrice * tax * Qty); //
    return totalPrice;
}
```

Create a unit test for the above example. The unit test code would contain the following code for the above method:

```
[TestMethod()]
public void CalculateTotalPriceTest()
{
    Class1 target = new Class1();
    double uPrice = 0F;
    int Qty = 0;
    double expected = 0F;
    double actual;
    actual = target.CalculateTotalPrice(uPrice, Qty);
    Assert.AreEqual(expected, actual);
}
```

Before setting the properties, we have to create the data source. The data source can be of different format like CSV, XML, Microsoft Access, Microsoft SQL Server Database or Oracle Database, or any other database. For this example, we will consider a CSV file having five records with **UnitPrice, Quantity, ExpectedTotalPrice**. These are values required in the test method.

Data.csv

```
UnitPrice,Quantity,ExpectedTotalPrice
5.99,12,80.5056
2.49,5,13.944
2.99,25,83.72
3.29,5,18.424
5.69,9,57.3552
```

Now the new unit test would also be listed in the **Test View** and **Test List Editor**. Open the **Test View** or **Test List Editor** using the **Test** menu option from the IDE. Select the test method from the list and open the **Properties** window. From the list of properties listed for the unit test, select the connection property, and choose the option to open the **Data Source** wizard. From the wizard, select the data source type as CSV file from the options. Select the CSV file we created from the location. This will show the preview of the data too. Now the property of the test would be like the window shown below:

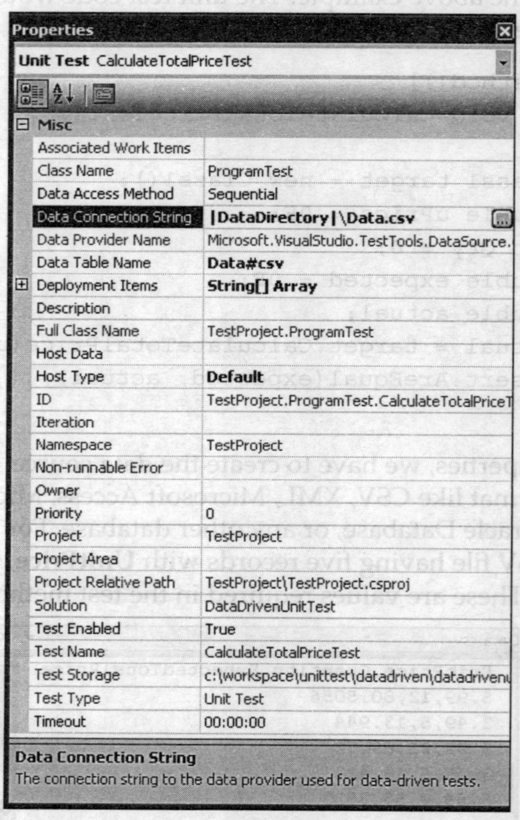

- **Data Provider Name**: This property is disabled as we have selected the file directly and made the connection. Visual Studio automatically assigns the **Data Provider Name** as **Microsoft.VisualStudio.TestTools.DataSource.CSV**.
- **Data Table Name**: After making the connection, we can see the tables listed from the database connected. The table that we select from the list will be the source of data for the testing.
- **Data Access Method**: This can be Sequential or Dynamic. This is the method that will be used for retrieving the data from the data source for the test.

When we keep changing the properties of the test, we can see the properties added as attributes to the test method.

```
[DeploymentItem("TestProject\\Data.csv"),
DataSource("Microsoft.VisualStudio.TestTools.DataSource.
CSV", "|DataDirectory|\\Data.csv", "Data#csv",
DataAccessMethod.Sequential), TestMethod()]
public void CalculateTotalPriceTest()
{
}
```

The data source which is a CSV file is added as the deployment item. The other attributes specify the method of data access and the namespace used. These are the method level attributes set for the test run.

To set the value of the data from the data source to the test method, modify the test method little bit as shown below. The `testContextInstance.DataRow` is used to fetch the value from the current row for the current instance of the test. For example, if we have five rows in the data source there would be five different instances of tests one for each row.

I have added a custom error message to the assert to get the actual and expected values in case if the test fails.

```
[DataSource("Microsoft.VisualStudio.TestTools.DataSource.
CSV", "|DataDirectory|\\Data.csv", "Data#csv",
DataAccessMethod.Sequential),
DeploymentItem("TestProject1\\Data.csv"), TestMethod()]
 public void CalculateTotalPriceTest()
 {
     Class1 target = new Class1();
     double uPrice = 0F;
     int Qty = 0;
     double expected = 0F;
     double actual;
     expected = Convert.ToDouble(testContextInstance.
          DataRow["ExpectedTotalPrice"]);
     actual = target.CalculateTotalPrice(Convert.ToDouble
         (testContextInstance.DataRow["UnitPrice"]),
          Convert.ToInt32(testContextInstance.
          DataRow["Quantity"]));
```

```
    Assert.AreEqual(expected, actual, "The expected value is {0}
    but the actual value is {1}", expected, actual);
    Trace.WriteLine("Expected:" + expected + "; Actual:"+ actual);
    }
```

Now open the **Test View** window and select the test method listed in the window.

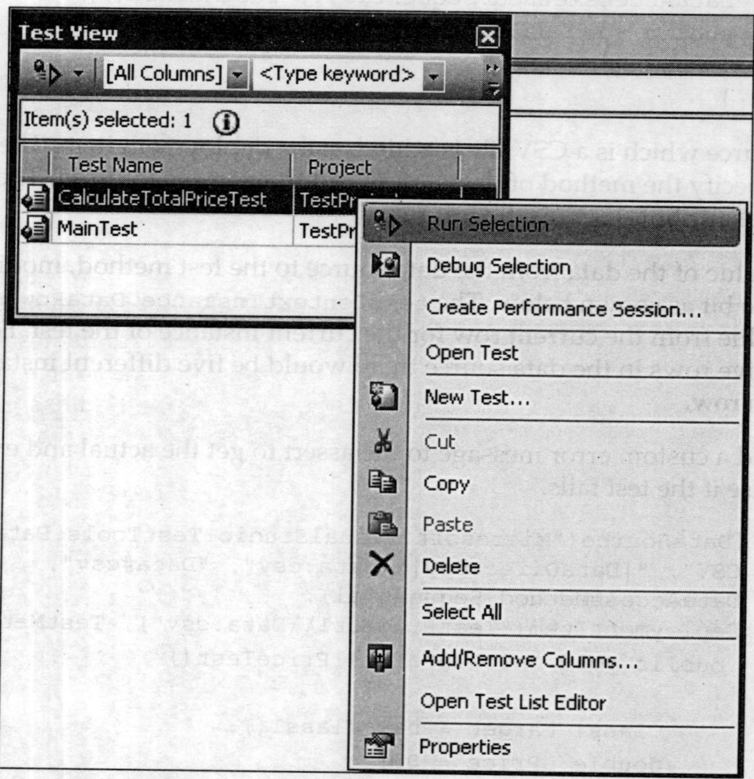

On running the test, we can see the test execution happening for each row in the data source. Once the test has been completed for all of the rows in the data source, we can see the test result based on the results of all individual tests. Even if one test fails, the end result of the test run will be a failure. To get the test run to pass, all of the individual tests within the selected test run should pass.

The output for the above test with the data source having five records in it, as shown in the previous screenshot, the test result would be:

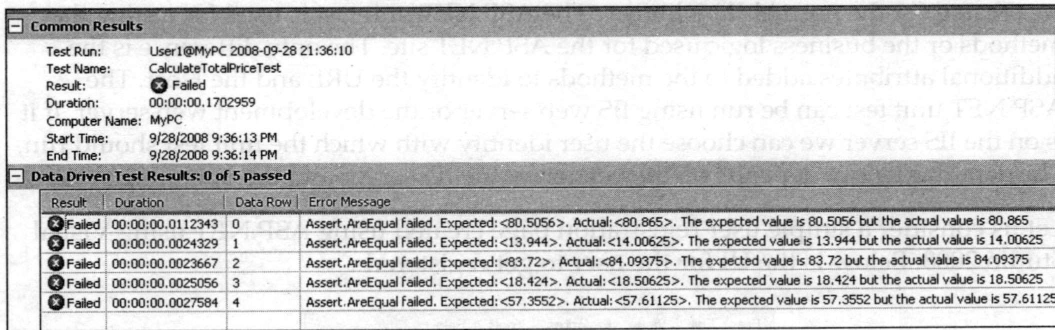

Common Results

Test Run:	User1@MyPC 2008-09-28 21:36:10
Test Name:	CalculateTotalPriceTest
Result:	Failed
Duration:	00:00:00.1702959
Computer Name:	MyPC
Start Time:	9/28/2008 9:36:13 PM
End Time:	9/28/2008 9:36:14 PM

Data Driven Test Results: 0 of 5 passed

Result	Duration	Data Row	Error Message
Failed	00:00:00.0112343	0	Assert.AreEqual failed. Expected:<80.5056>. Actual:<80.865>. The expected value is 80.5056 but the actual value is 80.865
Failed	00:00:00.0024329	1	Assert.AreEqual failed. Expected:<13.944>. Actual:<14.00625>. The expected value is 13.944 but the actual value is 14.00625
Failed	00:00:00.0023667	2	Assert.AreEqual failed. Expected:<83.72>. Actual:<84.09375>. The expected value is 83.72 but the actual value is 84.09375
Failed	00:00:00.0025056	3	Assert.AreEqual failed. Expected:<18.424>. Actual:<18.50625>. The expected value is 18.424 but the actual value is 18.50625
Failed	00:00:00.0027584	4	Assert.AreEqual failed. Expected:<57.3552>. Actual:<57.61125>. The expected value is 57.3552 but the actual value is 57.61125

We can see the total time taken for each test and the row picked for each test from the above result. All five tests fail and you can see the custom error message displayed with the expected and actual values applied to the formatters. All the tests fail because of the calculation mistake in the actual method. The data source contains the expected value based on the tax value as 0.12 but the actual method has the value as 0.125. If you change the value to 0.12 in the method `CalculateTotalPriceTest` and rerun the test, the test would pass.

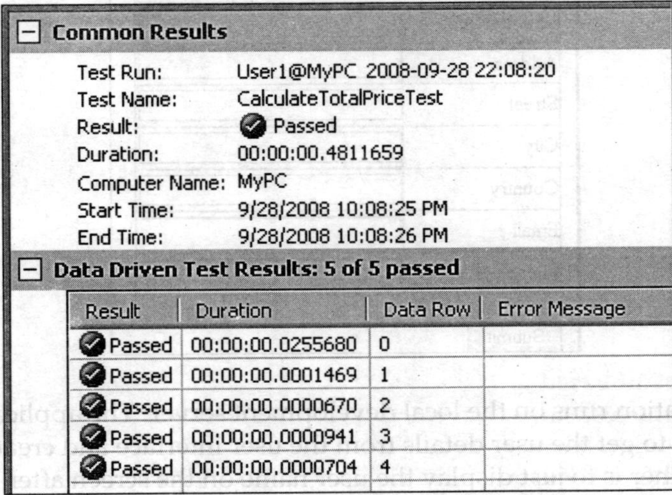

Common Results

Test Run:	User1@MyPC 2008-09-28 22:08:20
Test Name:	CalculateTotalPriceTest
Result:	Passed
Duration:	00:00:00.4811659
Computer Name:	MyPC
Start Time:	9/28/2008 10:08:25 PM
End Time:	9/28/2008 10:08:26 PM

Data Driven Test Results: 5 of 5 passed

Result	Duration	Data Row	Error Message
Passed	00:00:00.0255680	0	
Passed	00:00:00.0001469	1	
Passed	00:00:00.0000670	2	
Passed	00:00:00.0000941	3	
Passed	00:00:00.0000704	4	

The **Test Run** details window shows the status of each test run for each row in the data source.

Unit testing an ASP.NET application

Creating the unit test for an ASP.NET web site or application is similar to the one we created for the normal class library. The ASP.NET unit test is used for testing the methods or the business logic used for the ASP.NET site. The only difference is the additional attributes added to the methods to identify the URL and the Host. The ASP.NET unit test can be run using IIS web server or the development web server. If it is on the IIS server we can choose the user identity with which the unit test should run. The default identity depends on the version of the IIS server and the operating system.

Let us consider a simple user registration page created using ASP.NET using Visual Studio 2008. Below is the UI for the user to get registered.

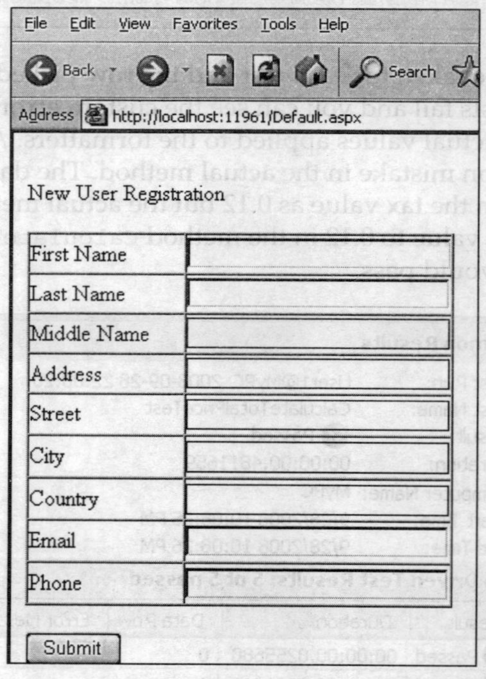

This web application runs on the local development server. The application has two methods. One is to get the user details from the user interface and create a new user object and the other is to just display the user name on the screen after submit. The application also has a class file for the user information.

```
protected void BtnSubmit_Click(object sender, EventArgs e)
{
    User usr = new User();
    GetUserDetails(usr);
    LabelOutput.Text = "Hello " + usr.FirstName + " " +
```

```
                    usr.LastName + " you are sucessfully
                      registered with the site";
        }
        public User GetUserDetails(User user)
        {
            user.FirstName = TextBoxFirstName.Text;
            user.LastName = TextBoxLastName.Text;
            user.MiddleName = TextBoxMiddleName.Text;
            user.Address = TextBoxCity.Text;
            user.Street = TextBoxStreet.Text;
            user.City = TextBoxCity.Text;
            user.Country = TextBoxCountry.Text;
            user.Email = TextBoxEmail.Text;
            user.Phone = TextBoxPhone.Text;
            return user;
        }
```

Before generating the unit test for the web application, let us build and run the application once to make sure it runs as expected.

Now to generate the unit test, open the code file of the web page, then right-click and select the **Create Unit Tests...** option which identifies all the classes and the methods for which the unit test can be generated as shown in the screenshot below:

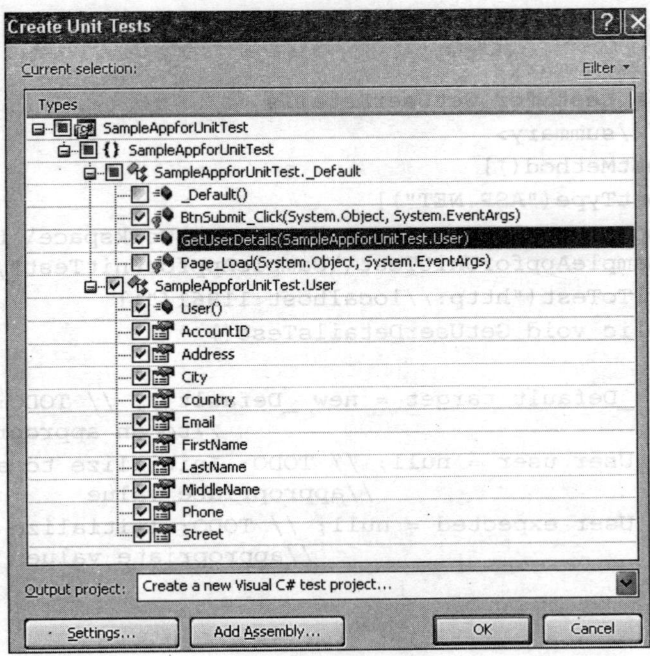

Select the methods and the user class for which the unit test can be generated and tested. Now Visual Studio creates the unit test class file for the new test with the required attributes and the base code for test. The unit test code for the two methods of the web page would be:

```
[TestMethod()]
[HostType("ASP.NET")]
[AspNetDevelopmentServerHost("C:\\Workspace\\UnitTest\\
  SampleAppforUnitTest\\SampleAppforUnitTest", "/")]
[UrlToTest("http://localhost:11961/")]
[DeploymentItem("SampleAppforUnitTest.dll")]
public void BtnSubmit_ClickTest()
{
    _Default_Accessor target = new _Default_Accessor();
      // TODO: Initialize to an appropriate value
    object sender = null; // TODO: Initialize to an
                              //appropriate value
    EventArgs e = null; // TODO: Initialize to an
                              //appropriate value
    target.BtnSubmit_Click(sender, e);
    Assert.Inconclusive("A method that does not return a
                              value cannot be verified.");
}

/// <summary>
///A test for GetUserDetails
///</summary>
[TestMethod()]
[HostType("ASP.NET")]
[AspNetDevelopmentServerHost("C:\\Workspace\\UnitTest\\
  SampleAppforUnitTest\\SampleAppforUnitTest", "/")]
[UrlToTest("http://localhost:11961/")]
public void GetUserDetailsTest()
{
    _Default target = new _Default(); // TODO: Initialize
                                    //to an appropriate value
    User user = null; // TODO: Initialize to an
                          //appropriate value
    User expected = null; // TODO: Initialize to an
                              //appropriate value
```

```
        User actual;
        actual = target.GetUserDetails(user);
        Assert.AreEqual(expected, actual);
        Assert.Inconclusive("Verify the correctness of this
        test method.");
    }
```

There are different attributes added to the unit test methods:

- `TestMethod`—attribute to identify the whether a method is a unit test method.
- `HostType`—the type of the host that takes care of running the unit test. In this case it is the ASP.NET.
- `AspNetDevelopmentServerHost`—this specifies the settings to be used when the development server is used as the host for the unit testing.
- `UrlToTest`—specifies the application URL to be used for the test context.
- `DeploymentItem`—this is to specify the items like files and folders to be deployed before the test.

After creating the test and setting the environment, set the expected values and include the required assert method for comparing the values and passing the test. For example, change the `GetUserDetailsTest` method as below:

```
[TestMethod()]
[HostType("ASP.NET")]
[AspNetDevelopmentServerHost("C:\\Workspace\\UnitTest\\
  SampleAppforUnitTest\\SampleAppforUnitTest", "/")]
[UrlToTest("http://localhost:11961/")]
public void GetUserDetailsTest()
{
    _Default target = new _Default();
    User user = new User();
    User expected = new User();
    expected.FirstName = "Subha";
    expected.LastName = "S";
    User actual;
    actual = target.GetUserDetails(user);
    Assert.AreEqual(expected.FirstName, actual.FirstName);
}
```

The test will pass if the value of `FirstName` and `LastName` properties of the expected object and the actual object returned by the method are equal. Right-click on the method and select **Run Tests...**

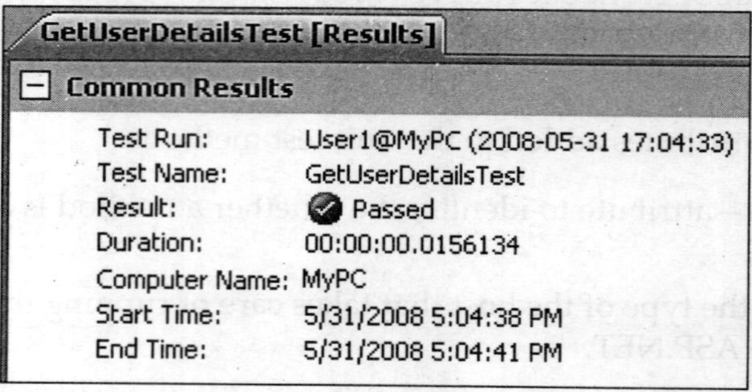
GetUserDetailsTest [Results]

Common Results

Test Run:	User1@MyPC (2008-05-31 17:04:33)
Test Name:	GetUserDetailsTest
Result:	Passed
Duration:	00:00:00.0156134
Computer Name:	MyPC
Start Time:	5/31/2008 5:04:38 PM
End Time:	5/31/2008 5:04:41 PM

We can use the different assert methods and test all different scenarios of the unit test with different expected values.

Unit testing web services

Web services are similar to any other method in the web application. We have to just add the reference of the web service and call the method, as we call any other method of the web application. All the methods and attributes required for testing the web service are available under the namespace **Microsoft.VisualStudio.TestTools.UnitTesting.Web**.

Similar to the web application, the web service can be hosted using IIS server or the local development server. If it is hosted in the IIS, just add the reference to the unit test application and call the web service method just like calling the method in the web application. If it is available in the local machine but not hosted in the web server, just add the attributes required to start the development server. This attributes takes care of hosting the service locally.

Let us create a simple web service which returns values based on the input parameter value that is passed to the web method. Given below is the sample code:

```
public class Service1 : System.Web.Services.WebService
{
    [WebMethod]
    public string HelloWorld()
    {
        return "Hello World";
    }
    [WebMethod]
    public string GetuserDetails(int id)
    {
        string name = "";
        if (id == 100)
            name = "Subha";
        if (id == 200)
            name = "Satheesh";
        return name;
    }
}
```

After creating the web method, right-click on the method and select **Create Unit Tests....** This will create the unit test with the attributes required for the web service test.

```
[TestMethod()]
[HostType("ASP.NET")]
[AspNetDevelopmentServerHost("C:\\Workspace\\UnitTest\\
  SampleAppforUnitTest\\WebService1", "/")]
[UrlToTest("http://localhost:15558/")]
public void GetuserDetailsTest()
{
    Service1 target = new Service1();
    int id = 100;
    string expected = "User Name";
    string actual;
    actual = target.GetuserDetails(id);
    Assert.AreEqual(expected, actual);
}
```

The above unit test method for the web method is very similar to the method for the ASP.NET application. This web service runs in a local development server. If it has to run under the IIS server, we can change the configuration settings.

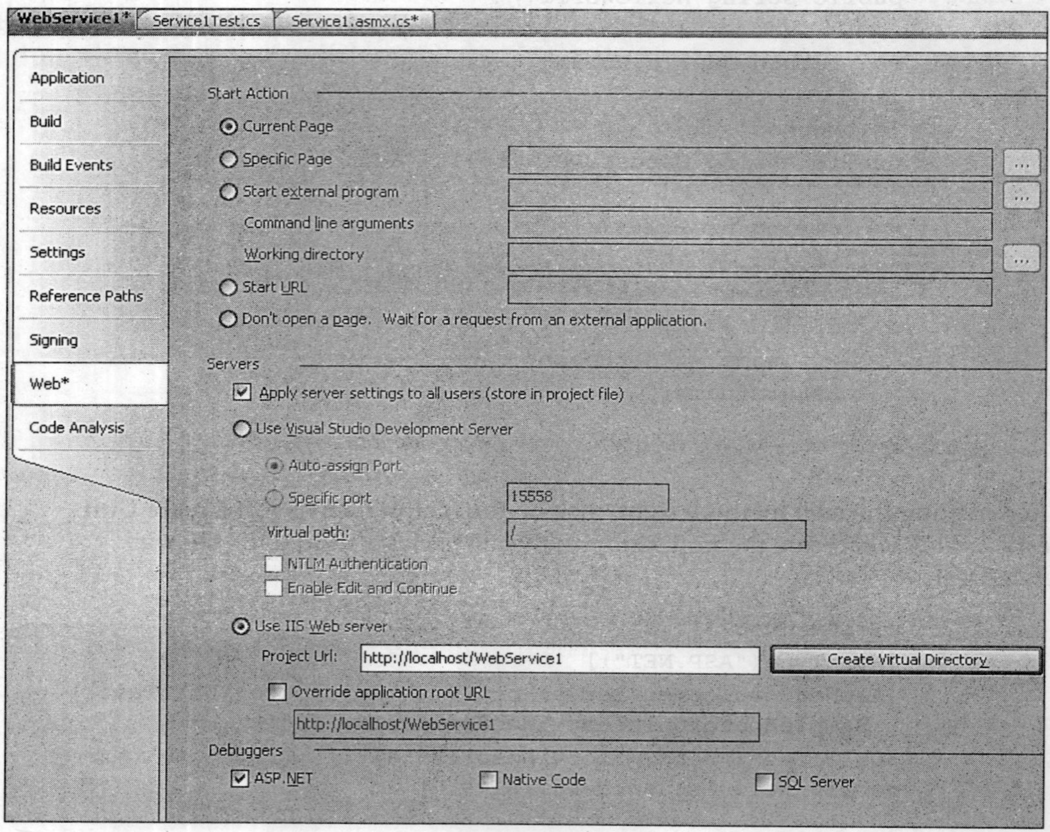

This is the property set for the **Web Service** project. The servers are by default set as **Visual Studio Development Server**. To change it to run on the IIS server, select the second option **Use IIS web server** and create virtual directory. Now the if we generate the unit test, the URL used for the unit test would be `http://localhost/WebService1`.

Just run the test similar to the other test by changing the expected value and using the required assert methods. Sometimes the test may fail because of unavailability of the web server or the server may not be running. In that case we can use the `TryUrlRedirection` method of the `WebServiceHelper` to try connecting to the URL before testing. The sample code for redirection would be

```
        Assert.IsTrue(WebServiceHelper.TryUrlRedirection(target,
                    testContextInstance,
                    "MyServer"
                   ),"Redirection failed."
           );
```

Code coverage unit test

This is to see the methods or the code has been covered by the unit test. This is the property we can set on the project level before starting the unit testing. Open the configuration file **localtestrun.testrunconfig** file under the solution. Select **Code Coverage** from the list shown on the left side. Now you can see the list of projects or artifacts to instrument options. Select the project for which the code coverage has to be turned and select apply and close the dialog.

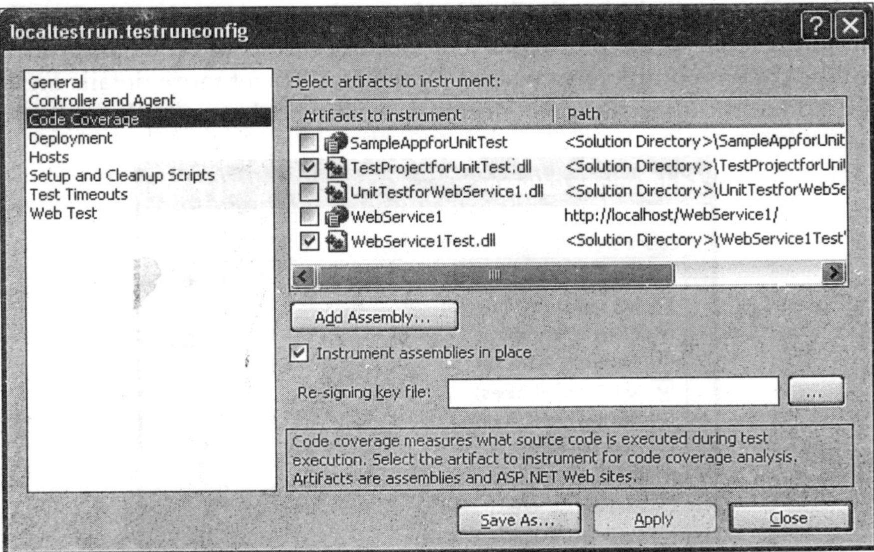

Now select the test and run the test again. Once the test is complete we can see the code coverage details from the code coverage window which can be opened using the option in the **Test** menu option.

The code coverage window shows the coverage details collected from the last test run. Below is the sample of the **Code Coverage Result**.

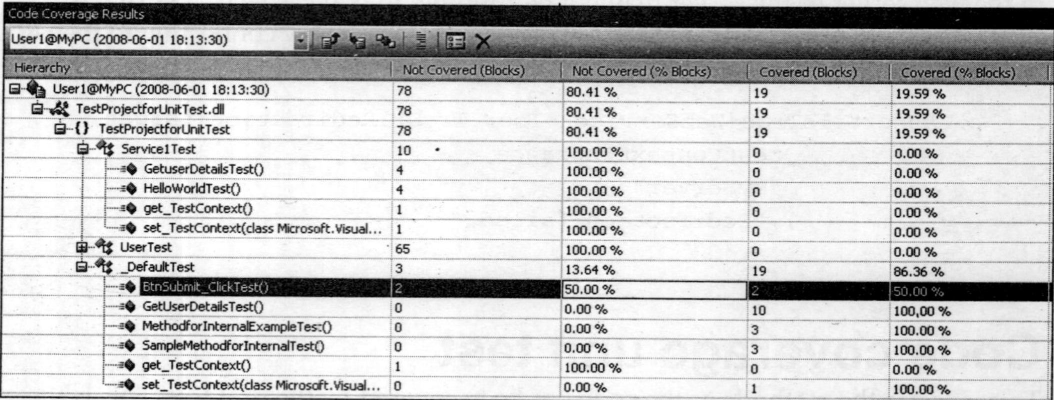

Code Coverage Results

User1@MyPC (2008-06-01 18:13:30)

Hierarchy	Not Covered (Blocks)	Not Covered (% Blocks)	Covered (Blocks)	Covered (% Blocks)
User1@MyPC (2008-06-01 18:13:30)	78	80.41 %	19	19.59 %
TestProjectforUnitTest.dll	78	80.41 %	19	19.59 %
TestProjectforUnitTest	78	80.41 %	19	19.59 %
Service1Test	10	100.00 %	0	0.00 %
GetuserDetailsTest()	4	100.00 %	0	0.00 %
HelloWorldTest()	4	100.00 %	0	0.00 %
get_TestContext()	1	100.00 %	0	0.00 %
set_TestContext(class Microsoft.Visual...	1	100.00 %	0	0.00 %
UserTest	65	100.00 %	0	0.00 %
_DefaultTest	3	13.64 %	19	86.36 %
BtnSubmit_ClickTest()	2	50.00 %	2	50.00 %
GetUserDetailsTest()	0	0.00 %	10	100,00 %
MethodforInternalExampleTest()	0	0.00 %	3	100.00 %
SampleMethodforInternalTest()	0	0.00 %	3	100.00 %
get_TestContext()	1	100.00 %	0	0.00 %
set_TestContext(class Microsoft.Visual...	0	0.00 %	1	100.00 %

There was an error during the unit test of the **BtnSubmit_ClickTest()** method which is why the code coverage is only **50.00%**. The other details are the percentage of the coverage of the code till the test failure.

If we know the fix for the test to complete 100% coverage of the method, we can just right-click on the particular method and select **go to source code**, which will takes us to the source code of the particular method. We can fix the code and rerun the test until the code is completely covered by the test. To get more details on the code coverage, add additional columns or remove existing columns to the output window.

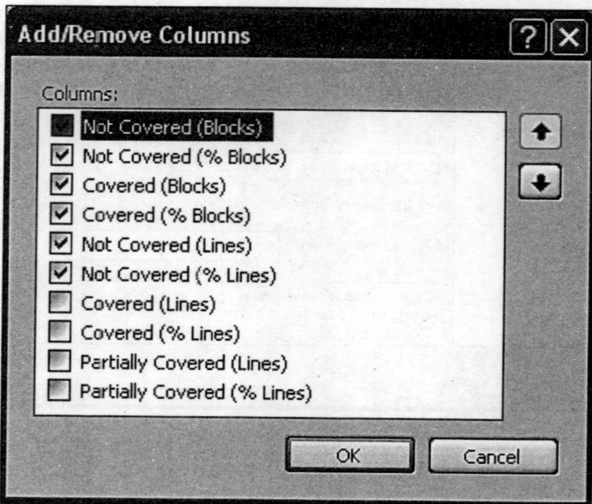

Summary

This chapter explained the different ways of unit testing the class library application, ASP.NET web application, and the web services created using Visual Studio. We have also seen the data-driven testing method which helps us to test the class methods using the data collected in a data source and attaching that to the test application. This chapter also covered the different settings and configurations that we can make on the application configuration file to get the basic code to be generated by default for the method and class under unit test. Different Assert methods and the usage of different assert methods are also explained in detail in this chapter. Lastly we have seen the method of collecting and analyzing the code coverage results for the unit tests.

So far we have seen the different ways of testing code developed by the developers. The next coming chapter concentrates on testing the actual web application using different features supported by Visual Studio Team System.

3
Web Testing

The previous chapter explained different ways of verifying the code to make sure it produces the expected functionality. This chapter concentrates on different ways to verify the web site responses for each request and the web site response in multiple scenarios like a slow network speed, different browsers, or with different number of users at given point in time. All these factors affect the web site performance and the response time. Web testing helps us to verify if the web site built produces the expected result with expected response time. This helps to identify the problems and rectify them before it happens in the actual production environment. Web testing also helps to find out if the hardware can handle the maximum expected requests at a time or needs additional hardware to handle the traffic and respond multiple user requests.

Discussed below are some of the main testing highlights that are performed on the web applications for better performance and availability:

- **Validation and verification test** helps verifying the inputs or the expected entries that satisfies the requirement. For example, if a field requires a date to be entered, the system should check for the date validation and should not allow the user to submit the page until the correct entry is made.
- **Web page usability test** is the method of simulating the practical user's way of using the application in production and testing the same as per requirement. This could be something like checking the help links, contents in the page, checking the menu options, and their links, think times between pages, and message dialogs in the pages.
- **Security Testing** helps us to verify the application response for different end users based on the credentials and other different resources required from the local system or a server in the network. For example, this could be writing/reading the log information to a file in the network share.

- **Performance Testing** verifies the web page responses as per the expectation based on the environment. This also includes the stress testing and load testing of the application with multiple user scenarios and volume of data explained in detail in Chapter 5, which talks about Load Testing
- **Testing web pages compatibility** with multiple browsers based on user requirements. The web page presentation depends on how well the components that are used are supported by different browsers the users may choose.
- **Testing web application using different networks**: This is because of the user location, which varies based on where the user is accessing the system from. The performance and the accessibility of the application are directly based on the network involved in providing the web pages to the user. This is also part of the performance testing. For example, it could be a local intranet or an internet with less network speed.

There are many more tests that can be performed as part of web testing, for example, using different operating systems or different databases, or installing the application on different versions of operating system.

All of the testing with many additional capabilities is supported by Microsoft VSTS. The dynamic web pages are created by any of the supported .NET languages by Visual Studio and using the ASP.NET web project and web page templates. Custom services, components, and libraries are used in the web application to get the functionality and make it more dynamic. Other scripting languages like JavaScript, Silverlight, and Flash are used in the web pages for validations and better presentation. Once we are ready with the web application, we need to test it, then deploy it if the web site functionality and qualities are satisfied as per the task requirements. To get to it, Microsoft VSTS provides tools for testing the web application. There are different ways of using the tool to test the application. One is to use the user interface to record and then add the validation rules and parameters to make it dynamic. The other way is to record the requests and then create the coded web test for the recorded web test and customize it using the code.

This chapter explains the basic way of web testing using VSTS and using the features like adding the rules and parameterize the dynamic variables.

Creating web test

Creating a web test is similar to any other test in Visual Studio. There are three different ways to create a new web test:

1. Select the test project, right-click, and choose **Add**. Then select the option **Web test** from the context menu.
2. Select the menu option **Test** and choose **New Test...** which opens the **Add New Test** window and it contains the different test type templates.
3. Select the menu option **Test** and choose **Windows** and then select the **Test View**, which opens the test view window listing all the available tests. Right-click on the surface of the **Test View** window to open the context-menu. Choose the **New Test** option which opens the **Add New Test** window.
4. After selecting one of the above three, select the **Web Test** template from the list of different test types.

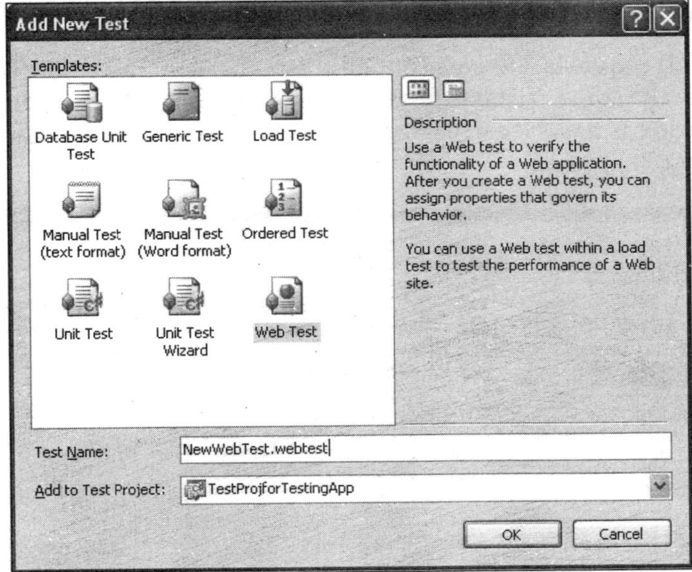

Once you select the **Web Test** and click **OK** you can see the test getting added to the selected test project and a new instance of a web browser opens. The browser contains the **Web Test Recorder** in the left pane.

Recording a test

Web applications can be easily tested by recording the requests with the recorder. This recorder will track all the web requests. We can easily find out the expected requests from the recorder and identify any defects coming along with the requested page. The user can request the web pages to record and create the test scenario. Once the scenario is created we can build the scenario or customize it to make it more dynamic.

As stated above, once after starting the web test, a new browser window opens with the web test recorder. Recorder has five different options discussed as follows:

- **Record** – to start recording the web page requests.
- **Pause** – this is used to pause the recording. In some cases we may not want to record some pages in the application. But we should have identified the pages for which we may have to pause the recording and restart the recording for the next coming pages.
- **Stop** – this is to stop the recording session. As soon as we click on the **Stop** button, the browser will close and the session will stop.
- **Add a Comment** – this option is used for adding any comments to the current request in the recording.
- **Clear all requests** – to clear out all the requests in the recording. Sometimes if we make some mistakes in the recording or if the web application that, we are testing is not the correct one, then we can clear all the requests and start from the beginning.

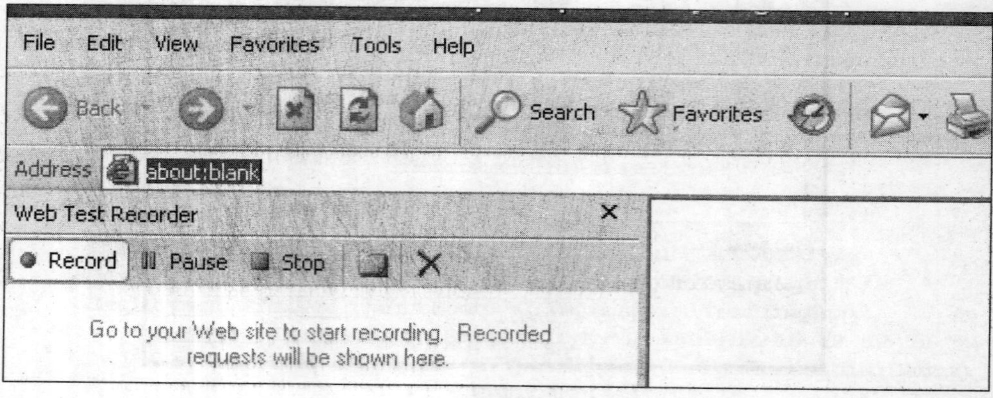

Before we proceed to the web testing let us create a sample web application for testing. Let's consider a user registration page where in the user has to provide the information like **First Name**, **Last Name**, **Middle Name**, **User ID**, and **Password**. This information is required to keep track of user activity in the web site, which is common in most of the web sites. For our example, let us consider only this registration page. It contains a **Register** option which collects all the information entered by the user and saves it to the database table. The user entries are validated as per the requirement, which we will see through the examples in subsections. The database is the SQL Server database with one table for storing all the information. We will use the SQL Server Express for all database operations. The next screenshot shows the database table for the sample application:

Register.aspx* | dbo.tableAcc...A\TESTDB.MDF)

Column Name	Data Type	Allow Nulls
AccountID	int	☐
FirstName	varchar(50)	☐
MiddleName	varchar(50)	☑
LastName	varchar(50)	☐
Address	varchar(50)	☑
Street	varchar(50)	☑
City	varchar(50)	☑
Country	varchar(50)	☐
Email	varchar(50)	☐
Phone	bigint	☐
		☐

The sample application web page user interface is as shown below with some required fields including a fields to show the validation error messages and the **Register** button to send the request:

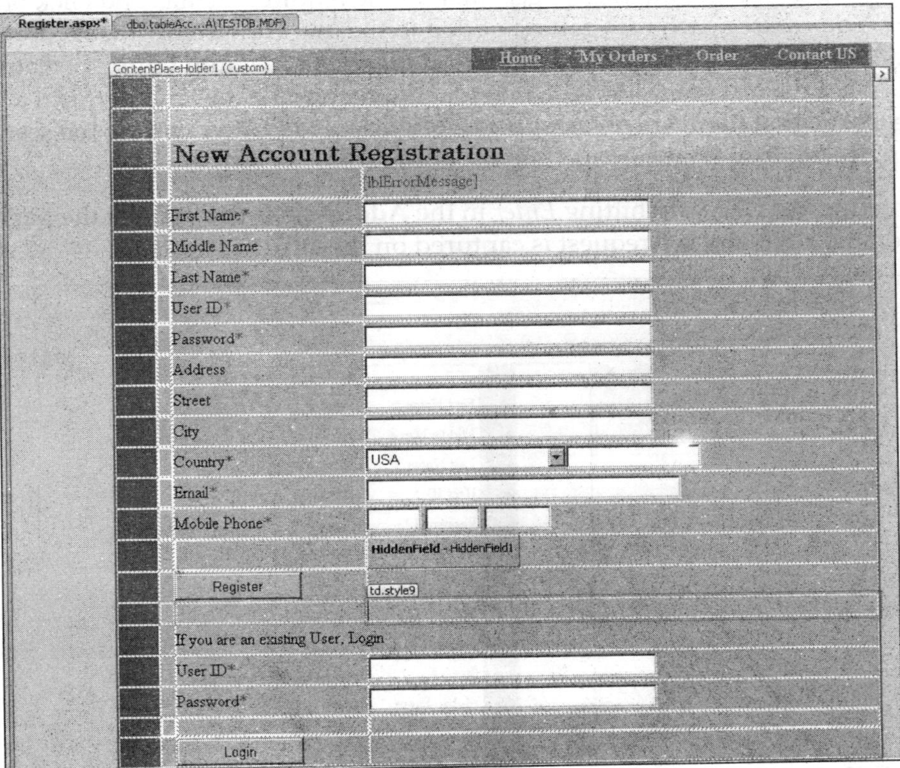

The application can be tested when it is hosted on a web server or when it is running on the local development web server within VSTS. The examples given in this chapter are based on the local VSTS development server. The approach is the same for hosted application on a web server like IIS 6.0.

As we are using the VSTS local development web server, build the new web project and keep it running. Get the web address from the running web application so that we have the web address with dynamic port assigned to it.

First let us look at the features of the web test and then we can go in detail about collecting information from test and the actual testing.

Create a new web test so that you get the new web test browser recorder window. The Web test tool opens the Microsoft Internet Explorer browser for the recording. Now in the **Address** bar enter the web page address and hit *Enter*. In this case it is going to be `http://localhost:49459/TestingApp/Register.aspx` (this is a test address using the local web server and will vary based on the dynamic port assigned to it). If you are planning to test the application from the hosted server, then record the test by browsing the web pages from the hosted server. Whether it is hosted server or a local development server, the web application should be up and running for testing. Once you get the web page, enter all the required details and click on **Register**. You can see each row getting added to the tree view below the recorder toolbar. All request details will get recorded until we hit the **Stop** button or **Pause** button. To get the test scenario right, enter all the required fields and perform a positive test so that there are no error messages displayed. After getting the scenario, we can perform invalid entries and test the application.

After entering the URL and hitting *Enter* in the **Address** bar you can see the page loaded on the right and the request is captured on the left.

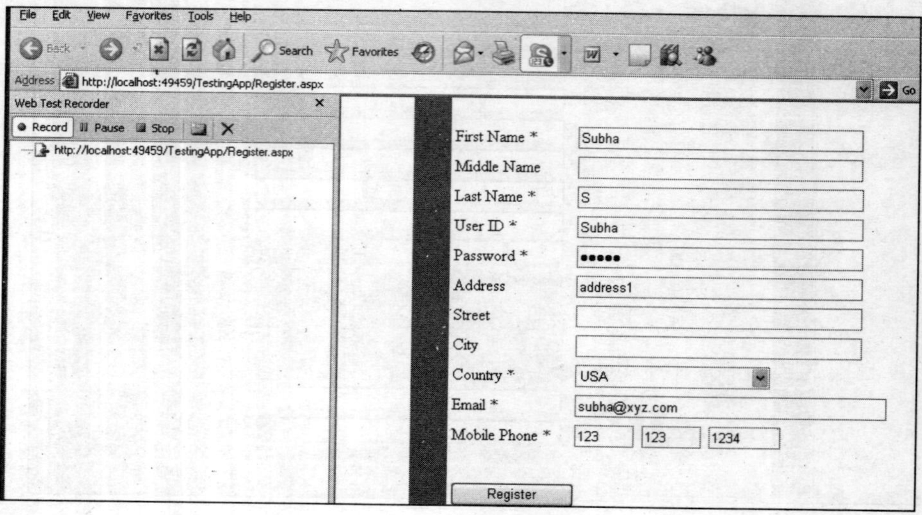

Enter all request details and then click on the **Register** button. As soon as the web page is submitted, we can see the second request captured by the recorder with the details and shown in the tree view.

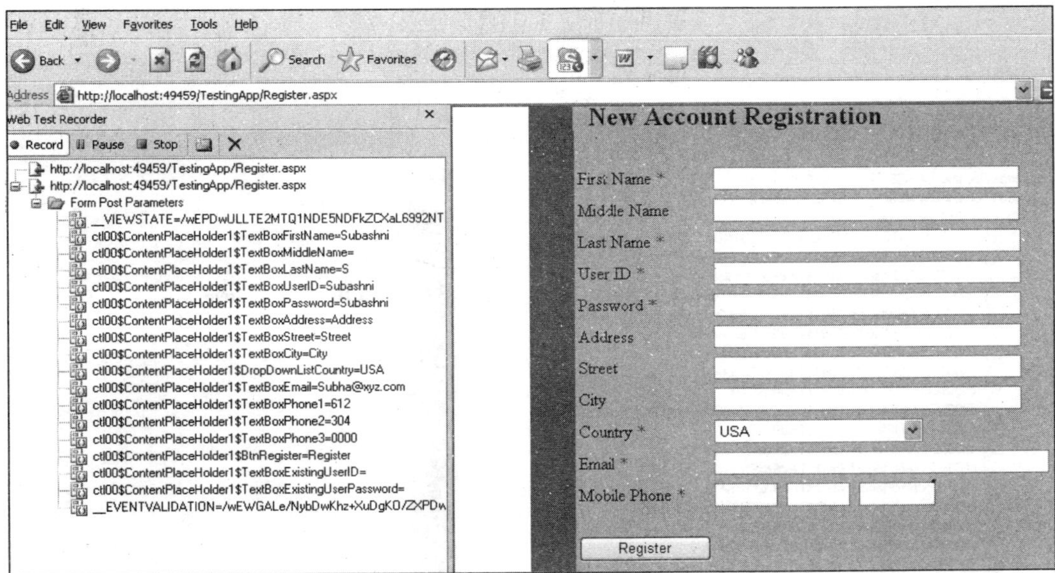

We had two requests during the recording—one for page display and the other for submitting the page or registering the details. The details of these requests are displayed in the tree view. If you expand the second root node in the tree view, you can find different values or strings passed by the web application by clicking **Register** button captured under the folder **Form Post Parameters**. You can also notice the event that took place by clicking the **Register** button in the web page. All other details are the parameter values posted by the request.

Below the **Register** button is the **Login** section. Here the user can enter the credentials and go to the **My Orders** section where user orders are displayed. This is a redirected request from the `Register.aspx` page to `MyOrder.aspx` submitted using HTTP-GET method by sending the `userid` in query string parameter. There are different protocols used for sending the requests: HTTP-GET, HTTP-POST, and SOAP.

- HTTP-GET: Hypertext Transfer Protocol-GET protocol appends the query strings to the URL. The Query string is the name and value pair, which created out of the parameters and data.
- HTTP-POST: Hypertext Transfer Protocol-POST protocol passes the name and value pairs in the body of the HTTP request message.

- SOAP protocol is an XML-based protocol used for sending the structured information. This is mostly used by the web services.

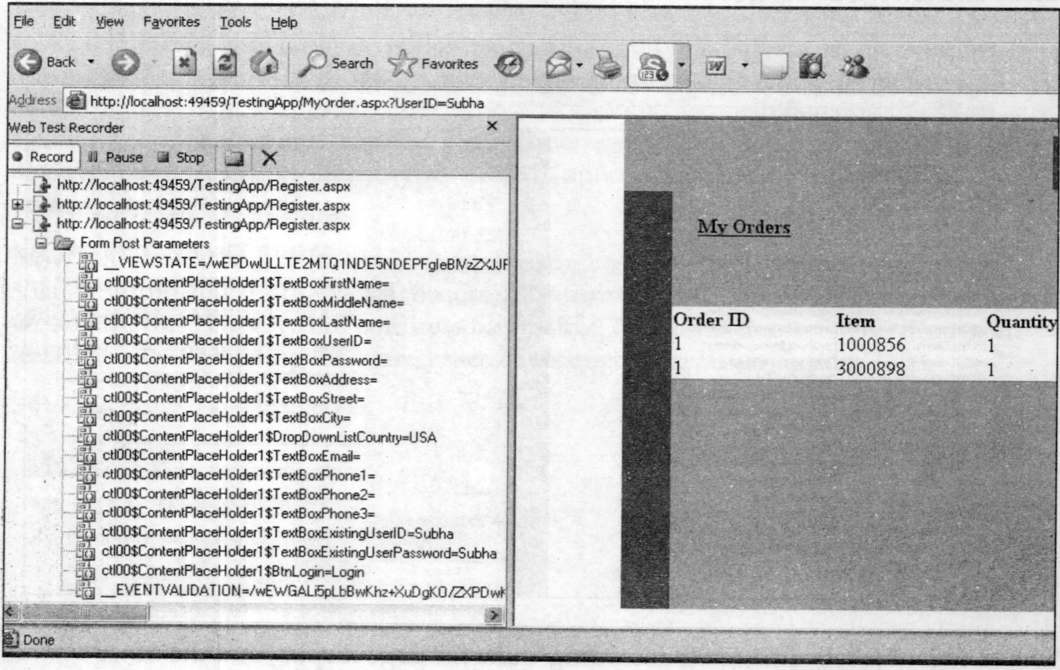

From the recording details you can see that only the independent requests (GET or POST) are recorded but not the dependent requests like getting the images and the other requests. These requests will be reported only when the test is run, but during recording it will not be shown or captured.

Adding comments

While recording the web page requests, we may need to add some comments about the page or the test. This comment could be any text with additional information for our reference. This is similar to the comments that we add to our code during development. Sometimes we may need to add information about the steps to follow during the test. Basically comments are to record the information about the task that we may have to do during the test but we easily forget to do. These comments can be added by just clicking the **Add Comments** button in the **Web Test Recorder** toolbar.

Cleaning the recorded tests

In the web test recording we might have requested many pages, but at the end of recording we may not need some of the requests to be part of testing. This is because we might have forgotten to stop and restart the test or we might have stopped and restarted the test at the wrong place. To remove the unwanted requests, we have to edit the recording. We should go through each recorded request and delete the requests which are not required.

Copying the requests

In some situations we may need the same requests to be tested multiple times. For example, page refresh. To simulate this, we can copy the recorded requests and place them into the recording list. We can copy the request any number of times.We need to select the request from the list in the tree view, right-click and **Copy** or use (*Ctrl* + *C*) and then select the destination folder and right-click and choose **Paste**.

By copying the requests we are also changing the order of testing. This is the easy way to change the order. Instead of copy, we can also cut and paste the requests to a different place just to change the order. But we should be careful in changing the order so that the dependent requests are not affected. For example, if request B is dependent on request A, then we should not move request B before A. We should take more care while copying and changing the order of tests.

Web test editor

After completing all requests recording, click on the **Stop** option in the **Web Recorder** pane which will stop recording and close the browser window. Now you can see the **WebTest** editor window is open and see the recording details in the **WebTest** editor.

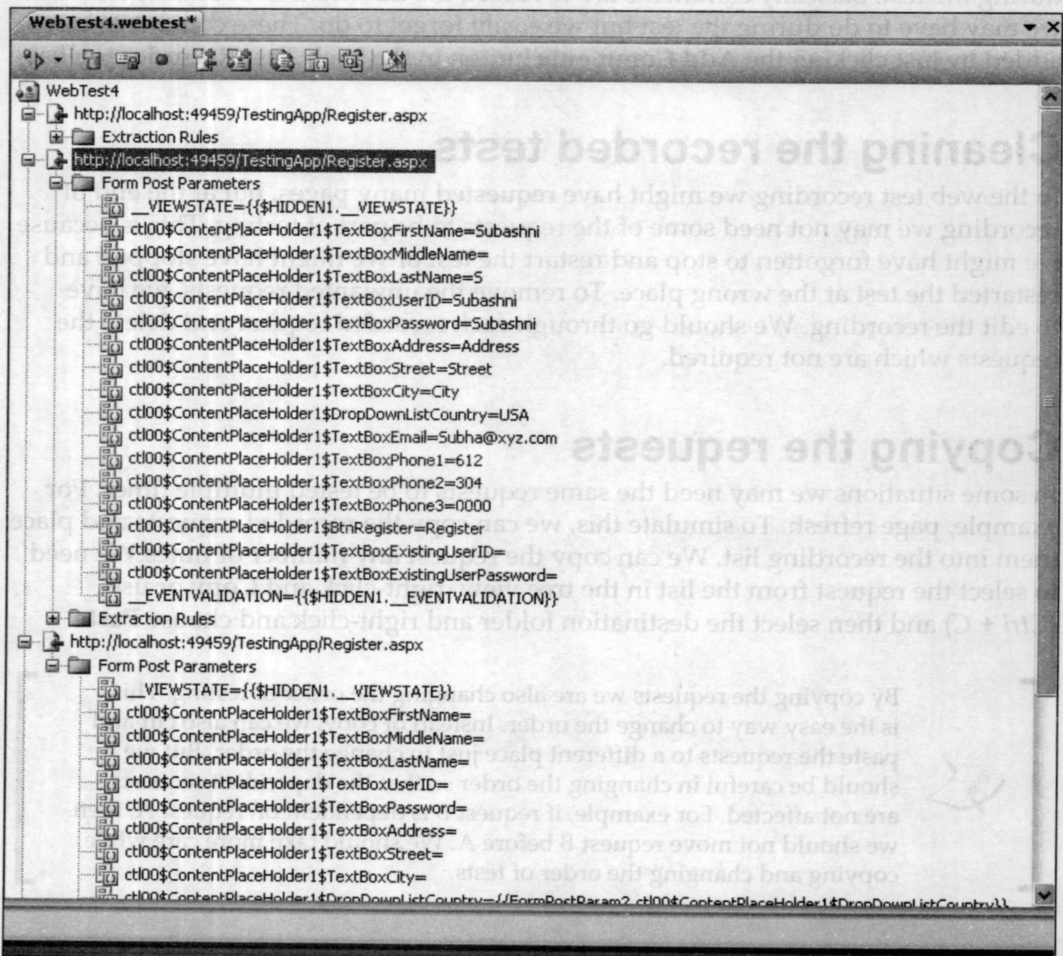

The editor shows the tree view of all requests captured during recording. This editor also exposes different properties of requests and parameters for each request. Not only the properties, but we can also set the **Extraction** and **Validation** rules using this editor. There are different levels of properties that we can set using the **WebTest** editor on the recorded requests.

- Properties at **WebTest** root level which applies to the entire web test. For example, setting the user credentials and giving a description to the test.
- Request level properties that applies to individual request within the web test. For example, we can set the timeout, think times, and recording result's properties on each request level.
- Properties for request parameter applies to the requests using HTTP-POST or HTTP-GET protocol. Each parameter in the request contains parameters like URL encode, value, and name.
- Setting the extraction and validation rules for the responses to make sure the request gets the expected result and are validated.

Apart from all of these the web test editor has a toolbar providing different functionalities like running the test, adding a new data source, and setting the credentials and parameters, explained in detail in coming sections.

Web test properties

Below are the different **Properties** of the **WebTest** that we can set using the editor.

Property	Description
Description	To specify the description for the current test.
Name	Name of the current **WebTest** application.
User Name	This is to specify the username of the user for this test, if we are using any user credential for this test. We can also associate this with the data source of any type like CSV file, XML file, or a Database.
Password	This field is useful in case of using any specific credentials for the test. This is the password for the username specified in the **Username** field.
PreAuthenticate	This is a Boolean field, which indicates whether the page has to be authenticated on every request or not. Only if this property is set to `true`, the authentication header is sent for each request. Otherwise headers are sent, if required. Default is **True**.

Property	Description
Proxy	In some cases, the requested web pages in the test might be outside the firewall which has to go through the proxy server. So we can use this field to set the proxy server name to be used by the test.
Test ID	This is the unique ID to identify the test. This ID is auto generated when we create the test. This can be used to define the test in the coded web test. This property gets the unique identifier when implemented in the derived class.
Stop On Error	This is useful to inform the application whether to stop the test or continue in case of any errors. If this value is true, the execution of complete test will stop in the first occurrence of the error. The default is **True**.

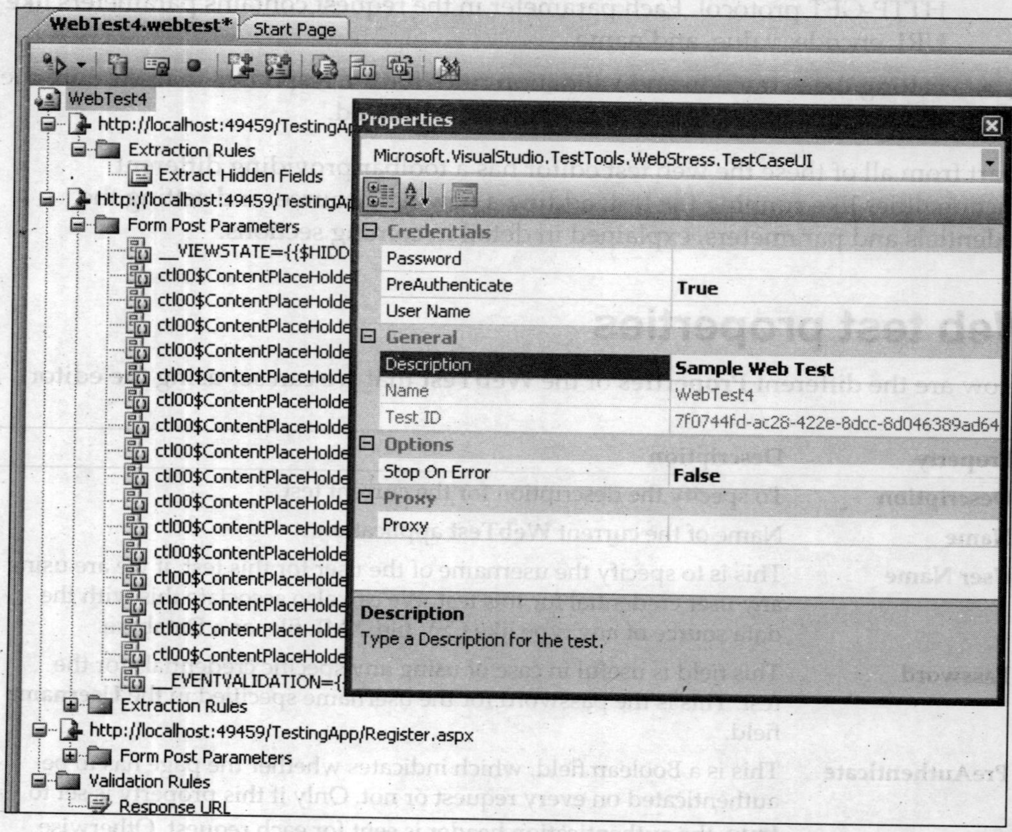

Web test request properties

The next screenshot shows the properties of the requests within the web tests. If you select any request from the tree view and open the properties, you can find these properties for each request.

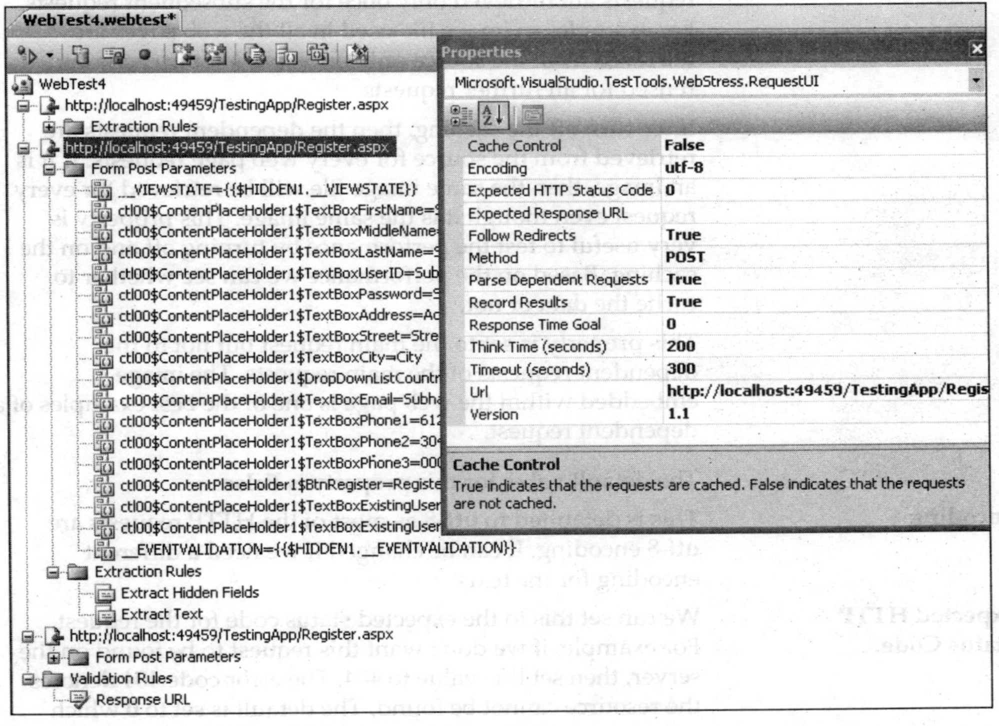

Property	Description
Cache Control	This property is to simulate the caching property of the web pages. The value can be true or false. If it is set to true it means that the caching is turned on, which means that the dependent requests are retrieved only once for the subsequent requests. For example, an image file used in all the web pages are retrieved from the source only once and kept in cache and reused for all further requests. If we turn off the caching, then the dependent requests are retrieved from the source for every web page requests. If it is an image, then the same image file will be retrieved for every request even though it is the same image. This property is very useful to test the performance by turning off and on the caching. Based on the performance we can see whether to cache the data or not. This property is set to the main request but not to the dependent requests of the main requests. The image embedded within the web page is one of the best examples of a dependent request. The default value for this property is **False**.
Encoding	This is defaulted to **utf-8** as most of the HTTP requests are utf-8 encoding. It can be changed if we need a different encoding for the texts.
Expected HTTP Status Code	We can set this to the expected status code for the request. For example, if we don't want this request to be found on the server, then set this value to 404. The error code 404 denotes the resource cannot be found. The default is set to **0** which returns pass for the return status 200 or 300 level and returns fail if the return status is 400 or 500 level.
Expected Response URL	This is set to the final URL response that we expect after the current request and redirects, if any, are made. This is to validate the response. The expected response is validated using the validation rule.

Property	Description
Follow Redirects	This is set to true or false based on whether we want to allow the page redirects made by the request to follow or not. If set to true then the request continues to its redirected web page and verifies if the status is the code entered for **Expected HTTP Status Code**. If it is false the redirects are not followed. For example, if the values of the **Expected HTTP Status Code** is set to any value between 200 and 300 and the **Follow Redirects** is set to **True**, then the end result status of the request after all redirects should be a success. Status code with 200 or 300 level is a pass and status level with 400 or 500 is a failure.
Method	This property is used to set the request method used for the current request. It can be either GET or POST.
Parse Dependent Requests	This property can be set to **True** or **False** to parse the dependent requests within the requested page. For example, we may not be interested in collecting the details for the images loaded in the web page. So we can turn off the requests for loading the images by setting this to False. Only the main request details will be collected. We should not get confused with this property and the Cache control property. Cache is to disable the dependent requests after caching the first occurrence of the request, but this property is to completely set-off the dependent requests or completely turn them on.
Record Results	This is a Boolean value which can hold true if the performance data has to be collected for this HTTP request. It is false if the data is not required to be collected.

Property	Description
Response Time Goal	There are situations where the users need the application to respond quickly without any delays. To test this scenario, we can set this property to the expected maximum response time and then test the pages to find out the ones which does not meet the requirement. This value is specified in seconds. The default value is **0** which means the property is not set.
Think Time(Seconds)	Think time is set for the think time required by the user between pages. This is not the exact time that the user can spend in thinking but it is a rough estimation. Also this property is not very useful for the normal single user web test. This is very useful in case of Load test where we can predict the load including the think time of user between the pages. The recorder automatically records the think times at the same time while recording the test
Timeout (Seconds)	This is the expiry time for the request. This is the maximum time for the request to respond back. If it doesn't return within this limit then the page gets timed out with the error. Default is **300.**
Version	This is to set the HTTP version to use for the request, which can be 1.0 or 1.1. The default is the **1.1** which is the normal or the latest of the HTTP versions.
Url	This is the URL address for the request

Other request properties

Each request in the web test has its own properties and there may be many dependent requests for each main request. We can get and set some properties even at the dependent request level. This is based on the request submit method GET or POST used for the request. We can set values for the parameters used in the request. Also there are some validation rules and extraction rules that can be used to extract the information from the request response.

Form post parameters

These are the parameters sent along with the request if the method used for the request is POST. All field entries made by the user in the web page are sent to the server as form POST parameters. After recording we can check the actual values of the parameters that were sent during the request.

- **Name** denotes the name of the component used for collecting the data.
- **Recorded Value** is the value entered by the user during recording. This is a read only field assigned while recording.
- **URL Encode** determines whether the **Name** and **Value** of the parameter should be URL encoded or not. The default is **True**.
- **Value** is the actual parameter value which should be used during testing. Initially it is set to the same value as recorded value but user can change it. This property also has the flexibility to bind it to a different data source such as Database or XML file or a CSV File. This is very useful in case of testing for different source of information and multiple test runs with different set of data. The next section covers more on how to add the new data source and point to the fields.

In the below screenshot the field **Middle Name** was not entered by the user before submitting the form so it contains nothing. The tester can change the parameter value by selecting the form parameter property and changing the value field.

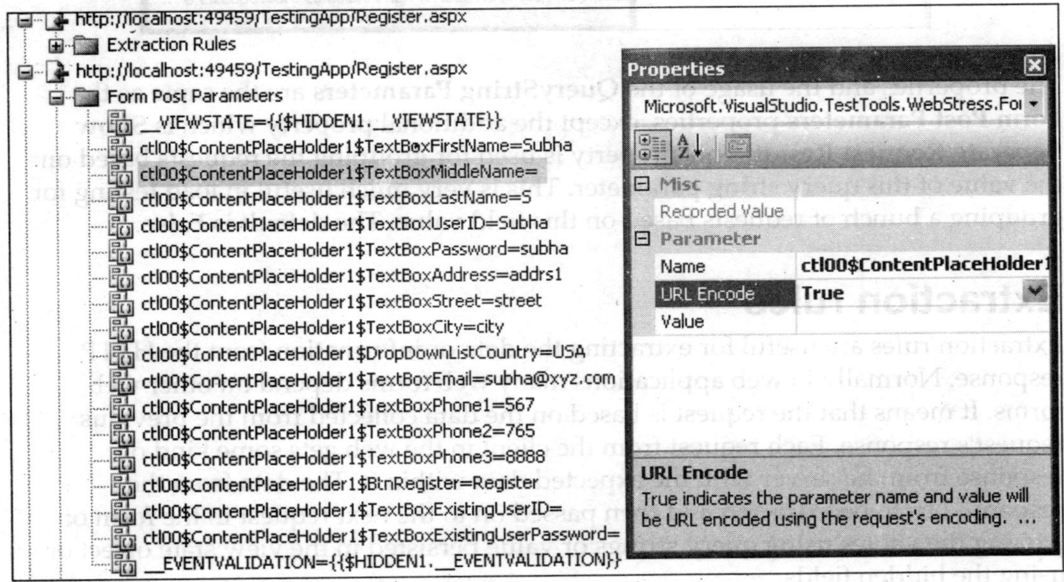

Sometimes, there are additional properties based on the type of control we use on the Web page. In that case we may have to set those properties as well. For example, if we use the **File Upload** control we may have to set the type of the file that we will be uploading.

Query string parameters

This is very similar to the **Form POST Parameters**. These query string parameters are listed under the request, which used the QueryString method for the request.

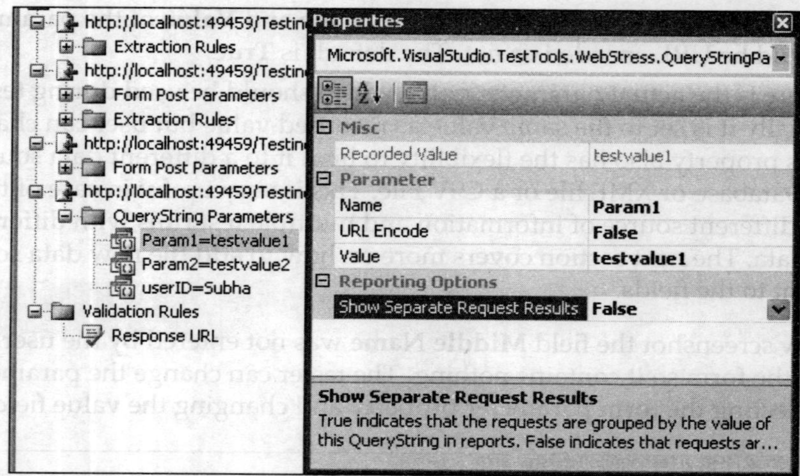

The properties and the usage of the **QueryString Parameters** are the same as the **Form Post Parameters** properties, except the additional property which is **Show Separate Request Result**. This property is used for grouping the requests based on the value of this query string parameter. This is very much useful in load testing for grouping a bunch of requests based on this field value. The default is **False**.

Extraction rules

Extraction rules are useful for extracting the data or information from the HTTP response. Normally in web applications many web forms depend on other web forms. It means that the request is based on the data collected from the previous request's response. Each request from the client in the web gets some kind of response from the server with the expected data within it. The data from the response has to be extracted and then passed on to the next request in the form of passing the values using query strings or value persisted in the view state object or using the hidden fields.

In our previous examples, we used the new user registration page where the user can enter all the details to get registered or the user can enter the user ID and password to log in to the page and get the orders placed earlier and also to place new orders. In this case, once the user enters the login details and clicks **Login** we have to validate the user and pass on the user information to the next `Orders.aspx` page where the orders for the user are displayed.

This validated user information is hidden somewhere in the request using `ViewState` or `Hidden` fields. In this case we can use the Extraction rules to extract the user information and pass it on to the next request or the further requests. We can extract the information and store it in the context parameter and use it globally across all requests, which are followed after this.

VSTS provides several built-in types of extraction rules. This helps us to extract the values based on the HTML tags or different type of fields available in the web form. If we need additional extraction behaviour, which is not supported by the existing one, then we can go for the custom rules. Given below are the existing Extraction rule types.

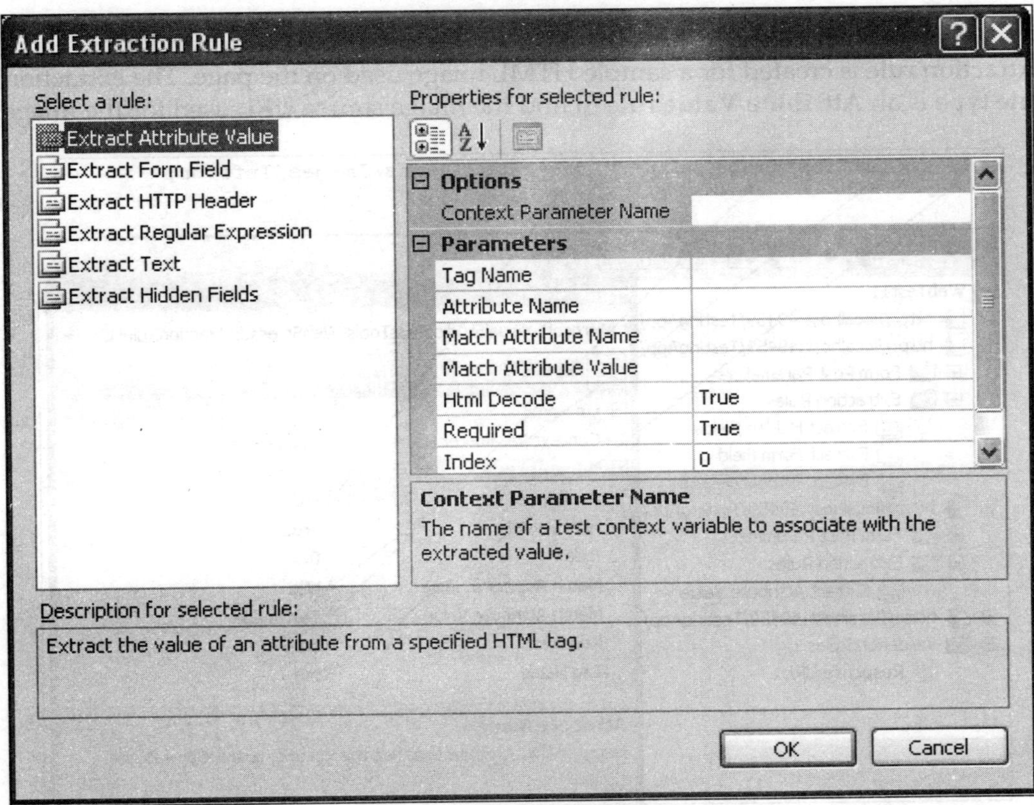

Rule Type	Description
Extract Attribute Value	This is to extract the attribute value from the request page based on the tag and the attribute name. We can also use the optional matching attribute name and value within the same tag to find out the required attribute easily. The extracted value will be stored in the context parameter.
Extract Form Field	To extract the value from any of the Form fields in the response. The field name is identified here.
Extract HTTP Header	To extract the HTTP message header value in the response page.
Extract Regular Expression	Extracts the value using the regular expression to find the matching pattern in the response
Extract Text	This is to extract the text from the response page. The text is identified based on its starting and ending value with text **Casing** as optional.
Extract Hidden Fields	Extracts all hidden field values from the response and assigns that to the context parameter

The screenshot below shows how to set the properties of the **Extraction Rules**. This extraction rule is created for a sample HTML image used on the page. The extraction rule type is an **Attribute Value** rule to find the image source URL used for the image.

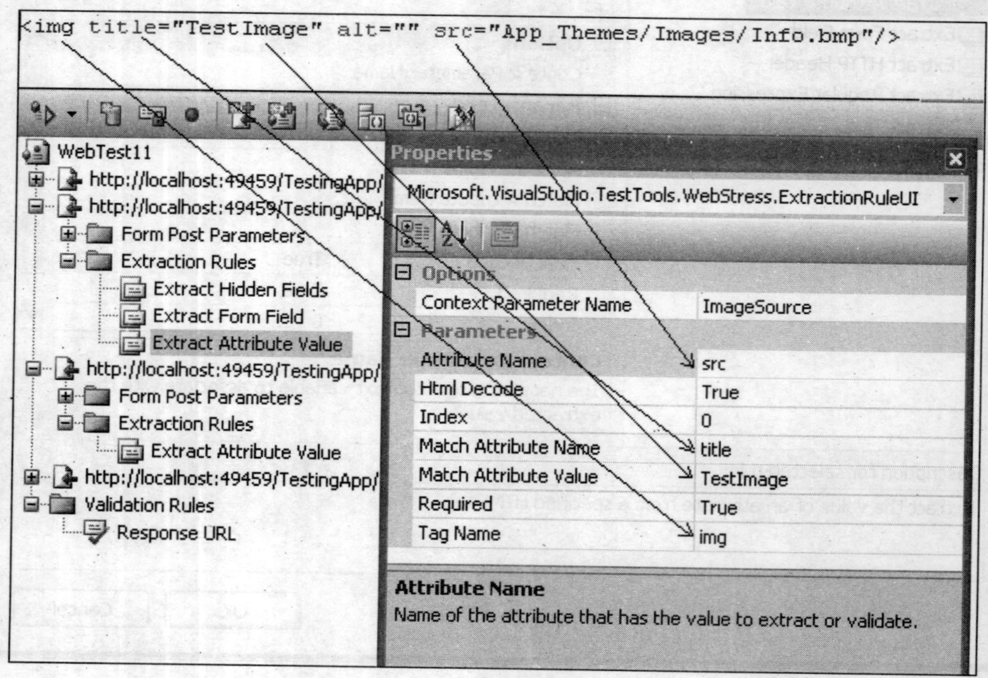

We can add as many rules as we want, but we should make sure the **Context Parameter Names** are unique across the application. It is like a global variable used in the application, which is referred in all the forms.

By default, Visual Studio adds extraction rules for hidden fields automatically. The references to the hidden fields are also automatically added to the **Form POST Parameters** and **Query String Parameters**.

For coded web tests we can create a custom extraction rule by deriving from `ExtractionRule` class.

Validation rules

Every application has some sort of validations done on the input and output data. For example, a valid email address or a valid username without any special characters or a valid password not less than six letters. All these validations are performed using the validation rule against the fields as per the expectation.

Validation rules are nothing but defining some criteria which the information contained in the response has to pass through. All the data collected from the response is validated against the set of defined rules. If it passes, it means that the response is validated otherwise the test fails. For example, if the user has to enter a specific value or if the user has to select a value from a set of values then we can define these validations as rules and use against the values returned in the response fields.

VSTS provides a set of predefined rules for validations. These rules are used for checking the text returned by the response.

For adding the validation rules, just right-click on the request and select the **Add Validation Rule** option which opens the validation rule's dialog. In here, select the type of validation rule required and fill the parameters required for the rule.

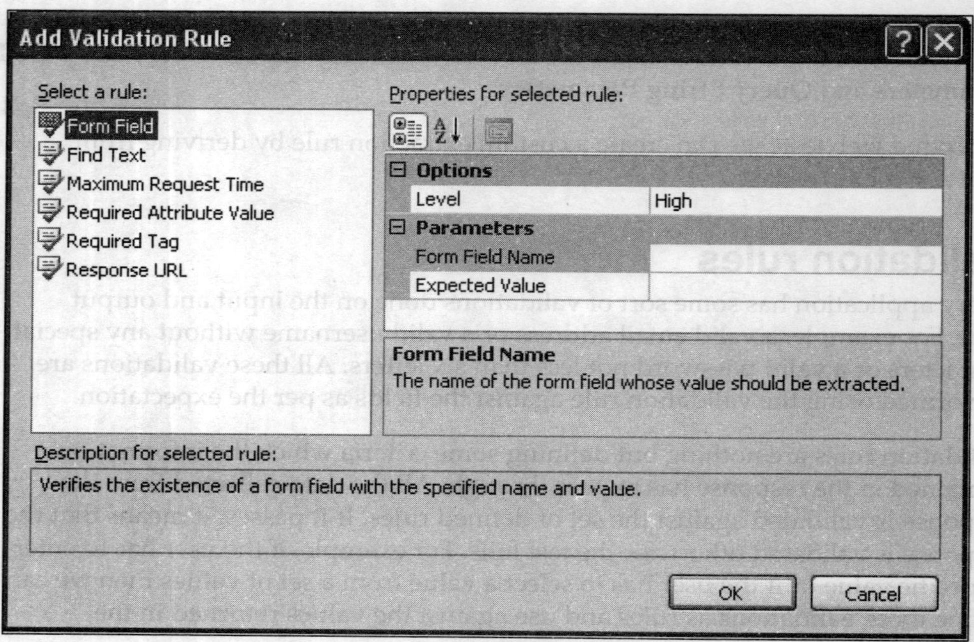

Validation Rule Type	Description
Form Field	The existence of the form field name and value is verified using this. The parameters are **Form Field Name** **Expected** value
Find Text	This is to verify the existence of a specified text in the response. The parameters used for this are: **Find Text** **Ignore Case** **Use Regular Expression** **Pass If Text Found**
Maximum Request Time	This is to verify whether the request finishes within the specified Maximum request Time **Max Request Time (milliseconds)**

Validation Rule Type	Description
Required Attribute Value	This is similar to the attribute used in the Extraction rules. In extraction rules, we just extracted the value of the specific attribute using the tag and the other attribute within the tag. But here in validation rules we use the same tag to find whether the attribute is returning the expected value. The parameters used here are the same as the one used in extraction rules with an additional field to specify the expected value. The properties are: **Tag Name** **Attribute Name** **Match Attribute Name** **Match Attribute Value** **Expected Value** **Ignore Case** **Index** The index is used here to indicate which occurrence of the string to validate. If this index is set to **-1**, then it checks any form field value in the form and passes the test if any one match is found.
Required Tag	To verify if the specified tag exists in the response. We can also set the minimum occurrence if there is a chance of getting the same tag many numbers of times in the response. The parameters are **Required Tag Name** **Minimum Occurences**
Response URL	This is to verify the URL is the same as the Expected URL. The property is the level for the response URL. The level can be any High or Medium or Low.

We can keep adding any number of validation rules we want, but as the number grows the performance or the time taken for the test will also grow. So we should decide which one is important in case of load testing, these rules will affect the time taken for the test.

In all the rule types, we have a special parameter known as the **Level** which can be set to **Low** or **Medium** or **High**. As mentioned earlier, the load test performance is directly affected by number of validation rules we have. So to control the execution of rules in a request during the load test, we can use the level property. The level does not mean the priority for the rule but it says when it should get executed based on the load test property. The load test also has similar property such as **Low** or **Medium** or **High.**

Based on the below load test property, the rules with the corresponding levels will get run during the load test:

- **Low**—all validation rules with level **Low** will be run.
- **Medium**—all validation rules with level **Low** and **Medium** will be run.
- **High**—all validation rules with level **Low, Medium**, and **High** will be run.

Based on the importance of the load test importance, we can set the property of the rules.

We will see more details about this in the chapter, which talks about load test.

Transactions

Transactions are very useful to group a set of activities. Here in this case, we can group a set of requests so that we can track the total time taken for the set of requests for our analysis. This is also helpful to collect the timing of the individual requests.

We just have to say the starting request and the ending request for the transaction so that all the requests in between these two requests will be part of the transaction including these two requests.

To add a transaction, select the starting request from where the transaction should start and right-click and choose **Insert Transaction** option.

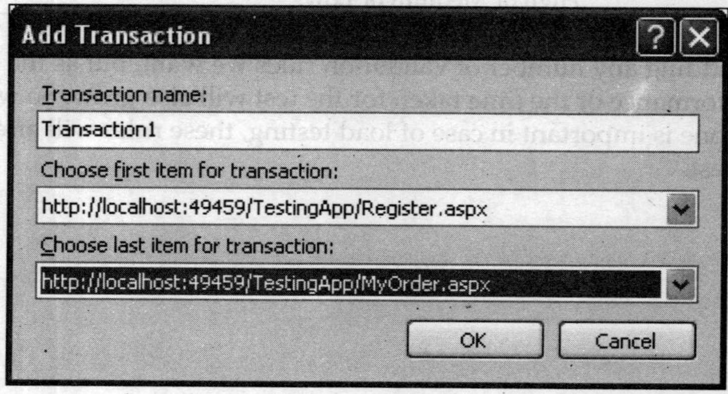

The Transaction dialog requires a name for the transaction and then the requests for the first item and last item for the transaction. When you choose both and say **OK,** the transaction is added before the first item selected for the transaction and all the other requests between the first and last item including first ad last are part of the transaction as shown below:

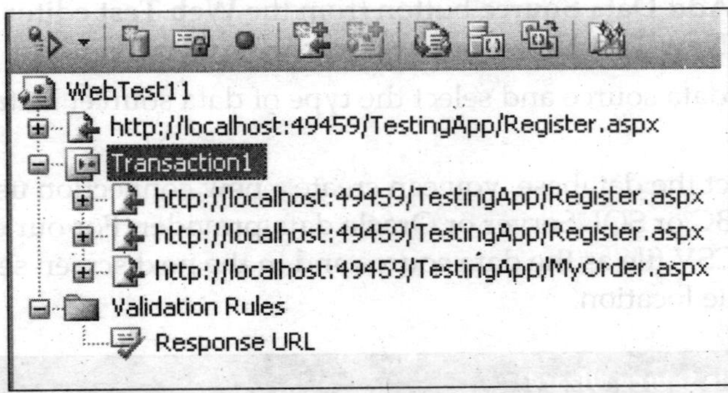

So when the test is run you can see the total time taken for all the requests under the transaction.

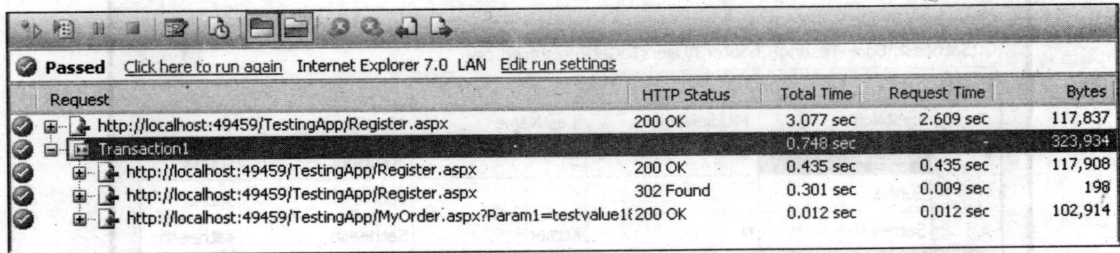

Toolbar properties

The web test editor has a toolbar on its own to work on the web tests. There are different options like adding a data source, set credentials, adding more requests recording, adding plug-ins to the test, generating code, parameterize the web servers, and creating the performance session for the test.

Add data source

We have seen the Form Post parameters and Query String parameters and how to set the values of the parameters using the property. Now each and every time we test the application, we have to change the property every time. In case of load testing too, it is difficult and time consuming process to test for more users. In this case, we can directly link the parameters to the available data in a different data source.

Visual Studio supports different type of data sources such as CSV, SQL Server database, XML File, Access, Excel, and any other database using OLE DB provider connection.

To add a new data source:

1. Select the **Add Data Source** button from the **Web Test** editor toolbar which opens the **New Test Data Source Wizard.**
2. Name the data source and select the type of data source(Database, CSV, XML File).
3. If you select the database, you can create a new connection using either OLE DB or ODBC or SQL Server or Oracle data provider. For our example here, select the CSV file as the data source and in the next screen select the CSV file from the file location.

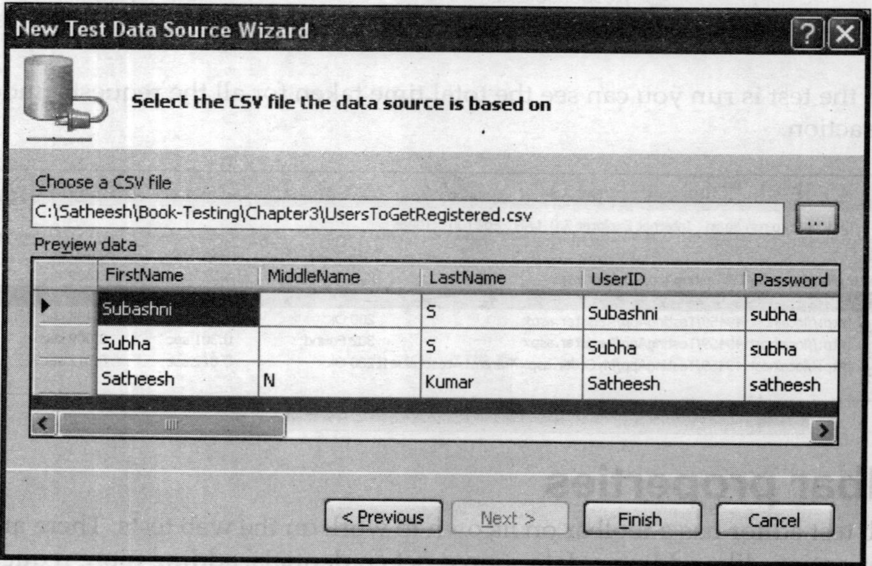

4. Once you select the file you can see the data in the preview data grid.
5. Once you say **OK** you can see the data source added to the test project.

You can add any number of data sources based on the requirement and based on the sources of data we have for testing.

The screenshot below shows two data sources, **CSVFileDataSource** is for the new user data and the second one **XMLCountriesDataSource** is for the list of countries for the user.

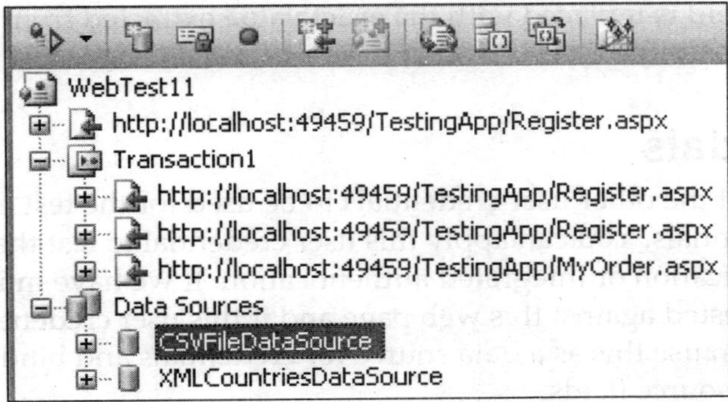

Once the data source is ready, we can change the source of the Form Post or Form Query String properties. For this, select the **Form Post Parameter** under the request, then right-click and choose the **Properties**. In the **Value** property select the data source and select the field from the data source.

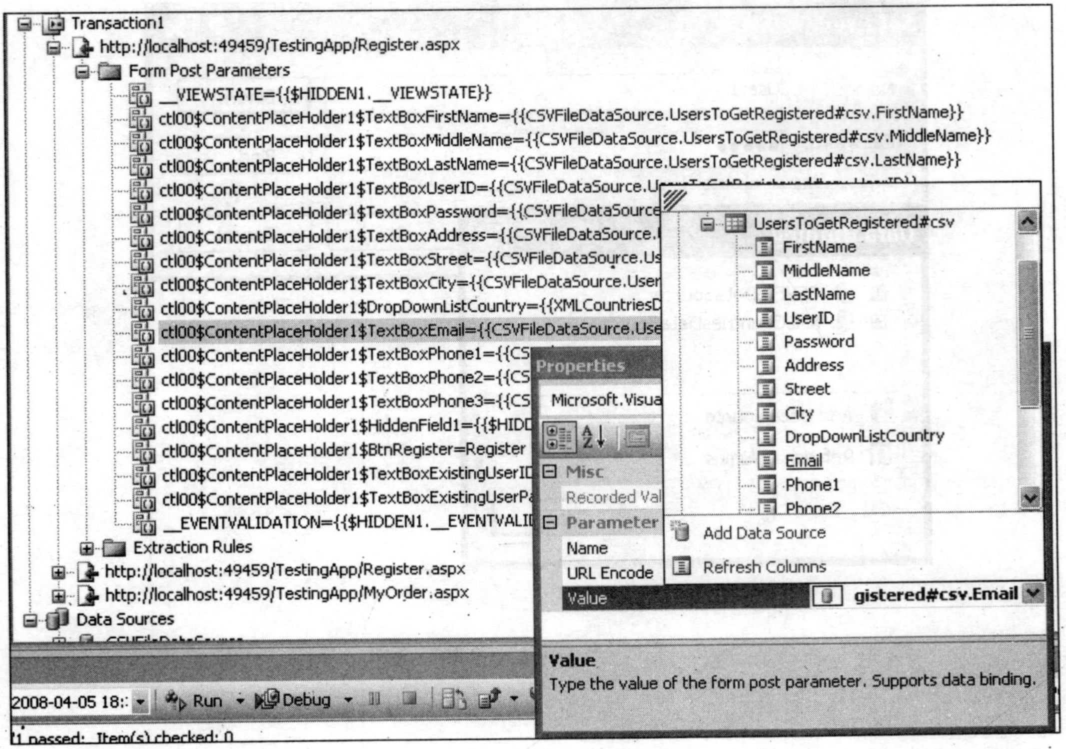

You can notice the value assigned to the form post parameters.
It is pointing to the field in the selected data source like:
{{CSVFileDataSource.UsersToGetRegistered#csv.FirstName}}

At run-time this field is replaced with the exact value extracted from the CSV file and the test runs successfully.

Set credentials

This is useful to set the other user credentials to be used for the test instead of the current user credentials. You can apply this user credential to test the page, which uses basic authentication or integrated authentication. If we have multiple user credentials to be tested against this web page and if this user credentials are stored somewhere, we can use this as a data source for credentials and bind the credentials field to these data source fields.

Credentials can be set using the option in the **Web Test** editor toolbar. Click the **Set Credentials** option and enter the **User Name** and **Password** values. If you have the data source already you can click on the **Bind...** option and choose the data source and the field for the multiple user credentials test for the test page.

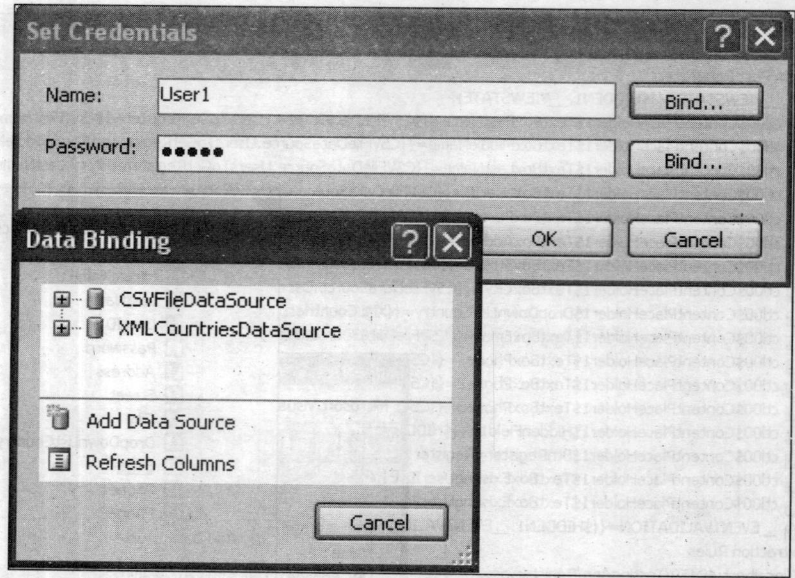

Add recording

This option adds a new request recording to the existing test. Sometimes we may forget to browse some web pages during the record, if we don't remember all the web pages. So after recording is done, we can still add requests to the recording using this option. On clicking the option **Add Recording** in the **Web Test** editor toolbar, you can see recording window opens for the new recording. After completing the recording, this current recording will get added to the existing Web test recording. This is one of the ways to edit the recording. We can also delete a request from the existing recording and add a new one.

Parameterize web server

All web tests are recorded and conducted using one web server. If we have to test the same test on another web server, then we were to re-record the whole testing on the new server and test again. But now the VSTS provides the feature of parameterizing the web servers. It means that the web server to which all the web test requests should point is identified at run-time using these parameters.

For example, this is required in case of performing same kind of testing but with different hardware configurations. The requests in the web test should point to different hardware every time the configuration is changed. The test scenario is the same in all of these cases but only the configuration changes based on the parameter values set at run-time. This is very useful when the application is tested for load testing, performance testing, and integration testing where the configuration is the only change.

To parameterize the web server in web test:

1. Select the **Parameterize Web Servers** option in the **Web Test** editor toolbar, which opens the dialog that lists different web servers used by the web test. The list contains the context parameter names and the web server URL associated to the context parameter.

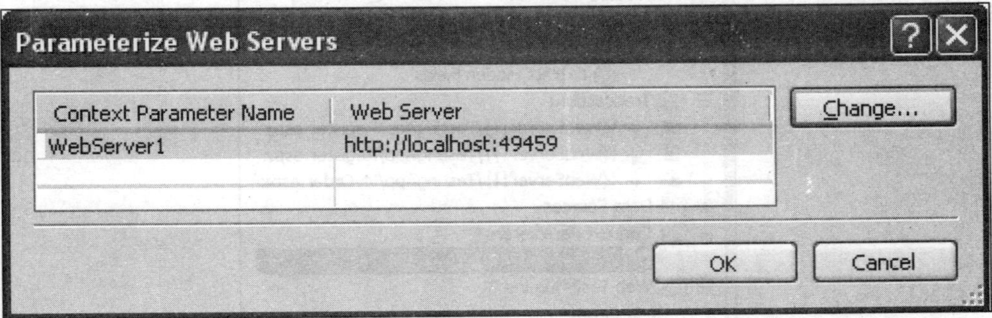

We can change the context parameter value to point to a different server by choosing the **Change...** option after selecting the context parameter name form the list. This opens the second dialog which helps us to change the name and the web server URL.

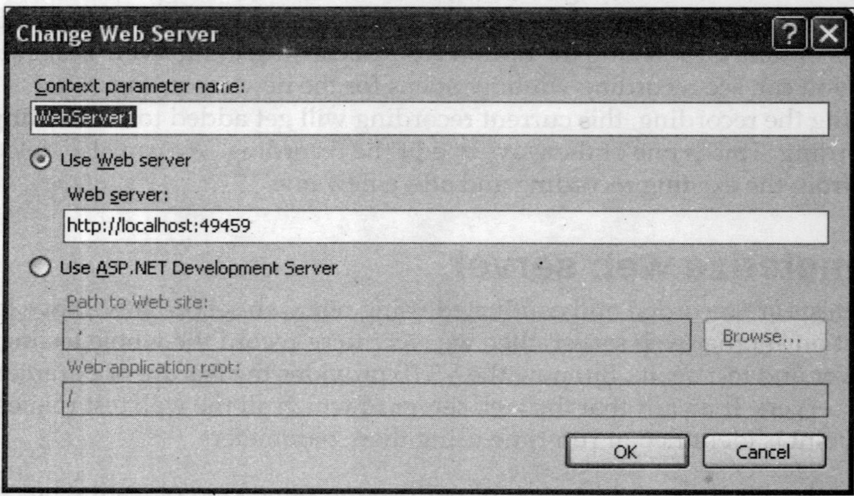

If you are planning to use the local ASP.NET development server, choose the second option which says **Use ASP.NET Development Server** and provide the local web site path and the application root.

After changing the value for the new context parameter, close the **Parameterize Web Server** dialog. Now we can see the context parameter added to the web test under the **Context Parameters** folder. Also we can notice that the server address in the entire request URLs in the web tests are replaced with this new parameter and the value is held by the context parameter.

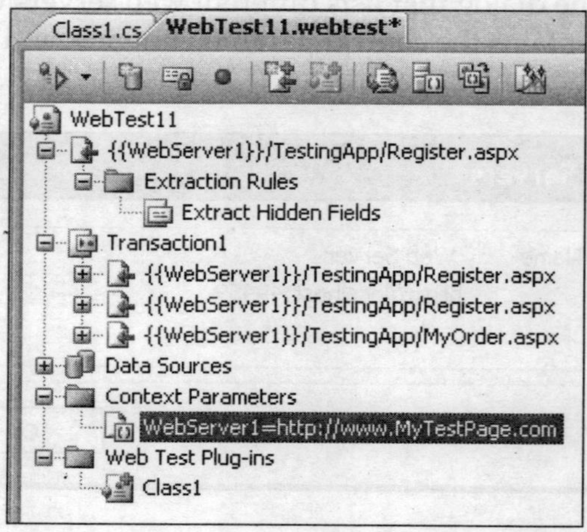

We can notice that the context parameters are used in the requests within the braces like **{{WebServer1}}**, which is replaced by the actual value at run-time.

Context parameters

There are different ways of creating context parameters:

1. By just right-clicking on the **Context Parameters** folder and selecting **Add Context Parameter**.
2. The plug-in can create the context parameter and assign the value in the event that runs before the web test.

For example, the plug-in assembly code below creates a new context parameter for the current windows **UserName** and adds the parameter to the web test. The code also assigns the **UserName** value to the existing **Form Post Parameter** field **TextBoxExistingUserID.**

```
public override void PreWebTest(object sender,
  PreWebTestEventArgs e)
{
    e.WebTest.Context["UserName"] =
      System.Environment.UserName.ToString();
    e.WebTest.Context["ctl00$ContentPlaceHolder1
    $TextBoxExistingUserID"] = e.WebTest.Context["UserName"];
}
```

When the Web test is run we can see the value assigned to the context parameter as well as the **TextBoxExistingUserID** form post parameter.

CSVFileDataSource.UsersToGetRegistered#csv.UserID	Subashni
ctl00$ContentPlaceHolder1$TextBoxExistingUserID	User1
EmailID	subashni@xyz.com
ImageSource	App_Themes/Images/Info.bmp
UserName	User1
WebServer1	http://localhost:49459
XMLCountriesDataSource.Data.Data_Text	USA

We can also have the context parameter added to the web test at design-time and assign the value at run-time using the plug-in.

Add web test plug-in

Plug-ins is the set of external libraries or assemblies written for some custom functionality which can run along the Web test. This plug-in runs once for every iteration of the test. For example, a currency converter could be an external service, which can be used as a plug-in to convert the currency value in the test.

To add a plug-in, we need to first create an assembly or a separate class library with a class containing the custom code. The class should inherit from the **Microsoft.VisualStudio.TestTools.WebTesting.WebTestPlugin** and should implement the methods `PreWebTest()` and `PostWebTest()`. Atleast one of these methods should be implemented:

- `PreWebTest()` – this code will run before the web test starts execution.
- `PostWebTest()` – this code will run after the web testing is over.

To get this namespace, we have to add the reference **Microsoft.VisualStudio.QualityTools.WebTestFramework** to the assembly. Now after completing the coding, add this assemble project reference to the Web test project. Then select the web test and choose the option **Add Web Test Plug-in** from the toolbar which will list the classes within the assembly. Select the class, it will get added to the test project.

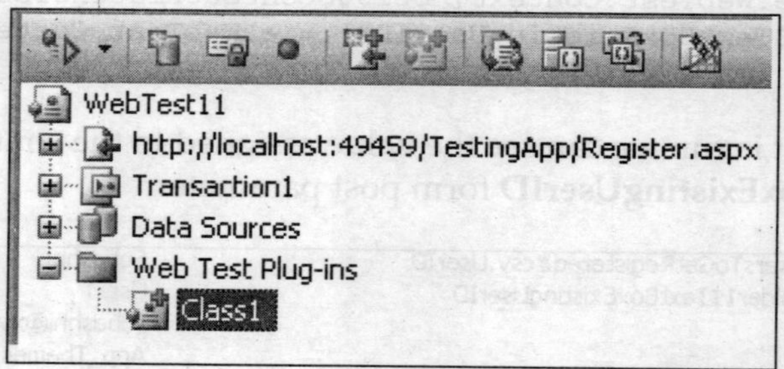

For example, if the class contains the following code in it, we can see the context variable with the value added to each request in the web test. The `e.WebTest.Context` contains the current context of the web test. The `e` is the current object which fires the event. The parameters and properties for the current context can be accessed using the `e.WebTest.Context` object.

```
using System;
using System.Collections.Generic;
using System.Linq;
using System.Text;
using Microsoft.VisualStudio.TestTools.WebTesting;
```

```
namespace WebTestPluginSample
{
    public class Class1 : WebTestPlugin
    {
        public override void PostWebTest(object sender,
          PostWebTestEventArgs e)
        {
        }

        public override void PreWebTest(object sender,
          PreWebTestEventArgs e)
        {
            e.WebTest.Context["TestParameter"] = "Test Value";
        }
    }
}
```

Now when the test is run, you can see the context variable added to each request's context.

Web Browser | Request | Response | Context | Details

Name	Value
CSVFileDataSource.UsersToGetRegi...	123
CSVFileDataSource.UsersToGetRegi...	123
CSVFileDataSource.UsersToGetRegi...	1234
CSVFileDataSource.UsersToGetRegi...	Street1
CSVFileDataSource.UsersToGetRegi...	Subashni
EmailID	subashni@xyz.com
ImageSource	App_Themes/Images/Info.bmp
TestParameter	Test Value
XMLCountriesDataSource.Data.Data...	USA

Add request plug-in

This is very similar to the web test plug-in but the only difference is that the plug-in code runs for every request in the web test. This is the custom code written for complex functionality which should run before or after every request in the web test.

The code assembly should reference the library **Microsoft.VisualStudio.QualityTools.WebTestFramework** and the class should inherit from **Microsoft.VisualStudio.TestTools.WebTesting.WebTestPlugin** and implement the methods `PreRequest()` or `PostRequest()` based on whether the code should execute before the request or after the request.

Performance session for the test

From running the test, we will come to know only the success or failure result of the test and different parameter values handled in the test. But to get the actual performance of the functions or method calls and the time taken for all the methods within the test, VSTS provides the performance session. This performance session is the profiling tool collecting run-time performance data for the application.

Performance session reports various information like the method calls, memory allocations, and the time spent in running the methods. To run the performance session:

1. Select the web test and choose the option **Create Performance Session for this Test** which opens the **Performance** wizard. The wizard provides two options for the session type.
    - **Sampling**: This technique collects information like the CPU time taken for the methods. Also the information collected is between the specific time intervals.
    - **Instrumentation**: This technique is used in case of collecting more information from the test and the external programs called within the test. This method is used in case of smaller tests as the information collected is more than sampling.
2. After selecting the required option, choose the current test application from the list.

The **Performance Explorer** opens with the new performance session for the selected test. The explorer contains two folders one says **Targets** and other says **Reports**. The targets are the application under profiling. The report contains the list of reports collected on every run of the test from the performance explorer.

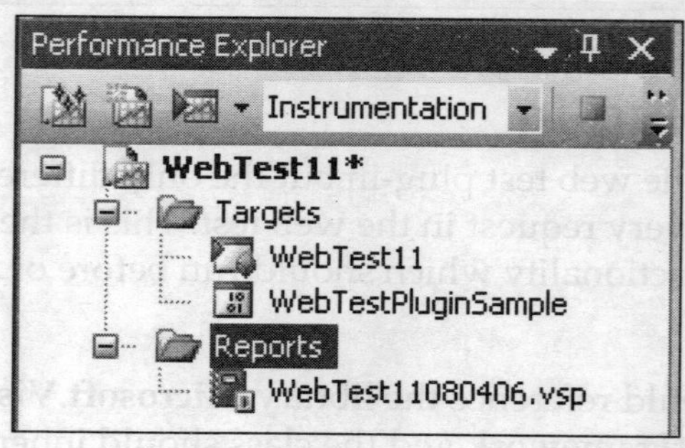

Now launch the test application from the **Performance Explorer** using the options in the explorer. It starts the application to run and at the same time the profiler starts collecting the execution data from the running application. At the end of completing the application run, the profiler produces a report, with all the information collected by grouping them based on the functionality as the one shown below. This is the default summary view of the report.

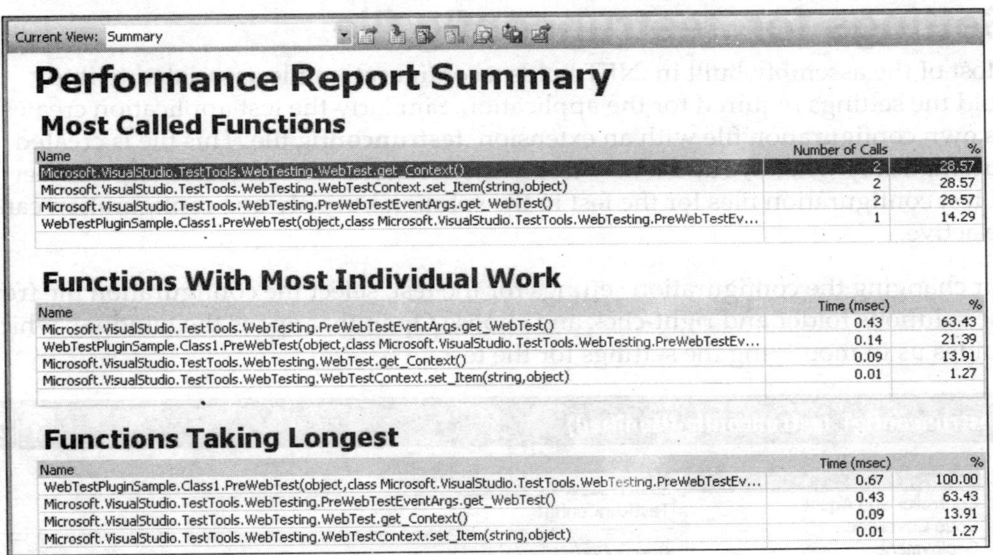

We can change the summary view to a different type of view by selecting the different options given in the toolbar. We can also export the result for further analysis.

The **Performance Explorer** also provides options to set or change different properties of the profiler. We can change the type of profiling and the data to be collected during data collection. For example, setting the clock cycles, Page faults, system calls, and performance counters in case of **Sampling** method of profiling. We can also set properties for **CPU Counters, Windows Events, Windows Counters**.

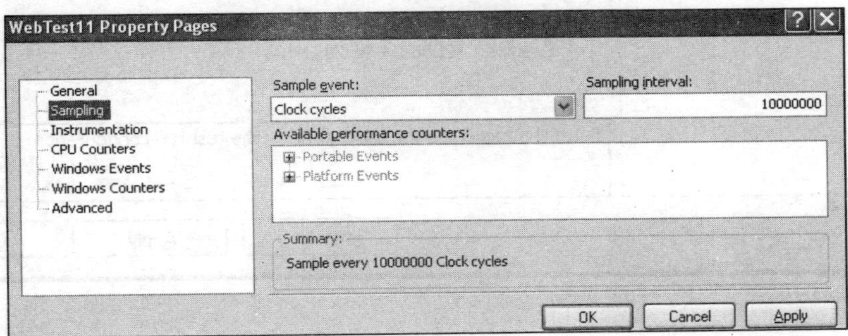

Debug/running web test

Once we finished recording the web test we need to verify that by running the test at least once to make sure it is working fine without any errors. But before running the test we need look at the configuration file associated to the test.

Settings for .testrunconfig file

Most of the assembly built in .NET holds a configuration file associated to it to hold the settings required for the application. Similarly the test application creates its own configuration file with an extension **.testrunconfig** file. This file is created automatically when we add a new test to the solution. We can create any number of test configuration files for the test in the solution but only one configuration can be active.

For changing the configuration settings for the test, select the configuration file from the solutions folder and right-click and choose **Open** that opens the window, which guides us in modifying the settings for the test.

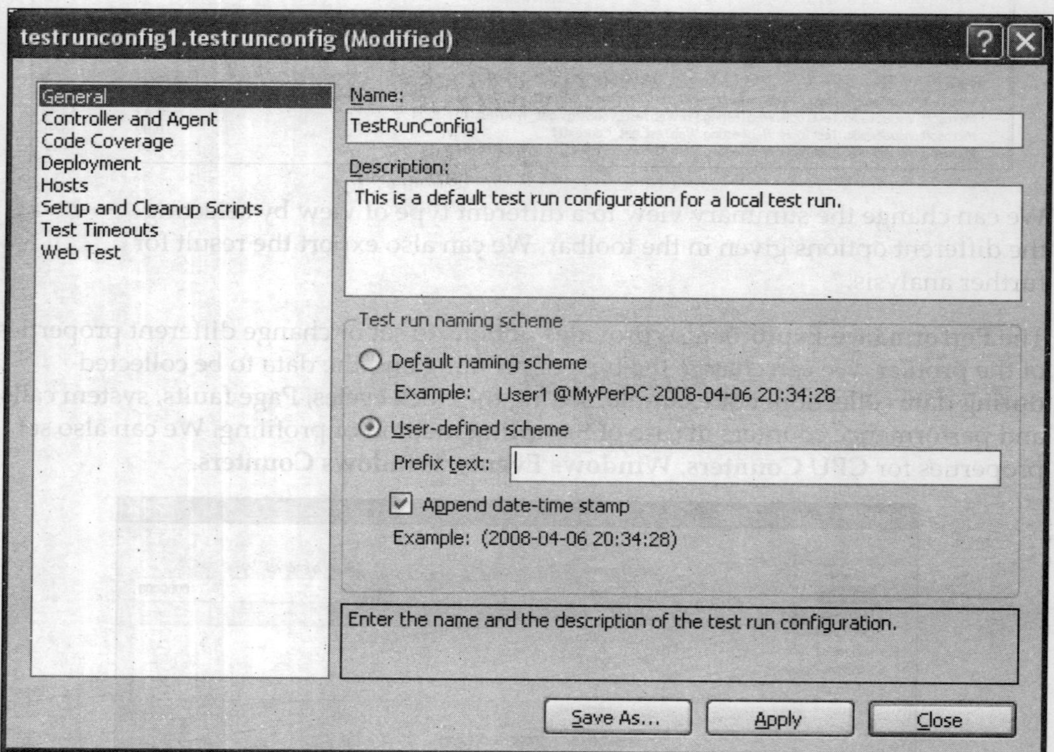

General

The **General** section contains the settings that are common for the test. They are:

- **Name**: This is to specify name for the configuration file.
- **Description**: short description of the test configuration. In case of maintaining multiple configuration files, we can use this field to briefly describe the changes from the previous settings.
- **Test run naming scheme**: When the test is run, the results are created and stored under a specific name in the application results folder. By default the name is the current windows user name followed by the @ symbol and then the machine name and current date and time. We can choose the next option which is the user defined schema text. We can also choose for appending the date time stamp with the user defined scheme.

Web test

This section describes all of the settings required for web testing. These settings are applied only for the web testing. Some of the properties will be overridden in case of load testing.

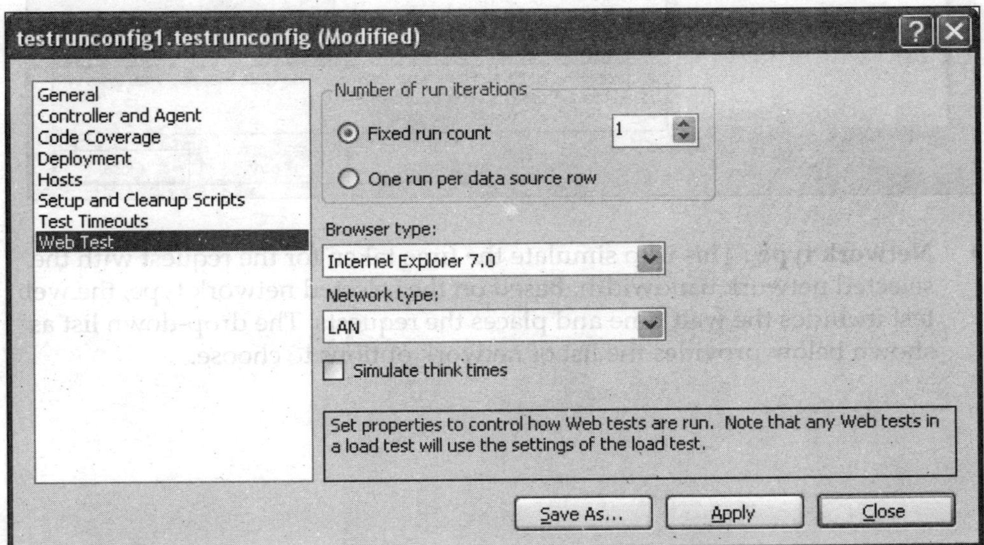

- **Number of run iterations**: This is to set the number of times the test has to run. There are two options for this: one is to set it to a specific number of times, which can be greater than **1**. The second option is to set it to take the number of rows available in the data source associated to the web test and run once per row. This property does not apply to load test as the load test is for number of users and scenarios not for iterations.
- **Browser type**: This property is to set the type of browser to use for the requests. The drop-down contains the list of different browser types to choose. The screenshot below shows the list of browsers to choose.

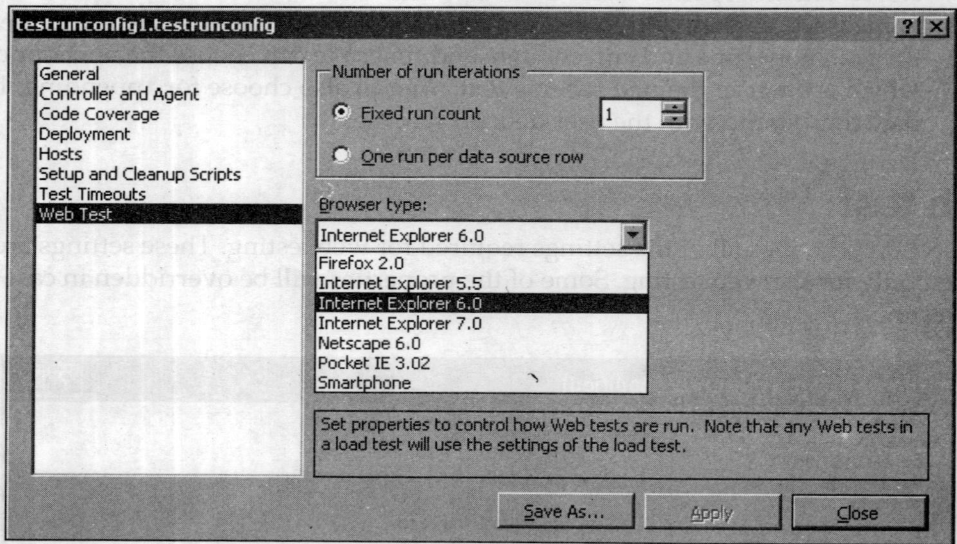

- **Network type** : This is to simulate the time taken for the request with the selected network bandwidth. Based on the selected network type, the web test includes the wait time and places the requests. The drop-down list as shown below provides the list of network options to choose.

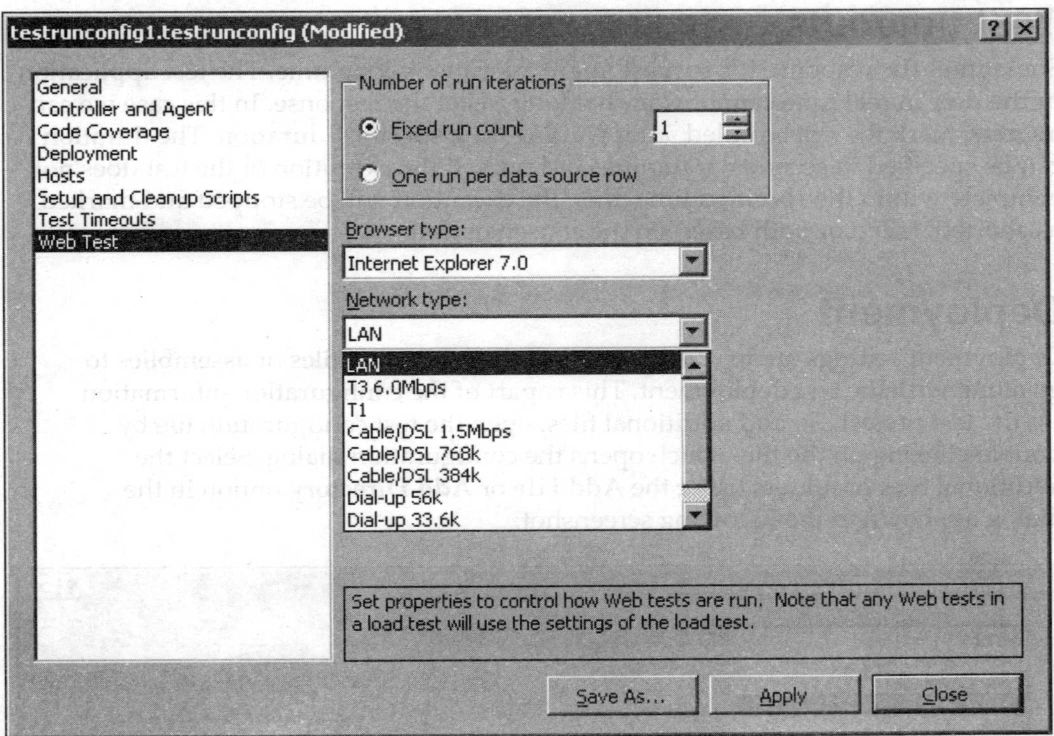

- **Think time**: If this property is selected, the test simulates the think time property set for the requests in the test. This is the time taken between the requests or the time taken for placing the next request after getting the response for the first request.

Controller and agent

This section is useful to specify the controller or the location where the tests will be processed. It can be a local machine or a remote machine. In the case of remote servers we can also specify the names of any agents required for hosting the web test.

Code coverage

This section is not very useful in case of web testing. This is used in Unit testing. Refer to the Unit testing chapter which explains more about this code coverage section.

Test timeouts

Sometimes the response for request might take a very long time. The test application or the user in real time cannot wait that long to get the response. In this case we can abort or mark the test as failed, after waiting for a specified duration. The duration can be specified in seconds or minutes or hours. If the execution of the test does not complete within the specified time, then the execution will be stopped and marked as aborted, failed or both based on the chosen option.

Deployment

Deployment settings are to specify or select the additional files or assemblies to go along with the test deployment. This is part of the configuration information for the test project. To add additional files, open the test configuration file by double-clicking on the file, which opens the configuration dialog. Select the additional files or folders using the **Add File** or **Add Directory** option in the dialog as shown in the following screenshot:

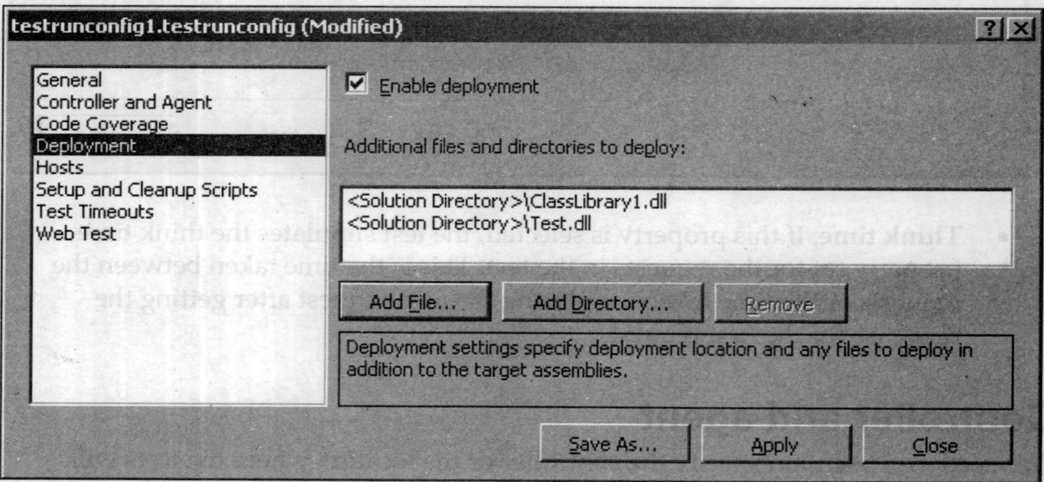

In case of coded web tests, the additional deployment items can be added using the `DeploymentItem` attribute. For example, the code below shows the deployment of the library files as part of deploying the test application.

```
[DeploymentItem("Test.dll")]
[DeploymentItem("ClassLibrary1.dll")]
public class WebTest11Coded : WebTest
{

}
```

Hosts

This specifies the default host for the test which cannot be hosted by the specified adapters. We can select either to run in the default host or not to run the test.

Setup and cleanup scripts

This property is to specify the script files, which can be used before and after the test. In some test scenarios, we might have to set the environment for the test using the setup scripts and in some cases we might have to clean up the environment by cleaning the files created by the test or the updates made by the system. This section takes care of setting the scripts to run. The screenshot below shows the script files that runs before and after the test run. The `SetEnvironment.bat` file contains the script which takes care of setting the environment for the test. The `CleanTestFolder.bat` is the file which contains the script that executes after the test completion to clean up the environment.

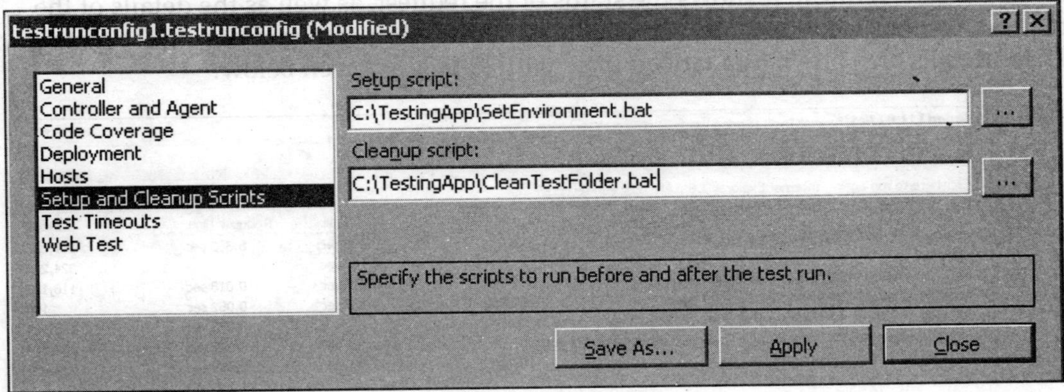

Running the test

Once we've made all the required settings and finished recording all the required requests, running the test is very easy. Before running, we can also define the context parameters, extraction, and validation rules, add the data sources, and bind the Form Post or Query String Parameters. But once we run the test we should take care of verifying all the results that we receive out of this test run. Use the **Run Test** option in the Web test editor toolbar to start running the test.

Now you can notice the test execution and the progress of each request in the web test window. After completing the execution, the result window displays success and failure information and marking against each request. If any one of the requests in the test fails, the entire test is marked as failed. The test result window shows the end result of the testing.

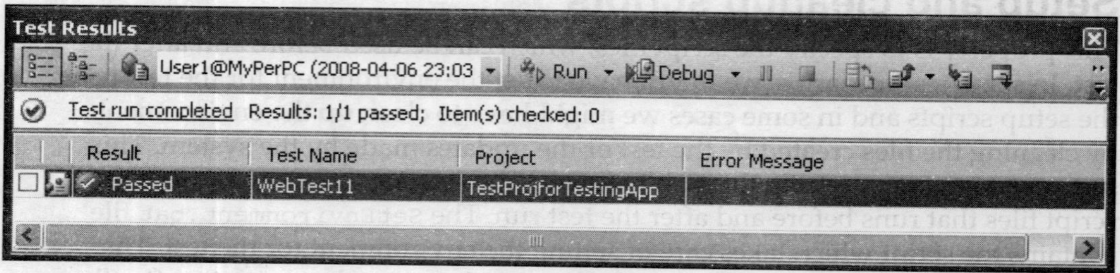

If there are multiple requests in the test, the test result details window shows the result for each request. It shows the status of the request, as well as the details of the request, response, context, and the details of information gathered during the testing. These details are shown as a tabbed page with details as given below:

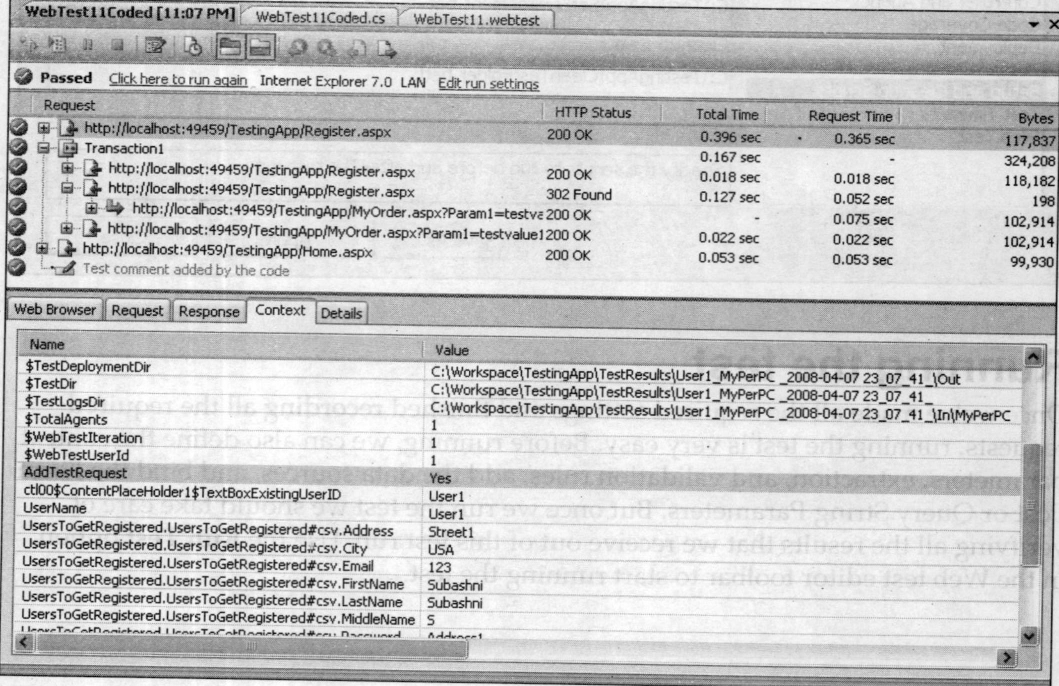

Web browser

This is the same web page used by the request. This tab displays the entire web page used just to get the view of the request.

Request

The **Request** tab contains all the information about the request like Headers, Cookies, Query String Parameters, Form Post Parameters. You can notice the Form Post Parameters with the values assigned to it and sent it with the request.

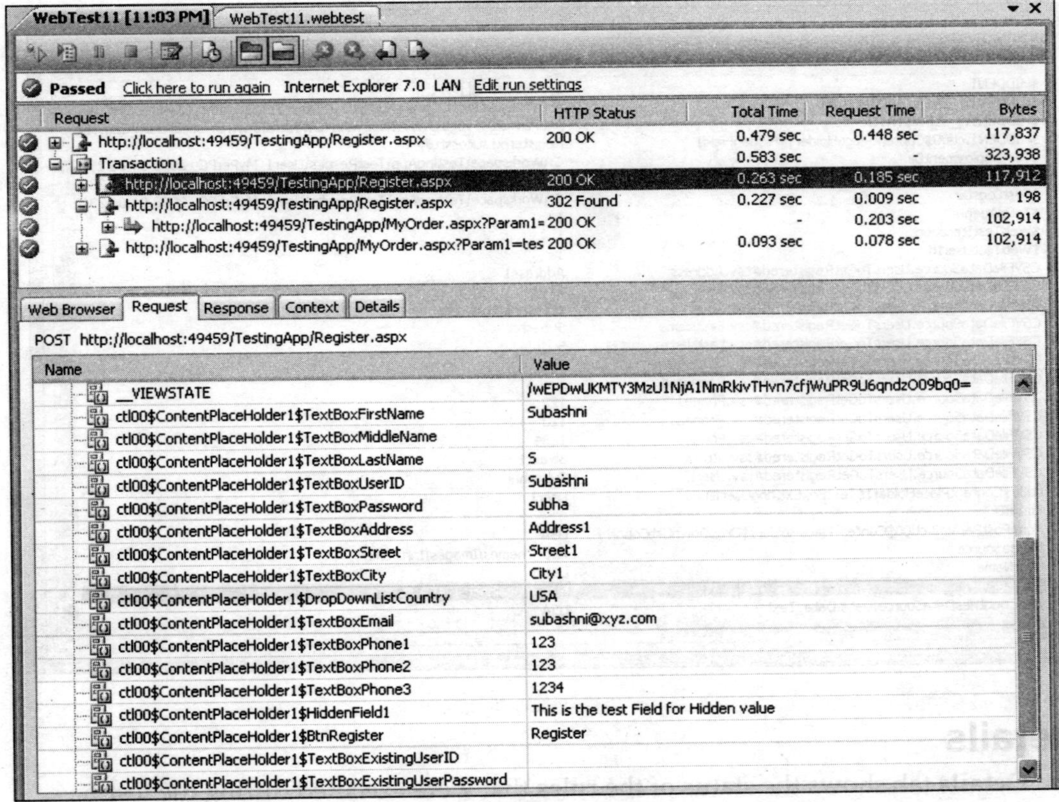

Response

This tab section shows the response for the requested web page. The result is shown as a plain HTML text with headers and body of the web response. There is also an option to view the response in an HTML editor.

Context

This section is very important to note as we have all the run-time details assigned to the test been captured here. Remember the data source we added in the **Add Data Source** section and binding the Form Post Parameters to the data source fields. We added the CSV file and bound the parameters. All the values picked from the data source and assigning the values to the parameters are shown here. Also the context parameters that we created before testing and the values assigned to the parameters during the run-time are also shown here. This is the place to verify visually all the values that are assigned to the context parameters and form fields.

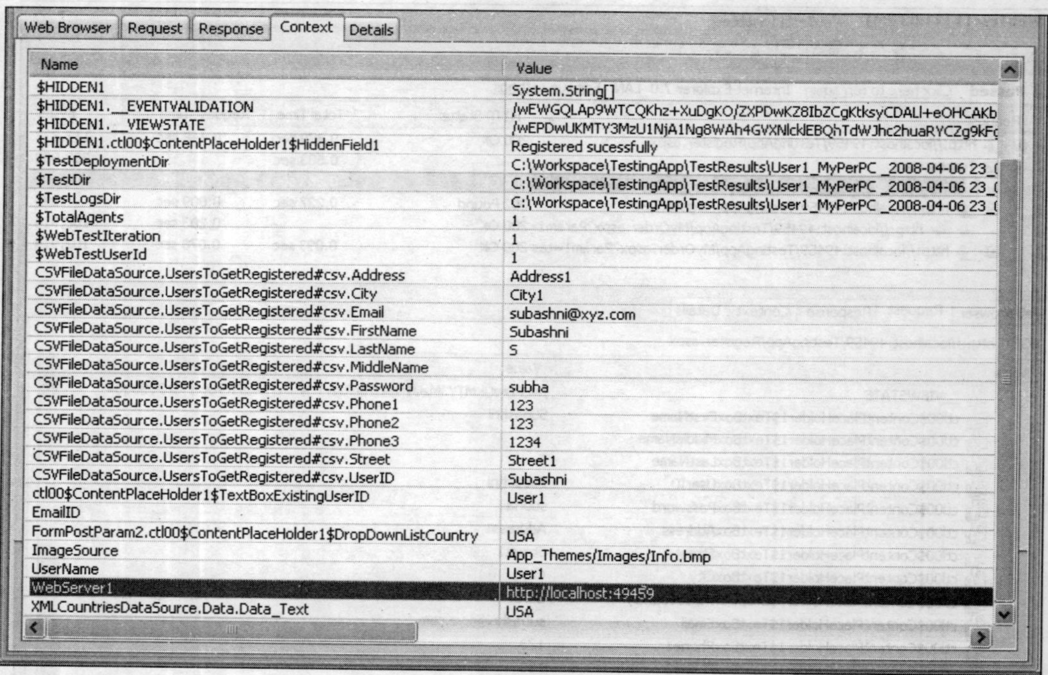

Details

The **Details** tab shows the status of the rules that were executed during the test. We can see from the below image that all the rules created as explained in the rules section got executed successfully. The details section also shows the type of the rule and the parameter values fetched during the execution of the rule. Looking at this details tab we can verify the parameters values returned by rules visually.

Below the toolbar in the web test window we can see the option for running the test again. This is useful to rerun the same test again and find the results, if there are any changes, to the source data or the configurations. There is another option to edit run settings. This option opens the same **Web Test Run Settings** window used by the configuration settings. This is another shortcut to change the web test settings.

Summary

This chapter explained in detail about how the web testing works and how the recording of web testing takes place for the web applications. We have gone through different properties of the web test including copying the tests, cleaning the unwanted recorded requests, and extracting the details from the request whether it has Form Post Parameters or Query String Parameters. In this chapter, we also learned about setting the rules for validating the details and extracting the details based on some conditions. Transaction helps us to group a set of similar requests and give it a name which we saw with an example. Many times during testing we may have to use the dynamic data, which we may not know while recording or creating the test. We have learnt the feature to include different data sources and mapping the fields to the data source fields and also parameterize fields and web server names as well.

At the end of this chapter we have seen the way to execute the tests and collect the test results. There are some more advanced web testing features using custom code in test. This is covered in detail in the next chapter.

4
Advanced Web Testing

This chapter is the continuation of the previous chapter, which explained web testing. There is another way of performing the same web testing using VSTS. The initial testing scenario is recorded as explained in Chapter 3. After the recording is completed, we can generate the code for the same testing using the **Generate Code** option in the **Web Test** toolbar. Without using this option, we should be able to create the same code by creating a new class file and using the namespace `Microsoft.VisualStudio.TestTools.WebTesting`, which contains all classes required for creating the web test. But it is too complex to create the test as compared to generating the code from the recording. Whether it is generated code or normal web testing using the user interface, the testing is the same. The only advantage is that we can customize the testing by using the .NET framework language. This chapter concentrates on creating the code from the recorded test and customizing it.

Dynamic parameters in web testing

Most of the web applications generate data dynamically and send it using the Query String Parameter or Form Post Parameter to subsequent requests. For example, the current user session ID, connection string, or parameter values to the method called are some of the dynamic data. Web tests can identify and detect these dynamic parameters from the request response and then bind it to the other requests. This process is also known as Promoting Dynamic Parameters.

Dynamic parameters are automatically detected by the web test after the web test recording is stopped. Visual studio web testing keeps track of the requests and finds the hard-coded values, which can be replaced by dynamic parameters. The advantage of using dynamic parameters is that we can pass different values to the parameter and verify the test. The other reason is to avoid the playback failure. If we don't promote the dynamic parameters, the playback of the test may fail as the parameter values, which are the same, are captured during the recording and the record would already exist in the system, or may not satisfy the test condition.

Once the web test recording is complete, all query string values used in the web page during test are hard-coded in the recording. So, if the values that are hard-coded are not valid during the playback of the test, then the test will fail. So the Visual Studio web test provides the feature to extract new values from the request and use the same in the dependent requests. This is the same extraction rule we saw in Chapter 3. But in this case, it is automatically added by the web test. At the same time, the parameters are also added to the subsequent request.

For example, the following screenshot shows the recording of the sample website which has the request to the orders page by passing the Query Strings, and the session ID that keeps changing every time the test is run.

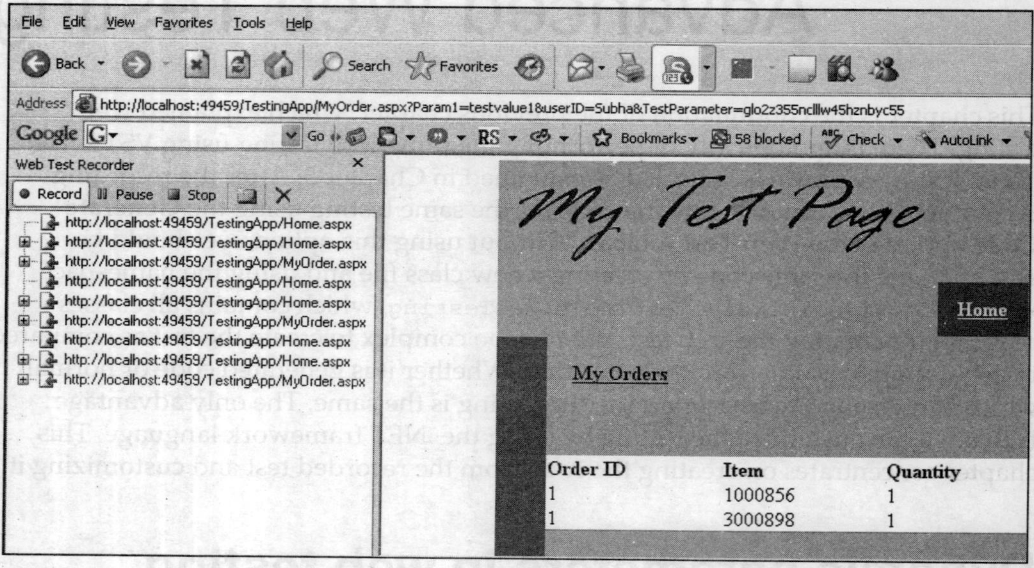

When the recording is stopped, we can see the dialog saying **Detecting dynamic parameters....** During this time, all the values that can be changed to a web test parameter are detected and listed on the next screen.

Visual Studio lists the parameters that can be promoted to web test parameters from normal hard-coded values and allows the choice to the tester who is recording the test. Either we can choose **OK** to promote the parameters, or we can **Cancel** the suggestion and keep it hard-coded.

But if we leave the parameters as it is, the next playback of the test might fail because of the hard-coded value, which may not be valid.

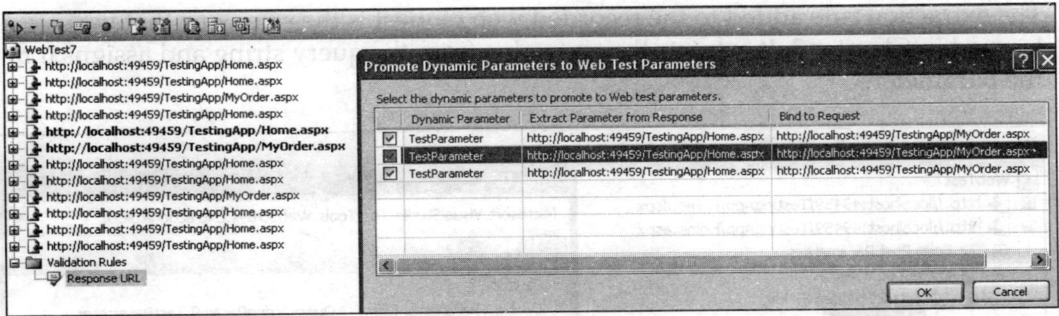

The above screenshot shows that there are three requests in which the value can be promoted as a dynamic parameter. If any parameter is selected from the list, the corresponding request from where the value is extracted and the request where the hard-coded value is replaced with the parameter are highlighted.

Now if the option **Cancel** is selected, nothing happens to the recording. The hard-coded values will be left as they are. But if we choose the option **OK**, it will change the requests by including the extraction rule and the dynamic parameter.

Visual Studio also provides the option for detecting dynamic parameters outside the recording. It means that we can find the parameters, which can be promoted to web test parameters after completing the recording of the test. The web test toolbar has this option to find out the dynamic parameters.

The extraction rule added to the recorded web request is the same one that we learned in Chapter 3. It extracts the text value from the query string and assigns it to the parameter.

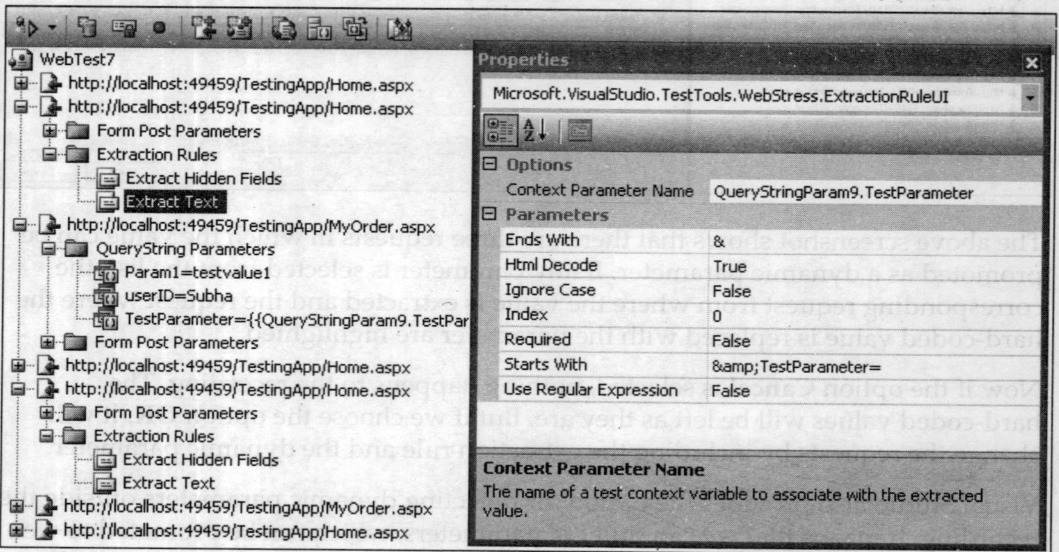

After saving the request, when the recorded test is run again, it should run without any issues as the parameter value is passed on to the requests as shown here:

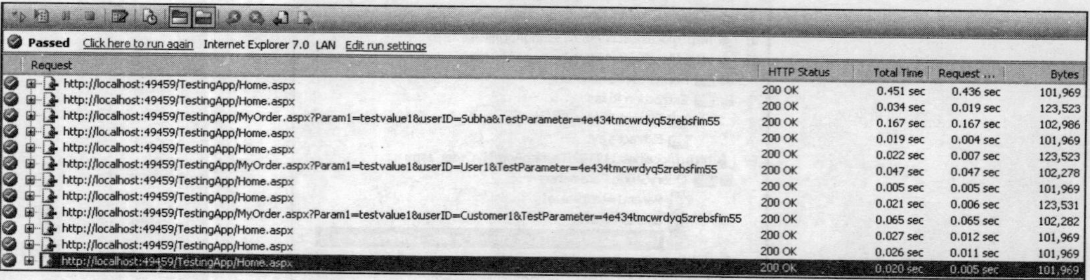

Coded web test

All the examples in the previous sections explain different features which are applicable to the recorded web test. Creating the same web test is also possible by writing code in VSTS. The recorded web test is simple, but the coded web test gives more flexibility. The coded web test generates the sequence of web test requests. The main advantage is that we can add more complex features such as looping, adding more request, or add any additional logic to the test using the .NET programming languages C# and Visual Basic.

The recorded web test can be converted to coded web test as it is always better to record the web test and then create the code out of it, for example, defining the data sources, extraction rules, validation rules, and binding the form post fields to the data source before creating the coded test. This is because we can let the tool generate the coding for all these works so that our job will be easier. We can concentrate only on customising the generated code with additional features.

The other advantage in coded test is the full control of the test execution. It's just a class file, which is created in the language of our choice. Once the class is created, we can include the required functionality and methods, whether it is a `for` loop or a different method call. We can also copy the requests and include it as many times as we want.

Creating a coded test from a recorded test

The recorded web test is very easy to create as there is no coding involved in it. WebTest editor provides features to create the code out of a recorded web test. Select the recorded web test, which you want to convert and then select the option **Generate Code** from the editor toolbar which opens a dialog asking for the name for the coded web test.

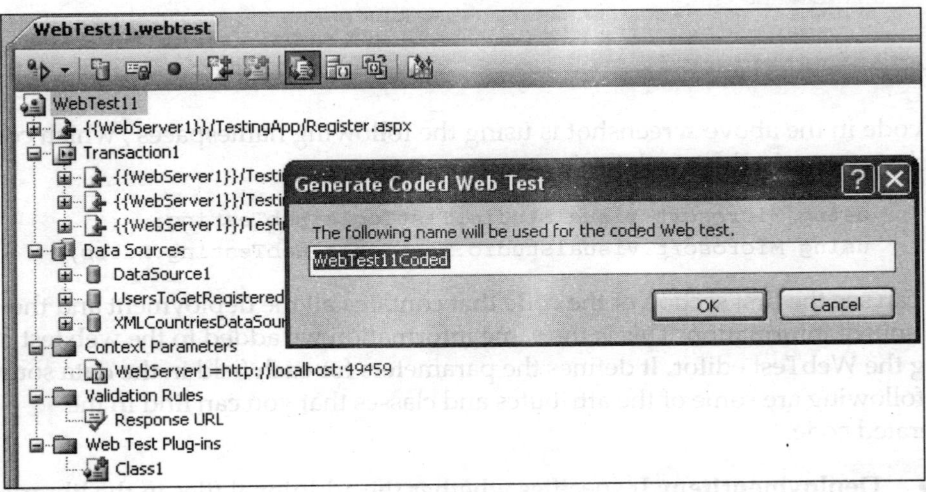

Now you can see the new code file created with the name given. The code file contains the code for the selected web test including the requests, data sources, rules and parameters. The following is a part of the code from the generated file:

```
namespace TestProjforTestingApp
{
    using System;
    using System.Collections.Generic;
    using System.Text;
    using Microsoft.VisualStudio.TestTools.WebTesting;
    using Microsoft.VisualStudio.TestTools.WebTesting.Rules;
    using WebTestPluginSample;

    [DeploymentItem("Test.dll")]
    [DeploymentItem("ClassLibrary1.dll")]
    [DeploymentItem("..\\testprojfortestingapp\\UsersToGetRegistered.xls", "..\\testprojfortestingapp")]
    [DeploymentItem("..\\testprojfortestingapp\\UsersToGetRegistered.csv", "..\\testprojfortestingapp")]
    [DataSource("DataSource1", "System.Data.Odbc", "Dsn=Excel Files;dbq=C:\\Workspace\\TestProjforTestingApp\\bin\\Debug\\UsersToGetRegistered" +
        ".xls;defaultdir=C:\\Workspace\\TestProjforTestingApp\\bin\\Debug;driverid=790;maxbuffersize=204" +
        "8;pagetimeout=5", Microsoft.VisualStudio.TestTools.WebTesting.DataBindingAccessMethod.Sequential, "Sheet1$")]
    [DataSource("UsersToGetRegistered", "Microsoft.VisualStudio.TestTools.DataSource.CSV", "C:\\Workspace\\TestProjforTestingApp\\bin\\Debug" +
        "\\UsersToGetRegistered.csv", Microsoft.VisuelStudio.TestTools.WebTesting.DataBindingAccessMethod.Sequential, "UsersToGetRegistered#csv")]
    [DataBinding("UsersToGetRegistered", "UsersToGetRegistered#csv", "FirstName", "UsersToGetRegistered.UsersToGetRegistered#csv.FirstName")]
    [DataBinding("UsersToGetRegistered", "UsersToGetRegistered#csv", "MiddleName", "UsersToGetRegistered.UsersToGetRegistered#csv.MiddleName")]
    [DataBinding("UsersToGetRegistered", "UsersToGetRegistered#csv", "LastName", "UsersToGetRegistered.UsersToGetRegistered#csv.LastName")]
    [DataBinding("UsersToGetRegistered", "UsersToGetRegistered#csv", "UserID", "UsersToGetRegistered.UsersToGetRegistered#csv.UserID")]
    [DataBinding("UsersToGetRegistered", "UsersToGetRegistered#csv", "Password", "UsersToGetRegistered.UsersToGetRegistered#csv.Password")]
    [DataBinding("UsersToGetRegistered", "UsersToGetRegistered#csv", "Address", "UsersToGetRegistered.UsersToGetRegistered#csv.Address")]
    [DataBinding("UsersToGetRegistered", "UsersToGetRegistered#csv", "Street", "UsersToGetRegistered.UsersToGetRegistered#csv.Street")]
    [DataBinding("UsersToGetRegistered", "UsersToGetRegistered#csv", "City", "UsersToGetRegistered.UsersToGetRegistered#csv.City")]
    [DataBinding("UsersToGetRegistered", "UsersToGetRegistered#csv", "Email", "UsersToGetRegistered.UsersToGetRegistered#csv.Email")]
    [DataBinding("UsersToGetRegistered", "UsersToGetRegistered#csv", "Phone1", "UsersToGetRegistered.UsersToGetRegistered#csv.Phone1")]
    [DataBinding("UsersToGetRegistered", "UsersToGetRegistered#csv", "Phone2", "UsersToGetRegistered.UsersToGetRegistered#csv.Phone2")]
    [DataBinding("UsersToGetRegistered", "UsersToGetRegistered#csv", "Phone3", "UsersToGetRegistered.UsersToGetRegistered#csv.Phone3")]
    public class WebTest11Coded : WebTest
    {
        private Class1 testPlugin0 = new Class1();
        public WebTest11Coded()
        {
            this.Context.Add("WebServer1", "http://localhost:49459");
            this.PreAuthenticate = true;
            this.PreWebTest += new EventHandler<PreWebTestEventArgs>(this.testPlugin0.PreWebTest);
            this.PostWebTest += new EventHandler<PostWebTestEventArgs>(this.testPlugin0.PostWebTest);
            this.Context["AddTestRequest"] = "Yes";
        }
```

The code in the above screenshot is using the following namespaces , which contain the classes required for web testing:

```
using Microsoft.VisualStudio.TestTools.WebTesting;
using Microsoft.VisualStudio.TestTools.WebTesting.Rules;
```

You can see the first section of the code that contains all the deployment and the data source information. This is the same information we added to the web test using the WebTest editor. It defines the parameters for each field in the data source. The following are some of the attributes and classes that you can find in the generated code.

- **DeploymentItem**: It specifies whether the additional files in the library should be deployed as part of the deployment. In the example above, there are two additional libraries `Test.dll` and `ClassLibrary1.dll` added as deployment items.

  ```
  [DeploymentItem("Test.dll")]
  [DeploymentItem("ClassLibrary1.dll")]
  ```

- **DataSource**: This attribute specifies if any data file or database is added as the source for dynamic data. The source can be an Excel, CSV, XML, or any other database. The attribute contains the data source name, the connection string to access the data source, location or the connection string to the data source, the mode for accessing the data such as `Sequential`, `Random`, or `Unique`, and the table name to access from the source. In the case of Excel, each spreadsheet can represent a table. For example, the following code shows the data source attribute for an Excel file and a CSV file.

```
[DataSource("DataSource1", "System.Data.Odbc",
        "Dsn=Excel Files;dbq=C:\\Workspace\\
            TestProjforTestingApp\\bin\\Debug
            \\UsersToGetRegistered" +
        ".xls;defaultdir=C:\\Workspace\\
                TestProjforTestingApp\\bin\\Debug;
                driverid=790;maxbuffersize=204" +
        "8;pagetimeout=5",
        Microsoft.VisualStudio.TestTools.WebTesting.
        DataBindingAccessMethod.Sequential, "Sheet1$")]
[DataSource("UsersToGetRegistered",
        "Microsoft.VisualStudio.TestTools.DataSource.CSV",
        "C:\\Workspace\\TestProjforTestingApp\\bin\\Debug"
        + "\\UsersToGetRegistered.csv",
        Microsoft.VisualStudio.TestTools.WebTesting.
        DataBindingAccessMethod.Sequential,
        "UsersToGetRegistered#csv")]
```

- **DataBinding**: This attribute denotes the fields in the data source. We can provide custom names for the fields by changing their names. For example, the following code denotes three fields `FirstName`, `MiddleName`, `LastName` in the above data source. The attribute contains the data source name, the table name to refer within the source, a custom name for the field within the table, the actual field name in the data source table.

```
[DataBinding("UsersToGetRegistered",
        "UsersToGetRegistered#csv", "FirstName",
        "UsersToGetRegistered.UsersToGetRegistered
        #csv.FirstName")]
[DataBinding("UsersToGetRegistered",
        "UsersToGetRegistered#csv", "MiddleName",
        "UsersToGetRegistered.UsersToGetRegistered
        #csv.MiddleName")]
[DataBinding("UsersToGetRegistered",
        "UsersToGetRegistered#csv", "LastName",
        "UsersToGetRegistered.UsersToGetRegistered
        #csv.LastName")]
```

- **WebTest**: This is the base class for all the web tests. Coded web tests are directly derived from this base class. In the example, the class **WebTest11Coded** is derived from this `WebTest` class.
- **Web Test Constructor**: The constructor is for initializing the new instance of the class. The constructor has the context variables for the test, for example the **WebServer1**.This is the main context variable used by all the requests within the test and replaced by the actual value during the test run. The next thing is to set the credentials for the web test to run. We can leave them as pre-authenticated or set the user credentials, if the Test has to run with different credentials. All the global declaration with respect to the web test is done at the constructor level.
- **Pre-and post-events for web test and requests**: The next is the **PreWebTest** and **PostWebTest** events to the test. The **PreWebTest** and **PostWebTest** are the events, which occur before and after the test. This is used for setting the environment for the test and cleaning the environment after the test is completed.

```
public WebTest11Coded()
{
    this.Context.Add("WebServer1",
                    "http://localhost:49459");
    this.PreAuthenticate = true;
    this.PreWebTest += new EventHandler
    <PreWebTestEventArgs>(this.testPlugin0.PreWebTest);
    this.PostWebTest += new EventHandler
    <PostWebTestEventArgs>(this.testPlugin0.
     PostWebTest);
}
```

The next set of code contains all the other request test details. The method is an `IEnumerator<WebTestRequest>` type, which runs for every request in the web test. This section also contains the `PreRequest` and `PostRequest` events which fire before and after every request in the web test.

```
public override IEnumerator<WebTestRequest>
  GetRequestEnumerator()
{
    // Initialize validation rules that apply to all
    //requests in the WebTest
    if ((this.Context.ValidationLevel> =
        Microsoft.VisualStudio.TestTools.
        WebTesting.ValidationLevel.Low))
    {
```

```
                ValidateResponseUrl validationRule1 = new
                        ValidateResponseUrl();
                this.ValidateResponse += new EventHandler
                  <ValidationEventArgs>
                   (validationRule1.Validate);
            }
            this.PreRequest += new EventHandler
               <PreRequestEventArgs>
               (this.testPlugin0.PreRequest);
            this.PostRequest += new EventHandler
             <PostRequestEventArgs>
               (this.testPlugin0.PostRequest);
```

We can say that the `PreWebTest`, `PostWebTest`, `PreRequest`, and `PostRequest` events for the web test and the requests are the same events that are accessed by the plug-ins. So both are used for the same purpose and are equivalent. For example, the code in the following screenshot is a plug-in with two different class files:

```
using System;
using System.Collections.Generic;
using System.Linq;
using System.Text;
using Microsoft.VisualStudio.TestTools.WebTesting;

namespace WebTestPluginSample
{
    public class ClassWebTest : WebTestPlugin
    {
        public override void PostWebTest(object sender, PostWebTestEventArgs e)
        {
            // Write code for deleting the temporary files created by test
        }

        public override void PreWebTest(object sender, PreWebTestEventArgs e)
        {
            e.WebTest.Context["UserName"] = "User1";
        }
    }

    public class ClassRequest : WebTestRequestPlugin
    {
        public override void PostRequest(object sender, PostRequestEventArgs e)
        {
           var RequestResult =  e.Request.Outcome.ToString();
            // log the RequestResult information
        }

        public override void PreRequest(object sender, PreRequestEventArgs e)
        {
            var Requesturl = e.Request.Url;
            // log the current Requesturl information
        }
    }
```

The class **ClassWebTest** derived from the **WebTestPlugin** has two methods, **PreWebTest** and **PostWebTest,** which are used for the same purpose and can be achieved by having these events in the coded web test. Similarly, the methods **PreRequest** and **PostRequest** in the **ClassRequest** class, which is derived from the **WebTestRequestPlugin** must override the base class method.

There are multiple methods which can be used by the class derived from the base class **WebTestPlugin**. They are:

- `PostPage` method: This method is called when the web page is completed with the request and all the dependent requests.
- `PrePage` method: This method is called before the primary request for the page.
- `PostTransaction`: This method is called after completing each transaction defined in the web test. Transactions are explained in more detail in a later section.
- `PreTransaction`: This method is called just before starting the transaction in the web test.

The next part of the code is for defining the request, extraction rules, validation rules, and the Form Post or the QueryString Parameters. These parameter values are set with values retrieved from the parameters bound with the data source fields. A part of the code looks like this:

```
WebTestRequest request2 = new WebTestRequest
  ((this.Context["WebServer1"].ToString() +
  "/TestingApp/Register.aspx"));
request2.ThinkTime = 6;
request2.Method = "POST";
FormPostHttpBody request2Body = new
  FormPostHttpBody();
request2Body.FormPostParameters.Add("__VIEWSTATE",
this.Context["$HIDDEN1.__VIEWSTATE"].ToString());
request2Body.FormPostParameters.Add
 ("ctl00$ContentPlaceHolder1$TextBoxFirstName",
 this.Context["UsersToGetRegistered.
 UsersToGetRegistered#csv.FirstName"].ToString());
request2Body.FormPostParameters.Add
("ctl00$ContentPlaceHolder1$TextBoxMiddleName",
this.Context["UsersToGetRegistered.
UsersToGetRegistered#csv.MiddleName"].ToString());
```

The first line in the above code defines the request and the rest of the code is assigning the values to the Form Post Parameters.

The coded web test provides all the properties of the web test and requests in the web test, which can be used to customize and add more functionality to the test.

Transactions in coded test

We have seen how inserting transactions for the set of requests for tracking the time taken for running all the requests, which were part of the transaction, was done. The same thing can be done using the code by using the transaction method in the web test. Transaction is the logical grouping of multiple requests in the web test. This is like a timer, which collects the start and end time of the group requests under the transaction. Given here is the code, which begins the transaction, requests for two web pages, and then ends the transaction:

```
this.BeginTransaction("Transaction1");

WebTestRequest request2 = new WebTestRequest
((this.Context["WebServer1"].ToString() +
"/TestingApp/Register.aspx"));
request2.ThinkTime = 6;
request2.Method = "POST";

ExtractHiddenFields extractionRule2 = new
            ExtractHiddenFields();
extractionRule2.Required = true;
extractionRule2.HtmlDecode = true;
extractionRule2.ContextParameterName = "1";
request2.ExtractValues += new EventHandler
 <ExtractionEventArgs>(extractionRule2.Extract);
ExtractFormField extractionRule3 = new
          ExtractFormField();
extractionRule3.Name =
             "ctl00$ContentPlaceHolder1$TextBoxEmail";
extractionRule3.HtmlDecode = true;
extractionRule3.Required = true;
extractionRule3.ContextParameterName = "";
extractionRule3.ContextParameterName = "EmailID";
request2.ExtractValues += new EventHandler
  <ExtractionEventArgs>(extractionRule3.Extract);
WebTestRequest request3 = new WebTestRequest
((this.Context["WebServer1"].ToString() +
"/TestingApp/Register.aspx"));
request3.ThinkTime = 5;
```

```
request3.Method = "POST";
request3.ExpectedResponseUrl = (this.Context["WebServer1"].
            ToString() + "/TestingApp/MyOrder.aspx?
            Param1=testvalue1&Param2
            =testvalue2&userID=Subha");

    this.EndTransaction("Transaction1");
```

Custom code

The main advantage of coded web test is customizing the code that is generated or creating a new class driving it from the `WebTest` base class and adding additional functionality. For example, the following code checks if the value of the context parameter `AddTestRequest` is yes, and adds a new web test request with think time and request method to the web test.

```
if (this.Context["AddTestRequest"].ToString() == "Yes")
     {
         WebTestRequest request5 = new WebTestRequest
         ((this.Context["WebServer1"].ToString() +
         "/TestingApp/Home.aspx"));
         request5.ThinkTime = 10;
         request5.Method = "POST";
         yield return request5;
     }
```

Adding comment

This class is used for adding comments to the web test. The code given here is an example for adding a comment to the test result from the web test code:

```
this.AddCommentToResult("Test comment added by the code");
```

Running the coded web test

We have created the code for the web test. Running or executing the code is very simple. This is not the same as running the other projects. We need to open the **Test View** window using the **Test** and **Windows** option in the main menu. The test view lists all tests in the current project including the coded web test.

From the list of tests, select the coded test and right-click and choose the **Run Selection** option, which starts running the coded web test.

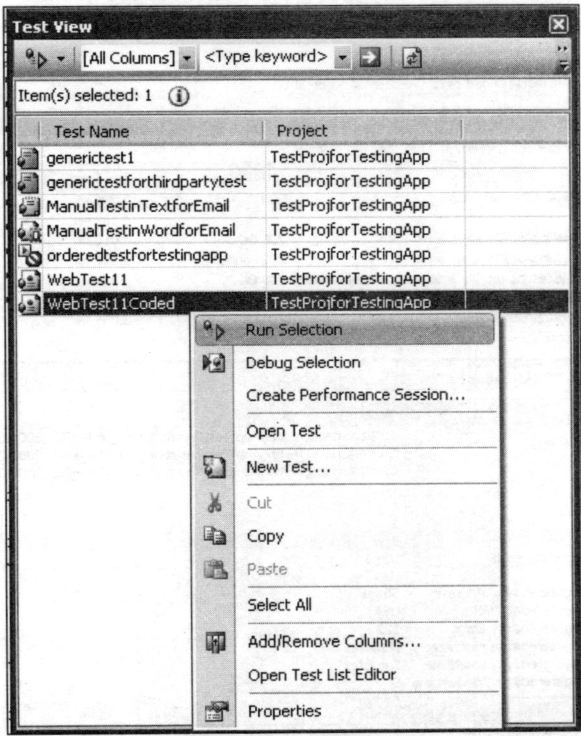

The result of the web test is shown in the **Test Results** window similar to that shown by the recorded web test. It shows the status of the test, whether it has successfully passed or failed, or has some errors.

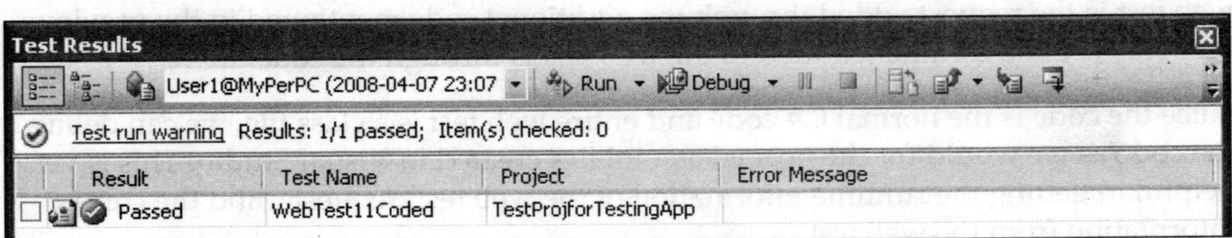

To know the details of the test result, select the result from the **Test Result** window, right-click and choose **View Test Result Details,** which opens a window depicting the details about the web code test. This is the same result details window that we saw for the recorded test.

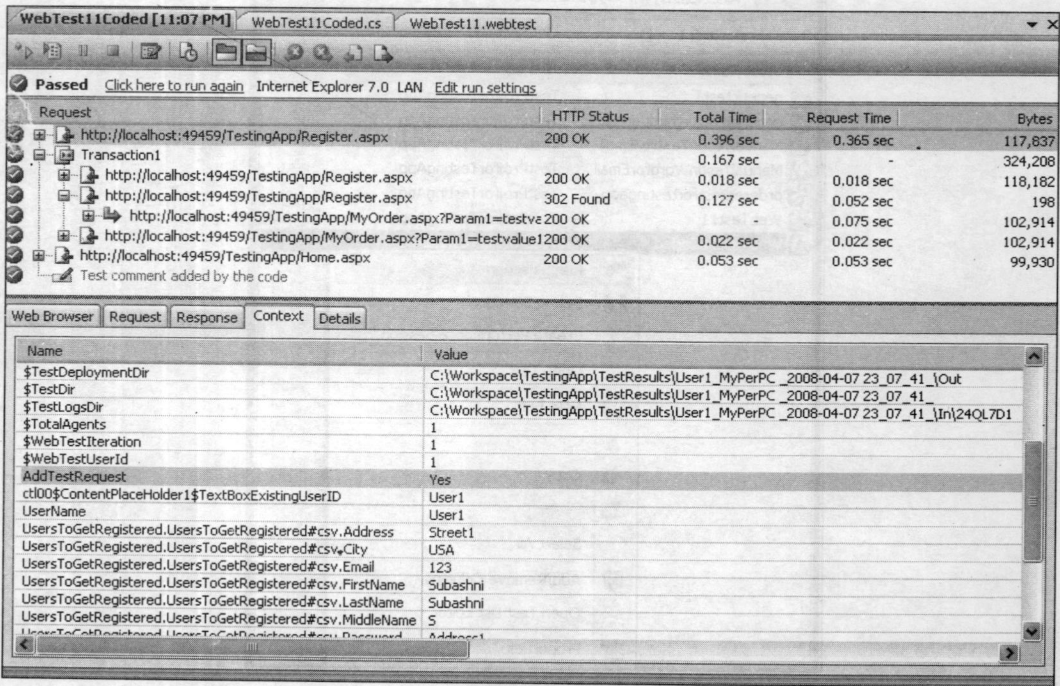

The result details window shows the result of each request in the web test. It also shows the information about the request, response, context parameters, and the rule execution details for each request. You can notice that the last request added to the web test is the request added through the additional code mentioned in the previous section. Also the comment added to the web test is through the code.

Since the code is the normal C# code and entire web test is a class file, we can debug the code as we would for the normal assemblies created in Visual Studio. This is very helpful in getting the runtime information of the web test, requests, and the context information from the web test.

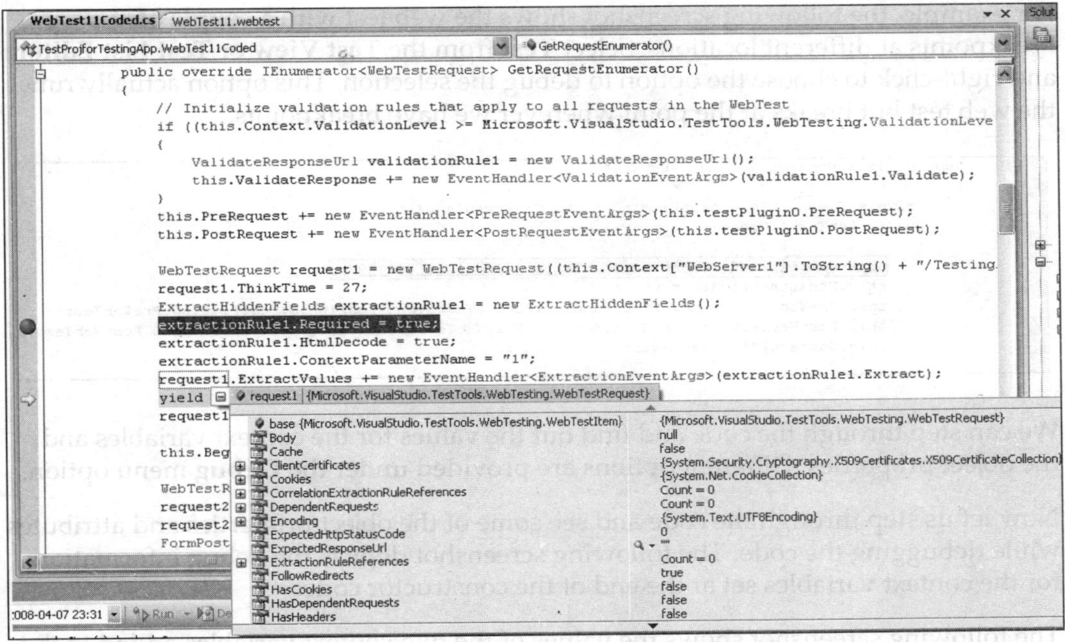

Debugging coded web test

Web testing is an integrated tool in Visual Studio, and the web test can be coded using the .NET languages. We know that we can debug the code while running the application during the application development. The same applies here, as creation of a web test is similar to developing another application, and we may have to debug sometimes when we want to find out the system behavior at runtime so that we can fix the issue easily. To do this, Visual Studio provides a debugging facility for the code.

Select the web test from the **Test View** or **Test List Editor** and double-click to open the web test code. Scroll to the method and the line where we want to include a breakpoint for the web test execution. Right-click on the line and select the option in the context menu to insert a new breakpoint. Continue doing this at all the places wherever breakpoints are required.

For example, the following screenshot shows the web test with a couple of breakpoints at different locations. Select **Test** from the **Test View** or **Test List Editor** and right-click to choose the option to debug the selection. This option actually runs the web test but breaks at the point wherever we have breakpoints.

```
public class WebTest11Coded : WebTest
{
    private ClassWebTest testPlugin0 = new ClassWebTest();
    public WebTest11Coded()
    {
        this.Context.Add("WebServer1", "http://localhost:49459");
        this.PreAuthenticate = true;
        this.PreWebTest += new EventHandler<PreWebTestEventArgs>(this.testPlugin0.PreWebTest);
        this.PostWebTest += new EventHandler<PostWebTestEventArgs>(this.testPlugin0.PostWebTest);
        this.Context["AddTestRequest"] = "Yes";
    }
```

We can step through the code and find out the values for the context variables and the object properties. Different options are provided under the **Debug** menu option.

Now let us step through the code and see some of the object properties and attributes while debugging the code. The following screenshot depicts the debug information for the context variables set at the end of the constructor code.

The following screenshot shows the values of the two context variables added to the context and the other properties set for the context.

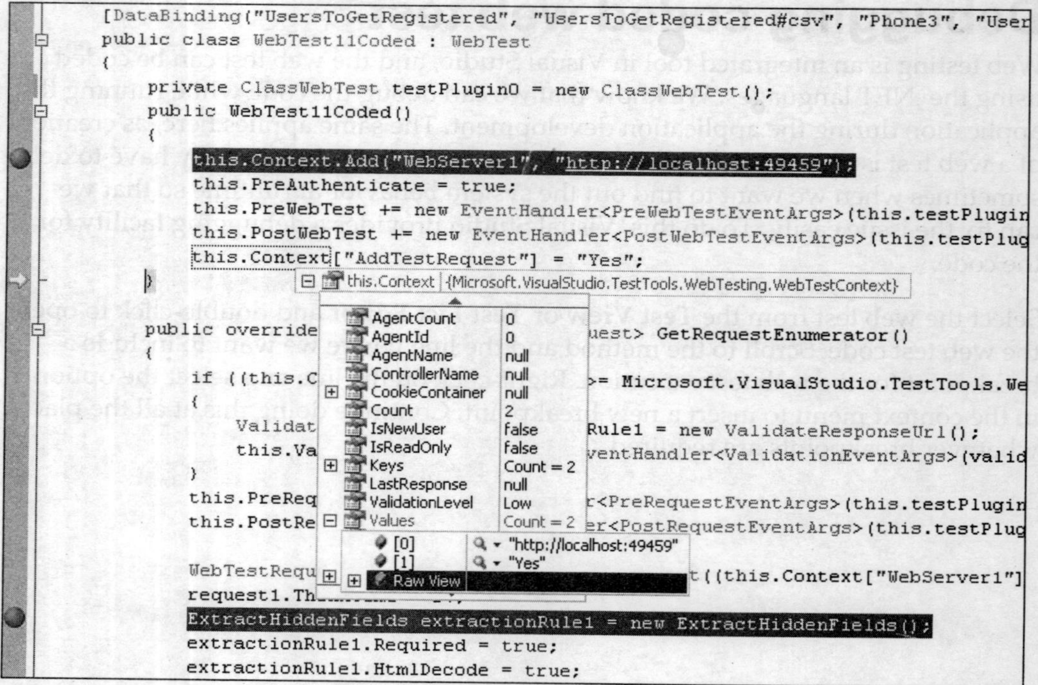

Similarly, we can step through the code line-by-line and find out if the current values depict the status of the objects and the properties. The following is another example of the **PostWebTest** event that refers to the methods in the plug-in `WebTestPluginSample.ClassWebTest`, which we discussed earlier in this chapter.

```
public class WebTest11Coded : WebTest
{
    private ClassWebTest testPlugin0 = new ClassWebTest();
    public WebTest11Coded()
    {
        this.Context.Add("WebServer1", "http://localhost:49459");
        this.PreAuthenticate = true;
        this.PreWebTest += new EventHandler<PreWebTestEventArgs>(this.testPlugin0.PreWebTest);
        this.PostWebTest += new EventHandler<PostWebTestEventArgs>(this.testPlugin0.PostWebTes
        this.Conte ⊟ this.PostWebTest {Method = {Void PostWebTest(System.Object, Microsoft.VisualStudio.TestTools.WebTesting.PostW
    }          ⊟ base {System.MulticastDelegate} {Method = {Void PostWebTest(System.Object, Microsoft.VisualStudio.TestTools
                  ⊟ base {System.Delegate} {Method = {Void PostWebTest(System.Object, Microsoft.VisualStudio.TestTools.Web
    public override IEn ⊞ Method {Void PostWebTest(System.Object, Microsoft.VisualStudio.TestTools.WebTesting.Post
    {                   ⊞ Target {WebTestPluginSample.ClassWebTest}
                        ⊞ Non-Public members
        if ((this.Context.ValidationLevel >= Microsoft.VisualStudio.TestTools.WebTesting.Valid
        {
            ValidateResponseUrl validationRule1 = new ValidateResponseUrl();
            this.ValidateResponse += new EventHandler<ValidationEventArgs>(validationRule1.Val
        }
        this.PreRequest += new EventHandler<PreRequestEventArgs>(this.testPlugin0.PreRequest);
        this.PostRequest += new EventHandler<PostRequestEventArgs>(this.testPlugin0.PostReques

        WebTestRequest request1 = new WebTestRequest((this.Context["WebServer1"].ToString() +
        request1.ThinkTime = 27;
        ExtractHiddenFields extractionRule1 = new ExtractHiddenFields();
        extractionRule1.Required = true;
```

Custom rules

When we generate the code for the recorded web test, Visual Studio creates the code for the rules that we added for the recorded test. But if we need more custom rules to be added to the web test, we can use the `Microsoft.VisualStudio.TestTools.WebTesting` namespace and create a new rule class which derives from the base class. This new class can be part of the managed class library which can be a plug-in. This can be an extraction rule or a validation rule.

Extraction rule

The extraction rules are used for extracting the data from the responses received for the web requests. Extracted data can be the values from text fields, headers, form fields, attributes, or hidden fields. The new custom extraction rule is a new class file derived from the base class `ExtractionRule`, which is in the namespace `Microsoft.VisualStudio.TestTools.WebTesting`. Add reference to the library `Microsoft.VisualStudio.QualityTools.WebTestFramework`, which contains the base classes. In the new class, implement the **RuleName**, **RuleDescripton**, and **Extract** methods and build the custom rule as per requirements. For example, the following screenshot shows a **CustomExtractionRule** for extracting the **Query String Parameter** value from the request.

```
CustomRules.CustomExtractionRule                    Extract(object sender, ExtractionEventArgs e)
using Microsoft.VisualStudio.TestTools.WebTesting;
using Microsoft.VisualStudio.TestTools.WebTesting.Rules;
using System.Globalization;

namespace CustomRules
{
    public class CustomExtractionRule :  ExtractionRule
    {
        public string ParameterName { get; set; }  // Name of the Query String Parameter to extract

        public override string RuleName  // to specify the Rule name for this rule
        {
            get { return "New Custom Extraction Rule";}
        }

        public override string RuleDescription  // to specify the Description for this rule
        {
            get {return "This is the custom rule for extracting the value of input field at index 1"; }
        }
        public override void Extract(object sender, ExtractionEventArgs e)
        {
            if (e.Request.HasQueryStringParameters)
            {
                foreach (QueryStringParameter parameter in e.Request.QueryStringParameters)
                {
                    if (parameter.Name.Equals(ParameterName, StringComparison.CurrentCultureIgnoreCase))
                    {
                        if (parameter.Value != null)
                        {
                            e.Success = true;
                            e.Message = String.Format("Parameter Found with value {0}: ", ParameterName);
                        }
                        return;
                    }
                }
                e.Success = false;
                e.Message = String.Format("Parameter {0} not Found ", ParameterName);
        }
```

- **ParameterName:** This is to specify the name of the Query String Parameter that we want.
- **RuleName**: This is to specify the name of the new Extraction Rule. The extraction rule dialog will show the input field for specifying the rule name.

```
public override string RuleName // to specify the Rule
                                //name for this rule
{
    get { return "New Custom Extraction Rule";}
}
```

- **RuleDescription**: This is to specify the rule description for the new rule. The **Extraction Rule** dialog will have a input field to specify the description.

```
public override string RuleDescription  // to specify the
                                        //Description for this rule
{
    get {return "This is the custom rule for extracting
            the value of input field at index 1"; }
}
```

- **Extract**: This is the method to extract the data. This method is applicable only for the Extraction Rule. This method contains two parameters: **object** and **ExtractionEventArgs**. The **ExtractionEventArgs** has the property response, which provides the response generated by the request. The response contains the QueryString, attributes, and the HTML documents alongwith all the other details about the response. Once the test is run, the extraction rule gets executed. In the example shown previously, the extract method will find the specified parameter in the QueryString and extract the value if a match is found. The method returns with a success or failure status along with the message. The extracted value can be added as the context variable using the code:

  ```
  e.WebTest.Context.Add(this.ContextParameterName,
    parameter.Value);
  ```

  The context contains the key value pair, where the key is equal to the `ContextParameterName` and the value is the parameter value that is extracted.

  ```
  // add the extracted value to the Web test context
  e.WebTest.Context.Add(this.ContextParameterName, fieldValue);
  e.Success = true;
  ```

The **ExtractEventArgs** object also contains a return value of either **Success** or **Failure**. We should set this to success or failure based on the extraction of the value. The following code shows the sample of an extraction rule which extracts the value of an input field with the given name.

```
public override void Extract(object sender,
                                ExtractionEventArgs e)
{
  if (e.Request.HasQueryStringParameters)
  {
     foreach (QueryStringParameter parameter in
                e.Request.QueryStringParameters)
     {
       if (parameter.Name.Equals(Name,
              StringComparison.CurrentCultureIgnoreCase))
       {
        if (parameter.Value != null)
        {
            e.Success = true;
            e.Message = String.Format("Parameter
                  Found with value {0}: ", Name);
            e.WebTest.Context.Add(this.ContextParameterName,
                  parameter.Value);
        }
          return;
       }
     }
    e.Success = false;
    e.Message = String.Format("Parameter {0} not Found ",
               ParameterName);
  }
```

After completing the class file with the code for the new extraction rule, compile the class library. Add the class library reference to the web test project and include the namespace to the web test code to make use of the new custom rule. Now to create a new rule for the request in the web test code, create a new instance of the `CustomExtractionRule`, which is the class that we created for the custom rule, and set the properties. The code in the following screenshot contains the sample for adding a new rule to the test. The extracted value will be added to the list of extracted values for the requests.

```
CustomExtractionRule extractionRulenew = new CustomExtractionRule();
extractionRulenew.Name = "Parameter1";
request2.ExtractValues += new EventHandler<ExtractionEventArgs>(extractionRulenew.Extract);
```

The custom rule can also be used in the recorded web test. To add the custom rule, open the **WebTest** project and add reference to the custom rule project.

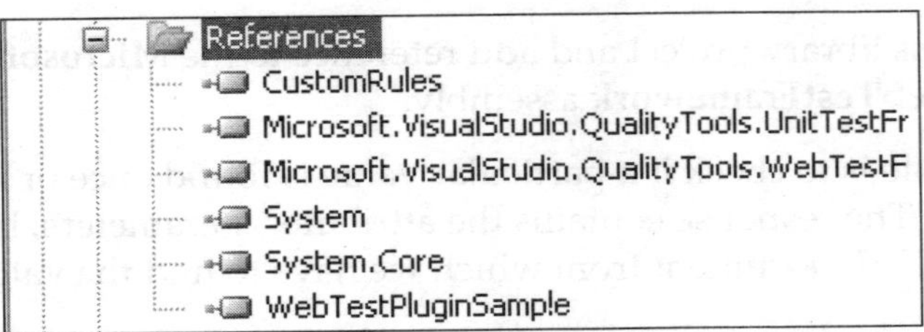

Now open the web test project and select the request for which the new extraction rule should be added. Expand the test recording and select the **Extraction Rules** folder for the request and select **Add Extraction Rule** option which will display all different types of extraction rules including the rule we created.

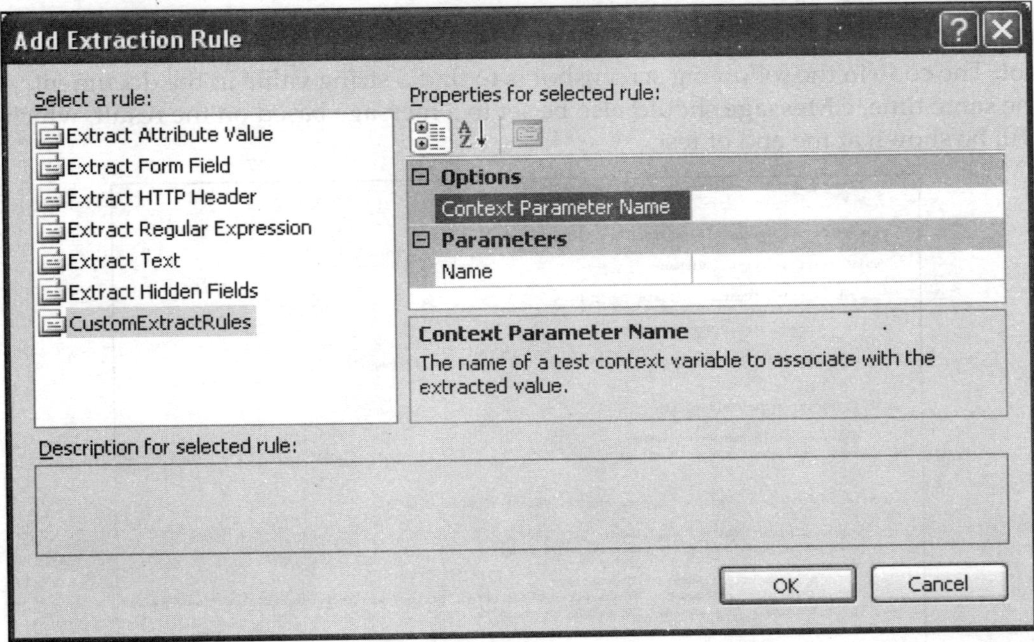

The `CustomExtractionRule` is just like the other rule, but is custom-built for the required functionality.

Validation rule

CustomValidationRule are written similar to extraction rules. It is the custom code written as a class, which is derived from the `ValidationRule` base class. This class is present in the namespace **Microsoft.VisualStudio.Testtools.WebTesting**. The new class can be a separate class library, which can be added to the web test project when required.

Create a new class library project and add reference to the **Microsoft.VisualStudio.QualityTools.WebTestFramework** assembly.

The validation rule is to check if a particular value is found once or more in the HTML response. The response contains the attributes, parameters, hidden values, and the entire HTML document from which we have to find the value to validate.

The validate rule also has similar properties and methods as **Rule Name, Rule Description,** and **Validate.**

The **Validate** method contains two parameters, **object** and **ValidationEventArgs**. The **ValidationEventArgs** object contains the response property that provides the response text for the request through which we can find out the string value and validate the response.

The validate method should set **e.IsValid** to **true** if the validation succeeds, or **false** if not. The code in the following screenshot is to find a string value in the document. At the same time, **e.Message** should also be set to a message based on the result, which will be shown at the end of test.

```
public class CustomValidationRule : ValidationRule
{

    private string stringValuetoFind;

    public override string RuleName
    {
        get { return "Custom Validate Tag"; }
    }
    public override string RuleDescription
    {
        get { return "Validates that the specified tag exists on the page."; }
    }

    public string StringValuetoFind
    {
        get { return stringValuetoFind; }
        set { stringValuetoFind = value; }
    }

    public override void Validate(object sender, ValidationEventArgs e)
    {
        string htmlDocument = string.Empty;
        if (!String.IsNullOrEmpty(e.Response.BodyString))
        {
            htmlDocument = e.Response.BodyString;
            e.IsValid = htmlDocument.Equals(stringValuetoFind, StringComparison.CurrentCultureIgnoreCase);
            e.Message = "Successful. The string is found.";
        }

        if (!e.IsValid)
        {
            e.Message = String.Format("String '{0}' is not found", stringValuetoFind);
        }

    }
}
```

Now compile the library and add the reference to the project similar to the extraction rule and add **include the namespace**. In the web test code, create a new instance of this custom rule and set the properties. Once the test is run, this rule gets executed and the result is added to the requested output.

```
CustomValidationRule validateRule = new CustomValidationRule();
validateRule.StringValuetoFind = "Test";
this.ValidateResponse += new EventHandler<ValidationEventArgs>(validateRule.Validate);
```

The custom rule can also be used in the recorded web test. To add the custom rule library created above, select the recorded web test project and add the reference to the library. Open the web test and select the validation rules folder, right-click and select the option **Insert Validation Rule**, which opens the dialog listing out all types of validation rules.

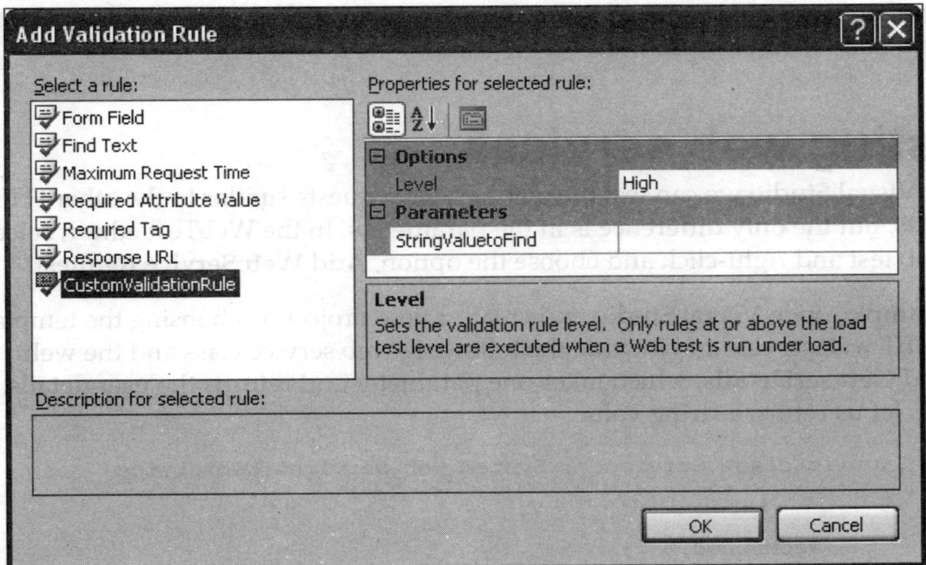

Now set the value of the **StringValuetoFind** parameter to something. Let us say the value is "Test". Run the web test again and check the results. The following is the sample of the test which returned failure and the message along with the result.

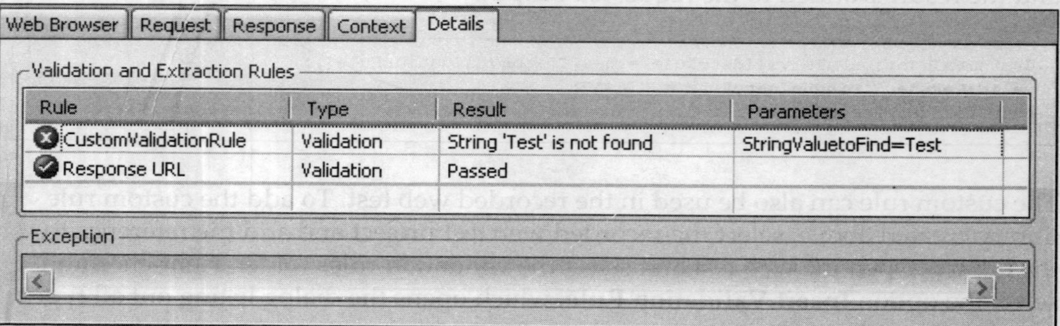

The message says: **String 'Test' is not found**. We can add as many custom rules like this and validate their responses.

Testing web services

Using Visual Studio we can test the web service requests similar to the other HTTP requests, but the only difference is in the parameters. In the WebTest editor, select the web test and right-click and choose the option, **Add Web Service Request**.

For example, open Visual Studio and create a new project by choosing the template ASP.NET web service and include the following web service class and the web method **GetuserDetails,** which takes one parameter and returns the user details. For testing, let us return a string value.

```
public class Service1 : System.Web.Services.WebService
{

    [WebMethod]
    public string GetuserDetails(string user)
    {
        // TODO: below code is a test. Replace with actual code.
        return "User details";

    }
}
```

Now build this and run the web service which will open IE with the web service method.

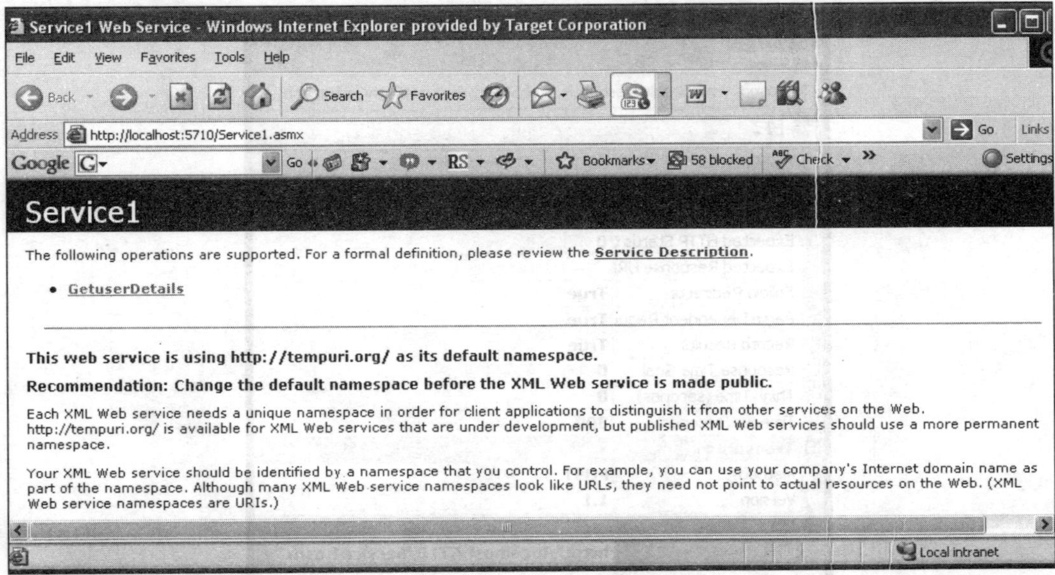

The web method takes one parameter and returns the user details. In this example, the return string is a constant to make the example simple.

Now create a new web test and when the browser opens, click on **Stop** in the recorder. Then select the web test in the editor, right-click and select the option **Add Web Service Request.**

The local default web address is added to the web test with the string body parameter. Now select the web URL and set the properties. Set the URL to the web service request that we are testing.

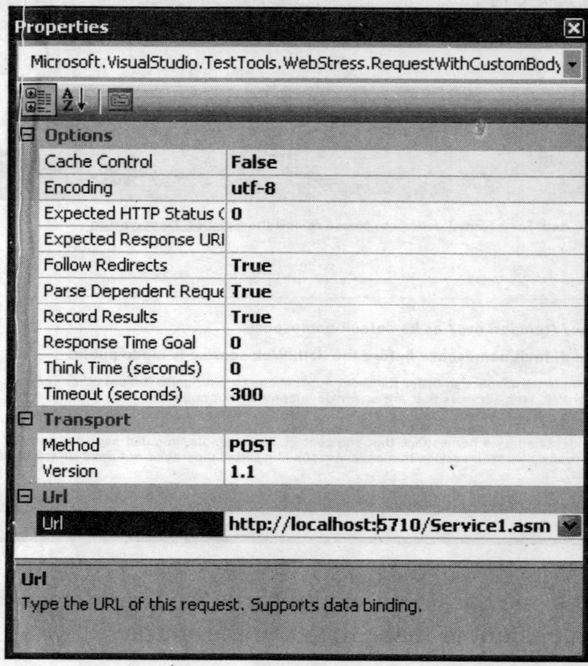

Now open a separate browser window and type the URL for the web service request in the address. Select the method **GetuserDetails** for which we are writing the test. This selection displays the SOAP message that contains the **SOAPAction**, which is required to set the properties.

In the WebTest editor select the request, right-click on it , and select **Add Header** to add a new header. Select the header and open the **Properties** window by right-clicking. Set the name to **SOAPAction**. Copy the **SOAPAction** value `http://tempuri.org/GetuserDetails` from the web service request into the value property of the header.

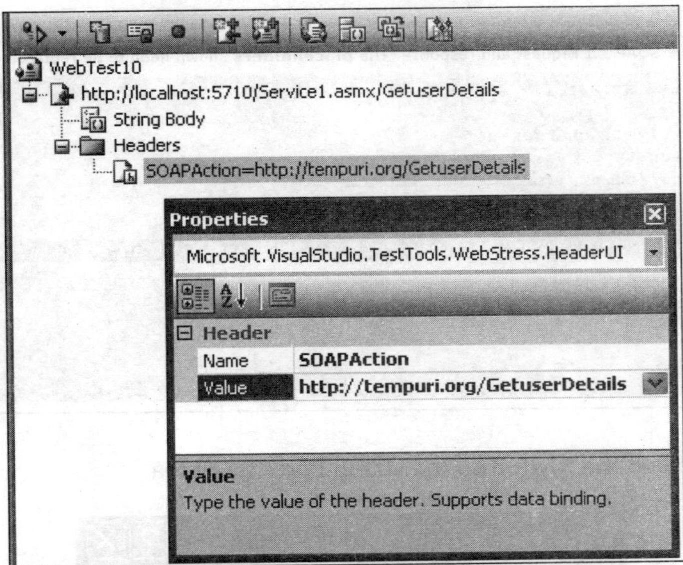

The **SOAPAction** can be found in the web service request.

The following is a sample SOAP 1.1 request and response. The **placeholders** shown need to be replaced with actual values.

```
POST /Service1.asmx HTTP/1.1
Host: localhost
Content-Type: text/xml; charset=utf-8
Content-Length: length
SOAPAction: "http://tempuri.org/GetuserDetails"

<?xml version="1.0" encoding="utf-8"?>
<soap:Envelope xmlns:xsi="http://www.w3.org/2001/XMLSchema-instance" xmlns:xsd="http://www.w3.org/2001/
  <soap:Body>
    <GetuserDetails xmlns="http://tempuri.org/">
      <user>string</user>
    </GetuserDetails>
  </soap:Body>
</soap:Envelope>
```

The next step is to set the parameter for the request. Select the empty **String Body** parameter added to the request, right-click and select **Properties**. Set the **Content Type** to **text/xml.** Now select the **String Body** in the **Parameters** window, and click on the option, which opens a new window to enter the **String Body** string. String Body is the XML portion of the SOAP request from the web service description page.

The following is a sample SOAP 1.1 request and response. The **placeholders** shown need to be replaced with actual values.

```
POST /Service1.asmx HTTP/1.1
Host: localhost
Content-Type: text/xml; charset=utf-8
Content-Length: length
SOAPAction: "http://tempuri.org/GetuserDetails"

<?xml version="1.0" encoding="utf-8"?>
<soap:Envelope xmlns:xsi="http://www.w3.org/2001/XMLSchema-instance" xmlns:xsd="http://www.
  <soap:Body>
    <GetuserDetails xmlns="http://tempuri.org/">
      <user>string</user>
    </GetuserDetails>
  </soap:Body>
</soap:Envelope>
```

Copy that and paste the XML into the string body text area.

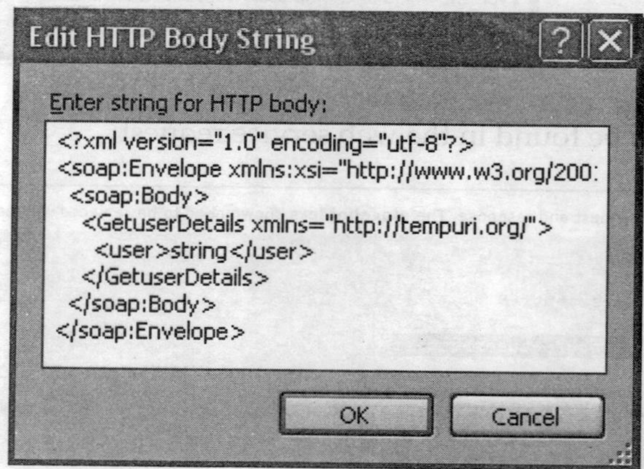

The value **string** is the static value that can be converted to dynamic by using the data bound values. We can use data binding in the SOAP body to replace any placeholder value with data bound values using the following syntax:

```
{{DataSourceName.TableName.ColumnName}}
```

For example, the value string we just saw can be converted to a data bound value as shown here:

```
<?xml version="1.0" encoding="utf-8"?>
<soap:Envelope xmlns:xsi="http://www.w3.org/2001/XMLSchema-instance" xmlns:xsd="http://www.w3.o
  <soap:Body>
    <GetuserDetails xmlns="http://tempuri.org/">
      <user>{{UsersToGetRegistered.UsersToGetRegistered#csv.UserName}}</user>
    </GetuserDetails>
  </soap:Body>
</soap:Envelope>
```

Now run the web test and see the results in the tabs in test result viewer. The web service request XML and the result of the operation will be displayed.

Summary

This chapter explained the advanced features of web testing using Visual Studio. All the features covered in this chapter explained customization of the web testing feature based on our requirements. Writing custom rules are the extension of the built-in Extraction and Validation rules that comes with the web testing. Generating code out of the recorded web testing gives more control to the tester to customize the testing. We can include looping, calling custom-written methods between the requests, adding transactions for requests and adding additional data sources. Further, we can copy and paste the same requests as many number of times as we want and modify them. We have also seen the web service testing, which is very similar to the normal web request with some differences in setting the parameters.

5
Load Testing

Load testing an application helps the development and management team understand the application performance under various conditions. Load testing can have different parameter values and conditions to test the application and check the application performance.

Each load test can simulate the number of users, network bandwidths, combinations of different web browsers, and different configurations. In the case of web applications, it is required to test the application with different sets of users and different sets of browsers to simulate multiple requests at the same time to the server. The following figure shows a sample of real-time situations for multiple users accessing the web site using different networks and different browsers from multiple locations.

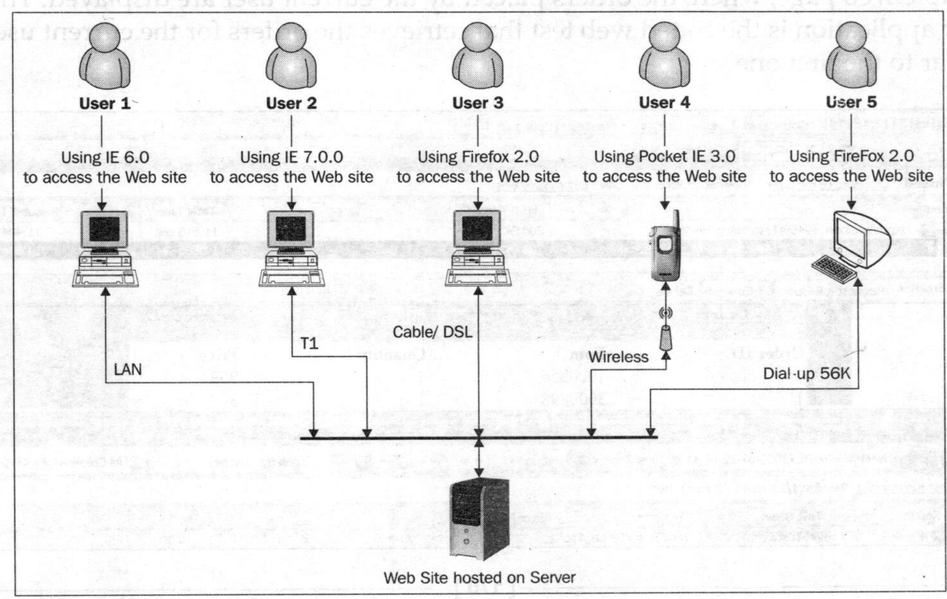

Load testing is meant not just for web applications. We can also test the unit tests under load tests to check the performance of the data access from the server. The load test helps identify application performance in various capacities, application performance under light loads for a short duration, performance with heavy loads, and different durations.

Load testing uses a set of computers, which consists of a **controller** and **agents**. These are called **rig**. The agents are the computers at different locations used for simulating different user requests. The controller is the central computer which controls multiple agent computers. The Visual Studio 2008 Test Load agent in the agent computers generates the load. The Visual Studio 2008 Test Controller at the central computer controls these agents. This chapter explains the details of creating test scenarios and load testing the application.

Creating load test

The load tests are created using the Visual Studio Load Test wizard. You can first create the test project and then add the new load test which opens the wizard, and guides us to create the test. We can edit the test parameters and configuration later on, if required.

Before we go on to create the test project and understand the parameters, we will consider a couple of web applications. Web applications or sites are the ones accessed by a large number of users from different locations at the same time. It is quite required to simulate this situation and check the application performance. Let's take a couple of web applications that we used in our previous chapters. It is a simple web page, where the orders placed by the current user are displayed. The other application is the coded web test that retrieves the orders for the current user, similar to the first one.

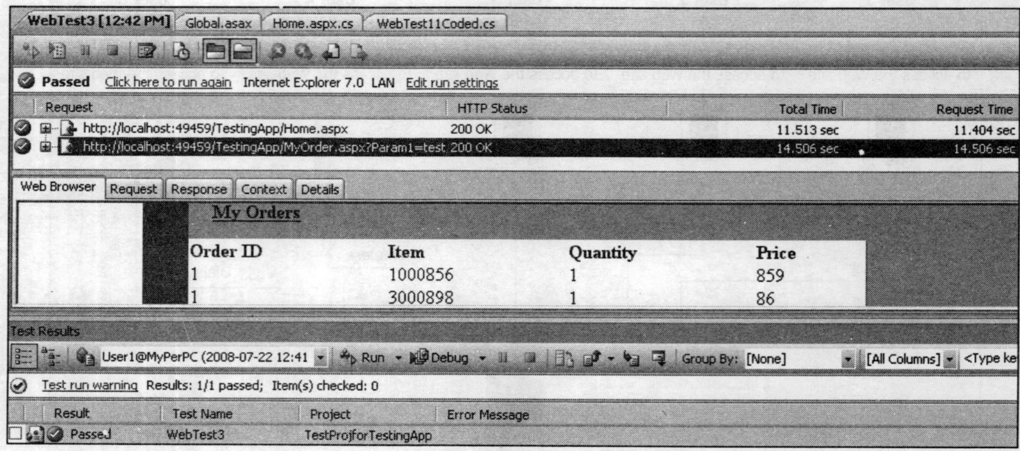

Using the above examples we will see the different features of load testing that is provided by Visual Studio. The following sections describe the creation of load testing, setting parameters, and load testing the application.

Load test wizard

The load test wizard helps us create the load test for the web tests and unit tests. There are different steps to provide the required parameters and configuration information for creating the load test. There are different ways of adding load tests to the test project:

- Select the test project and then select the option **Add | Load Test...**

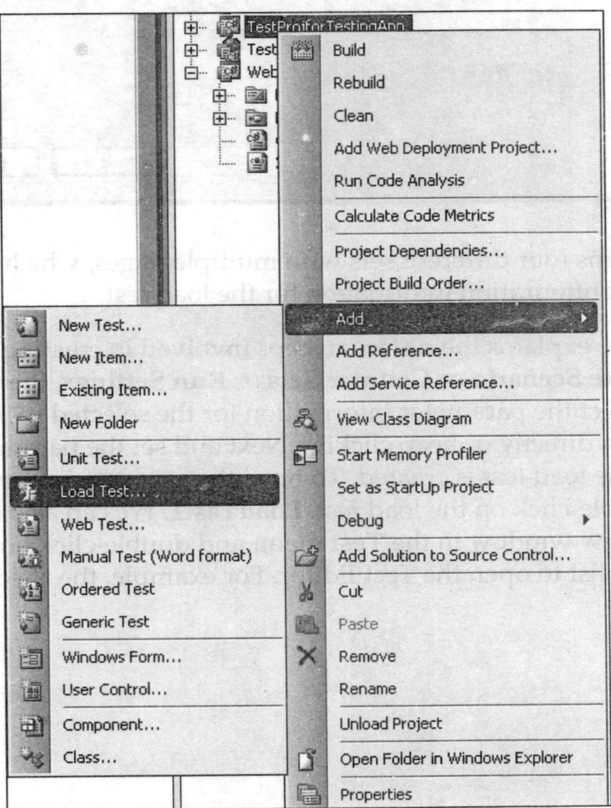

- Select the test menu in Visual Studio 2008 and select **New Test,** which opens the **Add | New Test...** dialog. Select the load test type from the list. Provide a test name and select the test project to which the new load test should be added.

Both the above options open the **New Load Test Wizard** shown as follows:

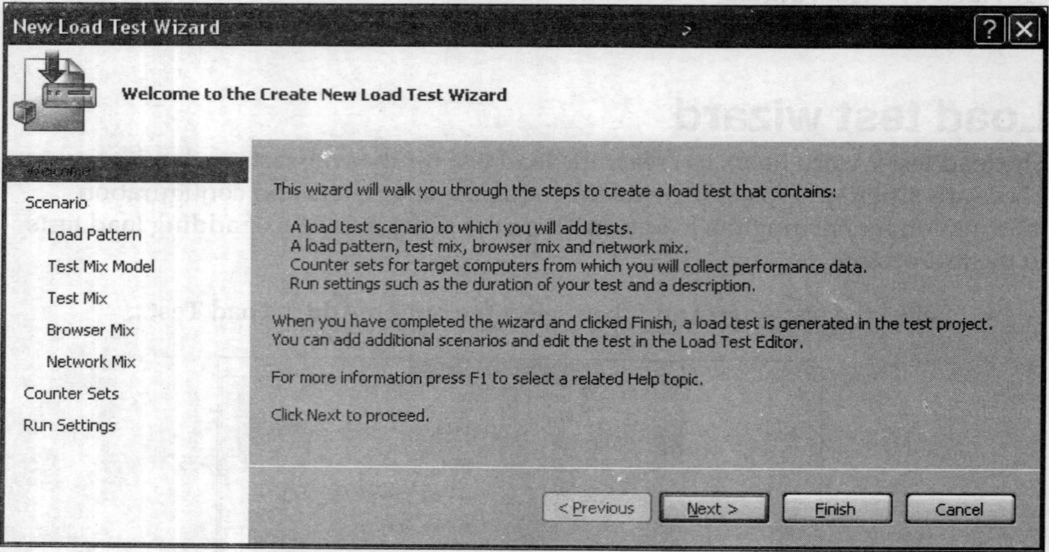

The wizard contains four different sets with multiple pages, which collects the parameters and configuration information for the load test.

The welcome page explains the different steps involved in creating a load test. On selecting a step like **Scenario** or **Counter Sets** or **Run Settings**, the wizard displays the section to collect the parameter information for the selected set option. We can click on the option directly or keep clicking **Next** and set the parameters. Once we click on **Finish**, the load test is created. To open the load test, expand the solution explorer and double-click on the load test, **LoadTest1.** We can also open the load test using the **Test View** window in the **Test** menu and double-click on the name of the load test from the list to open the Test Editor. For example, the following is a sample load test:

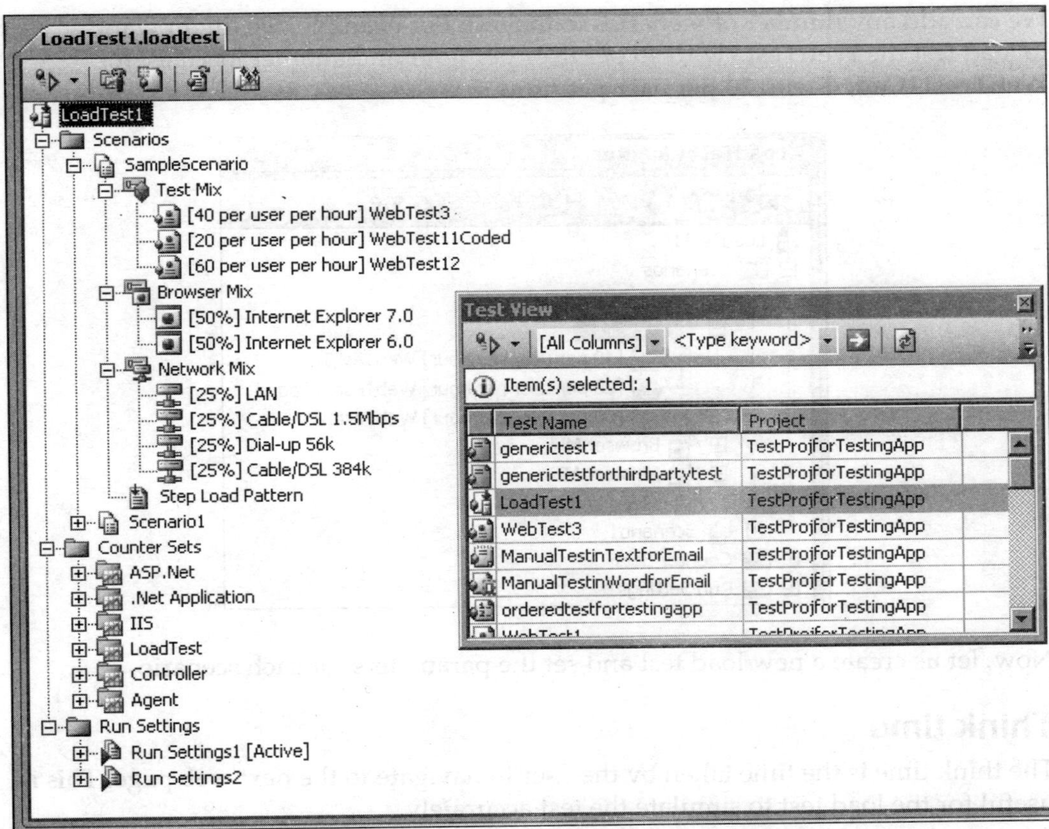

The following detailed sections explain setting the parameters in each step:

Specifying scenario

Scenarios are used for simulating the actual user tests. For example, there are different end users to any web application. For a public web site, the end user could be anywhere and there could be any number of users. The bandwidth of the connection and the type of browsers used by the users also differ. Some users might be using a high-speed connection, and some a slow dial-up connection. But if the application is an Intranet application, the end users are limited within the LAN network. The speed at which the users connect will also be constant most of the time. The number of users and the browsers used are the two main things which differ in this case. The scenarios are created using these combinations which are required for the application under test. Enter the name for the scenario in the wizard page.

We can add any number of scenarios to the test. For example, we might want to load test the **WebTest3** with **40 per user per hour** and another load test for **WebTest11Coded** with **20 per user per hour**.

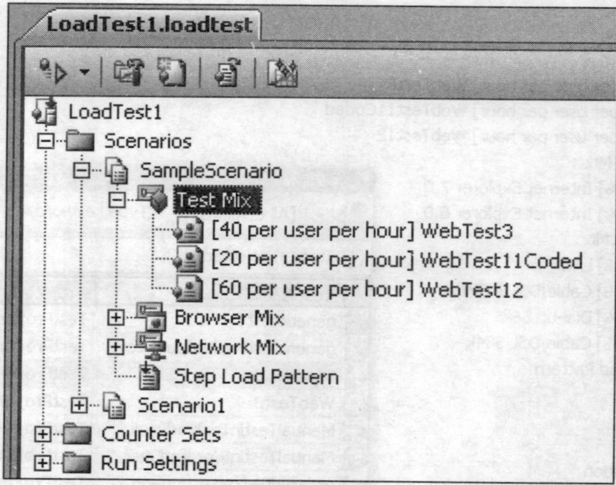

Now, let us create a new load test and set the parameters for each scenario.

Think time

The think time is the time taken by the user to navigate to the next web page. This is useful for the load test to simulate the test accurately.

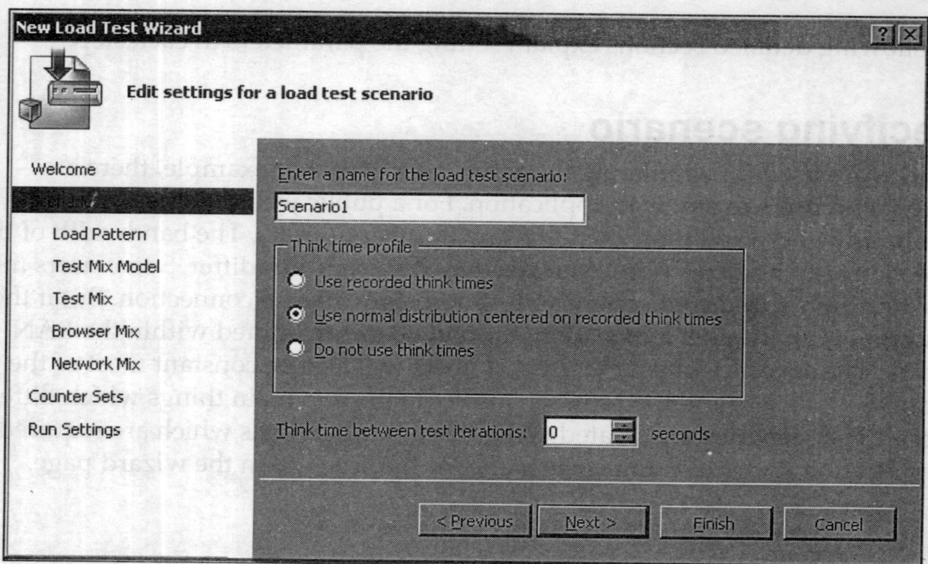

We can set the load test to use the actual think time recorded by the web test or we can give a specific think time for each test. The other option is to set the normal distribution of the think time between the requests. The time varies slightly between the requests, but is mostly realistic. There is a third option, which is configured not to use the think times between the requests.

The think times can also be modified for the scenario after creating the load test. Select the scenario and right-click and then open **Properties** to set the think time.

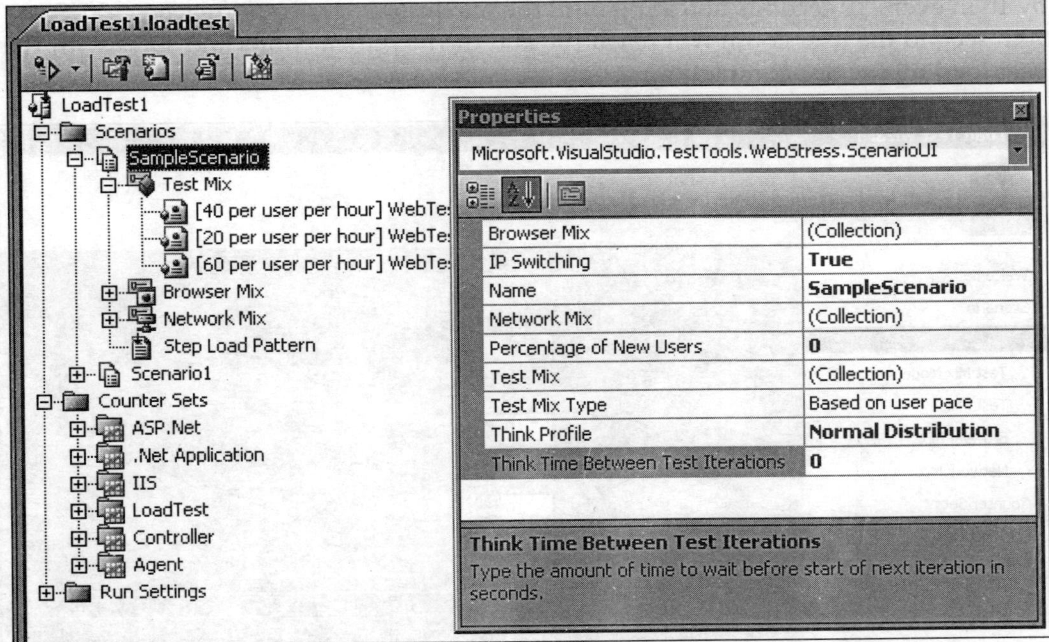

Now once the properties are set for the scenario, click **Next** in the **New Load Test Wizard** to set parameters for **Load Pattern**.

Load pattern

Load pattern is used for controlling the user loads during the tests. The test pattern varies based on the type of test. If it is a simple Intranet web application test or a unit test, then we might want to have a minimum number of users for a constant period of time. But in case of a public web site, the amount of users would differ from time to time. In this case, we might want to increase the number of users from a very small number to a large number with a time interval. For example I might have a user load of 10 initially but during testing I may want the user load to be increased by 10 in every 10 seconds of testing until the maximum user count reaches 100. So at 90th second the user count will reach 100 and the increment stops and stays with 100 user load till the test completion.

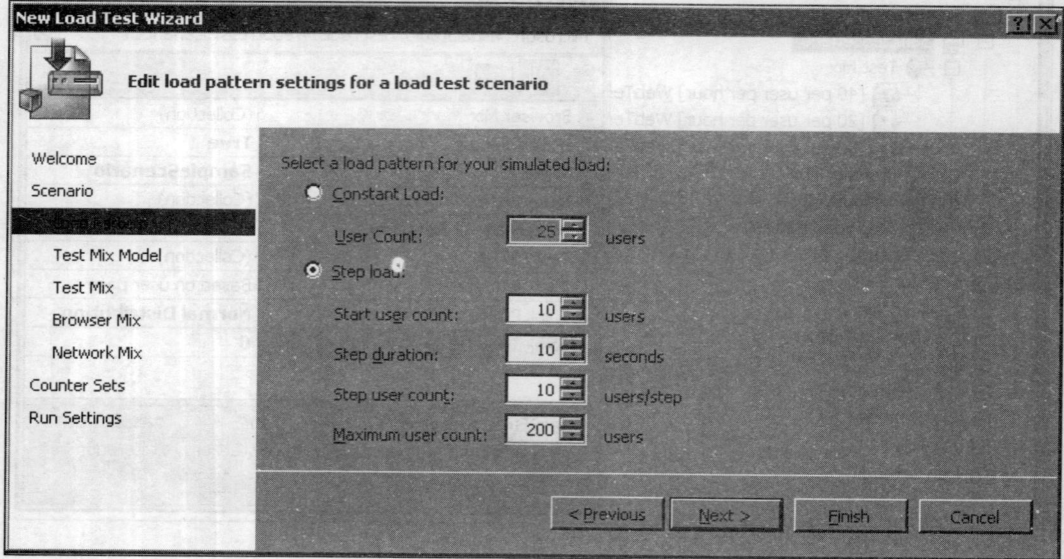

Constant load

The load starts with the specified user count and ends with the same number.

User Count: This is to specify the number of user counts for simulation.

Step load

The load test starts with the specified minimum number of users and the count increases constantly with the time duration specified until the user count reaches the maximum specified.

- **Start user count**: This specifies the number of users to start with
- **Step duration**: This specifies the time between the increases in user count

- **Step user count**: This specifies the number of users to add to the current user count
- **Maximum user count**: This specifies the maximum number of user count

We have set the parameters for the **Load Pattern**. The next step in the wizard is to set the parameter values for **Test Mix Model** and **Test Mix**.

Test mix model and test mix

The test load model has to simulate the accuracy of the end-users count distribution. Before selecting the test mix, the wizard provides a configuration page to choose the test mix model from three different options. They are based on the total number of tests, on the virtual users, and on user pace.

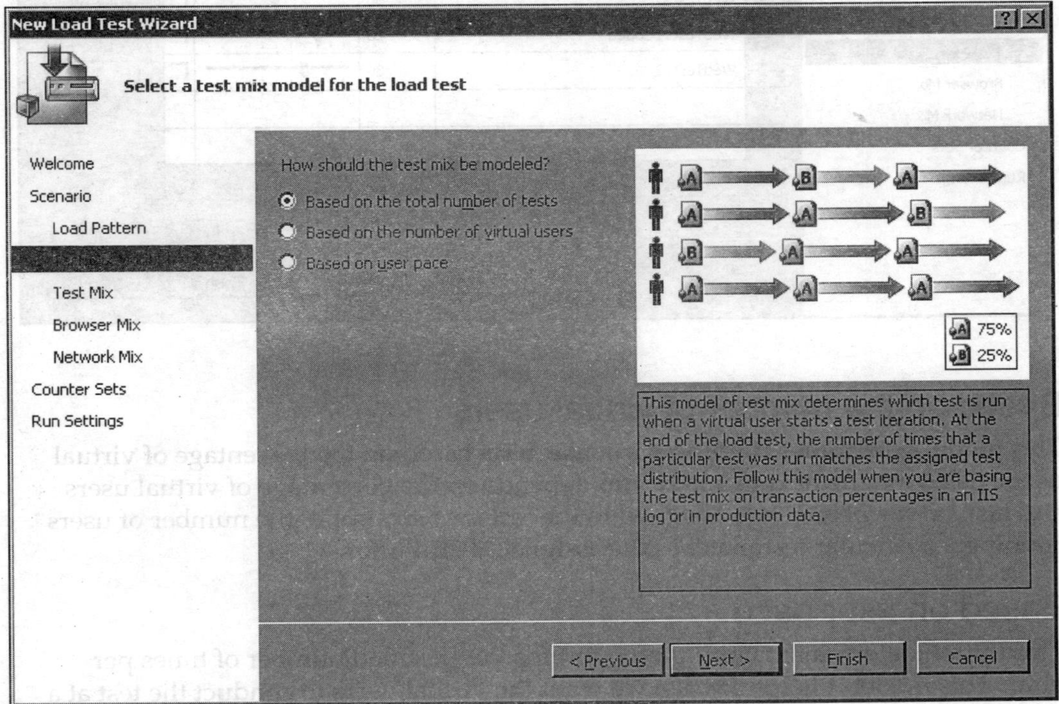

The next page in the wizard provides the option to select the tests and provide the distribution percentage, or the option to specify the tests per user per hour for each test for the selected model. The mix of tests is based on the percentages specified or the test per user specified for each test.

Based on the total number of tests

The next test to be run is based on the selected number of times. The number of times the tests is run should match the test distribution. For example, if the distribution is like the one shown in the image on the previous page, then the next test selected for the run is based on the percentage distributions.

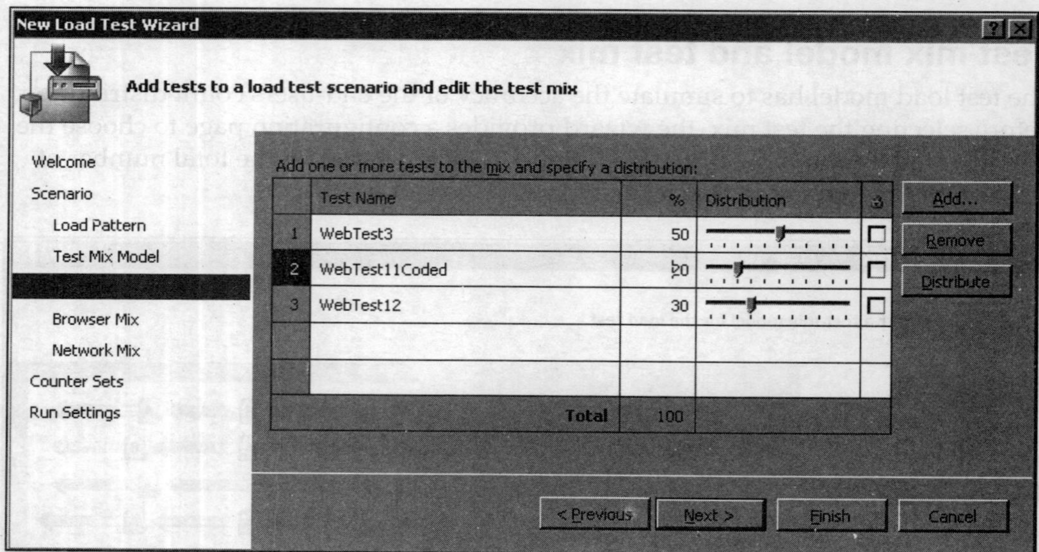

Based on the number of virtual users

This model determines running particular tests based on the percentage of virtual users. Selecting the next test to be run depends on the percentage of virtual users and also on the percentage assigned to the tests. At any point, the number of users running a particular test matches the assigned distribution.

Based on user pace

This option determines running each test for the specified number of times per hour. This model is helpful when we want the virtual users to conduct the test at a regular pace.

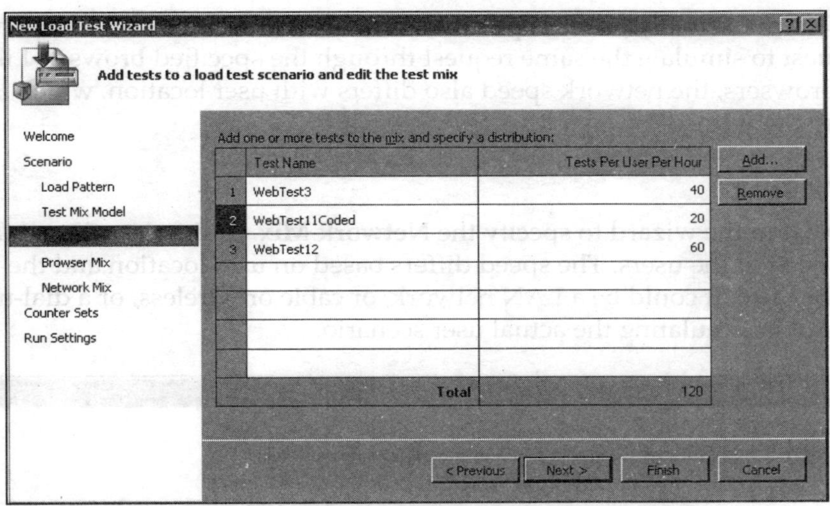

The test mix contains different web tests, each with different number of tests per user. The number of users is defined using load pattern. The next step in the wizard is to specify the **Browser Mix**, explained in the next section.

Browse mix

We have set the number of users and the number of tests, but there is always a possibility that all the users may not use the same browser. To mix the different browser types, we can go to the next step in the wizard and select the browsers listed and give a distribution percentage for each browser type.

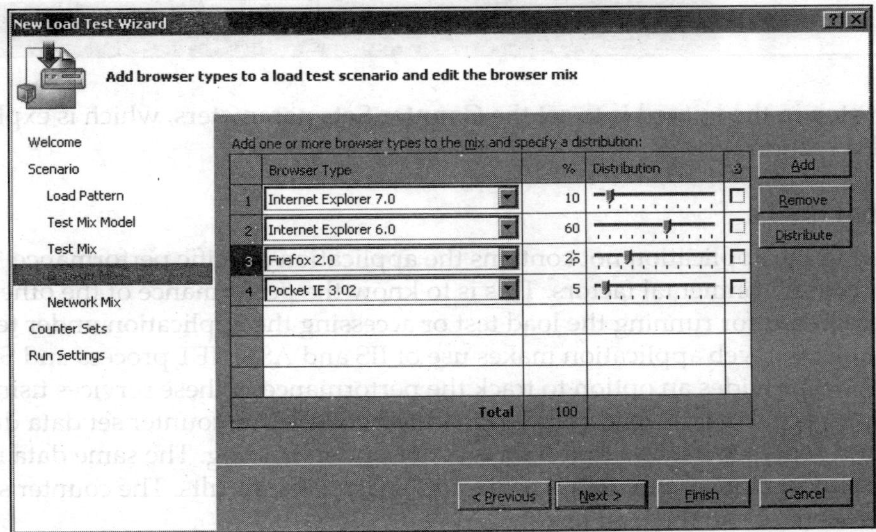

The test does not actually use the specified browser, but sets the header information in the request to simulate the same request through the specified browser. Like different browsers, the network speed also differs with user location, which is the next step in the wizard.

Network mix

Click on **Next** in the wizard to specify the **Network Mix,** to simulate the actual network speed of the users. The speed differs based on user location and the type of network they use. It could be a LAN network, or cable or wireless, or a dial-up. This step is useful in simulating the actual user scenario.

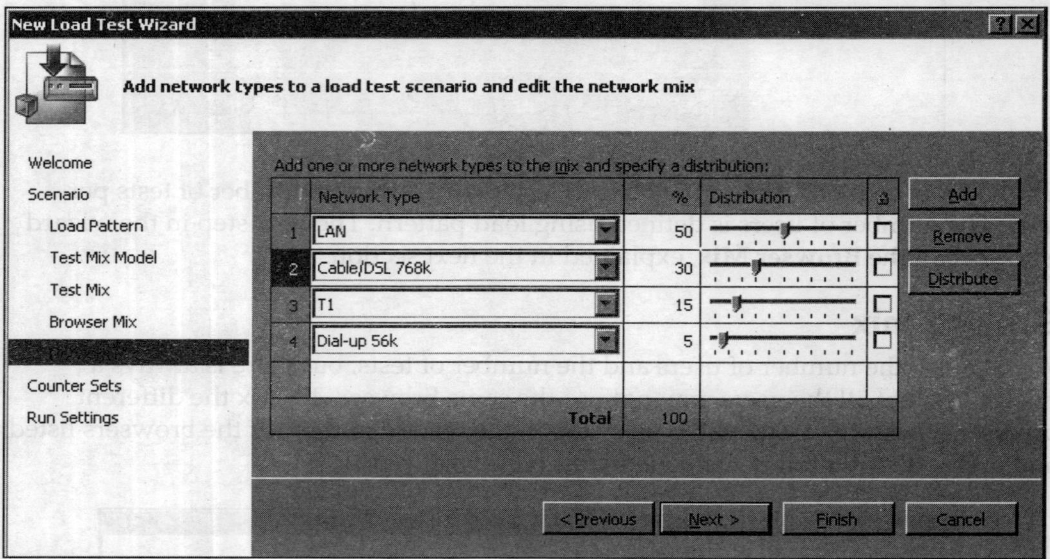

The next step in the wizard is to set the **Counter Sets** parameters, which is explained in the next sections.

Counter sets

Load testing the application not contains the application-specific performance but also the environmental factors. This is to know the performance of the other services required for running the load test or accessing the application under test. For example, the web application makes use of IIS and ASP.NET process and SQL Server. VSTS provides an option to track the performance of these services using counter sets as part of the load test. The load test collects the counter set data during the test and represents it as a graph for a better understanding. The same data is also saved locally so that we can load it again and analyze the results. The counter set is for all the scenarios in the load test.

The counter set data is collected for the controllers and agents by default. We can also add the other systems that are part of load testing. These counter set results help us to know how the services are used during the test. Most of the time the application performance is affected by the common services or the system services used.

The load test creation wizard provides the option to add the performance counters. The wizard includes the current system by default and the common counter set for the controllers and the agents. The following screenshot shows the sample for adding systems to collect the counter sets during the load test:

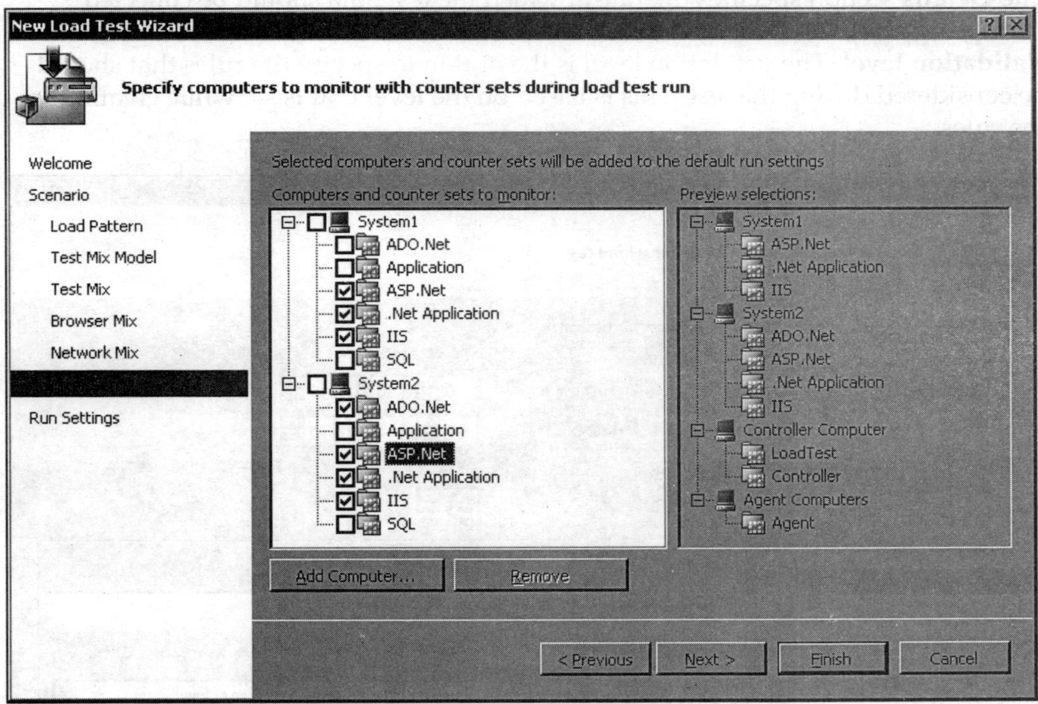

There are lists of counters listed for the system by default. We can select any of these for which we want to collect the details during the load test. For example, the above screenshot shows that we need the data to be collected for **ASP.NET**, **.Net Application**, and **IIS** from **System1**. Using the **Add Computer...** option, we can keep adding the computers on which we are running the tests and choose the counter sets for each system.

Once we are done with selecting the counter sets, we are ready with all the parameters for the test. But for running the test some parameters are required, which is done in the next step in the wizard.

Run settings

These settings are basically for controlling the load test run to specify the maximum duration for the test and the time period for collecting the data about the tests. The screenshot below shows the options and the sample setting.

There are two options for the test run. One is to control it by a maximum time limit and the other is to provide a maximum test iteration number. The test run will stop once it reaches the maximum, as per the option selected. For example, the screenshot below shows the option to run the test for 5 minutes.

The **Details** section specifies the rate at which the test data should be collected (**Sampling rate**), the **Description**, the **Maximum error details** to show, and the **Validation level**. The validation level is the option to specify the rules that should be considered during the test. This is based on the level that is set while creating the rules.

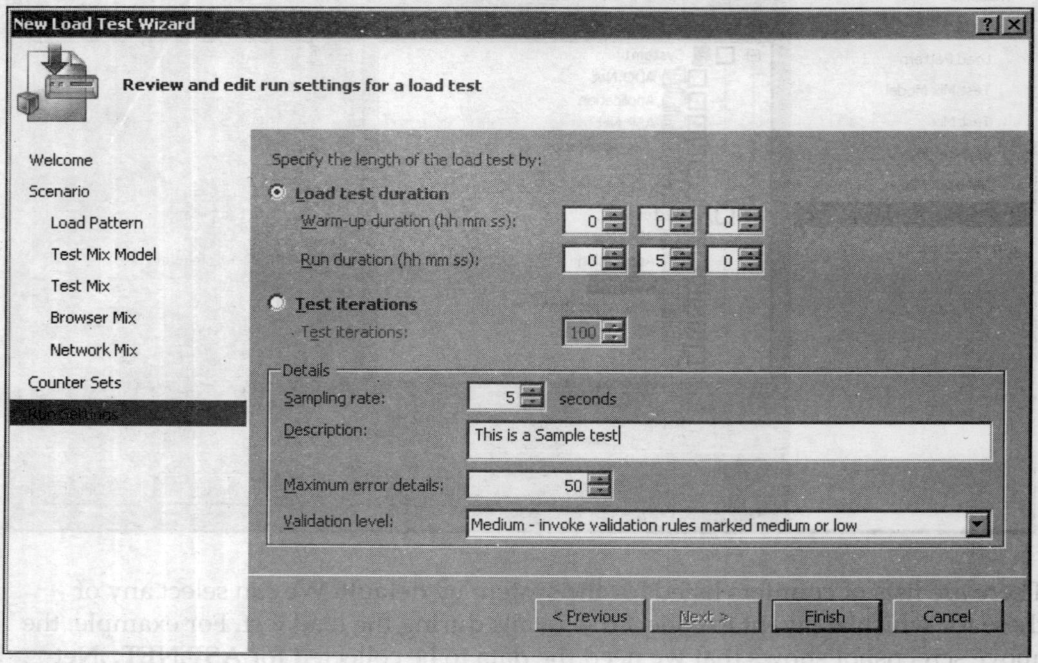

Now we are done with setting all the parameters required for load testing. Finish the wizard by clicking the **Finish** button, which actually creates the test with all the parameters from the wizard and shows the load test editor. The load test editor would look like the one shown here:

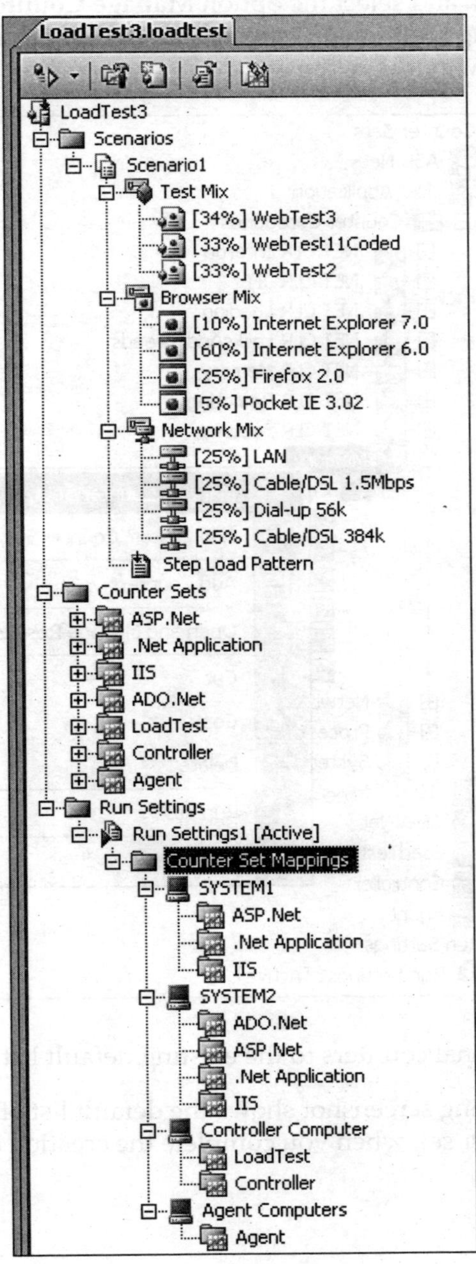

The actual run settings for the load test contains the counter sets selected for each system and the common run settings provided in the last wizard section. To know more about what exactly these counter sets contain and what the options are to choose in each counter set, select a counter set from the **Counter Sets** folder under the load test. Right-click and select the option **Manage Counter Sets...** for choosing more counters or adding additional systems. This option displays the same window that we saw as the last window in the wizard.

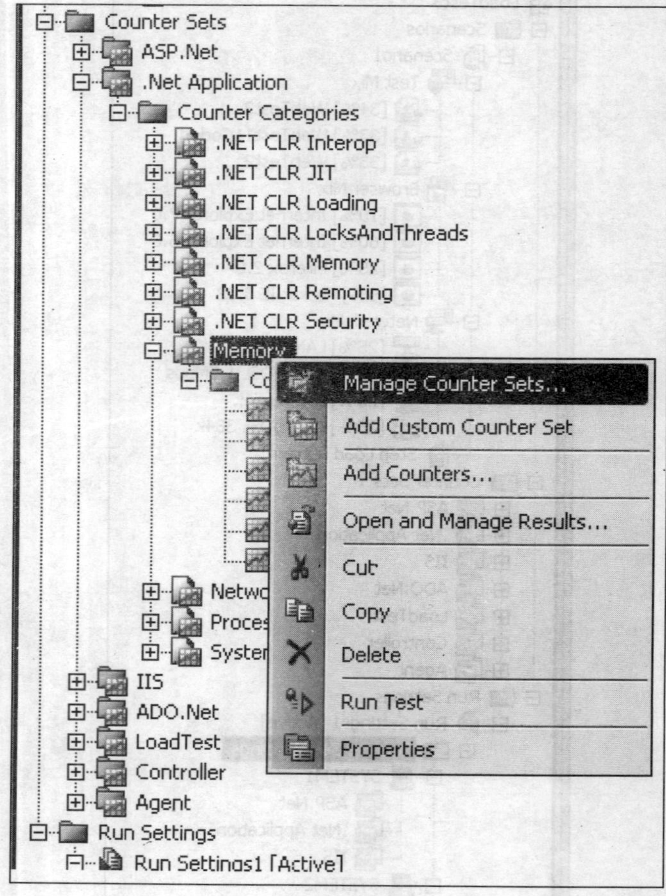

We can also add additional counters to the existing default list.

For example, the following screenshot shows the default list of categories under the .NET application counter set, when you complete the creation of the wizard.

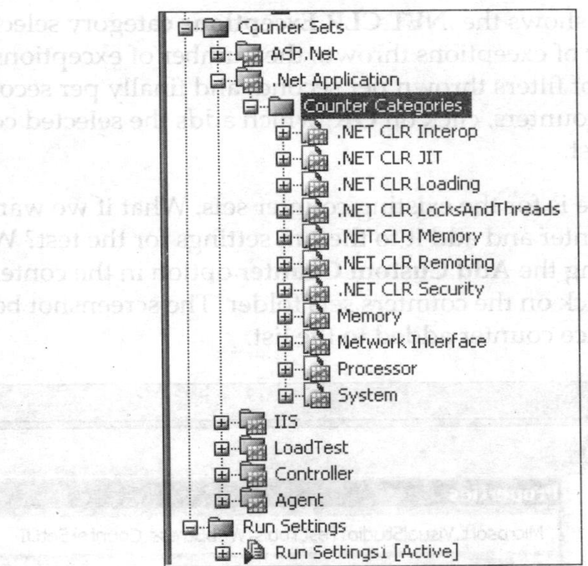

To add more counter categories, just right-click on the **Counter Categories** and select the **Add Counters** option and then choose the category you wish to add from the **Performance category** list. After selecting the category, select the counters from the list for the selected category.

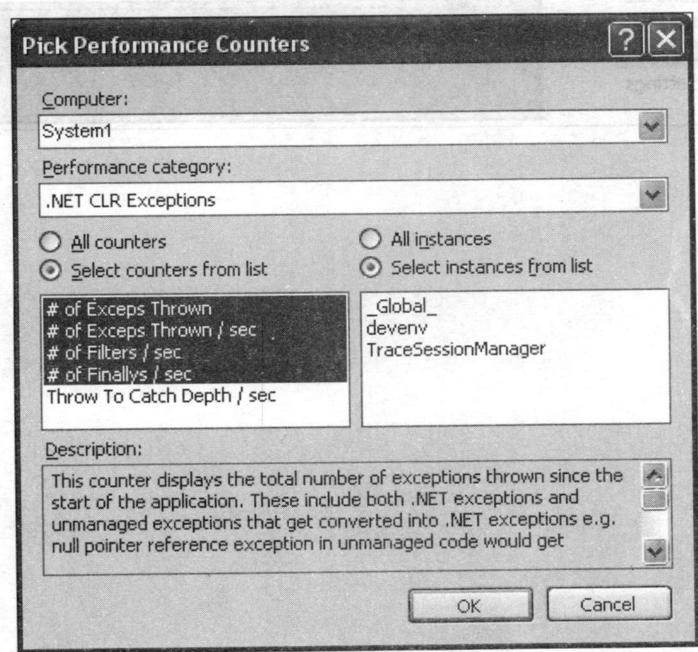

The previous screenshot shows the **.NET CLR Exceptions** category selected with the counters like the number of exceptions thrown, the number of exceptions thrown per second, the number of filters thrown per second, and finally per second. After selecting the additional counters, click on **OK**, which adds the selected counters to the existing list for the test.

What we have seen above is for the existing counter sets. What if we want to add the custom performance counter and add it to the run settings for the test? We can create a new counter by choosing the **Add Custom Counter** option in the context menu that opens when you right-click on the counters sets folder. The screenshot below shows a new custom performance counter added to the list.

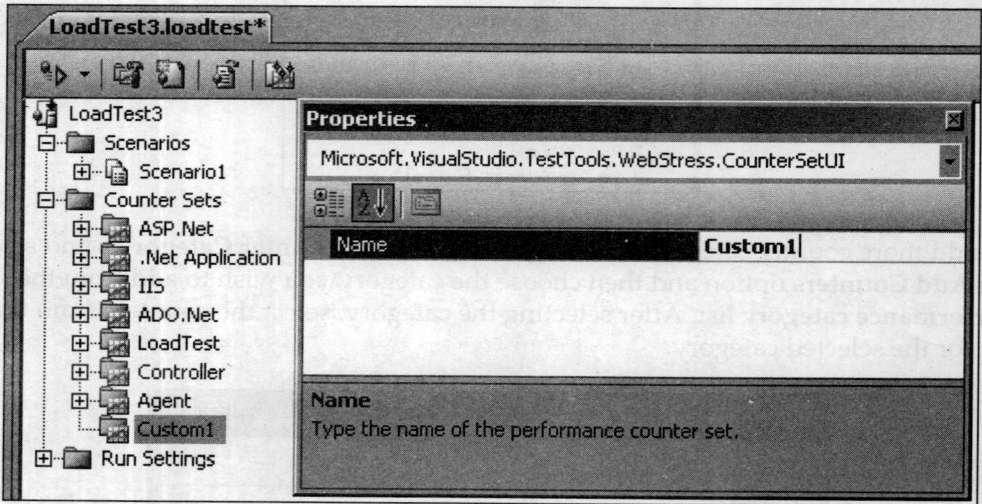

Now select the custom counter, right-click and choose the **Add Counters** option and select the category, and pick the counters required for the custom counter set. For example, we might want to collect the Network Interface counters such as the number of bytes sent and received per second and the current bandwidth during the test. Select these counters for the counter set.

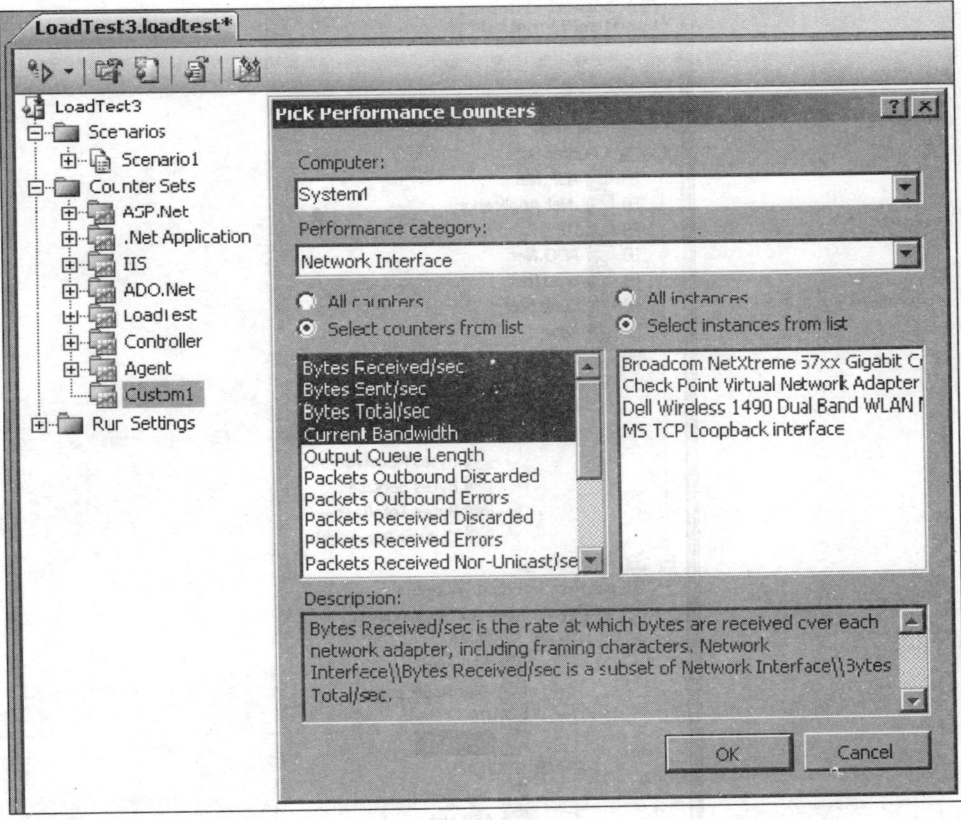

Once we are ready with the custom counter set, we need to add this as part of the run settings on all the systems that are part of the test. Select the **Run Settings** folder, right-click and choose the **Manage Counter Sets** option from the context menu and select the custom performance counter **Custom1** for the available systems. The final list of **Run Settings** would look like this:

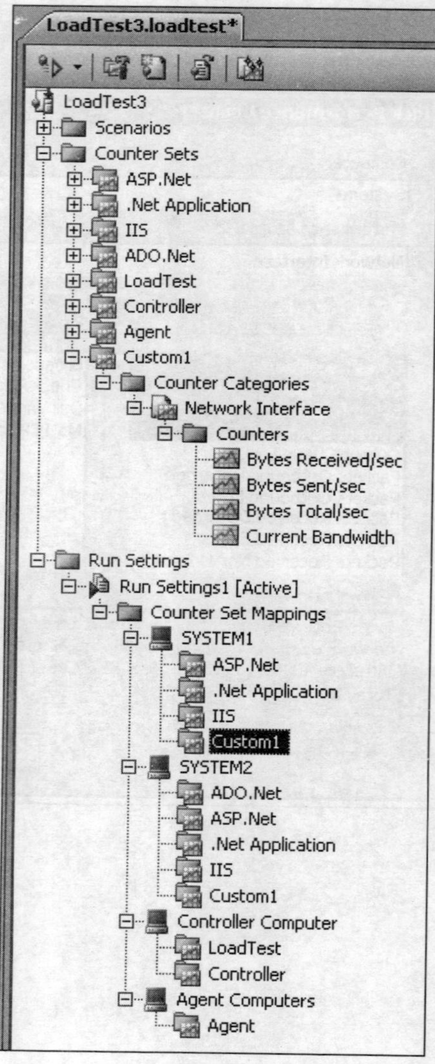

Keep adding all the custom counters and counter sets and select them for the systems used for running the test.

The main use of these counters is to collect the data during the test, but at the same time we can use it to track the readings. The load test has an option to track the counter data and indicate if it crosses the threshold values by adding rules to it. This is explained in the coming section.

Threshold rules

The main use of the counters and counter sets are to identify the actual performance of the current application under test and the usage of memory and time taken for the processor. There is another main advantage in collecting these counter data. We can set the threshold limits for each of these data collected during the test. For example, we may want to get an alert warning when the system memory is almost full. Also if any process takes more time than the expected maximum time, we may want the system to notify us so that we can act upon it immediately. These threshold rules can be set for each performance counters.

Select a performance counter and choose the **Add Threshold Rule** option, which opens a dialog for adding the rules.

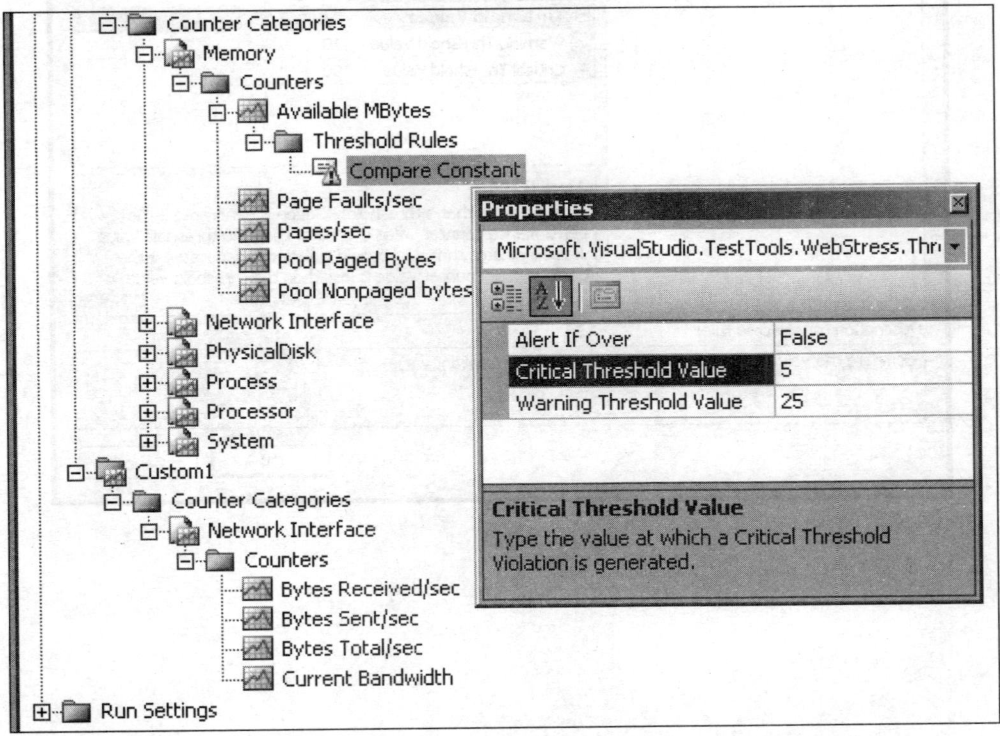

There are two different types of rules that can be added. One is to compare with constant values and the other is to compare the value with the other performance counter value. The following rules explain different ways of setting the threshold values:

- **Compare Constant**: This is to compare the performance counter value with a constant value. For example, we may want a violation, if the percentage of time taken for the processor is more than 70 and a critical message if it crosses 90. The **Alert If Over** option can be set to true or false, where true denotes that the violation would be generated if the counter value is greater than the specified threshold value and false denotes that the violation would be generated if the counter value is less than the specified threshold value.

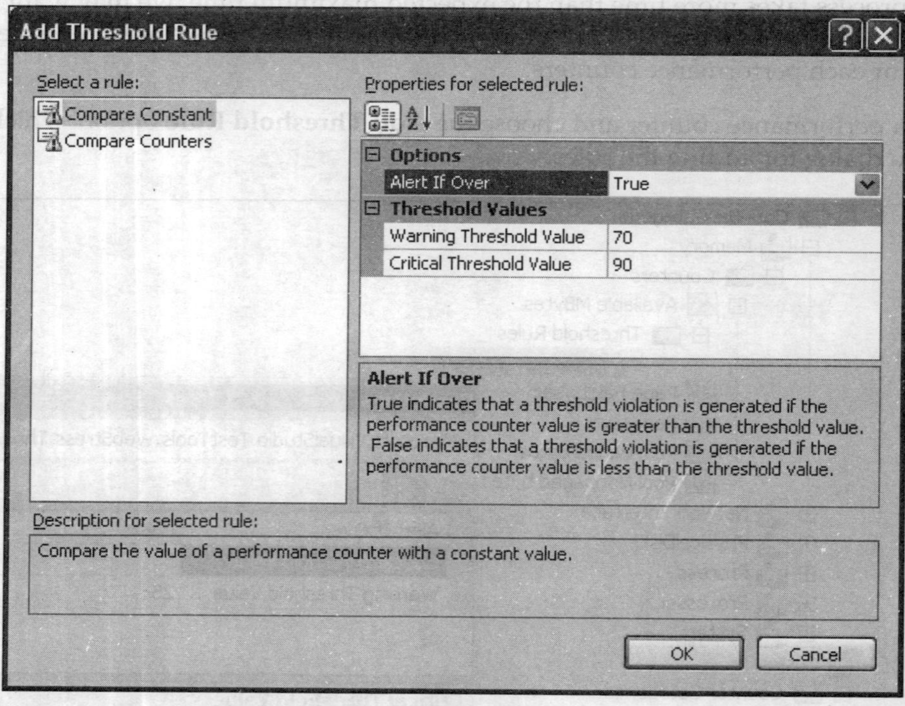

In the above screenshot, the threshold constant value is set to **70** to trigger the warning violation and the threshold value is set to **90** for the critical violation message.

- **Compare Counters**: This is to compare the performance counter value with another performance counter value. The functionality is the same as the above constants. But here the performance counter values are compared instead of constant.

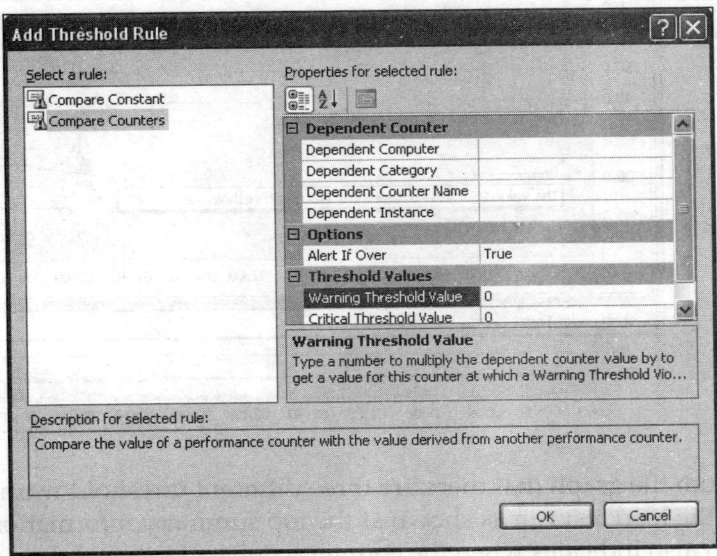

The above screenshot shows the options for adding **Compare Counters** to the counter set. The warning and critical threshold values are constants, which is multiplied by the dependent counter value and then compared with the current counter value. For example, if the dependent counter value is 50 and if the constant is set to 1.25 as the warning threshold, then the violation would be raised when the current counter value reaches a value of over 62.5.

The screenshot below shows the example of the threshold violation whenever the value exceeds the constant defined in the rule. The test is aborted because the test was stopped before it got completed.

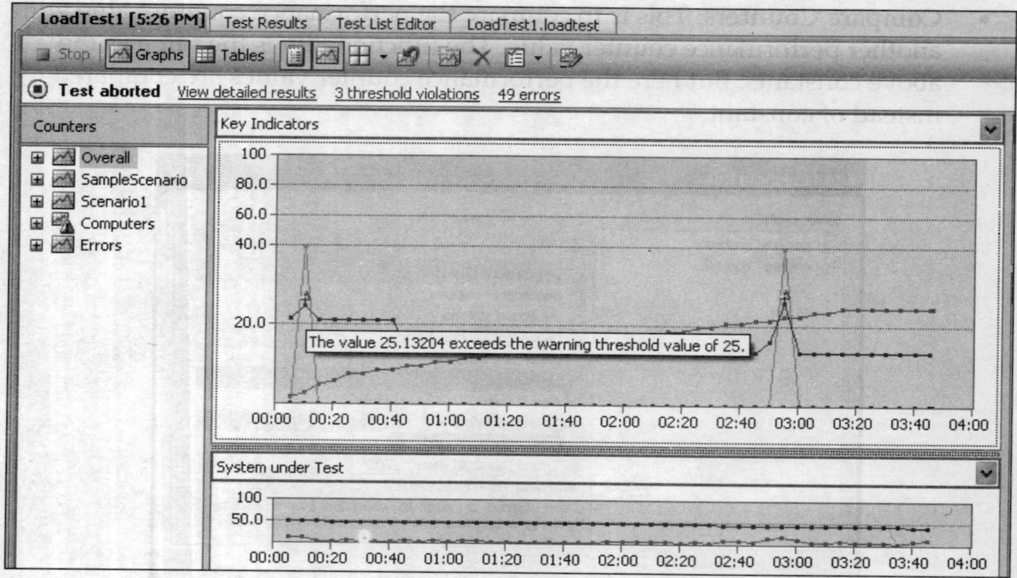

You can see from the graph that there are three different threshold warning messages raised during the load test run as shown at the top summary information about the test. The graph also indicates when the counter value had reached the value above the constant defined in the rule. As the graph shows, the value has reached the value **25.13204,** which is higher than the constant **25** defined in the rule. If the value is above the warning level, it is indicated as yellow and it is red, if it is above the critical threshold value. These rules will not fail the test but will provide the alert if the values are above the thresholds set.

Editing load tests

The load can contain one or more scenarios for testing. The scenarios can be edited any time during the design. To edit a scenario, select the scenario you want to edit and right-click to edit the test mix, browser mix, or network mix in the existing scenario or add a new scenario to the load test. The context menu has different options for editing as shown here:

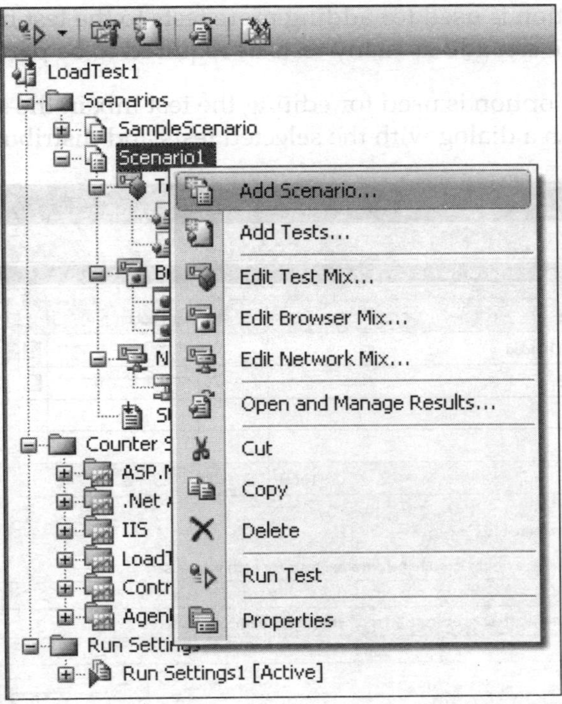

The **Add Scenario...** will open the same wizard, which we used before adding the scenario to the load test. We can keep adding the scenarios as much as we need. The scenario properties window also helps us modify some properties such as the **Think Profile** and the **Think Time Between Test Iteration** and the scenario **Name**.

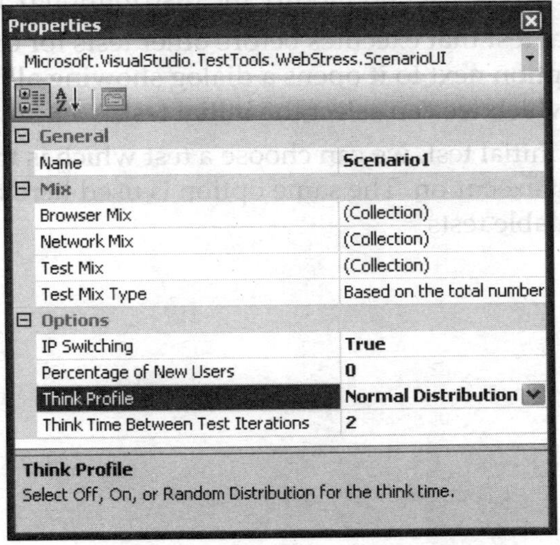

The **Add Tests...** option is used for adding more tests to the test mix from the tests list in the project. We can add as many tests as required to be part of the test mix.

The **Edit Test Mix...** option is used for editing the test mix in the selected scenario. This option will open a dialog with the selected tests and distribution.

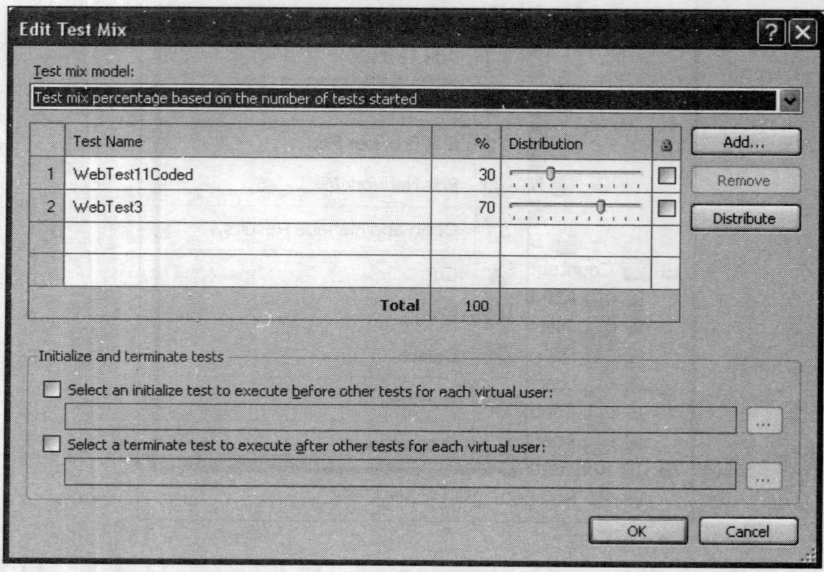

Using this **Edit Test Mix** window we can:

- Change the test mix model listed in the drop-down.
- Add new tests to the list and modify the distribution percentage.
- Select an initial test that executes before other tests for each virtual server. The browse option next to it opens a dialog showing all the tests from the project from which we can select the initial test.
- Similar to the initial test, we can choose a test which is the final test to run during the test execution. The same option is used here to select the test from the list of available tests.

The **Edit Browser Mix...** option opens the **Edit Browser Mix** dialog from where you can select the new browser to be included to the browser mix and delete or change the existing browsers selected in the mix.

The **Edit Network Mix...** option opens the **Edit Network Mix** dialog from where you can add new browsers to the list and modify the distribution percentages. We can change or delete the existing network mix.

For changing the existing load pattern, select the **Load Pattern** under the **Scenarios** and open the **Properties** window which shows the current patterns properties. You can change or choose any pattern from the available patterns in the list as shown in the following screenshots:

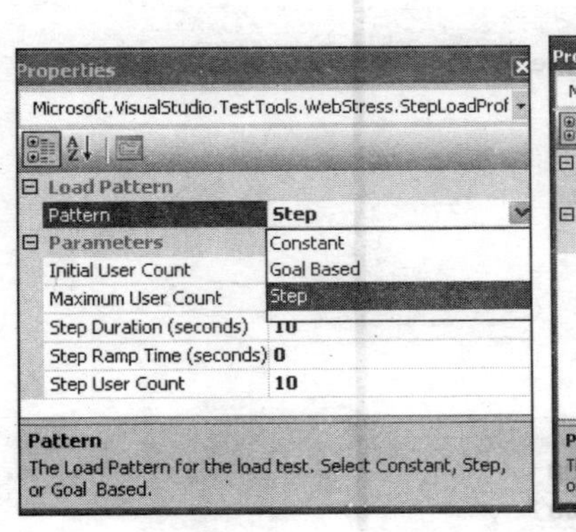

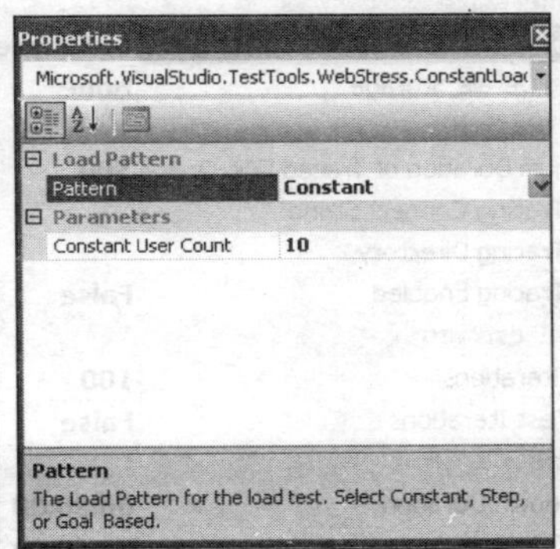

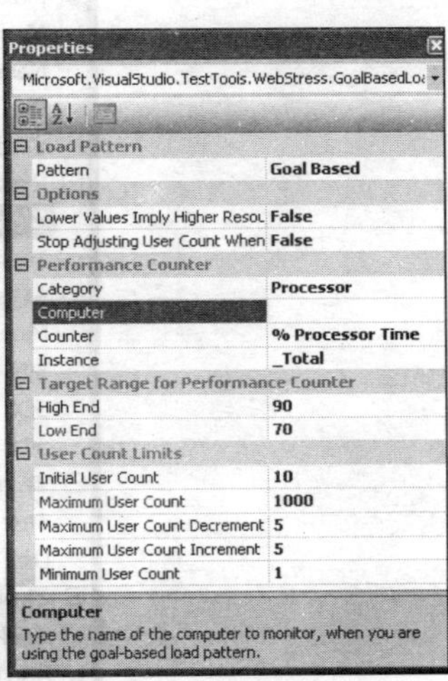

The **Run Settings** can be multiple for the load tests, but at any time only one can be active. To make the run settings active, select **Run Settings,** right-click and select **Set as Active**. The properties of the run settings can be modified directly using the properties window. The properties that can be modified include results storage, SQL tracing, test iterations, timings, and the web test connections.

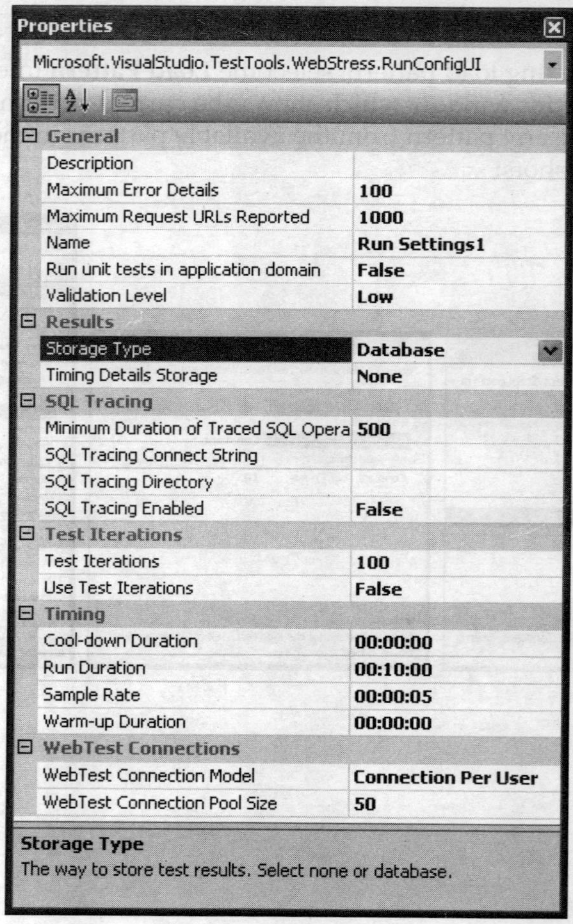

Adding context parameters

We have seen the context parameters in Chapter 3, which explain the web tests. The web tests can have context parameters added to them. The context parameter is used in place of the common values of multiple requests in the web test. For example, every request has the same web server name, which can be replaced by the context parameters. So whenever the web server changes, we can just change the context parameter value, which replaces all the requests with the new server name.

We know that the load test can have web tests and unit tests in the list. If there is a change in the web server for the load test other than what we used for web tests then we will end up modifying the context parameter values in all the web tests used in the load tests. Instead of this, we can include another context parameter in the load test with the same name used in the web tests. The context parameter added to the load test will override the same context parameter used in the web tests. To add new context parameter to the load test, select the **Run Settings** and right-click to choose the **Add Context Parameter** option, which adds a new context parameter. For example, the context parameter used in the web test has the web server value as

```
this.Context.Add("WebServer1", "http://localhost:49459");
```

Now to overwrite this in load tests, add a new context parameter with the same name as shown below:

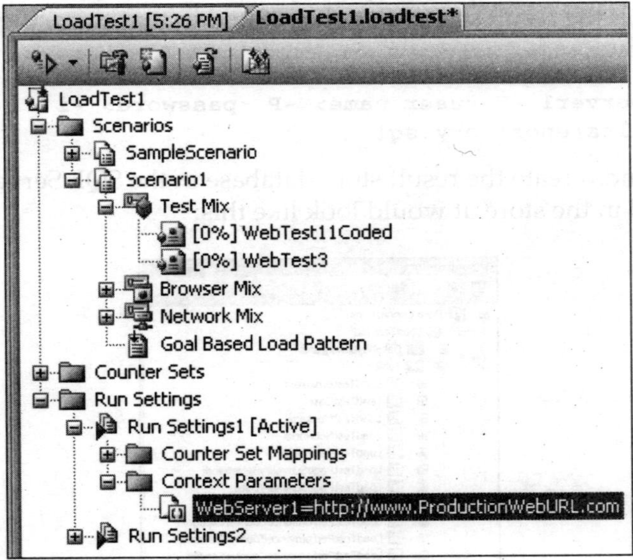

Results store

All information collected during the load test run is stored in the central result store. The load test results store contains the data collected by the performance counters and the violation information and errors that occurred during the load test. The result store is the SQL server database created using the script `loadtestresultsrepository.sql`, which contains all the SQL queries to create the objects required for the result store.

If there are no controllers involved in the test and if it is the local test, we can create the results store sql database using SQL Express. Running the script creates the store using SQL Express. Running this script once on the local machine is enough for creating the result store. This is a global central store for all the load tests in the local machine. To create the store, open the visual studio **command prompt** and run the command with the actual drive where you have installed the visual studio.

```
cd c:\Program Files\Microsoft Visual Studio 9.0\Common7\IDE
```

In the same folder, run the following command which creates the database store

```
SQLCMD /S localhost\sqlexpress /i loadtestresultsrepository.sql
```

If you have any other SQL Server and if you want to use that to have the result store then you can run the script on that server and use that server in connection parameters for the load test. For example, if you have the SQL Server name as **SQLServer1** and if the result store has to be created in that store, then run the command as below:

```
SQLCMD /S SQLServer1 -U <user name> -P <password> -i
  loadtestresultsrepository.sql
```

All these commands create the result store database in the SQL Server. If you look at the tables created in the store, it would look like this:

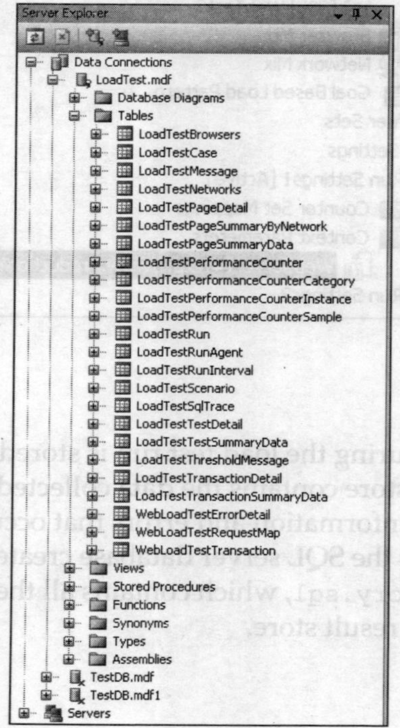

If you are using a controller for the load tests, the installation of the controller itself takes care of creating the results store on the controller machine. The controller can be installed using the Visual Studio 2008 Team Test Load agent Product.

To connect to the SQL Server result store database, select the **Test** option from the Visual Studio IDE and then select the **Administer Test Controller** window. This option would be available only in the controller machine. If the result store is on a different machine or the controller machine, select the controller from the list or select **<Local-No controller>,** if it is in the local machine without any controller. Then select the **Load Test Results** store using the browse button and close the **Administer test Controller** window.

The controllers are used for administering the agent computers and these controller and agents form the rig. Multiple agents are required to simulate a large number of loads from different locations. All the performance data collected from all these agents are saved at the central result store at the controller or any global store configured at the controller.

Running the load test

Load tests are run like any other test in Visual Studio. Visual Studio also provides multiple options for running the load test.

One is through the **Test View** window where all the tests are listed. We can select the load test, right-click and choose the option **Run Selection** option, which starts the load tests to run.

The second option is to use the **Test List Editor**. Select the load test from the test list in the test lists editor and choose the option to run the selected tests from the test list editor toolbar.

The third option is the built-in run option in the load test editor toolbar. Select the load test from the project and open the load test. This opens the load test in the load test editor. The toolbar for this load test editor has the option to run the currently opened load test.

The fourth option is through the command line command. MS Test command line utility is used for running the test. This utility is installed along with the Visual Studio Team System for Test. Open the Visual Studio command prompt. From the folder where the load test resides, run the following command to start the load test

```
mstest /testcontainer:LoadTest1.loadtest
```

In all the above cases, the load test editor will show the progress during the test run. But the other option does not show the progress instead stores the result to the result store repository. It can be loaded later to see the test result and analyze it. You can follow these steps to open the last run tests:

1. Open the menu option **Test | Windows | Test Runs**.
2. From the **Connect** drop-down, select the location for the test results store. On selecting this, you can see the trace files of the last run tests getting loaded in the window.
3. Select the test run name from the list and double-click to open the test results for the selected run.
4. Double-click the test result shown in the Results window that connects to the store repository, fetches the data for the selected test result, and presents in the load test window.

The end result of the load test editor window will look like the one shown in the following screenshot with all the performance counter values and the violation points.

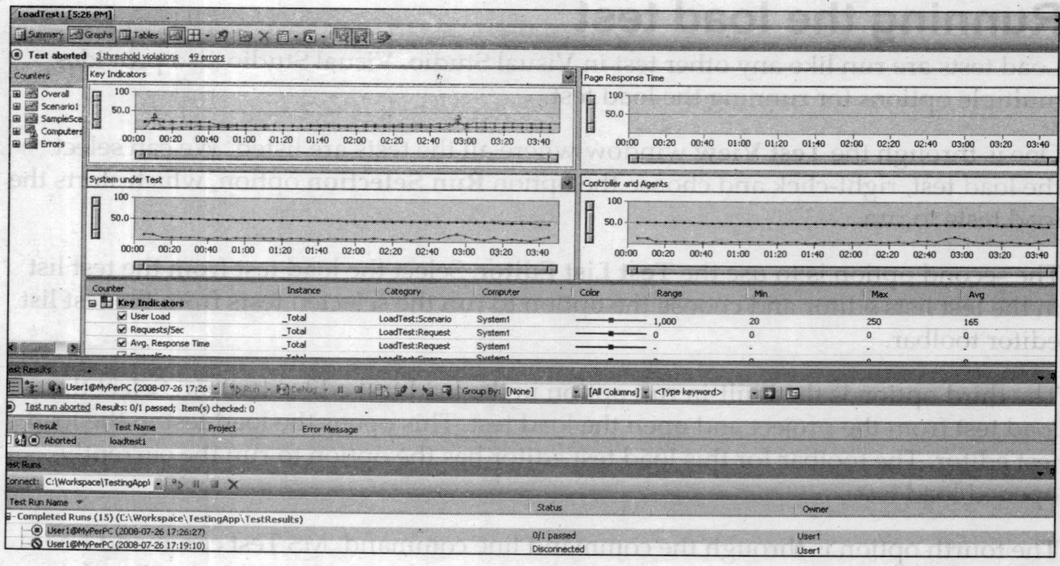

More details about the graph are given under the *Graphical View* subsection.

Running load test using rig

The rigs are used to simulate the load test with a large number of computers at different locations. The rig consists of one central controller that controls multiple agent computers at different locations. These computers together form a rig. The rig is used for generating heavy load from multiple machines instead of load testing with single machine. Any time that we want the load test simulation to be increased, we can simply add more agents to the controller. All these agents added to the rig are controlled by a single controller. When these controller and agents are involved in running the load test and collecting the data, the client will monitor and present the data to the user.

The agents run the test and the controller controls all these agents and collects the data and stores it into the central repository from which the client fetches the data and presents it to the user. The controller keeps track of sending messages to the agents about when to start the load test.

The controller and agents are configured using the controller and agent tabs in the configuration window. Before configuration, the controller and the agents should be installed on the computers. This can be done only through the **Microsoft Visual Studio 2008 Team Test Load Agent** disc.

After installation of the controller and the agents on the respective machines, the client has to be configured with the controller and the agents for the load test. This can be done through the menu option **Test** and the **Administer Test Controllers...** option in Visual Studio. This option opens the window to select the controller and add the agents to the list for the controller. The list of agents should be added to this list.

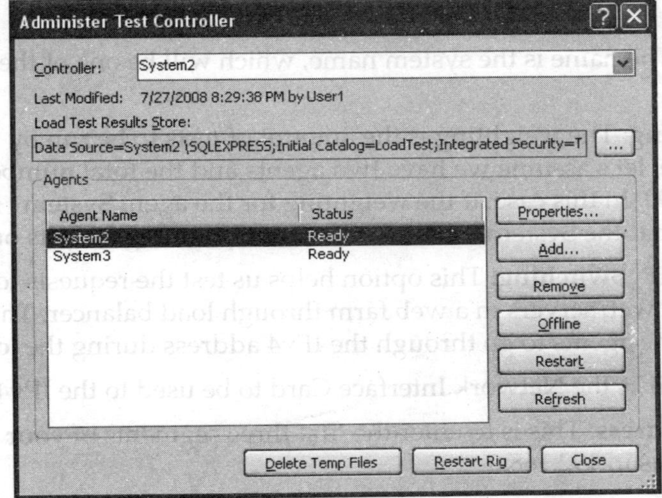

The **Add...** option in the **Administer Test Controller** windows has the option to add, remove, restart, and set the properties for the agent. Select the **Add...** option, which opens the dialog for adding new agent. Set the agent properties such as the name and the attributes for the agent.

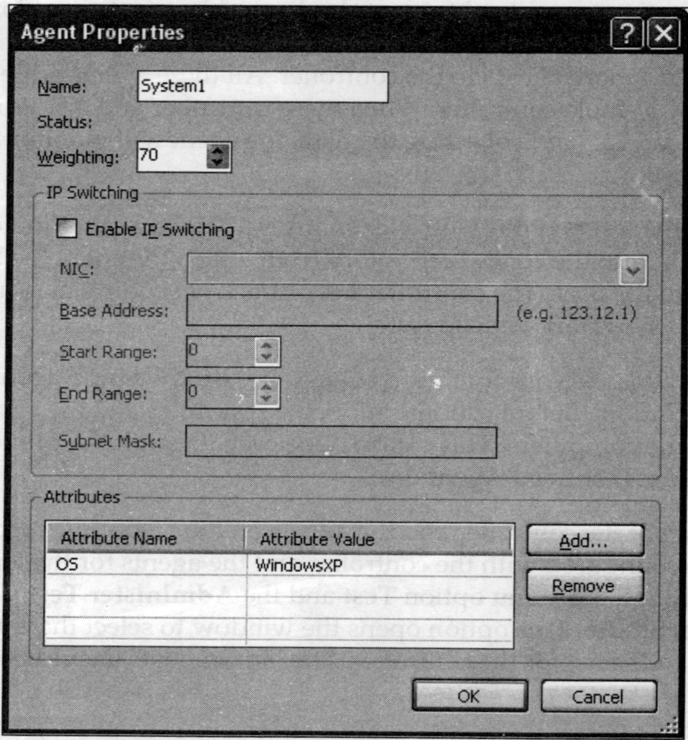

- **Name**: The name is the system name, which will be one of the agents for the test.
- **Weighting**: The weighting is the amount of tests to be run by this agent. For example, let's assume we have two agents and the total number of tests to run is 100. In this case, if the weighting for the agent System1 is 70, then it means that the System1 should take care of running 70 tests out of 100.
- **Enable IP_Switching:** This option helps us test the requests to multiple backend web servers in a web farm through load balancer. This option allows the agents to go through the IPv4 address during the load test.
- **NIC**: This is the Network Interface Card to be used to the IPv4 address.
- **Base Address**: This is to enter the first three segments of your base IPv4 address as in 192.168.0.

- **Start Range**: This is to enter the starting number to be used in the IPv4 address. For example, if the starting number is 15, then the first IPv4 address would be the base address with the first number in the start range which is 192.168.0.15.
- **End Range**: This is the final or the end range for the IPv4 addresses. For example, if the end range is 20, then the agent will generate addresses from the start range to the end range where the end range address would be 192.168.0.20.
- **Subnet Mask:** This is to enter the subnet mask.
- **Attributes:** The attributes are the properties of the agent, which will be used for the selection of a suitable agent for the test, if any constraints are specified. This is the name value pair. The name represents the name given for the attribute and the value is the value given for the attribute. The following are some examples of attributes:

  Example 1

  - Attribute Name: OS
  - Attribute Value: WindowsXP

  Example 2

  - Attribute Name: RAM
  - Attribute Value: 2GB

These attributes are used when the test configuration has the constraints for selecting the agents for the tests. The configuration file will have the properties such as shown in the following screenshot:

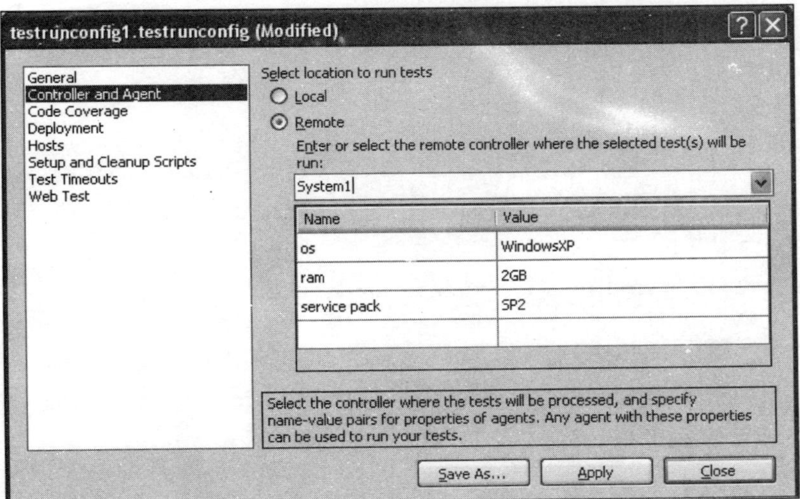

The controller will consider the agents whose properties match with the properties mentioned in the name value for the agents on the screen for selecting the location to run tests.

Working with test result and analyzing test results

The result that we get out of the load test contains a lot of information about the test. All of these details get stored in the results repository store. The graph and indicators shown during the test run contain only the important cached results. The actual detailed information will get stored to the store. We can load the test result later from the store and analyze it.

There are different ways to see the test results using the options in the Test Editor toolbar. At any time we can switch between the views to look at the results. The one that follows is the graphical view of the test results. The graphical view window contains different graphs shown for different counters.

Graphical view

The graphical view of the result gives a high-level view of the test result, but the complete test result data is stored in the repository. By default, there are four different graphs provided with different readings. We can select the drop-down and choose any other counter reading for the graphical view.

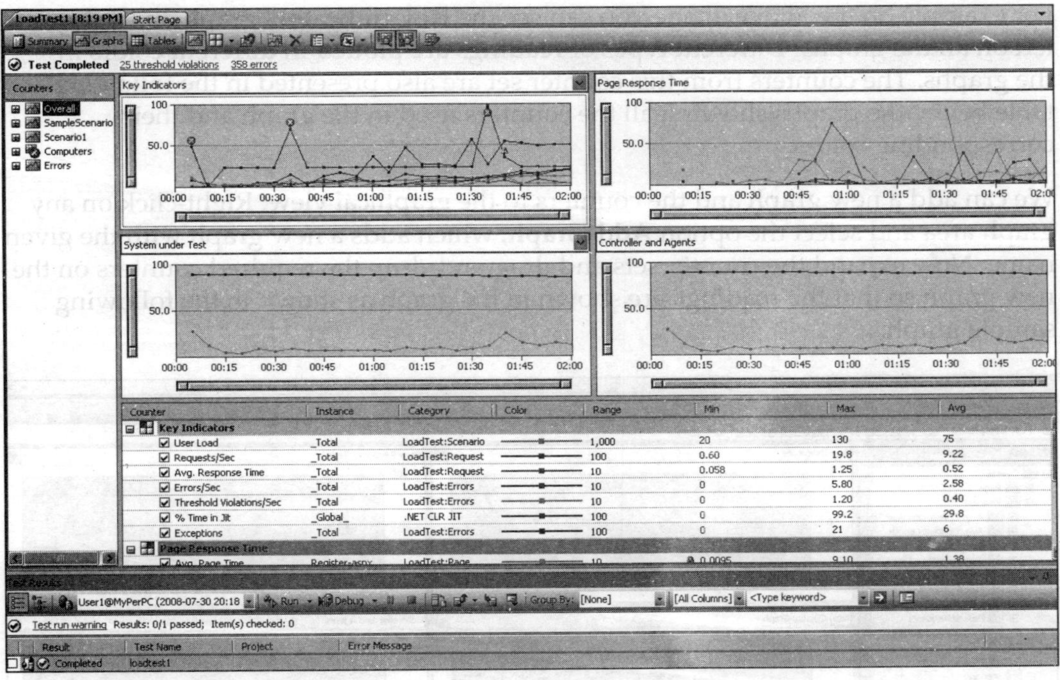

- **Key Indicators**: This graph shows the data collected on average response time, Just-In-Time (JIT) percentage, threshold violations per second, errors per second, and the user load. The details about the graph are given below the four graphs section, which describes the actual counter data collected during the test.
- **Page Response Time**: This graph explains how long the response for each request took in different URLs. The details are given below the graphs.
- **System Under Test**: This is the graph, which presents the data about different computers or agents used in the test. The data include readings such as the available memory and the processing time.
- **Controller and Agents**: The last graph will present the details about the system or machine involved in the load test. The data collected would be the processor time and the available memory in MB.
- **Transaction Response Time**: This indicates the average time taken by the transactions in load testing.

For all the graphs, we have more detailed information on each counter in the following grid with the color legends. The details shown contain information on the counter name, category, range, min, max, and average readings for each counter. The legend grid can be made visible or invisible using the option in the toolbar.

For example, in the above image you can see the **Key Indicators** graph on the top left on all the graphs. Different types of readings are plotted in different colors in the graphs. The counters from this counter set are also presented in the following table below the graphs showing all the counters used in the graph and their corresponding colors.

We can add a new graph and the counters to the graphical view. Right-click on any graph area and select the option **Add Graph,** which adds a new graph with the given name. Now expand the counter sets and drag-and-drop the required counters on the new graph so that the readings are shown in the graph as shown in the following sample graph:

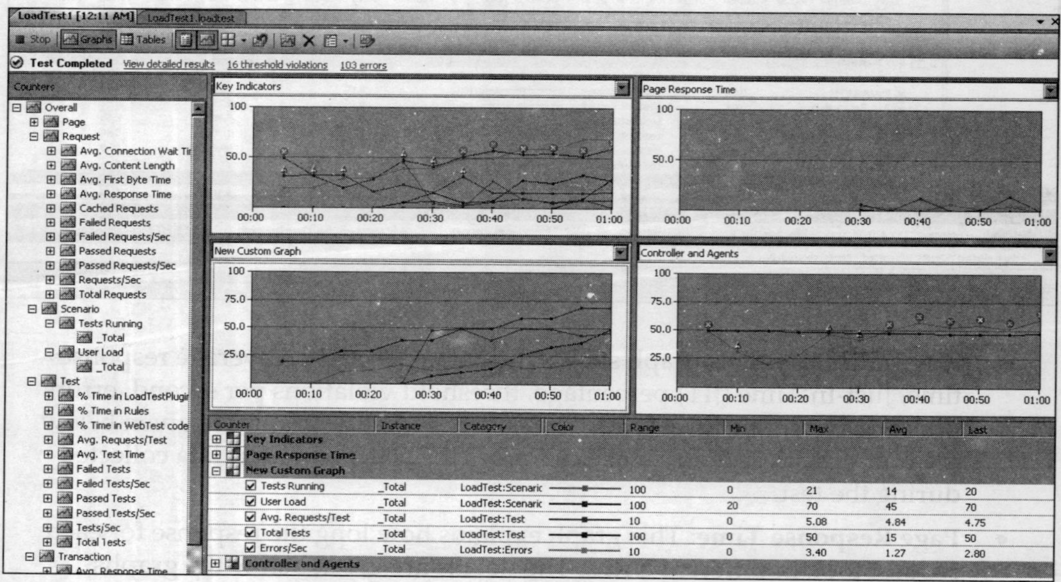

The **New Custom Graph** is the new graph added to the result and counters are added to the graph. The counters and readings are listed in the table below the graphs.

Summary view

The summary view option in the load test editor window toolbar presents more information on the overall load testing.

The very important information is the top five slowest pages and tests. The tests are ordered based on the average test time taken for each test and the time taken for each page request.

- **Test Results**: This section gives the status information such as the number of tests conducted on each test selected for load testing. For example, out of 100 web tests selected for load testing, what is the number of passed tests and failed tests?
- **Page Results**: This section gives information about the test conducted for each URL used in the test. This result shows the number of times the page is requested, and the average time taken for each request. The detail includes the test name to which the URL belongs.
- **Transaction Results**: The transaction is the set of tasks in the test. This section in the summary view gives the information like scenario name, test name, the elapsed time for testing this transaction, the number of times this transaction tested, and so on.
- **System under Test resources and controller and agents resources**: This section gives the information about the systems involved in testing, the processor time for the test, and the amount of memory available at the end of test completion.
- **Errors:** This section details the list of errors that occurred during the test. It gives information such as the error type, the sub type, and the number of times the same error occurred during the test, the last message from the error stack, and so on.

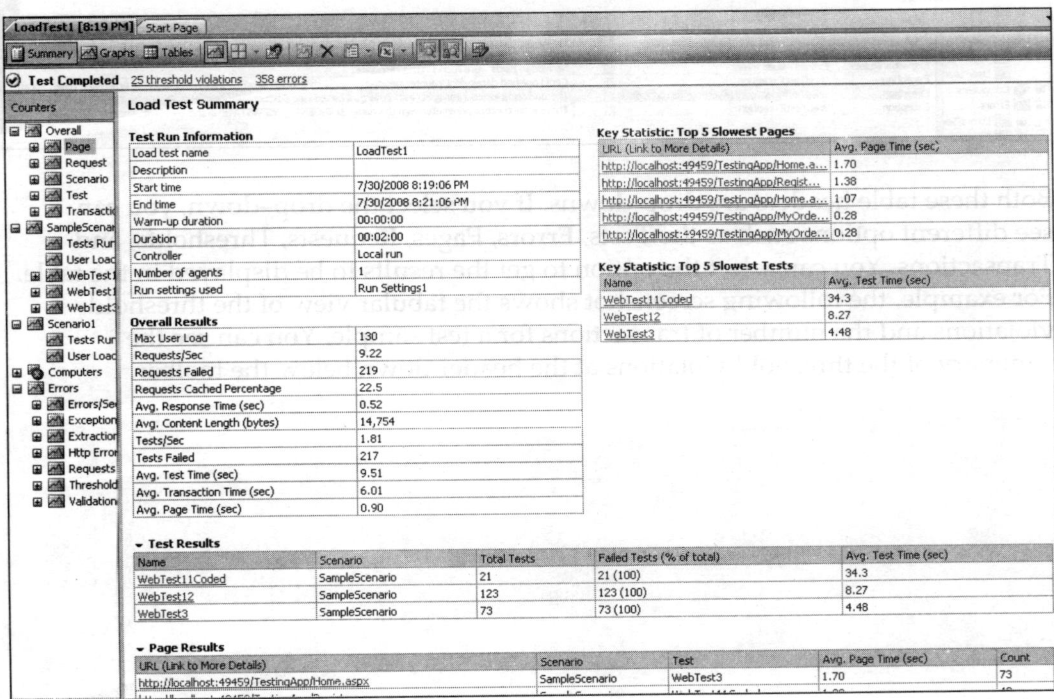

We have seen the Summary view and Graphical view and how to customize the Graphical view by adding custom graphs and counters to it. The tool bar provides a third view to the results, which is the tabular view.

Table view

In this tabular view, you can see the summarized result information in table format. By default there are two tables shown on the right pane with the table on top showing the list of tests run and their run details such as the scenario name, the total number of tests run, tests passed and the number of tests failed, and the time. The second tab down shows the **Errors** that occurred while testing. The details shown are the type of exceptions, the sub type of the exception, the number of exceptions raised, and the detailed error message.

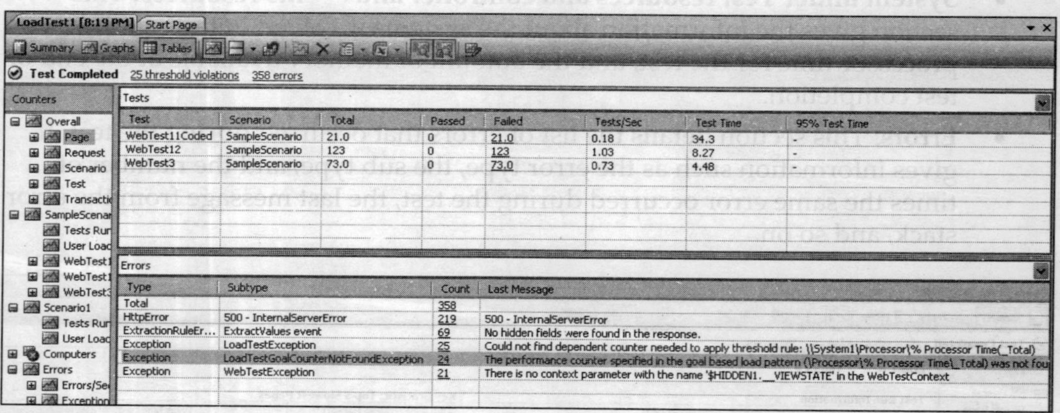

Both these table headers are drop-downs. If you select the drop–down, you can see different options such as the Tests, Errors, Pages, Requests, Thresholds, and Transactions. You can select the option to get the results to be displayed in the table. For example, the following screenshot shows the tabular view of the threshold violations and the number of transactions for a test sample. You can see the summary of the threshold violations at the header down below the toolbar.

The Threshold violation table shows the detailed information about each violation that occurred during the test. The counter category, the counter name, the instance type, and the detailed message explain the reasons for the violation showing the actual value and the threshold value set for the counter.

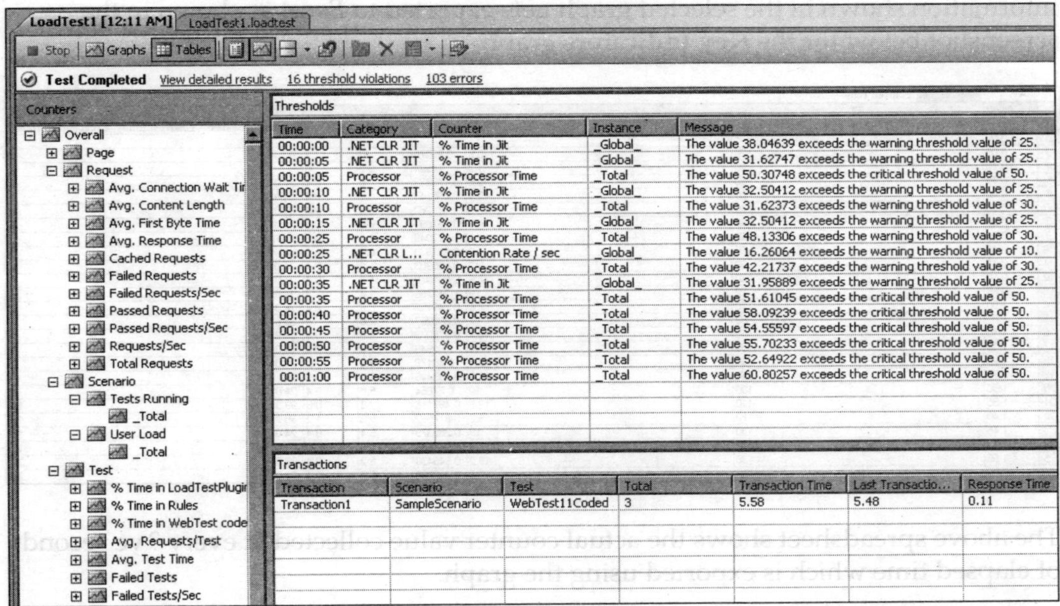

The other details provided by the tabular view are:

- The Requests table view shows the different pages requested during the tests with their statuses and the response time and content length for each request during the test.
- The Pages table view shows the number of pages involved during the test. The result table shows information on the page names, scenario, test names, total pages for the entire test, and page time.

Exporting to Excel

We can export part of the results view to Excel using the **Export to Excel** option in the toolbar of the load test editor. You can select a particular graph from the four different graphs shown here and then select the option to **Export**. All counter information shown in the selected graph gets exported to Excel as shown in the screenshot below for the **Key Indicators** graph.

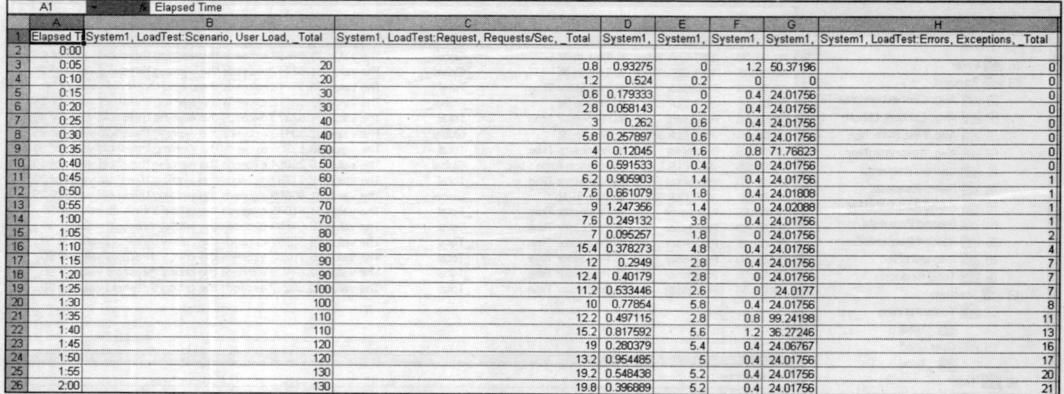

A1 | Elapsed Time

	A	B	C	D	E	F	G	H
1	Elapsed Ti	System1, LoadTest:Scenario, User Load, _Total	System1, LoadTest:Request, Requests/Sec, _Total	System1,	System1,	System1,	System1,	System1, LoadTest:Errors, Exceptions, _Total
2	0:00							
3	0:05	20	0.8	0.93275	0	1.2	50.37196	0
4	0:10	20	1.2	0.524	0.2	0	0	0
5	0:15	30	0.6	0.179333	0	0.4	24.01756	0
6	0:20	30	2.8	0.058143	0.2	0.4	24.01756	0
7	0:25	40	3	0.262	0.6	0.4	24.01756	0
8	0:30	40	5.8	0.257897	0.6	0.4	24.01756	0
9	0:35	50	4	0.12045	1.6	0.8	71.76623	0
10	0:40	50	6	0.591533	0.4	0	24.01756	0
11	0:45	60	6.2	0.905903	1.4	0.4	24.01756	1
12	0:50	60	7.6	0.661079	1.8	0.4	24.01808	1
13	0:55	70	9	1.247356	1.4	0	24.02088	1
14	1:00	70	7.6	0.249132	3.8	0.4	24.01756	1
15	1:05	80	7	0.095257	1.8	0	24.01756	2
16	1:10	80	15.4	0.378273	4.8	0.4	24.01756	4
17	1:15	90	12	0.2949	2.8	0.4	24.01756	7
18	1:20	90	12.4	0.40179	2.8	0	24.01756	7
19	1:25	100	11.2	0.533446	2.6	0	24.0177	7
20	1:30	100	10	0.77854	5.8	0.4	24.01756	8
21	1:35	110	12.2	0.497115	2.8	0.8	99.24198	11
22	1:40	110	15.2	0.817592	5.6	1.2	36.27246	13
23	1:45	120	19	0.280379	5.4	0.4	24.06767	16
24	1:50	120	13.2	0.954485	5	0.4	24.01756	17
25	1:55	130	19.2	0.548438	5.2	0.4	24.01756	20
26	2:00	130	19.8	0.396889	5.2	0.4	24.01756	21

The above spreadsheet shows the actual counter value collected at every ? ve seconds of elapsed time which is exported using the graph.

Summary

This chapter explained the steps involved in creating the load test using sample web tests. We have seen the details of each step and the parameter values to set in each step in the load test creation wizard. There is always a chance of going back to edit the test to change the parameters set or add additional counters and scenarios, which is explained in this chapter. Creating custom performance counters, including the ones for load testing for different systems, setting the threshold rules for counters, and creating rules in different ways are some of the other topics we covered. After creating the load test, we have seen the different methods of running the tests and collecting the test results. And ? nally this chapter explained the multiple ways of looking at the results such as Summary view, Graphical view, and Tabular view, and how useful they are in analyzing the test results. Having all these results in the test repository may not solve our purpose sometimes. So we may have to export the results for detailed analysis purposes. From this chapter, we have also gotten some idea of how to export the test results.

6

Manual, Generic, and Ordered Tests

It is not always possible to conduct the automated tests. There are situations where we may need the manual tests. Manual testing is a document or a text file, which contains a set of steps for the tester to follow. Manual testing can be conducted in between automated tests or anywhere between a series of different tests. For example, after some sets of automated tests, we may have to check log files or configuration information or settings based on the tests executed to continue with the remaining automated tests. We can group all these tests together, order them, and create an ordered test to execute the tests in an order.

In some cases, we may need to execute the tests that are not created by using Visual Studio but required for this current application. In that case, we go for the generic test, which acts as a wrapper for the tests written by some third-party tool and executes that test inside Visual Studio IDE. Once it is wrapped, it is executed normally like any other test inside Visual Studio.

This chapter talks about the manual, generic, and ordered test types in detail. We will go through the steps to create and manage these tests types in VSTS. The following screenshot describes a simple web application, which has a page for the new user registration. The user has to provide the necessary field details. After entering the details, the user will click on the **Register** button provided in the web page to submit all the details so that it gets registered to the site. To confirm this to the user, the system will send a notification with a welcoming email to the registered user. The mail is sent to the email address provided by the user.

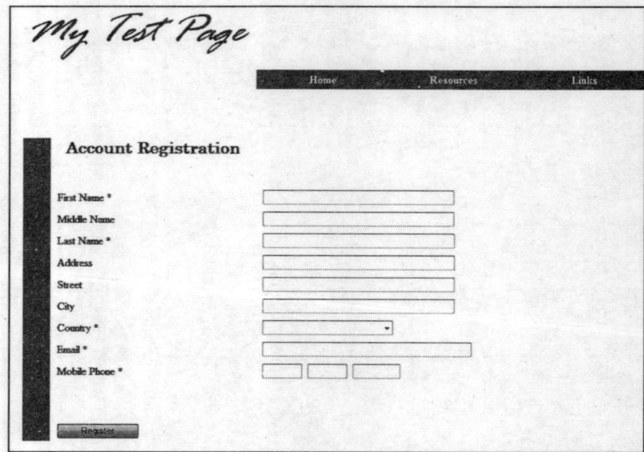

In the application shown in the above screenshot, the entire registration process cannot be automated for testing. For example, the email verification and checking the confirmation email sent by the system will not be automated as the user has to go manually and check the email. This part of the manual testing process will be explained in detail in this chapter.

Manual tests

Manual testing, as described earlier, is the simplest type of testing carried out by the testers without any automation tool. This test may contain a single or multiple tests inside. Manual test type is the best choice to be selected when the test is too difficult or complex to automate, or if the budget allotted for the application is not sufficient for automation.

Visual Studio 2008 supports two types of manual tests file types. One as text file and the other as Microsoft Word.

Let's take our example `TestingApp` application for writing the manual test. You can refer to Chapter 1 for the detailed steps involved in creating the sample test application. Before we start to create the manual tests, we should learn about the two manual test formats in detail.

Manual test using text format

This format helps us to create the test in the text format within Visual Studio IDE. The predefined template is available in Visual Studio for authoring this test. This template provides the structure for creating the tests. This format has the extension of `.mtx`. Visual Studio servers act as an editor for this test format.

For creating this test in Visual Studio, either create a new test project and then add the test or select the menu option **Test | New Test...** and then choose the option to add the test to a new project. Now create the test using the menu option and select **Manual Test (Text Format)** from the available list as shown in the picture below. You can see the list **Add to Test Project** drop-down, which lists the different options to add the test to a test project.

If you have not yet created the test project and selected the option to create the test, the drop-down option selected will create a new test project for the test to be added. If you have a test project already created, then we can also see that project in the list to get this new test added to the project. We can choose any option as per our need. For this sample, let us create a new test project in C#. So the first option from the drop-down of **Add to Test Project** would be selected in this case. After selecting the option, provide the name for the new test project the system will ask for. Let us name it **TestingAppTest** project.

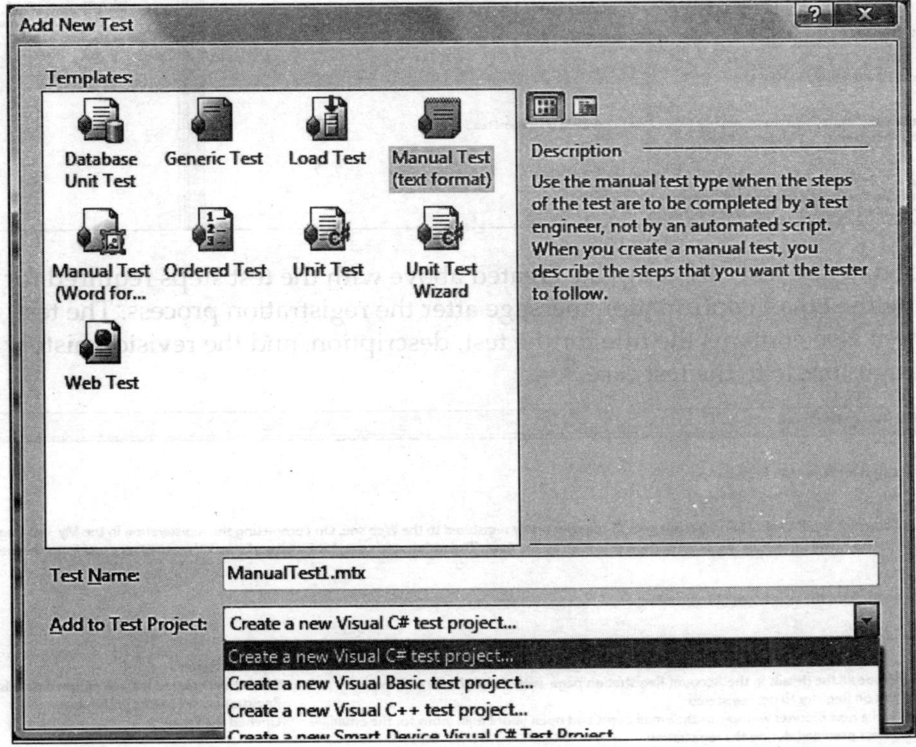

Now you can see the project getting created under the solution and the test template is also added to the test project as shown next. The template contains the detailed information for each section. This will help the tester or whoever is writing the test case to write the steps required for this test.

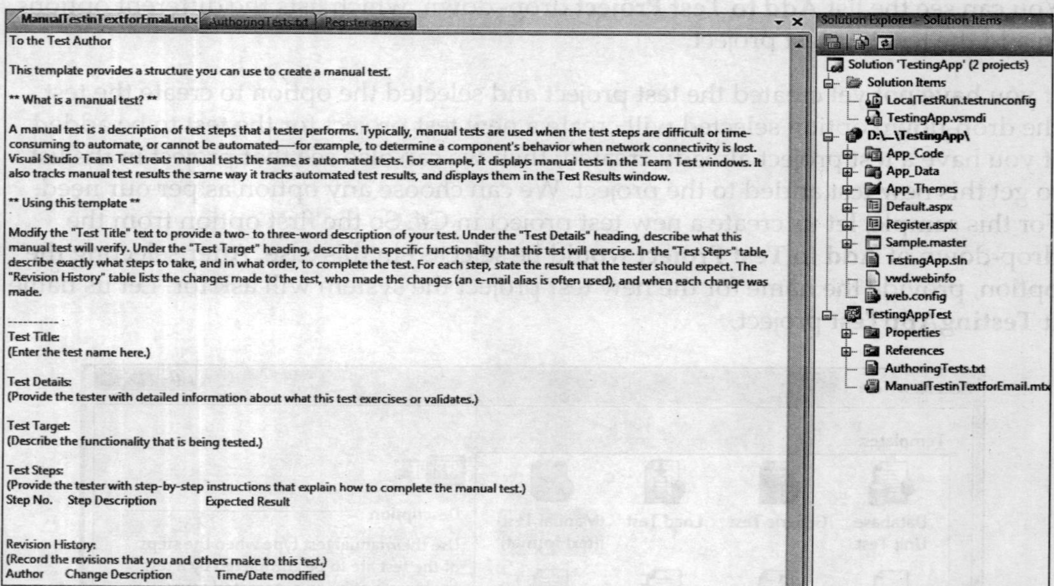

Now update the test case template created above with the test steps required for checking the email confirmation message after the registration process. The test document also contains the title for the test, description, and the revision history for the changes made to the test case.

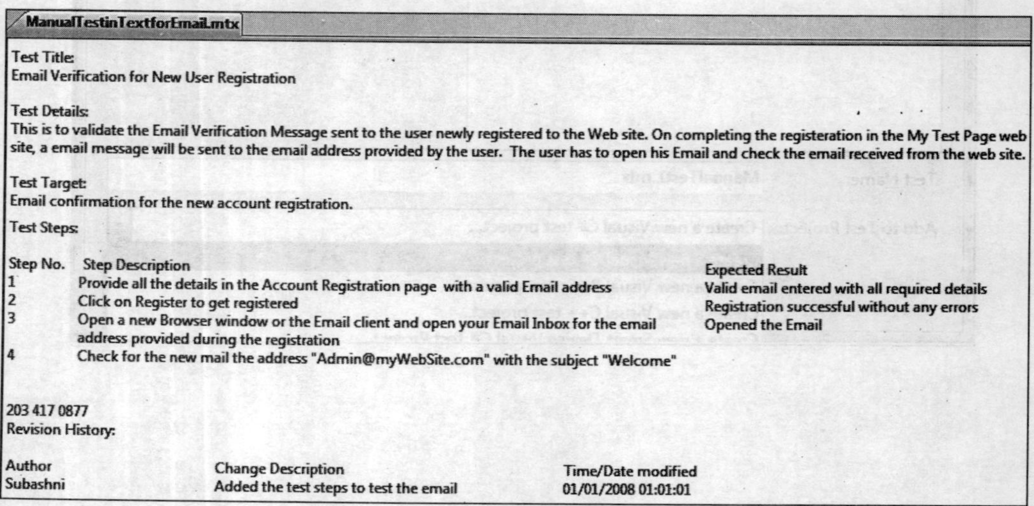

Before executing the test and looking into the details of the run and the properties of the test, we will create the same test using Microsoft Word format as described in the next section.

Manual test using Microsoft Word format

This is similar to the manual test that was created using text format, except that the file type is Microsoft Word with extension `.mht`. While creating the manual test choose the template **Manual Test (Word format)** instead of the **Manual Test (Text Format)** as explained in the previous section. This option is available only if Microsoft Word is installed in the system. This will launch the Word template using the MS Word installed (version 2003 or later) in the system for writing the test details as shown in the following screenshot. The Word format helps us to have richer formatting capabilities with different fonts, colors, and styles for the text with graphic images and tables embedded for the test.

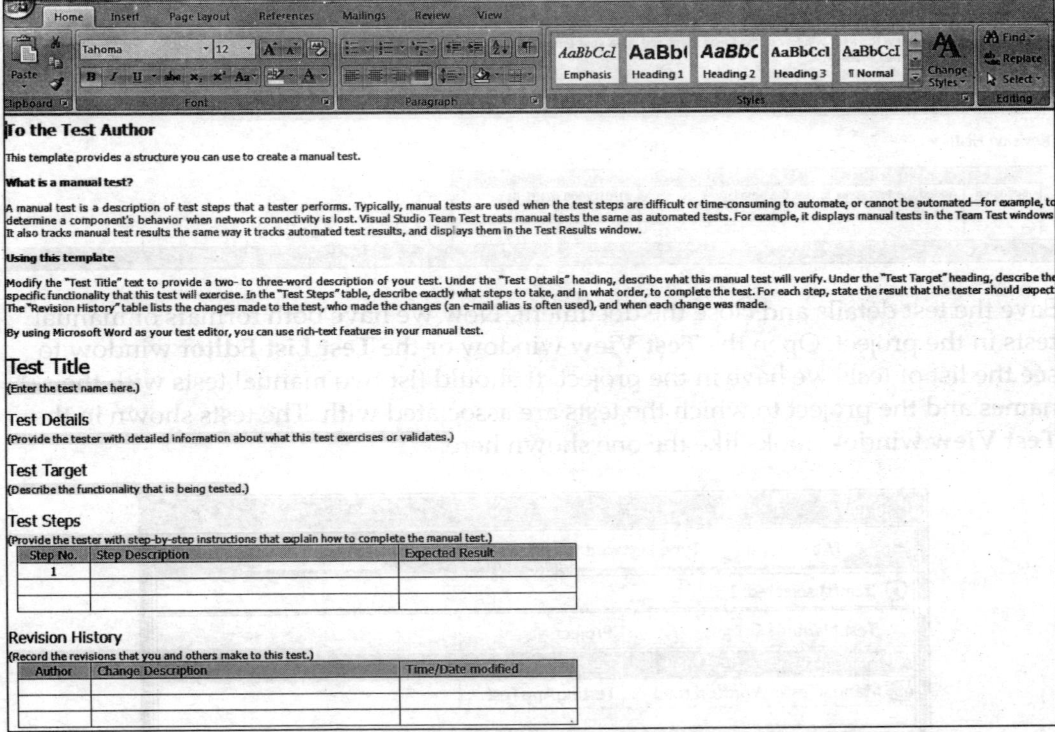

To the Test Author

This template provides a structure you can use to create a manual test.

What is a manual test?

A manual test is a description of test steps that a tester performs. Typically, manual tests are used when the test steps are difficult or time-consuming to automate, or cannot be automated—for example, to determine a component's behavior when network connectivity is lost. Visual Studio Team Test treats manual tests the same as automated tests. For example, it displays manual tests in the Team Test windows. It also tracks manual test results the same way it tracks automated test results, and displays them in the Test Results window.

Using this template

Modify the "Test Title" text to provide a two- to three-word description of your test. Under the "Test Details" heading, describe what this manual test will verify. Under the "Test Target" heading, describe the specific functionality that this test will exercise. In the "Test Steps" table, describe exactly what steps to take, and in what order, to complete the test. For each step, state the result that the tester should expect. The "Revision History" table lists the changes made to the test, who made the changes (an e-mail alias is often used), and when each change was made.

By using Microsoft Word as your test editor, you can use rich-text features in your manual test.

Test Title

(Enter the test name here.)

Test Details

(Provide the tester with detailed information about what this test exercises or validates.)

Test Target

(Describe the functionality that is being tested.)

Test Steps

(Provide the tester with step-by-step instructions that explain how to complete the manual test.)

Step No.	Step Description	Expected Result
1		

Revision History

(Record the revisions that you and others make to this test.)

Author	Change Description	Time/Date modified

This document not only provides the template but also the help information for each and every section so that the tester can easily understand the sections and write the test cases. This help information is provided in both the Word and Text format of the manual tests.

In the test document seen in previous screenshot, we can fill the **Test Details, Test Target, Test Steps,** and **Revision History** similar to the one we did for the text format. The completed test case test document will look like this:

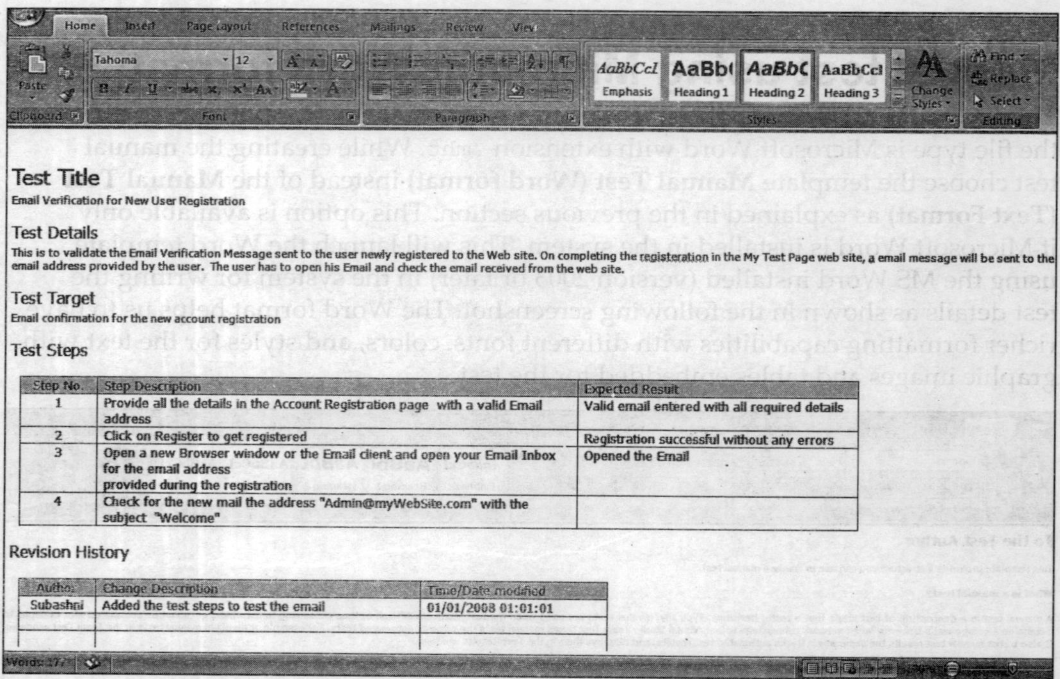

Test Title

Email Verification for New User Registration

Test Details

This is to validate the Email Verification Message sent to the user newly registered to the Web site. On completing the registeration in the My Test Page web site, a email message will be sent to the email address provided by the user. The user has to open his Email and check the email received from the web site.

Test Target

Email confirmation for the new account registration

Test Steps

Step No.	Step Description	Expected Result
1	Provide all the details in the Account Registration page with a valid Email address	Valid email entered with all required details
2	Click on Register to get registered	Registration successful without any errors
3	Open a new Browser window or the Email client and open your Email Inbox for the email address provided during the registration	Opened the Email
4	Check for the new mail the address "Admin@myWebSite.com" with the subject "Welcome"	

Revision History

Author	Change Description	Time/Date modified
Subashni	Added the test steps to test the email	01/01/2008 01:01:01

Save the test details and close the document. Now we have both formats of manual tests in the project. Open the **Test View** window or the **Test List Editor** window to see the list of tests we have in the project. It should list two manual tests with their names and the project to which the tests are associated with. The tests shown in the **Test View** window looks like the one shown here:

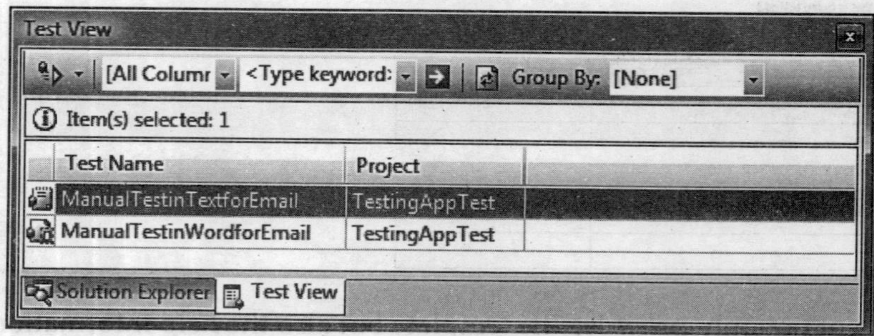

The same tests list shown by the **Test List Editor** would look like the one shown below. The additional properties like test list name, the project name the test belongs to, is also shown in the list editor. There are options for each test either to run or get added to any particular list.

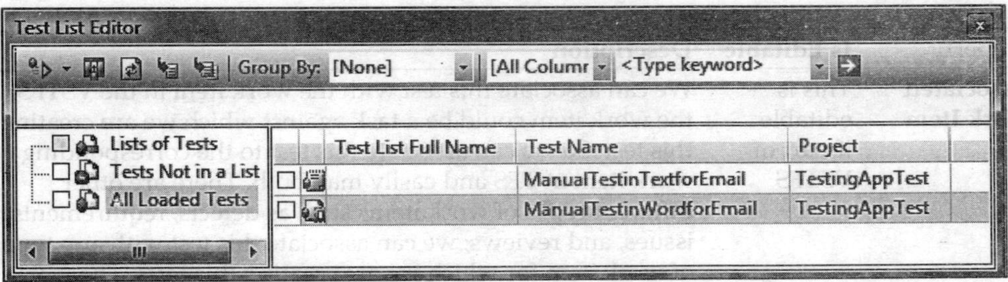

Manual tests also have other properties, which we can make use of during testing. These properties can be seen in the **Properties** window, which can be opened by choosing the manual test either in the **Test View** or in the **Test List Editor** windows by right-clicking the test and selecting the **Properties** option. The same window can also be opened by choosing the menu option **View | Properties** window. Both formats of manual testing have the same set of properties.

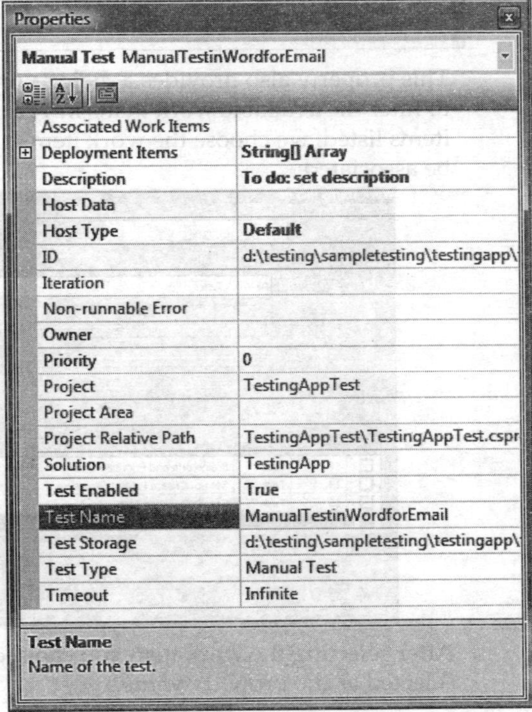

Some of these properties are editable while some are read-only, which will be set by the application based on the test type. Some properties are directly related to TFS. The VSTFS is the integrated collaboration server, which combines team portal, work item tracking, build management, process guidance, and version control into a unified server.

Property	Is Editable	Description
Associated Work Item	This is editable if part of VSTFS	We can associate this test with the work item in the VSTFS; the work item could be a task against which we are creating this test. So we can associate this test to the corresponding work item in TFS and easily map both. There are other different types of work items such as defects, requirements, issues, and reviews; we can associate this test with any type of work item for which we are creating this tests. The work item of type **Task** in TFS would look like this:

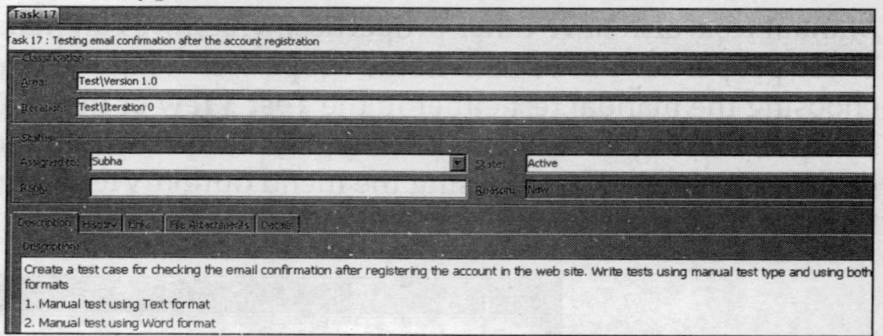

This property also provides a dialog window, which helps us to filter the available work items in TFS; based on the work items listed, we choose the work item to which this test has to be associated:

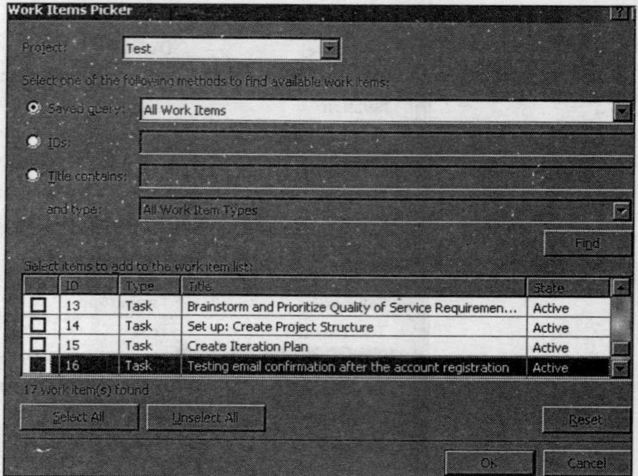

After selecting the work item you can see the work item **ID** is selected as the property value.

Property	Is Editable	Description
Deployment Items	Editable	Files or folders that need to be deployed along with this test; we need to give the full path of the files or folders that we are going to deploy. When **...** button is pressed it opens the **String Collection Editor** dialog box. In the string collection editor, enter the path of the files and folders Each line of text is considered as a separate string String Collection Editor Enter the strings in the collection (one per line): D:\SampleTesting\Deploy\Settings.XML D:\SampleTesting\Deploy\Readme.txt OK Cancel
Description	Editable	This property is used for giving the detailed description of the test
Host Data	Editable	This explains the custom data to pass to the host adapter; this is very useful in deploying the test under a different host. By by default, the test is hosted under `VSTestHost.exe`
Host Type	Editable	This property explains the test execution environment It contains the value **Default**, which means the default test host environment (`VSTestHost.exe`)
ID	Read-only	This property gives us the unique name of the test; it gives the full path of the manual test, that is, where it resides

Property	Is Editable	Description
Iteration	This is editable if part of VSTFS	This property explains which iteration in the software project life cycle these tests belongs to; these values are based on the iterations set in the TFS. This property will provide a dialog with the list of iterations in TFS. From this, we can select the iteration for which we want to associate this test.
Non-runnable Error	Read-only	This property explains the reason of the manual test that cannot be executed in this test run. Even though a test is included in a test project, if this test cannot be executed in this test for some reason, then we can enter the reason in this property This property will be empty if the test is executable for this test run
Owner	Editable	This gives the name of the owner for the test
Priority	Editable	This property explains the priority of the test; this is an integer value explaning the relative importance of the test and tells which test needs to be executed first
Project	Read-only	This is the test project name to which the test belongs
Project Area	This is Editable if part of VSTFS	This property maps to the Area Path in the VSTFS. This property also provides the dialog similar to the Iteration with list of Areas created in TFS; from the list we can select the area path for this test

Property	Is Editable	Description
Project Relative Path	Read-only	This property tells the file name of the project where the test resides; the path is relative to the location of the solution
Solution	Read-only	This property denotes the name of the solution that contains the test project to which this test belongs
Test Enabled	Editable	This property allows us to make a test disabled for this test run; if you set this property as **False** this test won't be available for execution The default value is **True**
Test Name	Read-only	To specify the name of the test.
Test Storage	Read-only	This property gives us the complete path of this test in the hard disk; for manual tests, this property is the same as the test **ID** property
Test Type	Read-only	This property tells us the type of the test as to whether the test is manual, or load, or web, or generic, or ordered In this case, the value displayed is **Manual**; using this property we can filter to see all the tests that belong to the manual test type
Timeout	Read-only	This property tells us about the timeout value for the test, that is, it will specify how long the test can take to run before it is marked as failed, and aborted For a manual test, this property is **Infinite** a as manual test doesn't have a timeout value

After selecting the properties for the selected tests, the property window would look like the one shown below. These properties are the same for a manual test with the Word format.

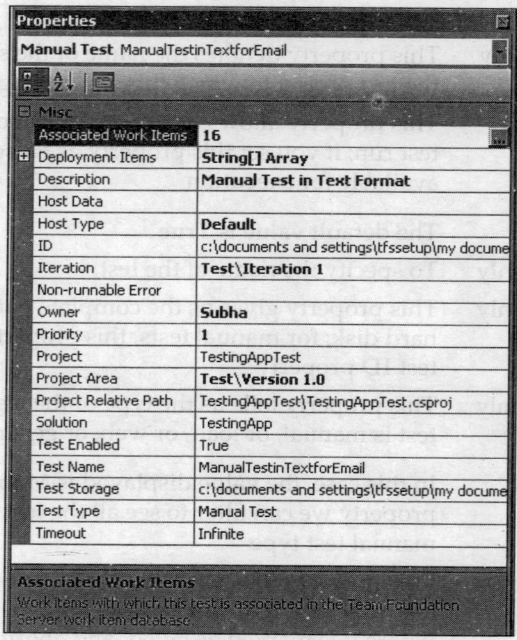

Some of these properties are also useful in grouping or ordering the tests in the Test View window and the Test List Editor. Open the **Test View** window and on the column header of the window right-click and select the **Add/Remove Columns...** option.

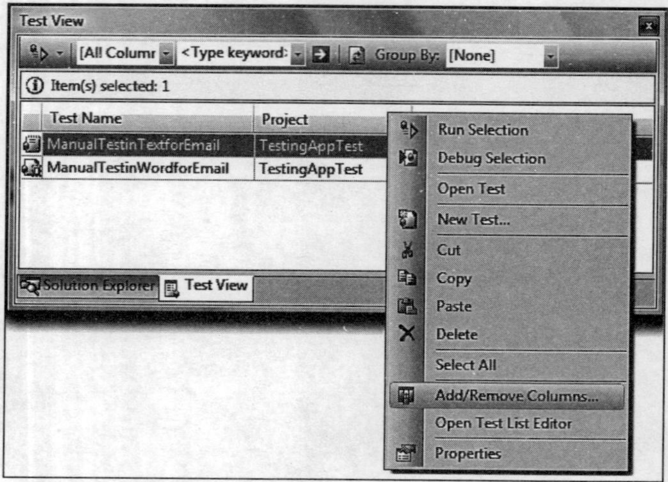

This selection would open a dialog with all the properties of the tests from which we can select the properties to be listed in the **Test View** or the **Test List Editor** window.

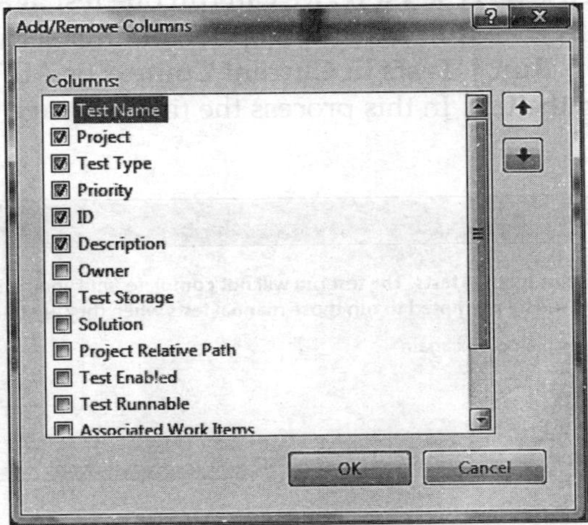

On clicking **OK,** we can see the selected properties listed in the **Test View**. Now we can use these values to sort the tests listed in the grid.

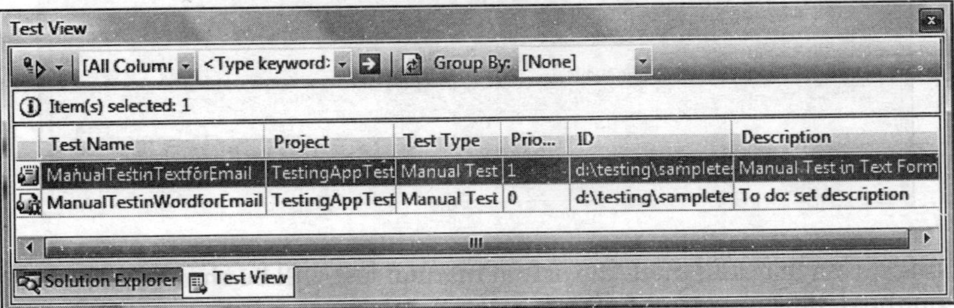

Running a manual test

We are now ready with the test project, and manual test cases in different formats by setting the properties. We should now start with testing the test application by running the manual tests. Let us consider that the tests for creating the new user account using sample web application is complete, and now we should test the email confirmation sent to the email address provided during the account creation.

We can run the tests from the **Test View** window or the **Test List Editor** window. In case of multiple tests, we can use the Test List Editor so that we can select all the tests at once and run it. In case of **Test View**, we can run one test at a time. Select the test and right-click and select the **Run Selection** option or after selecting the tests choose the menu option **Test | Run | Tests in Current Context** or **All Tests in Solution**. This will start running the test. In this process the first message given by the system would be:

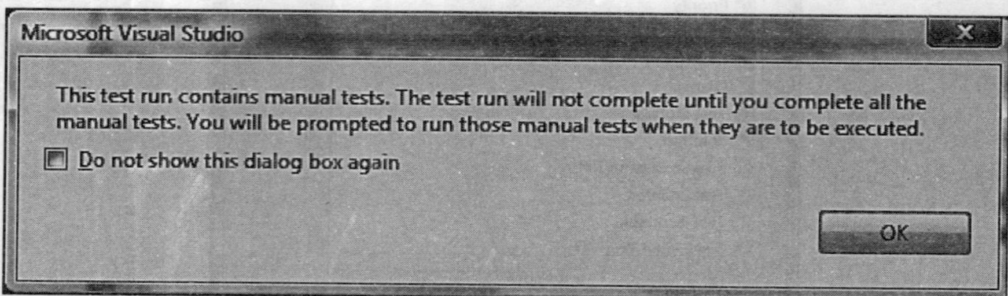

Click **OK** to accept the message, and upon accepting the message you would see another message saying the test is ready for execution.

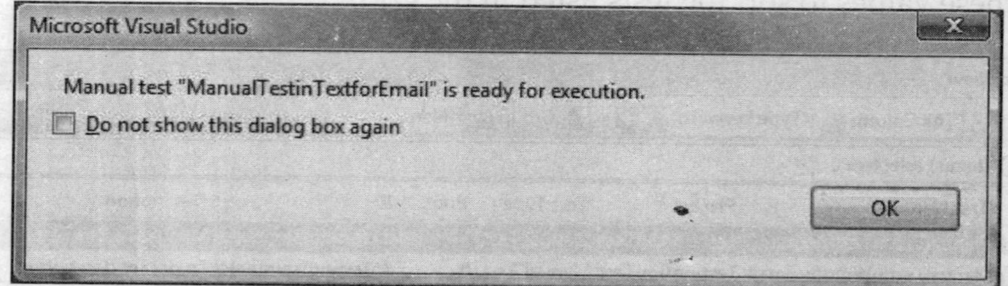

When this message is accepted, the actual manual test will be shown to the tester. Based on the details provided in the test, the tester has to follow the steps mentioned in the test. In this example, the tester has to open the mail client that was provided during the registration process and check whether notification mail is there in the inbox.

Before actually completing the test, let us look at the **Test Results** window. Open the window using the menu option **Test | Windows | Test Results.** By default, it will show the result window with the current test status. Since we have started the test but not completed it yet, the status will be shown pending. You can check the status of all the tests run so far by changing the option in the **Test Results** window and selecting the option **All** in the **Select Run** drop-down.

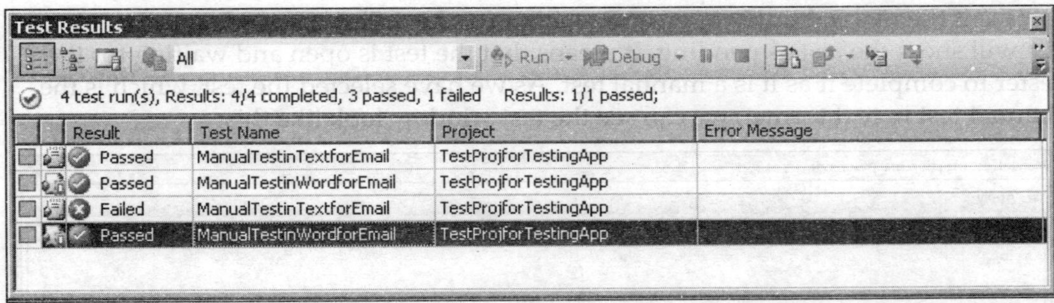

In the **Test Results** window shown above, we can see different statuses for the tests run. They are also shown with different images to represent the status:

- **Aborted**: This one denotes that the test has been aborted during the run.
- **Failed**: This status denotes that the test run has failed because of some reason.
- **Passed**: This is the status for a successful run of the test with an expected result.
- **Pending**: This means that the test is still in progress. It has neither completed, nor failed or aborted. It is waiting for the tester or system to complete the test.

The individual test can be run from this window by selecting the test result from the Test Result drop-down. Choose the checkbox option against the test result and rerun the test using the **Run** option in the toolbar.

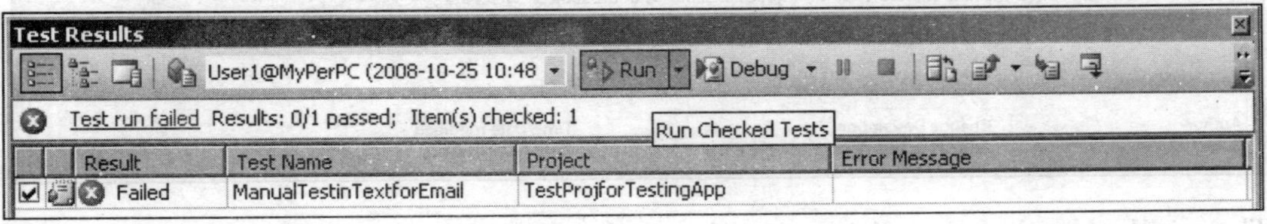

In case if the manual test is open and waiting for the tester to complete it, Test run list will show the test as pending. It means that the test is open and waiting for the tester to complete it as it is a manual test. As we have selected the test, which is the manual test in text format, we can see the test window look like this:

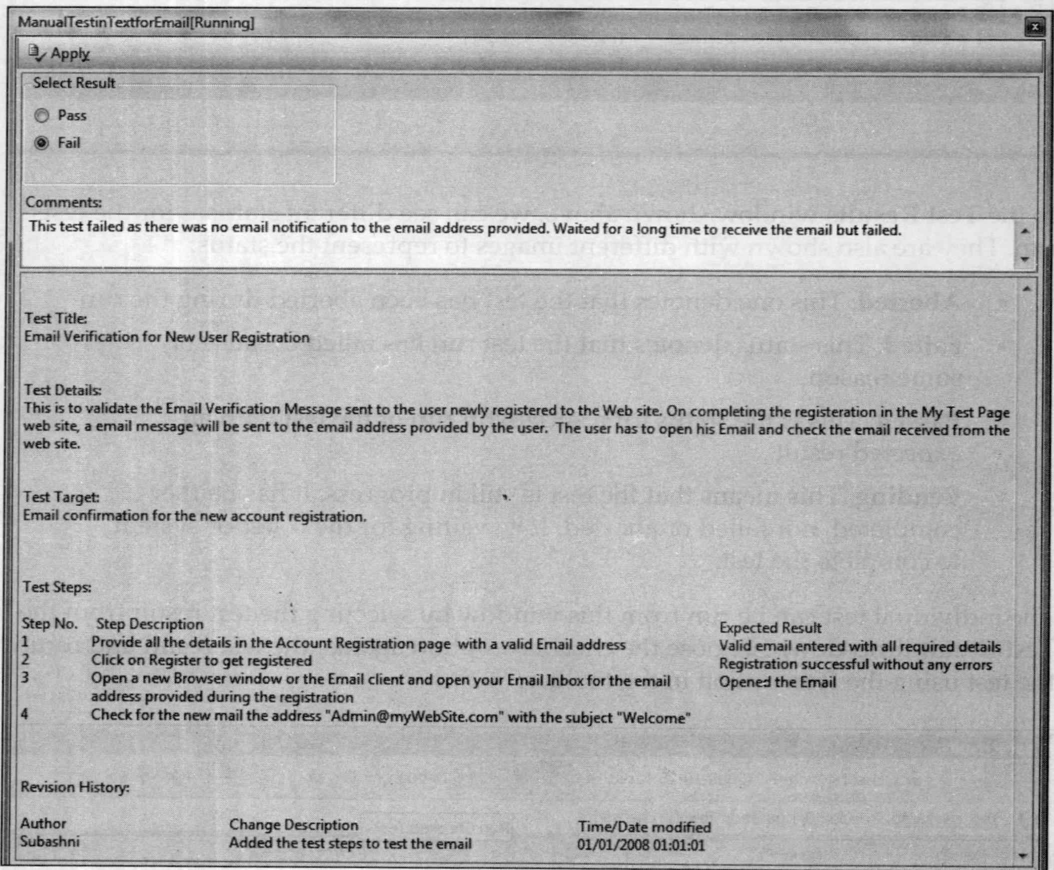

The window in the preceding screenshot is the same that we created during the design time of the manual test in text except the **Comments**, **Select result**, and **Apply** options. These are the options for submitting the result of the manual test performed by the tester. For example, in the test result shown in the preceding screenshot, you can see the checkbox **Fail** selected and the comment says that the email is not received. It means that the test has failed. So the tester has chosen the option **Fail** and put in the comments about the result from this test. After entering all the details, the tester has to complete the test by clicking the apply button on top left corner of the test window. Once the **Apply** button is pressed, the test window becomes read-only, and the test is completed. Now the manual test in the text format is executed with the result Failed. We can also see the status in the **Test Results** window.

The next manual test format in Word is almost similar to the text format, the only difference being the test opens in Microsoft Word, where we can have additional formatting and documentation features. The test run of the manual test in Word would look like this:

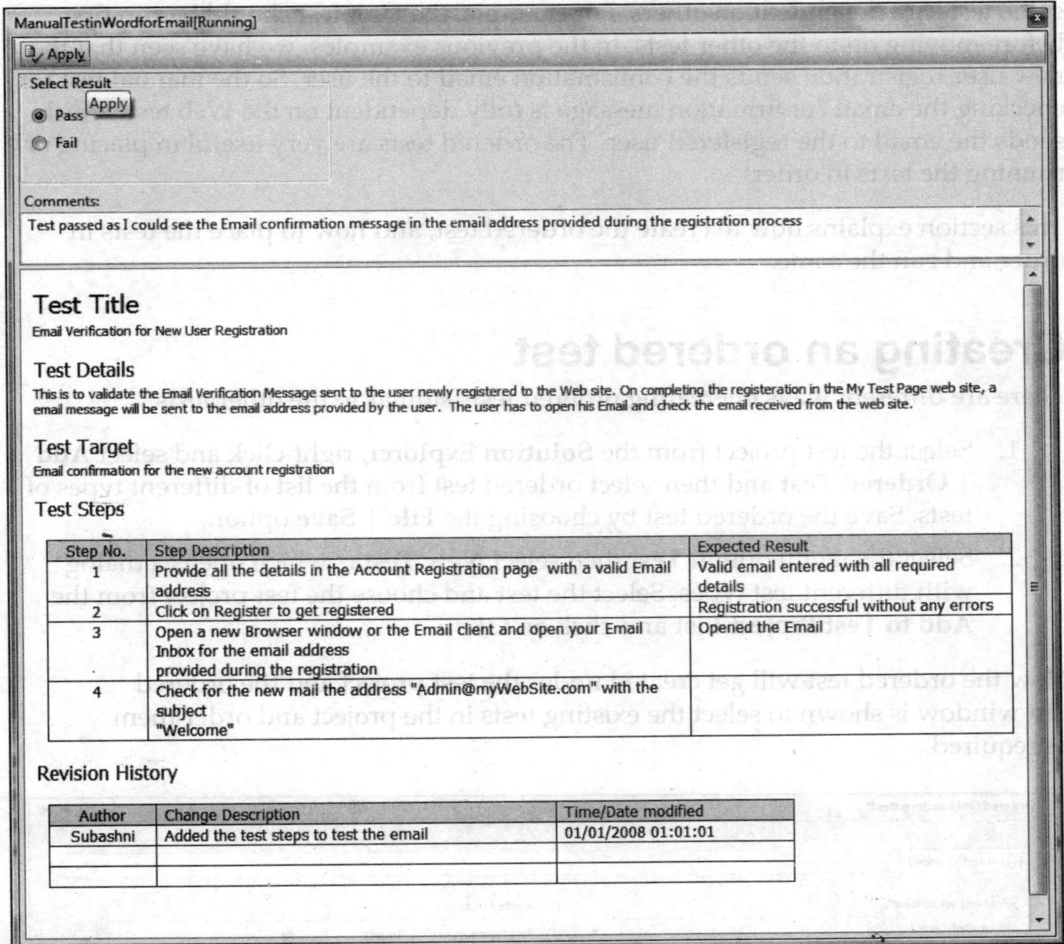

Test Title

Email Verification for New User Registration

Test Details

This is to validate the Email Verification Message sent to the user newly registered to the Web site. On completing the registeration in the My Test Page web site, a email message will be sent to the email address provided by the user. The user has to open his Email and check the email received from the web site.

Test Target

Email confirmation for the new account registration

Test Steps

Step No.	Step Description	Expected Result
1	Provide all the details in the Account Registration page with a valid Email address	Valid email entered with all required details
2	Click on Register to get registered	Registration successful without any errors
3	Open a new Browser window or the Email client and open your Email Inbox for the email address provided during the registration	Opened the Email
4	Check for the new mail the address "Admin@myWebSite.com" with the subject "Welcome"	

Revision History

Author	Change Description	Time/Date modified
Subashni	Added the test steps to test the email	01/01/2008 01:01:01

Manual tests are used for tracking the test steps, history, and the results. The actual testing of the application is done by the tester. This indirectly means that these tests cannot be run remotely, or by using the command line execution, as it always requires human intervention to carry out the testing. In case this is required, the tester has to note the steps and then go to the remote machine and execute the test as per the steps and then come back and apply with the results.

Ordered tests

In the previous chapters we have seen different types of tests that we can perform on applications using Visual Studio 2008. Let us say we have created Unit tests, Web tests, Load tests, and other different types of tests. We might have a situation where some tests are dependent on others. For example, the Unit test should be run first before moving on to the other tests. In the previous examples, we have seen that the new user registration sends the confirmation email to the user. So the manual test for checking the email confirmation message is fully dependent on the Web test, which sends the email to the registered user. The ordered tests are very useful in placing or running the tests in order.

This section explains how to create the ordered test, and how to place the tests in order and run the same.

Creating an ordered test

There are different ways of creating ordered tests similar to the other tests:

1. Select the test project from the **Solution Explorer**, right-click and select **Add | Ordered Test** and then select ordered test from the list of different types of tests. Save the ordered test by choosing the **File | Save** option.
2. Select the menu option **Test** then select **New Test...**, which opens a dialog with different test types. Select the test and choose the test project from the **Add to Test Project List** and click on **OK**.

Now the ordered test will get created under the test project and the ordered test window is shown to select the existing tests in the project and order them as required.

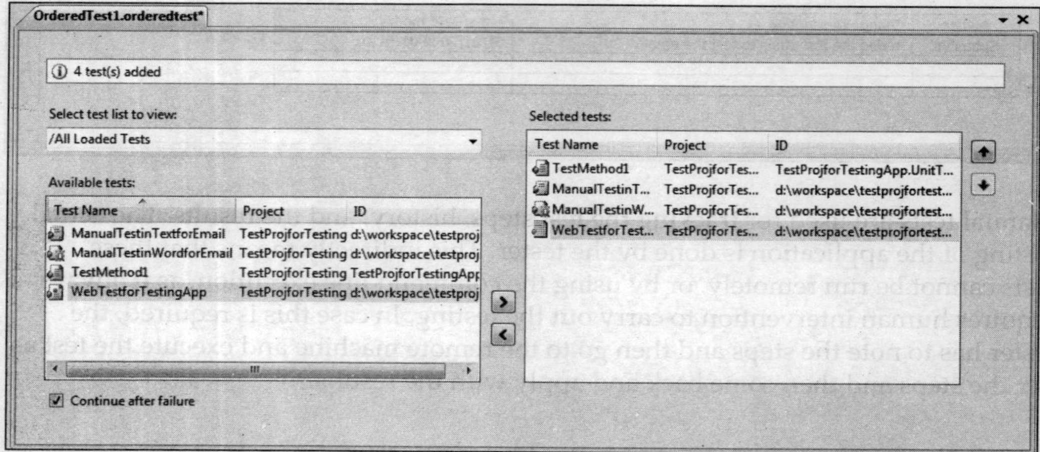

The above window shows different options for ordering the tests.

The first line is the status bar, which shows the number of tests selected for the ordered test.

The **Select test list to view** drop-down has the option to choose the display of tests in the available test lists. This drop-down has the default **/All Loaded Tests**, which displays all the tests under the project. The other options in the drop-down are **Lists of Tests** and **Tests Not in a List**. The List of Tests will display the test lists created using the Test List Editor. It is easier to include the number of tests grouped together and order them. The next option **Tests Not in a List** will display the available tests, which are not part of any test lists.

The **Available tests** list displays all the tests from the project based on the option chosen in the drop-down.

The **Selected tests** contains the tests that are selected from the available tests list to be placed in order.

The two right and left arrows are used for selecting and unselecting the tests from the **Available tests** list to the **Selected Tests** list. We can also select multiple tests by pressing the *Ctrl* key and selecting the tests.

The up-down arrows on the right of the **Selected Tests** list are used for moving up or down the tests in the **Selected tests** list.

The last option **Continue after failure** checkbox at the bottom of the window is to override the default behavior of the ordered tests aborting the execution after the failure of any test. The tests in the order are dependent on the previous tests run result. If the option **Continue after failure** is unchecked, and if any test in the order fails, then all remaining tests will get aborted. In case the tests are not dependent, we can check this option and override the default behavior to allow the application to continue running the remaining tests in order.

Properties of an ordered test

Ordered tests have properties similar to the other test types, in addition to some specific properties. To view the properties, select the ordered test in **Test View** or **Test List Editor** window and right-click and select the **Properties** option. The **Properties** dialog box displays the available properties for the ordered test.

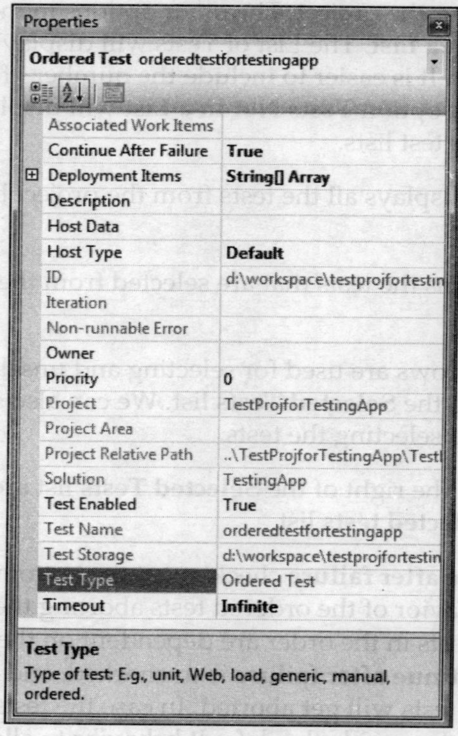

The above screenshot depicts that most of the properties are the same as the properties of the other test types. We can associate this test with the TFS work items, iterations, and area.

Executing an ordered test

An ordered test can be run like any other test. Open the **Test View** window or the **Test List Editor** and select the ordered test from the list, then right-click and choose the **Run Selection** option from Test View or **Run Checked Tests** from the **Test List Editor**. Once the option is selected, we can see the tests running one after the other in the same order in which they are placed in the ordered test. After the execution of the ordered tests, the **Test Results** window will show the status of the ordered test. If any of the tests in the list fails, then the ordered test status would be **Failed.** The summary of the status of all the tests in the ordered test is shown below the toolbar. The sample test application had five tests in the ordered tests, but two of them failed.

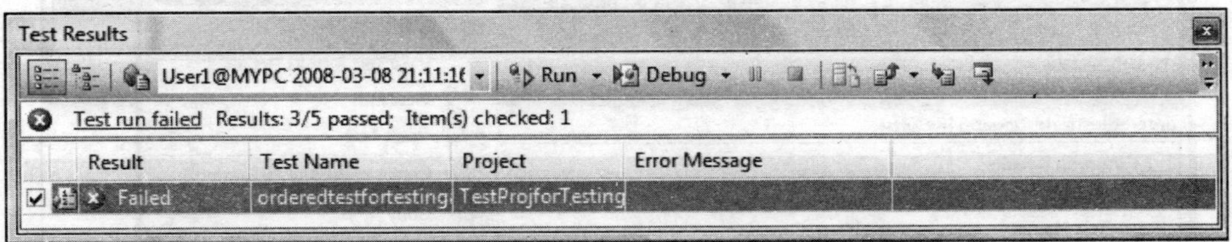

Clicking the **Test run failed** hyperlink in the status bar will show a detailed view of the test run summary:

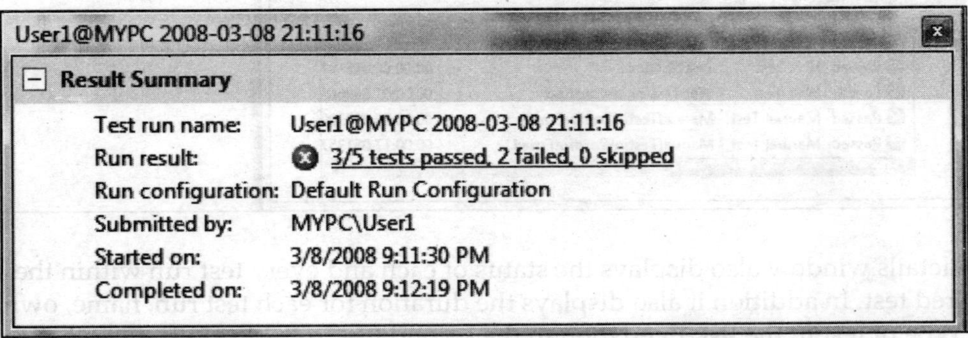

The **Test Results** window also provides detailed information about the tests run so far. To get these details, choose the test from the **Test Results** window and then right-click and choose the option **View Test Results Details,** which will open the details window and the common results information such as test name, result, duration of the test run, start time, and end time.

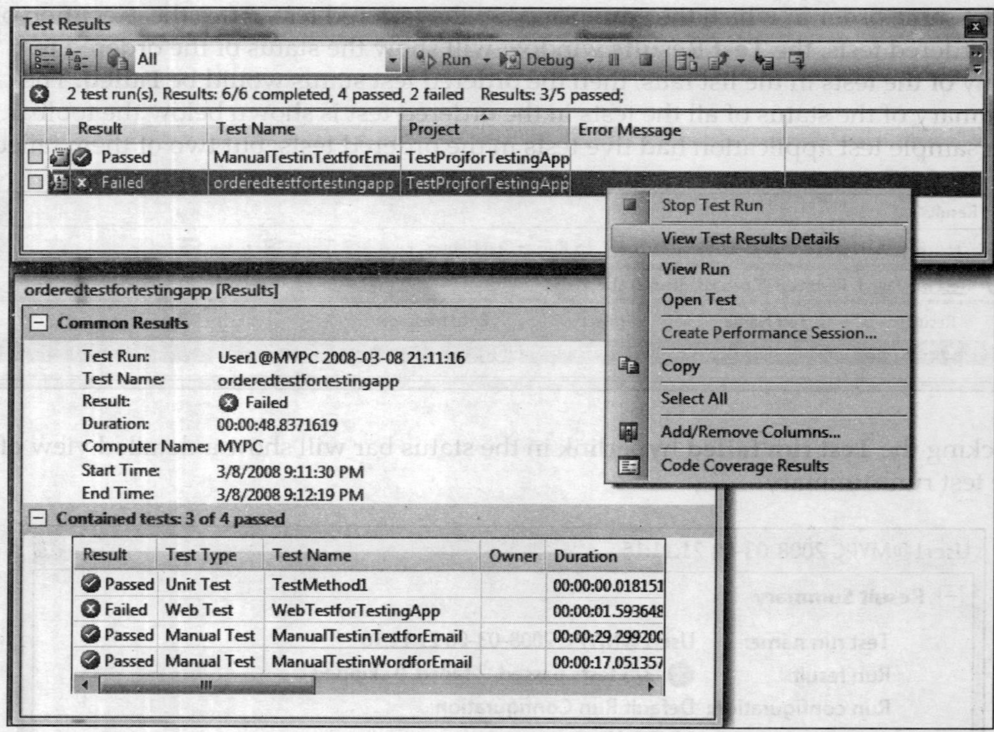

The details window also displays the status of each and every test run within the ordered test. In addition it also displays the duration for each test run, name, owner, and type of test in the list. Even though the second test in the list fails, the other tests continue to execute as if the **Continue after failure** option were checked.

Generic tests

Generic tests are ways to integrate third-party tests into Visual Studio. There are situations where we would be dependent on third-party tests because of business requirements or because those tests were created when Visual Studio was not available in the organization. The generic tests act as wrappers for executing these third-party tests within the boundary of Visual Studio. Once it is wrapped, we can execute these generic tests like any other test in Visual Studio IDE.

The third-party tests should adhere to the following conditions to be categorized under the generic tests in Visual Studio:

1. We must be able to execute the third-party tests from the command line.
2. The third-party tool must return a Boolean value of either True or False when executed in the command line.
3. It is preferred that the third-party test tool writes an XML file, which contains the list of individual tests. The XML file is the summary results file, which contains the details of all the tests run.

Creating a generic tests

This is similar to any other test in Visual Studio. Either use the **Test** menu and choose the options of creating a new test or right-click on the test project in the **Solution Explorer** and add a generic test, or open the **Test View** window and then right-click from there and add a new test. Then provide a name for the generic test. For this example, name it **GenericTestforThirdPartyTest**. A new window opens to set the values or parameters for the generic test.

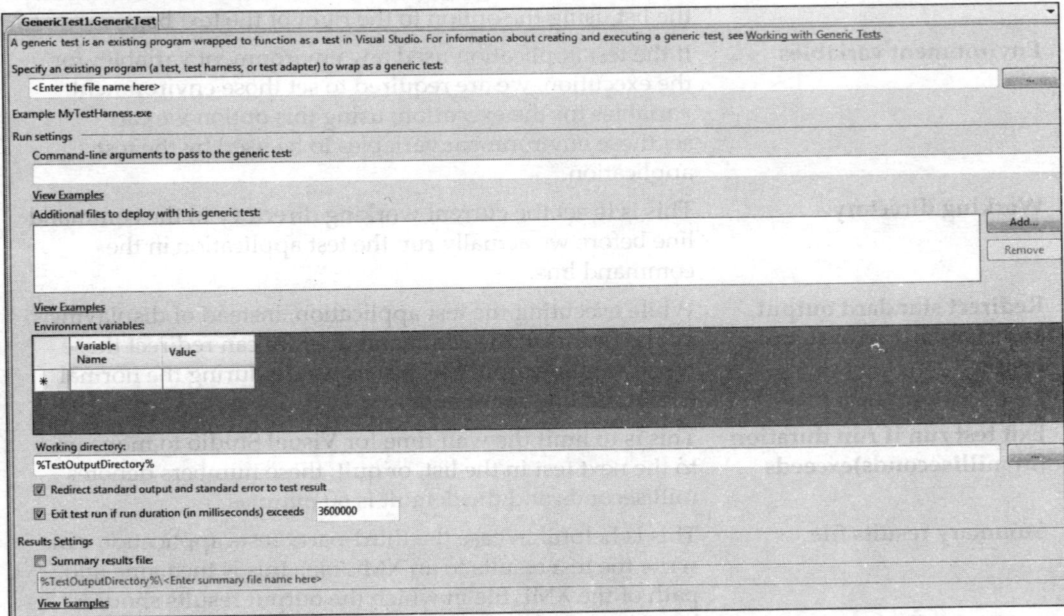

You can see from the form that all the values we have to enter are for executing another test application from the command line by passing parameters. For a command line execution , we may have to set the environment variables, execution parameters, set the working directory, copy or deploy some files, and set the output directory and the file. All these details can be set using the generic test.

The following table explains the different options and their uses:

Parameters for Generic Test	Description
Specify an existing program	This is the name and path of the third-party test application to be executed at the command line; it is the name of the executable application. We can also use the browse button to the right of the text box to find the application and select it.
Command-line arguments to pass to the generic test	This is the place to specify the command line parameters required for the third-party test application; these parameters totally depend on the testing tool's expected value.
Additional files to deploy with this generic test	In some cases, there might be other files required for this test execution; add those files or remove the selected files in the list using the option to the right of the text box.
Environment variables	If the test application used any environment variables for the execution, we are required to set those environment variables for the execution; using this option we can set those environment variables to be used by the test application.
Working directory	This is to set the current working directory in the command line before we actually run the test application in the command line.
Redirect standard output and standard error to test result	While executing the test application, instead of displaying all the results at the command line, we can redirect those results to the output file, just as we do during the normal command line commands.
Exit test run if run duration (in milliseconds)exceeds	This is to limit the wait time for Visual Studio to move on to the next test in the list, or quit; these numbers denotes milliseconds and the default is 60 minutes.
Summary results file	This is helpful in case the third-party tests application can write the test results to an XML file; this is the name and path of the XML file in which the output results should be written. If the number of tests in the test application is more in number, then it will be easy to track the result of these individual tests by having the results in the XML file. Not only the result but also detailed information of the test result would be written to this file.

The following is an example of a generic test that executes the **Test.exe**, which is a third-party test application capable of writing the output to the XML file. The command-line parameter for this application is also provided along with the supporting file to be deployed, which is the **Readme.txt** file. You can see the **Output.xml**, which is to store the output details of the test by the **Test.exe**.

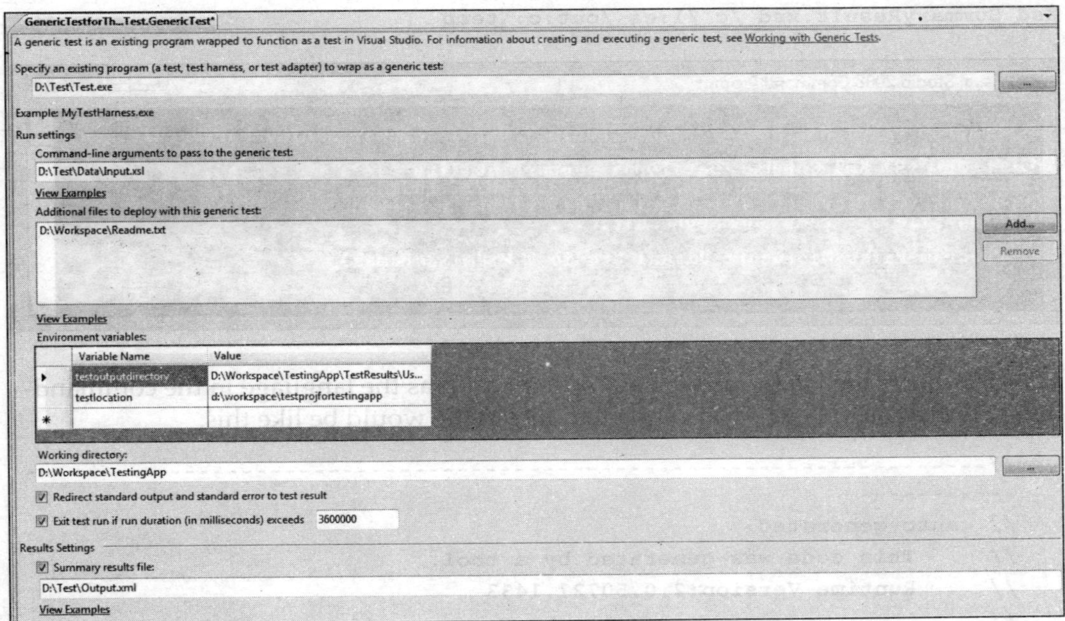

Summary results file

When we execute the above generic test, the third-party **Test.exe** will get executed at the command line. The generic test by Visual Studio will get the result back from the third-party **Test.exe** application, which is a single test. But we do not know how many tests are executed internally within the test, and it is not easy to track the results of all the tests of the third-party application using the generic test. But Visual Studio supports the third-party application with a summary results file, which can be used by the application to write the details of the internal test results.

The third-party applications can make use of the class file, which can be generated by using the schema file provided by Visual Studio. The schema file is located at the Visual Studio command-line. If Visual Studio is installed in the default `c:` drive, then the path would be:

```
C:\Program Files\Microsoft Visual Studio 9.0\Xml\Schemas\
SummaryResult.xsd
```

The class file can be generated from this schema file using the `xsd.exe` utility on any .NET supported languages. The following is an example for generating the default **SummaryResult.cs** class file out of an XSD file. The output folder should exist before the command can be run. The `c:\temp` is the output folder used in the following sample:

```
Xsd SummaryResult.xsd /c /l:cs /out:c:\temp
```

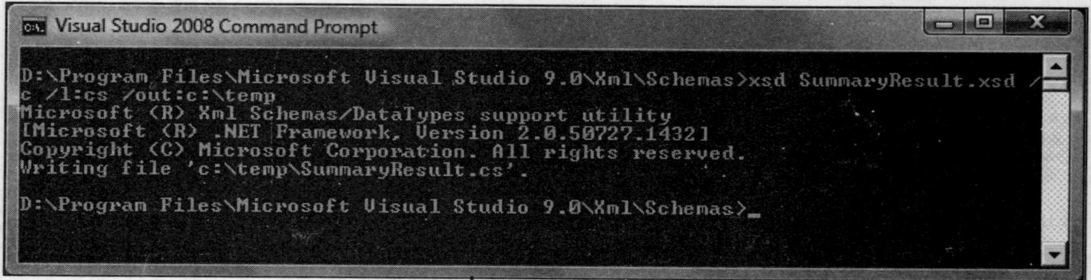

The class file is the C# file as we have specified C# as the language in the command-line parameter as `/l:cs`. The generated output file would be like this:

```
//------------------------------------------------------------------------
-----------
// <auto-generated>
//      This code was generated by a tool.
//      Runtime Version:2.0.50727.1433
//
//      Changes to this file may cause incorrect behavior and will be
lost if
//      the code is regenerated.
// </auto-generated>
//------------------------------------------------------------------------
----------

using System.Xml.Serialization;

//
// This source code was auto-generated by xsd, Version=2.0.50727.1432.
//


/// <remarks/>
[System.CodeDom.Compiler.GeneratedCodeAttribute("xsd",
"2.0.50727.1432")]
[System.SerializableAttribute()]
```

```
[System.Diagnostics.DebuggerStepThroughAttribute()]
[System.ComponentModel.DesignerCategoryAttribute("code")]
[System.Xml.Serialization.XmlTypeAttribute(AnonymousType=true)]
[System.Xml.Serialization.XmlRootAttribute(Namespace="",
IsNullable=false)]
public partial class SummaryResult {

    private string testNameField;

    private testResultType testResultField;

    private string errorMessageField;

    private string detailedResultsFileField;

    private SummaryResultInnerTest[] innerTestsField;

    /// <remarks/>
    public string TestName {
        get {
            return this.testNameField;
        }
        set {
            this.testNameField = value;
        }
    }

    /// <remarks/>
    public testResultType TestResult {
        get {
            return this.testResultField;
        }
        set {
            this.testResultField = value;
        }
    }

    /// <remarks/>
    public string ErrorMessage {
        get {
            return this.errorMessageField;
        }
        set {
            this.errorMessageField = value;
```

```
            }
        }

        /// <remarks/>
        public string DetailedResultsFile {
            get {
                return this.detailedResultsFileField;
            }
            set {
                this.detailedResultsFileField = value;
            }
        }

        /// <remarks/>
        [System.Xml.Serialization.XmlArrayItemAttribute("InnerTest",
          IsNullable=false)]
        public SummaryResultInnerTest[] InnerTests {
            get {
                return this.innerTestsField;
            }
            set {
                this.innerTestsField = value;
            }
        }
    }

    /// <remarks/>
    [System.CodeDom.Compiler.GeneratedCodeAttribute("xsd",
    "2.0.50727.1432")]
    [System.SerializableAttribute()]
    public enum testResultType {

        /// <remarks/>
        Aborted,

        /// <remarks/>
        Error,

        /// <remarks/>
        Inconclusive,

        /// <remarks/>
        Failed,

        /// <remarks/>
        NotRunnable,

        /// <remarks/>
        NotExecuted,
```

```
        /// <remarks/>
        Disconnected,

        /// <remarks/>
        Warning,

        /// <remarks/>
        InProgress,

        /// <remarks/>
        Pending,

        /// <remarks/>
        PassedButRunAborted,

        /// <remarks/>
        Completed,

        /// <remarks/>
        Passed,
    }

    /// <remarks/>
    [System.CodeDom.Compiler.GeneratedCodeAttribute("xsd",
    "2.0.50727.1432")]
    [System.SerializableAttribute()]
    [System.Diagnostics.DebuggerStepThroughAttribute()]
    [System.ComponentModel.DesignerCategoryAttribute("code")]
    [System.Xml.Serialization.XmlTypeAttribute(AnonymousType=true)]
    public partial class SummaryResultInnerTest {

        private string testNameField;

        private testResultType testResultField;

        private string errorMessageField;

        private string detailedResultsFileField;

        /// <remarks/>
        public string TestName {
            get {
                return this.testNameField;
```

```
        }
        set {
            this.testNameField = value;
        }
    }

    /// <remarks/>
    public testResultType TestResult {
        get {
            return this.testResultField;
        }
        set {
            this.testResultField = value;
        }
    }

    /// <remarks/>
    public string ErrorMessage {
        get {
            return this.errorMessageField;
        }
        set {
            this.errorMessageField = value;
        }
    }

    /// <remarks/>
    public string DetailedResultsFile {
        get {
            return this.detailedResultsFileField;
        }
        set {
            this.detailedResultsFileField = value;
        }
    }
}
```

The third-party tool can make use of the above class file to write the test result details, or the test application should take care of writing the test result details into the XML file based on the XML schema used. The results output XML file should look like this:

```
<?xml version="1.0" encoding="utf-8" ?>
<SummaryResult>
  <TestName>Third party test Application</TestName>
  <TestResult>Failed</TestResult>
  <InnerTests>
    <InnerTest>
      <TestName>Export the Data to Excel</TestName>
```

```
        <TestResult>Passed</TestResult>
        <ErrorMessage></ErrorMessage>
        <DetailedResultsFile></DetailedResultsFile>
      </InnerTest>
      <InnerTest>
        <TestName>Import Data from Excel</TestName>
        <TestResult>Failed</TestResult>
        <ErrorMessage>Data Not in Expected format</ErrorMessage>
        <DetailedResultsFile>D:\Testing\Trace.txt</DetailedResultsFile>
      </InnerTest>
    </InnerTests>
  </SummaryResult>
```

In the previous example, we can see that there are two different tests within a single test. One is to export the data to Excel, which is passed, and the other test is to **import** the details from Excel, which is failed. The second test which failed writes detailed information about the test result to the text file. Writing into the log file should be taken care of by the third-party test application in the required format.

Now the **Test Results** window for this generic test would show the result as **Failed** as shown in the following screenshot:

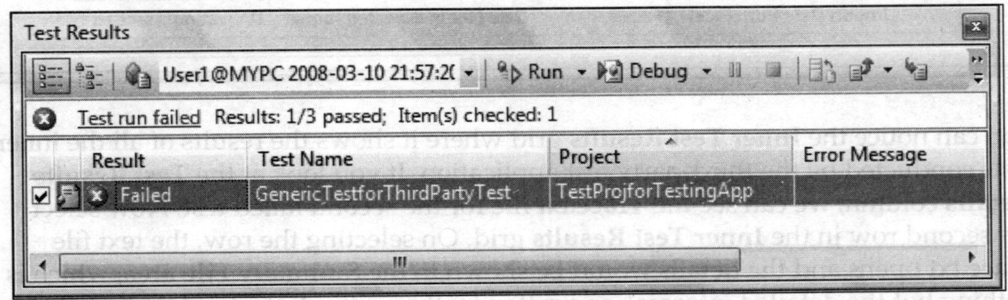

Select the result in the **Test Results** window, then right-click and select **View Test Results Details**. This would show all the summary and detailed results based on the XML output as shown here:

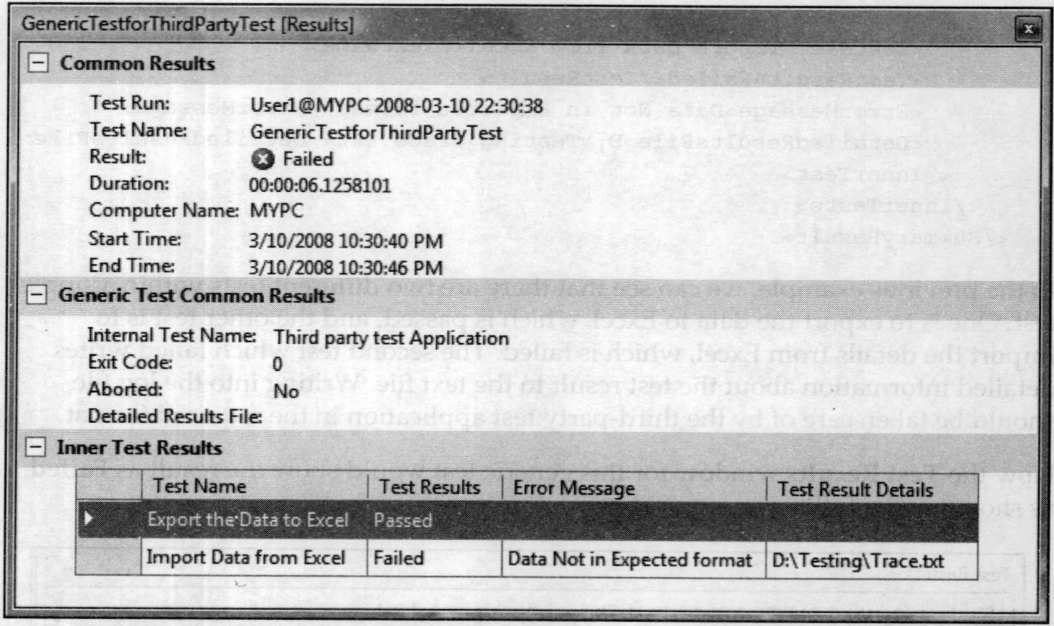

You can notice the **Inner Test Results** grid where it shows the results of all the inner tests conducted by the third-party test application. If you look at the **Test Results Details** column, we can see the **Trace.txt** file for the second failed test. Now select the second row in the **Inner Test Results** grid. On selecting the row, the text file **Trace.txt** opens and the details would be shown in the **Summary File** area, which is nothing but the detailed information written by the application about the failed test:

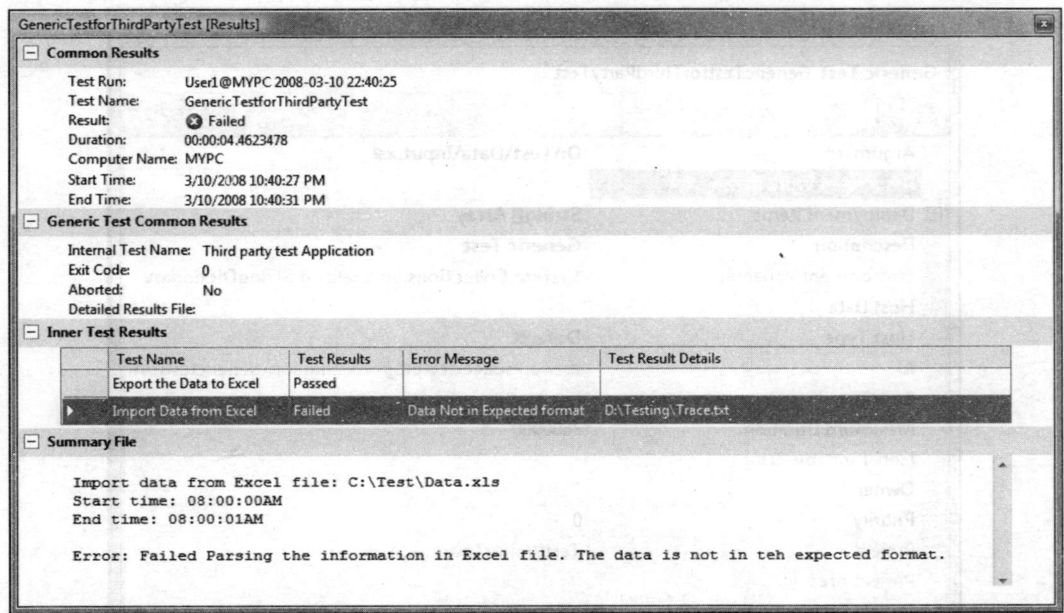

The **Summary File** information is just the content of the text file given in the DetailedResultsFile, in the XML output file.

Properties of a generic test

Besides having some properties common with the other tests, generic tests also have some specific properties. To view the properties, select the generic test in **Test View** or **Test List Editor** window and right-click to select the **Properties** option. The **Properties** dialog box is then displayed with the available properties for the generic test:

Using the **Properties** window we can associate a test to a work item, an iteration, or a project area defined in the TFS. We can also set the input file as arguments, specify deployment items, and set the maximum duration for the test run and many other properties. Most of the properties such as deployment items, description, owner, priority, work item, iteration, and solution are common for all test types, whereas properties such as arguments and target executable are specific to the generic test type.

Summary

This chapter explained the details and usage of different formats of manual testing using Text and Word. Even though both the tests are similar, the Word format gives better formatting features. The section on ordered test explained how to order the tests and execute them in the same order irrespective of their type. The generic test explained the ways of executing the third-party tests within Visual Studio and shows the tests results collected within the third-party tests.

Each of these different test types has its own properties. Some of them are common, while some are specific to the individual test. There are some common properties to associate the tests to the work items in the TFS. This is very helpful in mapping the test and tracking a set of related work items.

7

Managing and Configuring the Test

The previous chapters explained the different ways of testing the application. We could have created a lot of testing applications, but we also needed to group the tests and manage them. There are different common properties that we can set for the tests using the test run configuration file, which is used by the tests during execution. VSTS provides a utility to edit the common test configuration stored in the `testrunconfig` file. VSTS provides different tools that support easy ways of managing the tests. Using these tools, we can enable and disable the tests, select them to run, filter the required tests from the list of all the tests created for the project, and set the properties for individual tests.

Managing tests using test lists

The test solution can contain any number of tests. If the number is small, we can manage the tests easily; but if it is too high, it will be difficult to identify the tests within the large list of tests. We need to group the tests based on some property to identify and filter them easily. The Test List Editor is the main interface provided by Visual Studio for managing all tests under the solution. On opening the **Test List Editor**, using the **Test** menu option in VSTS, you can see all the tests listed in the editor under **All Loaded Tests**, by default. The Test List Editor is divided into two panes. The left pane has the options to choose the list of tests to be displayed on the right side.

By default, the editor displays all tests in the solution irrespective of the type, the project it belongs to, and whether the test is enabled or disabled.

The **Test List Editor** has a toolbar with options for grouping the tests, filtering the tests, and loading the metadata.

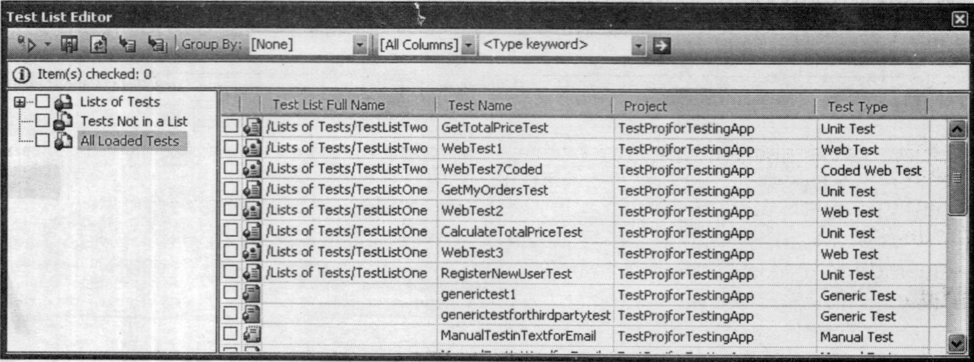

We can select the tests from the list and run them using the **Run** option in the toolbar. We can add or remove the columns to be displayed in the list.

Organizing test list

The editor window has three different top-level nodes in the left pane to show the test groups based on some property.

Lists of Tests: This is where we have to maintain the tests under the new lists. Initially there won't be any list created.

Select the **New Test List...** option after selecting and right-clicking the **List of Tests** node. There will be a new screen for entering the test list **Name** and **Description**. The window will also provide the flexibility to choose the node in the tree to place this new list node. For example, the following screenshot shows the new test list with the name **TestListThree** added to the root node.

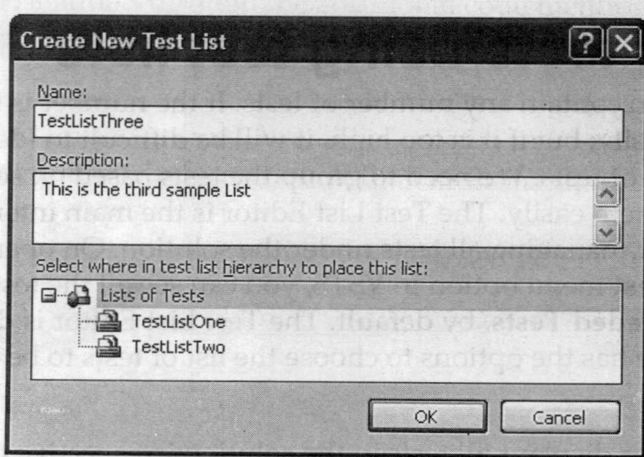

After clicking on **OK**, we can see the new list name added as a new node to the parent node **Lists of Tests**. This is the same screen used for editing as well. We can edit only the **Name** and the **Description**. We can also delete, remove, and rename the list node from the lists.

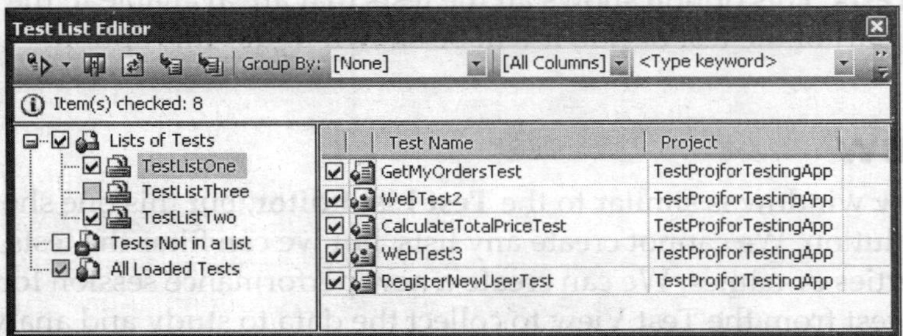

The preceding screenshot shows the **Lists of Tests** added to the solution. If the main node is selected, all the subnodes or the lists under the root node will also get selected by default. The new list **TestListThree** is not selected, but grayed out because there are no tests added to the list yet. It's an empty list now.

To add the tests to the list, select the tests from the list under **Tests Not in a List,** which are not yet added to any list. After the selection, drag-and-drop the selected tests on the test list name. We can also use the cut, copy, and paste commands to move the tests under the lists. Now you can see the selected tests added to the list.

Each test can belong to many lists. To copy the tests to the list, without removing it from the original list, press *Ctrl* key while dragging the test to the new list.

To remove a test from all the tests lists to which the test is added, select the test from any test list and right-click and choose the option **Remove from All Test Lists**. For example, the following screenshot shows the option to remove the **GetMyOrdersTest,** which is added to the lists **TestListOne** and **TestListTwo**.

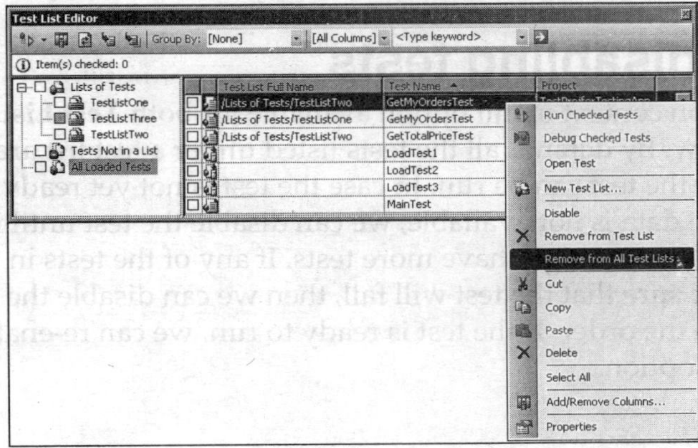

Tests Not in a List: This is to list the tests that are not part of any of the List. Using this list, we can identify the tests that we need to organize and place under a particular test.

All Loaded Tests: This option shows all the tests that are available in the solution. Whether it is part of the test or not, it will be shown under this option.

Test view

The **Test View** window is similar to the **Test List Editor,** but this one shows all the tests in the solution. We cannot create any lists, but we can filter the tests based on test properties or names. We can create a new performance session for the load test and web test from the Test View to collect the data to study and analyze the application performance. The Test View toolbar is similar to the toolbar available for Test List Editor, which provides group by, filter, run, and debug options.

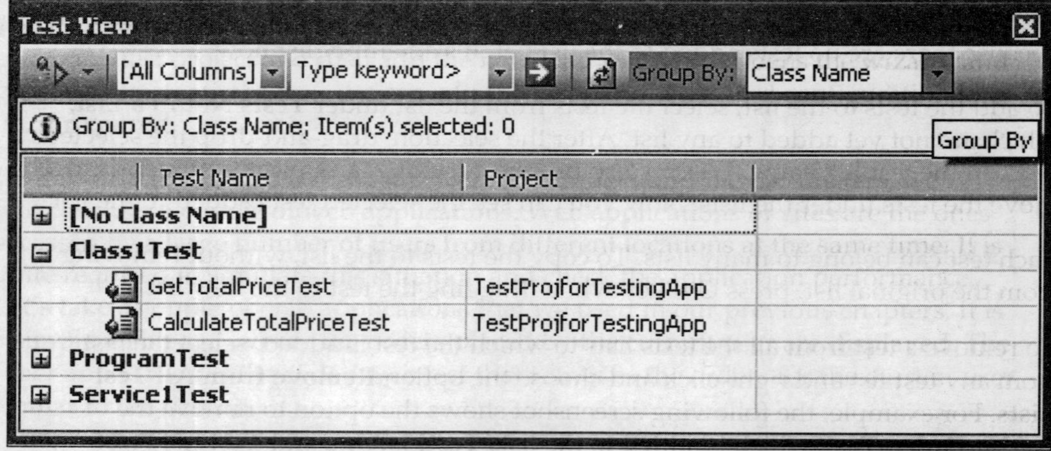

Enabling/disabling tests

This is the common context menu option available for both **Test List Editor** and **Test View** window. By default, all the tests listed under a test list are enabled, which means that the test can be run. In case the test is not yet ready to run or if any supporting source data is not available, we can disable the test until it is ready. In the case of ordered tests, we might have more tests. If any of the tests in the order is not ready, or if we are sure that the test will fail, then we can disable the test and run the remaining tests in the order. If the test is ready to run, we can re-enable the test using the context menu option.

Toolbar options

The toolbar options provided by Test List Editor and the Test View window are almost the same with features such as filtering and grouping the test based on test properties.

Filtering tests

Displaying of tests in the Test List Editor and Test View window can be controlled using the **Apply Filter** option in the toolbar. Filtering is useful in finding specific types of tests from the huge list of tests available in the solution. The developers might want to list only the unit tests that requires re-testing the code fix/enhancements. On the other side, the test team might want to list only the web test to see if the defect fixed by the developer still exists, or if it is fixed and working as expected.

To filter the tests, use the drop-down provided in the toolbar of the Test List Editor or Test View window and select the property by which you want to filter the tests. After selecting the property in the drop-down, enter the string in the **Filter Text** box to find a matching string in the selected property of all the tests. Now click on the **Apply Filter** button which is next to the **Filter Text** box control. Now, the filter is applied and the editor lists only the test which has matching text in the property selected and the string entered in the **Filter Text** as shown here:

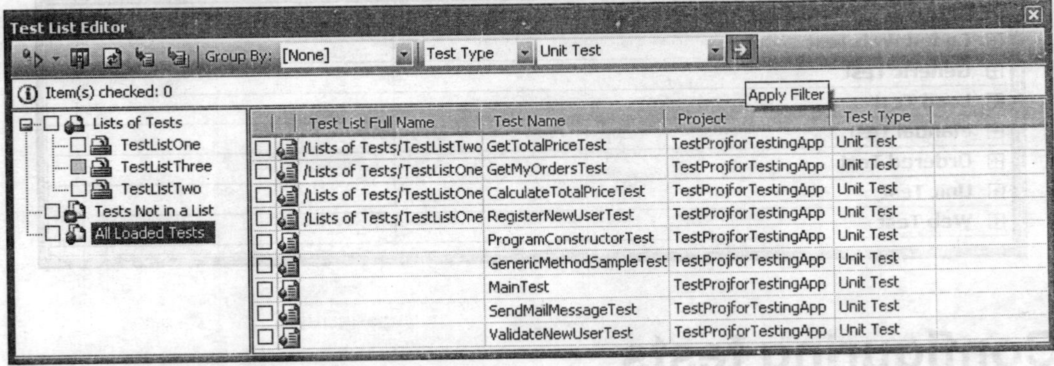

Group By

The **Group By** option is used for displaying the test list by grouping them based on a selected property. For example, the following screenshot shows the Test List Editor and Test View window in which tests are grouped based on properties. The Test List Editor groups the tests by the test property that identifies if the test is enabled or disabled. The Test View window groups the tests based on the test type.

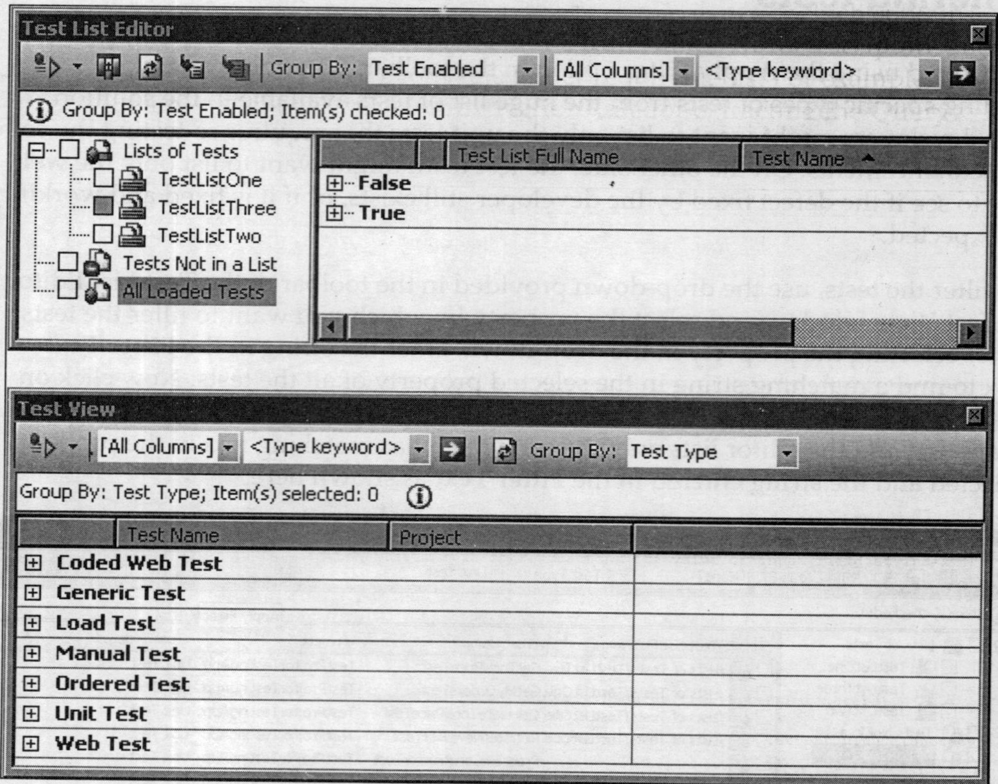

Configuring tests

Configuration is the setting used for controlling the application execution. In .NET all the applications are generally controlled using the configuration files. The name of the configuration file differs with the type of application and the operation system in which the application is deployed. Similarly, all the test applications in the solution are also controlled by a separate, default configuration file created by the solution. This file is created under the solution with the extension `.testrunconfig`. We can have multiple configuration files, but at any point in time only one configuration file can be active from which the settings are applied to each test run.

Test run configuration

To specify or modify the settings in the configuration, we can use the test configuration editor which opens up on double-clicking the configuration file. It has different pages for different sets of configurations.

General

This is the general page for specifying the **Name** of the configuration file and the **Description** for the configuration. We can also define the naming scheme used for storing the test run results. By default, it takes the current user name and the name of the machine with the run date and time added to the file name. We can also customize and specify the user-defined file name schema to be used. We can also specify whether or not to add the current date-time stamp to the name.

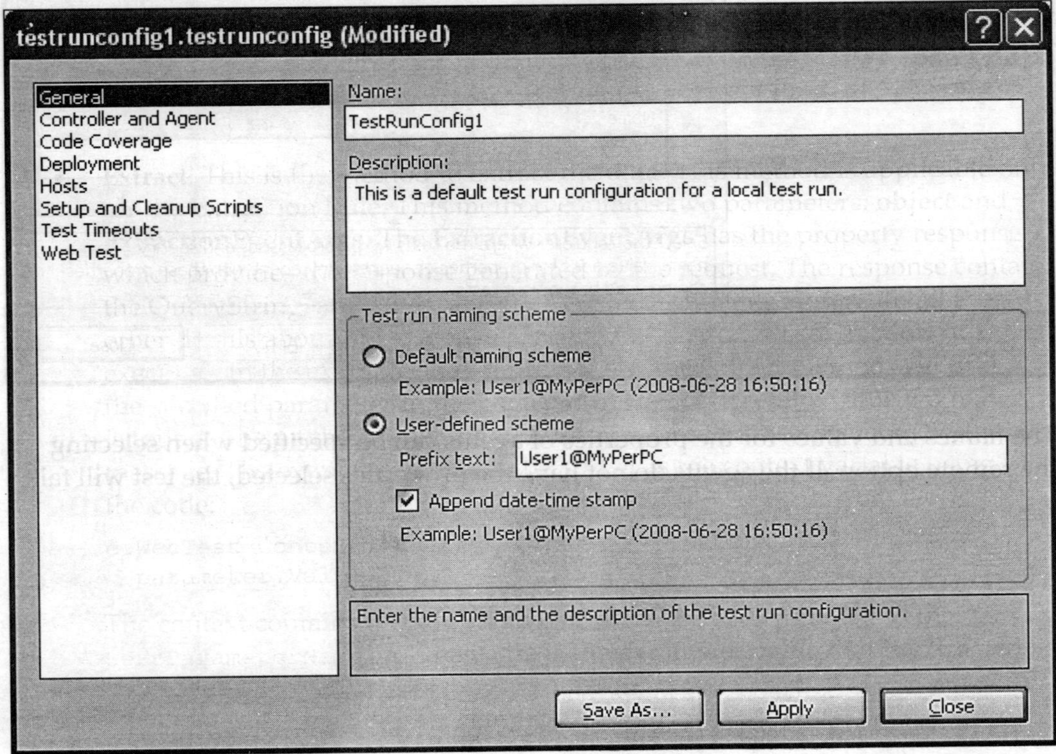

Controller and agent

This is to set whether the test has to be run in the local machine or in a remote machine. By default, it is set to run on the local machine. If it is a remote machine, we need to provide the controller and the agents name for the test. Running the test in remote machine proves useful in reproducing the multiple user tests using multiple remote machines. This group of remote machines is controlled by a single controller, and one or many agents. This is used for simulating the load test. You can refer to Chapter 5 *Load Testing*, for more details on testing using multiple remote machines.

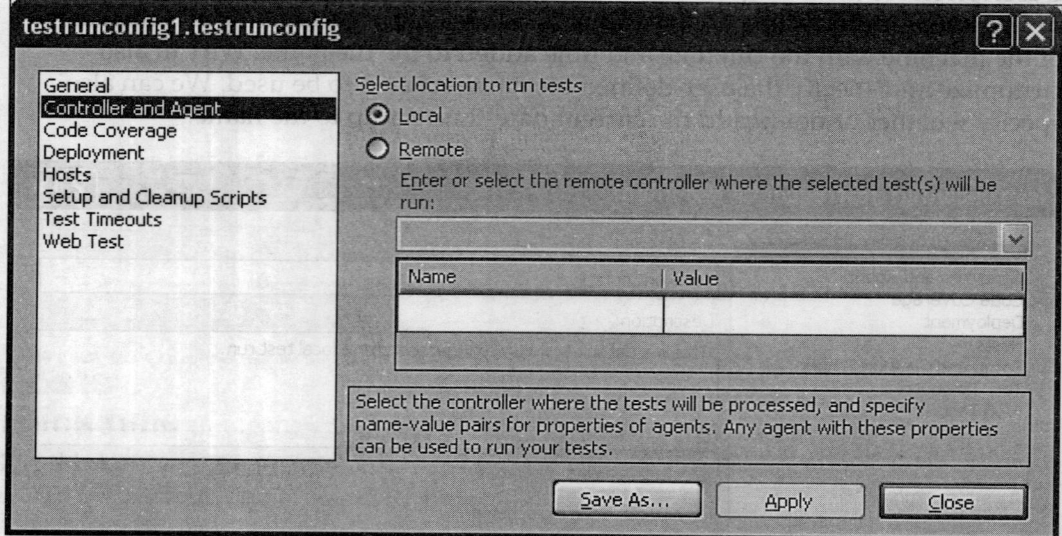

The names and values for the properties of agents can be specified when selecting the remote option. If the agents do not have the properties selected, the test will fail.

Code coverage

In the **Code Coverage** section, you can select the `.dll` and `.exe` test files from where the code coverage data can be collected. Code coverage is used for collecting the statistics of the code not covered during the test. This setting takes care of collecting the details when the selected test application actually runs.

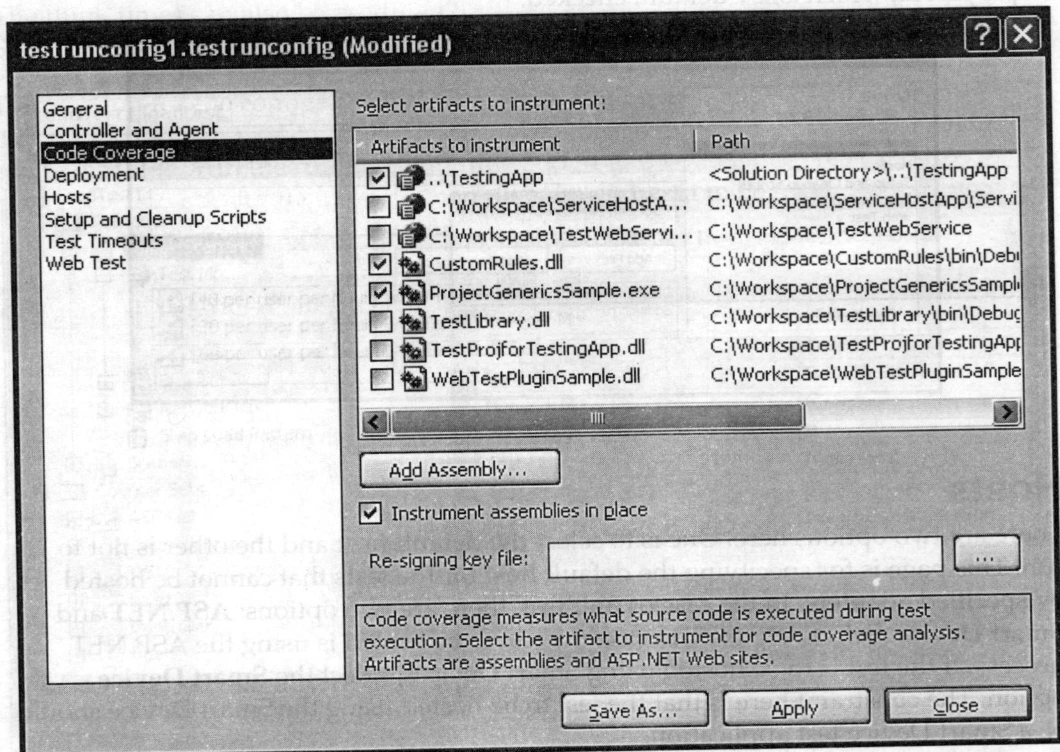

Using this page, we can also select the **Instrument assemblies in place** checkbox and re-sign the key file (**Re-signing key file**). This is to make the copy of the file and then change it to collect the code coverage data during testing.

Deployment

Using this page, we can add files and the folder containing multiple files to be deployed along with the application. Whatever is specified here are the additional files copied along with the application files that are going to be deployed. We can also enable or disable the deployment using the checkbox option **Enable Deployment,** which is, by default, checked.

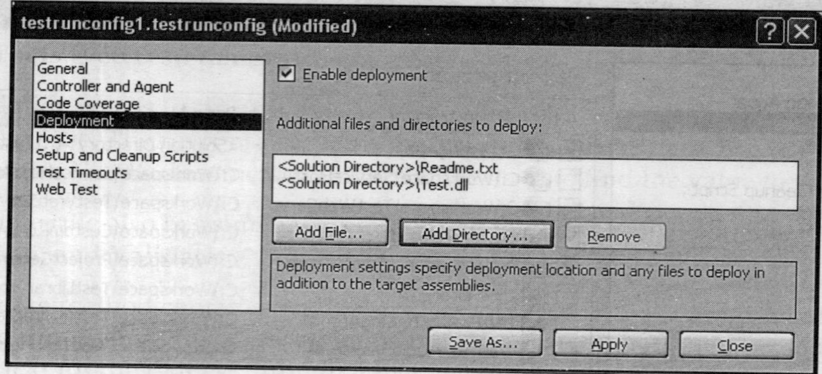

Hosts

There are two options here. One is to select the default host and the other is not to run. This page is for specifying the default host for the tests that cannot be hosted by specified adapters. In the case of unit test, there are two options: **ASP.NET** and **Smart Device**. Select ASP.NET in case the test to be hosted is using the ASP.NET process. If the test is to be hosted using Smart Devices, select the **Smart Device** option. The constraint here is that the test to be hosted using the Smart Device should be a Smart Device test application.

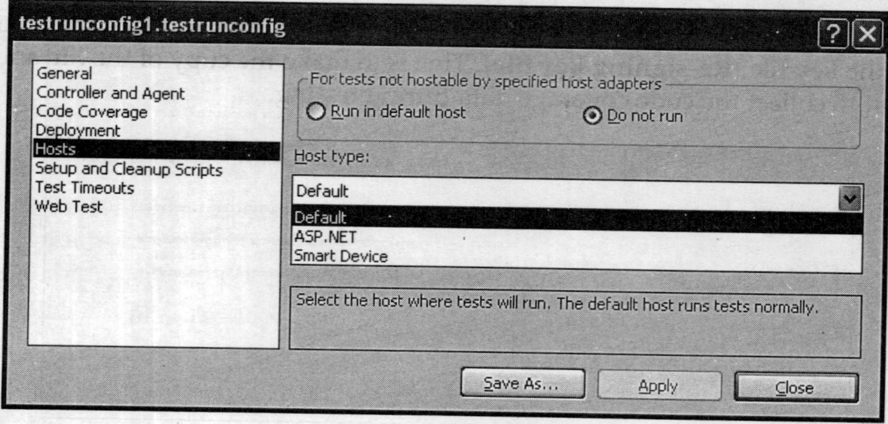

If we are selecting the **Host type** as ASP.NET, we should provide the following information about the URL address and the path for the application in the local machine. Also select the option, **Run in default host**.

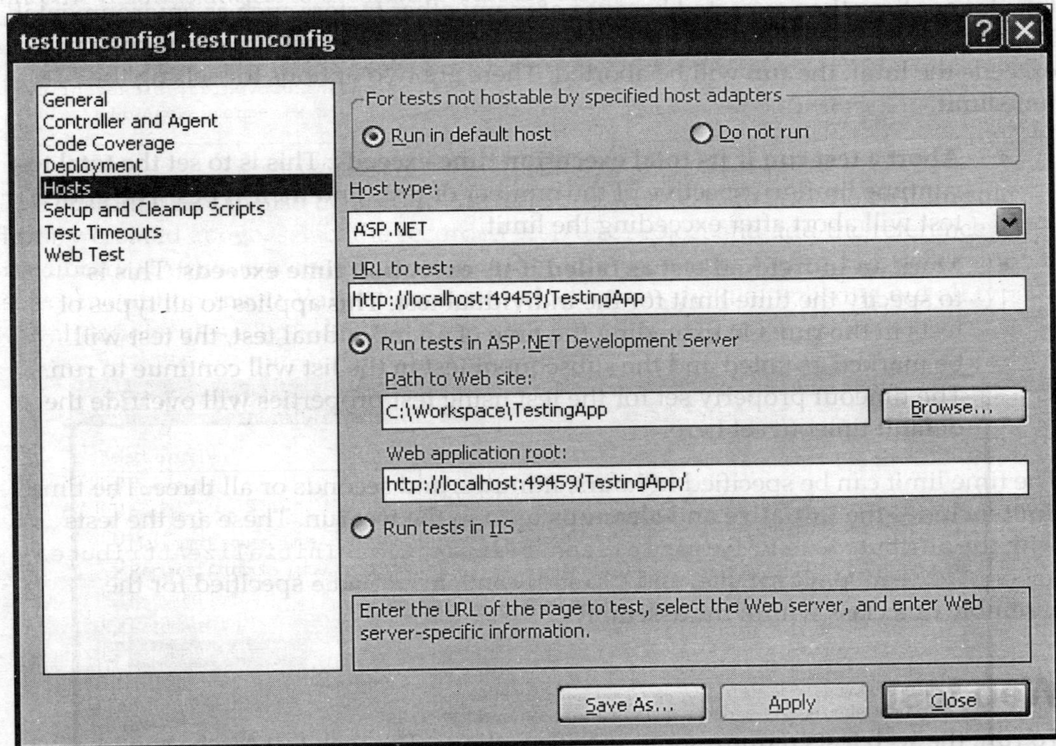

After setting the URL and the path to the application, you can run the test as normal. The local development server will take care of running the test.

Setup and cleanup scripts

Here in this section, we can specify the script files to be run before and after running the test. This script file is useful in setting the environment for running the test and also in cleaning up the files or other objects used during testing. These are the common scripts for all the tests under the solution. So we should take extra care while writing the script in such a way that it should be common to all types of tests.

Test timeouts

These values are specified to set the time limit value during the test run. We cannot wait for long for the test to complete. There are situations where some tests might take longer time than expected because of many other factors such as environmental issues. In that case, we can set the maximum time limit the test run can take. If it exceeds the limit, the run will be aborted. There are two options for setting the time limit:

- **Abort a test run if its total execution time exceeds**: This is to set the total test runtime limit irrespective of the number of tests and their types. The entire test will abort after exceeding the limit.
- **Mark an individual test as failed if its execution time exceeds**: This is to specify the time limit for the individual test. This applies to all types of tests in the run. On exceeding the time of an individual test, the test will be marked as failed and the subsequent test in the list will continue to run. The timeout property set for the test using test properties will override the default timeout set here.

The time limit can be specified in hours, minutes, and seconds or all three. The time limit includes the **initialize** and **cleanups** used in the test run. These are the tests with the attribute `AssemblyInitializeAttribute`, `ClassInitializeAttribute`, `AssemblyCleanUpAttribute`, and `ClassCleanUpAttribute` specified for the assembly or a class within the assembly.

Web test

To run, the web tests require some specific settings. The web test can be run in different browsers and with different sets of data. This page has the option to specify the required setting.

Using the first option, we can specify the number of run iterations. It can be a fixed run count where the count is specified, or it can be **one run per data source row**. If the number of run iterations is fixed, the test will run for the specified number of times. If it is mentioned as one row per data, the test will run for each row in the data source attached to the test.

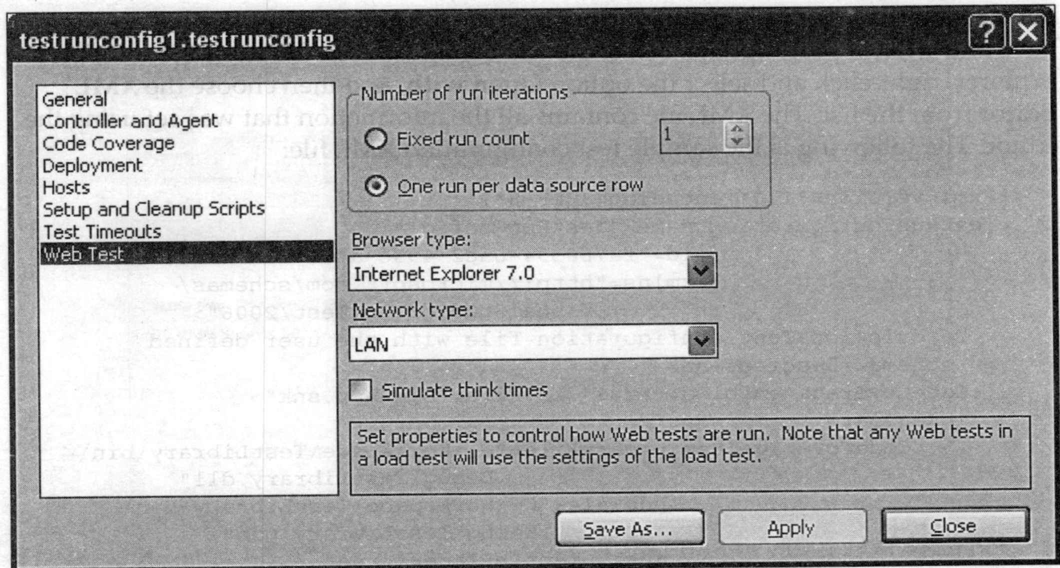

The second option is for selecting the **Browser type** used for testing.

The other option is to select the **Network type**. This is to specify the speed at which the test has to run.

The page also has the option to simulate the think times.

Editing test run configuration file

The test configuration file is not something new here. It is the same configuration information we saw in the previous section. There it is, the editor which takes care of writing the information into the file. But here we are going to see how we can edit the file directly without using the editor. The information edited from both places is going to the same file. It is the normal XML version of the file, which can be opened using any XML Editor. As we are not using the editor, we should be careful to update the file without breaking the syntax format.

Let us open the test configuration file using the XML Editor and see what we have and what we can update. Select the test configurations file from the solution explorer, right-click and select the option **Open with**, and then choose the **XML Editor** from the list. The XML file contains all the information that was set using the editor. The following is the sample test configuration XML file:

```
<?xml version="1.0" encoding="UTF-8"?>
<TestRunConfiguration name="TestRunConfig1"
                     id="fa788594-6aç2-495e-a484-2229faa94326"
                     xmlns="http://microsoft.com/schemas/
                            VisualStudio/TeamTest/2006">
  <Description>Test configuration file with the user defined
    scheme</Description>
  <CodeCoverage enabled="true" keyFile="SignApp.snk">
    <Regular>
      <CodeCoverageItem binaryFile="C:\Workspace\TestLibrary\bin\
                                    Debug\TestLibrary.dll"
                       pdbFile="C:\Workspace\TestLibrary\bin\
                                 Debug\TestLibrary.pdb"
                       instrumentInPlace="true" />
      <CodeCoverageItem binaryFile="C:\Workspace\
                                    ProjectGenericsSample\bin\
                                    Debug\ProjectGenericsSample.exe"
                       pdbFile="C:\Workspace\ProjectGenericsSample\
                                 bin\Debug\ProjectGenericsSample.pdb"
                       instrumentInPlace="true" />
      <CodeCoverageItem binaryFile="C:\Workspace\
                                    TestProjforTestingApp\bin\Debug\
                                    TestProjforTestingApp.dll"
                       pdbFile="C:\Workspace\TestProjforTestingApp\
                                 bin\Debug\TestProjforTestingApp.pdb"
                       instrumentInPlace="true" />
      <CodeCoverageItem binaryFile="C:\Workspace\
                                    WebTestPluginSample\bin\
                                    Debug\WebTestPluginSample.dll"
                       pdbFile="C:\Workspace\WebTestPluginSample\
                                 bin\Debug\WebTestPluginSample.pdb"
                       instrumentInPlace="true" />
    </Regular>
    <AspNet>
      <AspNetCodeCoverageItem
        id="42fb46b4-063e-43d2-a50d-b44e3620c817"
        name="..\TestingApp" applicationRoot="/TestingApp"
        url="http://localhost:0/TestingApp" />
    </AspNet>
  </CodeCoverage>
  <Timeouts runTimeout="1800000" testTimeout="2700000" />
  <Deployment>
    <DeploymentItem filename="Test.dll" />
```

```
    <DeploymentItem filename="ClassLibrary1.dll" />
    <DeploymentItem filename="Readme.txt" />
  </Deployment>
  <NamingScheme baseName="User1@MyPerPC" useDefault="false" />
  <TestTypeSpecific>
    <WebTestRunConfiguration
       testTypeId="4e7599fa-5ecb-43e9-a887-cd63cf72d207">
      <Browser name="Internet Explorer 7.0">
        <Headers>
          <Header name="User-Agent" value="Mozilla/4.0 (compatible;
                                 MSIE 7.0; Windows NT 5.1)" />
          <Header name="Accept" value="*/*" />
          <Header name="Accept-Language"
               value="{{$IEAcceptLanguage}}" />
          <Header name="Accept-Encoding" value="GZIP" />
        </Headers>
      </Browser>
      <Network Name="LAN" BandwidthInKbps="0" />
    </WebTestRunConfiguration>
  </TestTypeSpecific>
</TestRunConfiguration>
```

To open the configuration file select the **testrunconfig** file, right-click and open with the **XML Editor**. Once the file is opened in the selected XML Editor, we can start editing the XML file as we would normally do with any XML file.

Editing the deployment section

For example, the following is the section that identifies the additional files to be deployed along with the application:

```
<Deployment>
  <DeploymentItem filename="Test.dll" />
  <DeploymentItem filename="ClassLibrary1.dll" />
  <DeploymentItem filename="Readme.txt" />
</Deployment>
```

If we have to include more files to be added, we can simply edit it and add the file with the correct attribute. The following code shows the additional files added to the section:

```
<Deployment>
  <DeploymentItem filename="Test.dll" />
  <DeploymentItem filename="ClassLibrary1.dll" />
  <DeploymentItem filename="Readme.txt" />
  <DeploymentItem filename="ClassLibrary2.txt" />
  <DeploymentItem filename="Test.exe" />
</Deployment>
```

Editing the code coverage

The following code shows the code coverage section for the assemblies selected using the configuration editor. To include more assemblies, we can simply edit the XML and save it. This code illustrates the additional two libraries added to it by editing the configuration file using the XML Editor.

```
<CodeCoverage enabled="true" keyFile="SignApp.snk">
  <Regular>
    <CodeCoverageItem binaryFile="C:\Workspace\TestLibrary\bin\
                                Debug\TestLibrary.dll"
                  pdbFile="C:\Workspace\TestLibrary\bin\
                             Debug\TestLibrary.pdb"
                  instrumentInPlace="true" />
    <CodeCoverageItem binaryFile="C:\Workspace\
                                ProjectGenericsSample\bin\
                             Debug\ProjectGenericsSample.exe"
                 pdbFile="C:\Workspace\ProjectGenericsSample\
                         bin\Debug\ProjectGenericsSample.pdb"
                  instrumentInPlace="true" />
    <CodeCoverageItem binaryFile="C:\Workspace\
                                TestProjforTestingApp\bin\
                              Debug\TestProjforTestingApp.dll"
                pdbFile="C:\Workspace\TestProjforTestingApp\
                         bin\Debug\TestProjforTestingApp.pdb"
                  instrumentInPlace="true" />
    <CodeCoverageItem binaryFile="C:\Workspace\
                                WebTestPluginSample\bin\Debug\
                                WebTestPluginSample.dll"
                  pdbFile="C:\Workspace\WebTestPluginSample\
                           bin\Debug\WebTestPluginSample.pdb"
```

```
                    instrumentInPlace="true" />
  <CodeCoverageItem binaryFile="C:\Workspace\
                          WebTestPluginSample\bin\Debug\
                          WebTestPluginSampleTwo.dll"
                    pdbFile="C:\Workspace\WebTestPluginSample\
                      bin\Debug\WebTestPluginSampleTwo.pdb"
                    instrumentInPlace="true" />
  </Regular>
  <AspNet>
    <AspNetCodeCoverageItem
      id="42fb46b4-063e-43d2-a50d-b44e3620c817"
      name="..\TestingApp" applicationRoot="/TestingApp"
      url="http://localhost:0/TestingApp" />
  </AspNet>
</CodeCoverage>
```

Test properties

Properties are the configurations meant for individual tests that are required for running the test. These properties can be set from the Test List Editor or the Test View window. Some of these properties are directly related to the Team Project Information available in the Visual Studio Team Foundation Server (**VSTFS**). The projects that are controlled by VSTFS contain properties such as the iteration, project area, and work items. If the current test project is maintained by the VSTFS integrated version control system, we can specify the test properties to maintain the test under a specific work item, specific iteration, and specific project area. The following list explains the properties available for tests. You can select the test from the Test List Editor or Test View and right-click to open the **Properties**. Some properties are specific to the test based on its type.

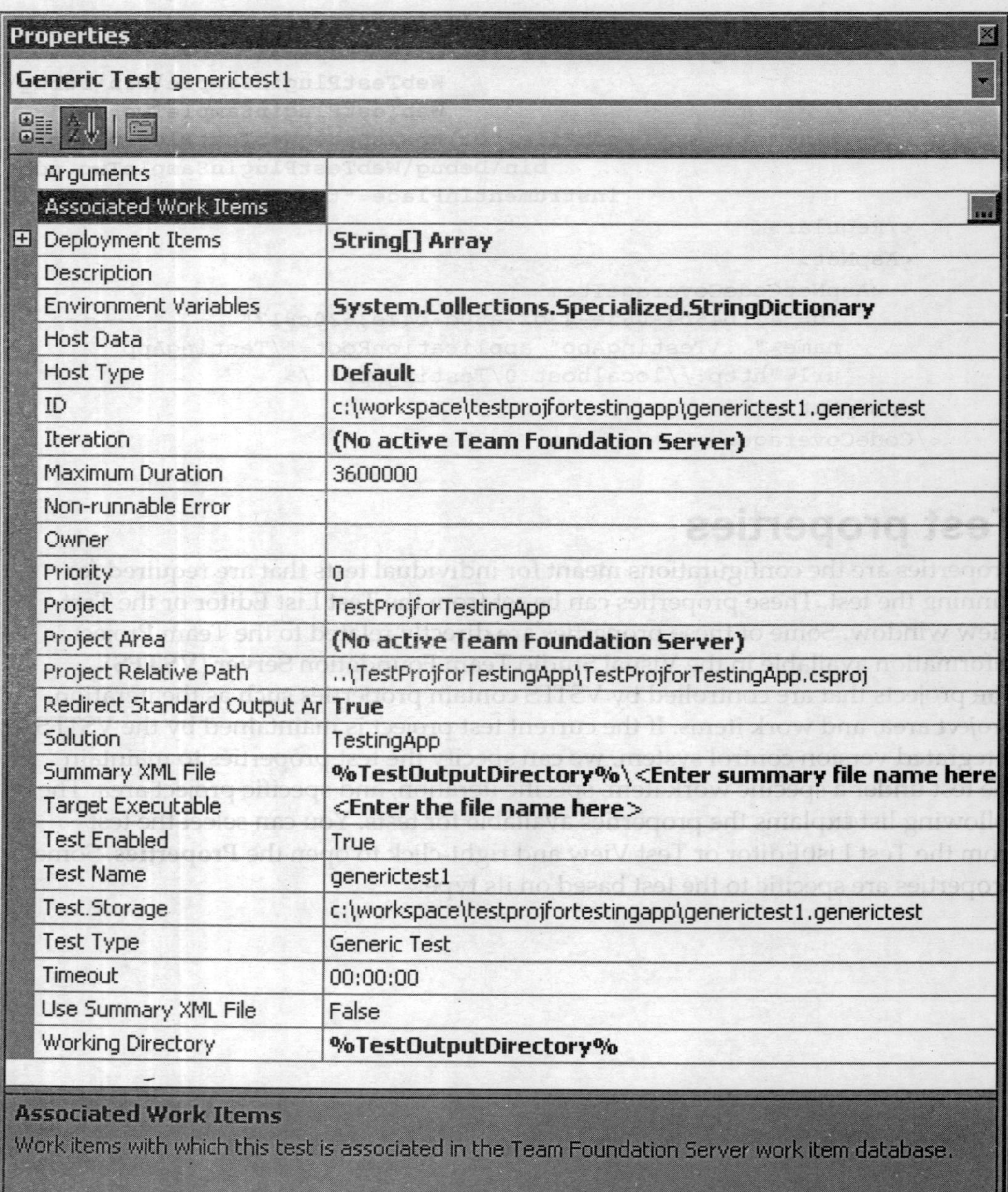
Properties
Generic Test genericktest1
Arguments
Associated Work Items
Deployment Items
String[] Array
Description
Environment Variables
System.Collections.Specialized.StringDictionary
Host Data
Host Type
Default
ID
c:\workspace\testprojfortestingapp\generictest1.generictest
Iteration
(No active Team Foundation Server)
Maximum Duration
3600000
Non-runnable Error
Owner
Priority
0
Project
TestProjforTestingApp
Project Area
(No active Team Foundation Server)
Project Relative Path
..\TestProjforTestingApp\TestProjforTestingApp.csproj
Redirect Standard Output Ar
True
Solution
TestingApp
Summary XML File
%TestOutputDirectory%\<Enter summary file name here
Target Executable
<Enter the file name here>
Test Enabled
True
Test Name
generictest1
Test.Storage
c:\workspace\testprojfortestingapp\generictest1.generictest
Test Type
Generic Test
Timeout
00:00:00
Use Summary XML File
False
Working Directory
%TestOutputDirectory%
Associated Work Items
Work items with which this test is associated in the Team Foundation Server work item database.

Property	Edit Capability	Description
Arguments	Editable	This property allows us to set the command line argument to be passed to the target program for the test execution.
Associated Work Items	This is Editable if part of VSTFS	We can associate this generic test to the Work item in VSTFS; the work item can be a task, or a defect, or a requirement.
Deployment Items	Editable	Refers to the files and folders that need to be deployed along with this test; we have to provide the full path of the files or folders that has to be deployed; there is an option in the property that opens the file open dialog to select the files.
Description	Editable	This property gives us a detailed description of the test.
Environment Variables	Read Only	This property is to set the environment variables for command line execution.
ID	Read only	This property gives us the unique name of the test; it gives the full path of the generic test where it resides.
Iteration	This is Editable if part of VSTFS	This property explains which iteration in the software project life cycle these tests belongs to; you can set the iterations in TFS.
Maximum Duration	Editable	This property tells how long a generic test can be allowed to execute before terminating the test. Default Value is '3600000' in milliseconds.
Non-runnable Error	Read only	This property explains the reason of the generic test that cannot be executed in this test run; even if a test is included in a test project but for some reason or the other, this test cannot be executed in this test run; you can enter the reason in this property. This property will be empty if the test is executable for this test run.
Owner	Editable	This property holds the name of the person who is the owner of the test or who is maintaining it.
Priority	Editable	This property is to set the priority of the test; it explains the relative importance of the test and tells which test needs to be executed first; this is also useful for grouping the tests based on priority.
Project	Read Only	This property holds the test the project name to which the test belongs.

Property	Edit Capability	Description
Project Area	This is Editable if part of VSTFS	This property tells the node in the team project to which this test belongs.
Project Relative Path	Read Only	This property tells the file name of the project where the test resides; the path is relative to the location of the solution.
Redirect Standard Output and Error	Editable	This property allows us to redirect the standard output and the error messages from the target program. The value 'TRUE' enables the standard output and error message to be redirected. The value 'FALSE' disables the redirection.
Solution	Read Only	This property identifies the name of the solution that contains the test project to which this test belongs.
Summary XML File	Editable	Identifies the path of the Summary XML Result file. This Summary XML result file contains the details of the results from the tests executed within the main test.
Target Executable	Editable	Identifies the path of the third-party command line utility that will be used to execute the tests.
Test Enabled	Editable	This is to enable or disable the test for this run Its default value is 'TRUE'.
Test Name	Read Only	This property identifies the name of the test.
Test Storage	Read Only	This gives us the complete path of the file that contains this test; for generic test, this property is the same as the test 'ID' property.
Test Type	Read Only	This is to identify the type of the test. In this case the value is 'Generic'; this property is used for Grouping and filtering the tests in the Test view and Test List Editor.

Property	Edit Capability	Description
Timeout	Read Only	This property sets the timeout value for the test; how long the test can take to run before it is marked as failed and abort. For a generic test this property has a value of '00:00:00', where we can overwrite by typing the new value.
Use Summary XML File	Editable	By using this property, we can decide whether to use the Summary XML result file, which contains the detailed result of the test execution. If 'TRUE' then the summary XML result file is used. If 'FALSE' then the summary XML result file is not used.
Working Directory	Editable	This property tells the working directory of the Target program.

Summary

This chapter explained the different ways of managing the tests in the solution and ways of filtering the tests and grouping the tests in the solution. This chapter also explained about editing the test run configuration using the configuration editor supported by Visual Studio. We have also seen ways of editing the configuration file directly without using the editor.

8

Deploying and Running Tests

The earlier chapters explained how to create different types of tests, execute the tests and collect the test results. Once we are ready with the expected test application, we need to deploy the application to the test machines as per the testing requirements. The test project contains the assemblies in the form of libraries and executables, similar to the class library or any other .NET application. The deployment of the test project assemblies is the same as any other .NET application, whether it is a local deployment or a deployment to remote machines. We may have to set the environment or deploy the supporting files or assemblies to execute in the target machine. This chapter explains how to deploy the test application using VSTS based on the type of the application.

VSTS provides multiple options for deploying the test application. The deployment differs based on the type of the original application. The environment could be a local machine, an IIS server, or a smart client. The configuration is set based on the type of application. Visual Studio provides a configuration editor tool and a test configuration file for holding all the information about deployment and the settings for deploying the test application. Chapter 7 touched upon this a little bit to understand how the deployment configuration works, and what are the different ways to edit the configuration file.

The configuration file not only holds information about deployment, but also other details such as the data source, the host process on which the application should run, timeouts for the test run, location to run the tests, start up and clean up scripts, and many more. There are two different ways of deployment. One is the default, which is the local deployment, and the other is to deploy in the remote machine.

Local deployment

Every time the test application is executed, the execution files are created in the default folder created by Visual Studio. The **Test Results** folder under the current solution is the default folder by Visual Studio. Visual Studio creates this folder when the binaries are built during the test run. On each test run, the Visual Studio creates a new folder specific to this test run under the **Test Results** folder. This folder is named after the current user running the test, machine name, date, and time of test run. Visual Studio creates it and copies the binaries and deployment files to this folder. The **Test Results** folder also contains test result files for each test run. This is a single file with the extension `.trx` for each test run. For example, the following screenshot shows the successful execution of a test in the solution:

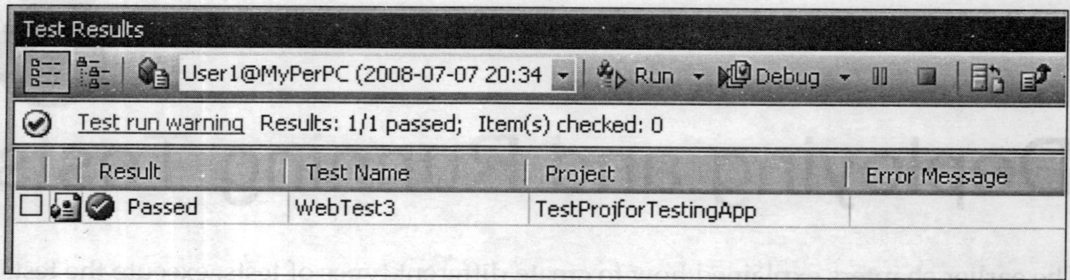

The **Test Results** window displays the execution result and the name of the execution result. This is the actual result file name created for the test under the **TestResults** folder as shown in the following screenshot. The corresponding folder for the test result is also shown.

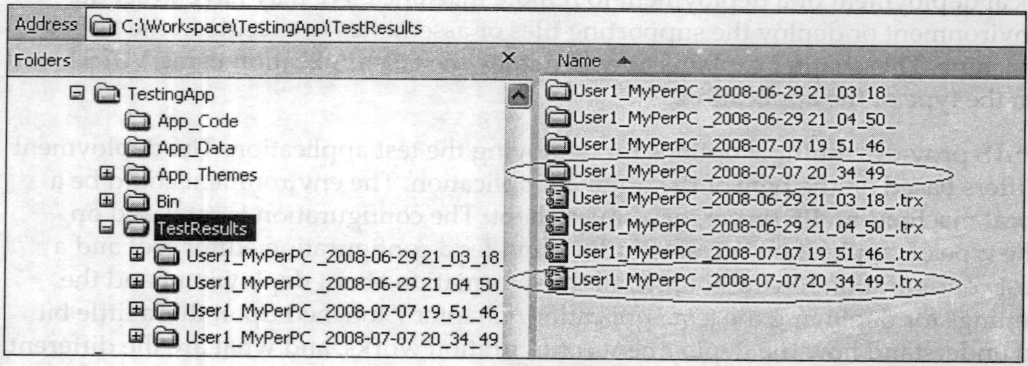

The folder name and the test result files are named as `<current user>_<machine name>_<date and time>.trx`. This name can be customized using the option in the test configuration file. You can refer to the chapter about test configurations to know more about the deployment configurations.

As mentioned above, each test run creates its own subfolder under the **TestResults** folder. Let us see what that folder contains and about the use of the files and folders under this test folder.

Each test run folder contains two subfolders: **In** and **Out**. These folders contain the files to be deployed and the output files from the tests.

In: All the files produced by the test run are stored in this folder. For example, the following screenshot shows a file named **data.coverage**, which is the code coverage result of the current test run.

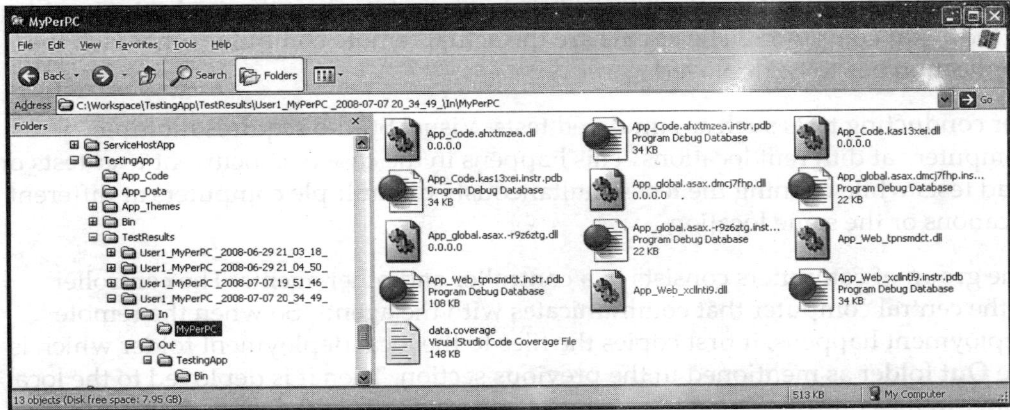

Out: This is the actual output folder that contains the deployment files. These are the files required for the test to run. This folder also contains the additional files added to be part of the deployment.

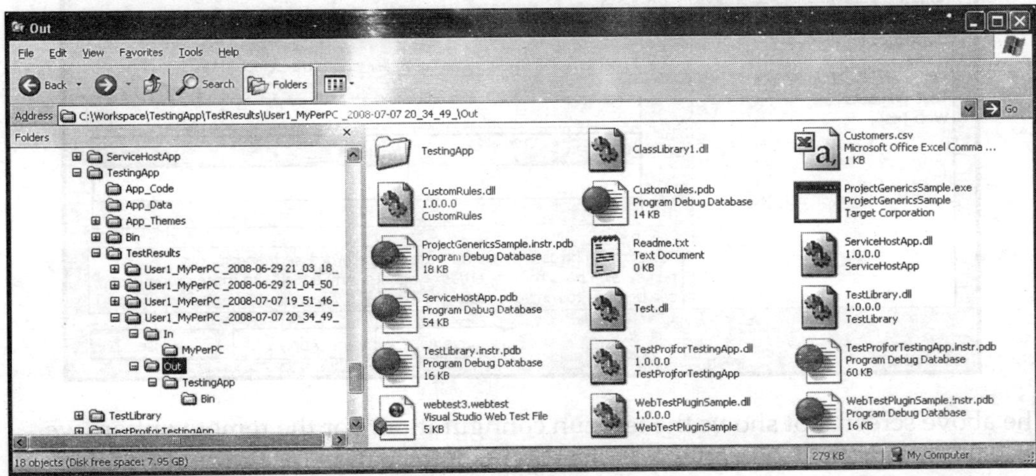

The image shows the **Out** folder, which contains all the files required for the test run and also the additional files added to the deployment, for example, **Readme.txt** and **Test.dll**.

Remote deployment

This type of deployment involves deploying the testing application and the supporting files to the remote machines, which are used for testing or running the test application. This deployment is not a direct or automatic deployment as we do with the local deployment. The first deployment happens in the centralized system called **controller**, which then distributes and deploys the application or files to the agent computers. The **agents** are the actual remote computers on which the application has to be deployed.

For conducting tests such as simulated tests, Visual Studio requires multiple computers at different locations. This happens in the case of concurrent user tests or load tests while running the test simultaneously on multiple computers at different locations or the same location.

The group of computers consists of a controller and other agents. The controller is the central computer that communicates with the agents. So when the remote deployment happens, it first copies the files to the local deployment folder which is the **Out** folder as mentioned in the previous section. Then it is deployed to the local folder in the controller computer, which then distributes the files to the agents. The agents are the real computers which conduct the tests.

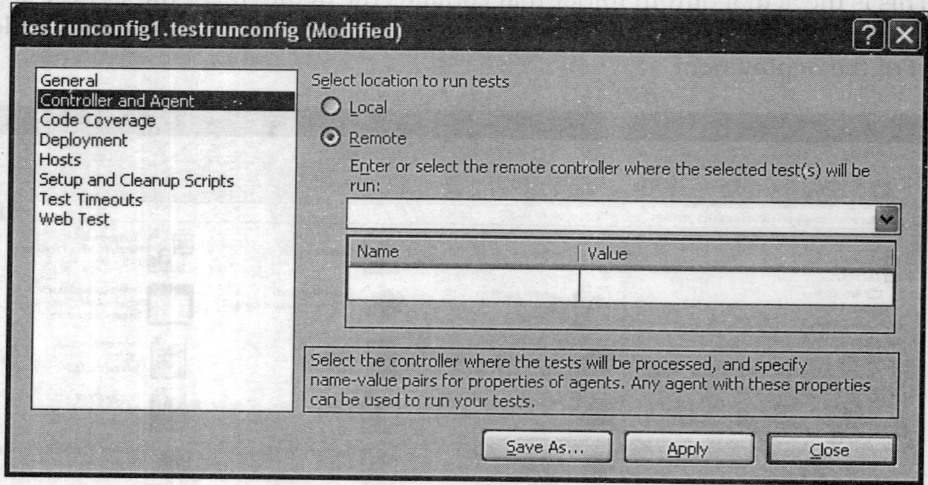

The above screenshot shows the test run configuration. For the remote option, we have to provide the **Controller and the Agents** information for the deployment.

Deploy additional files

The configuration settings contain the list of additional items to be deployed as part of test deployment. Open the test configuration file, which opens in a configuration editor tool which is the inbuilt tool in Visual Studio used for easy editing of the configuration information. In the screenshot below, the **Deployment** section shown in the configuration editor tool specifies the additional files or folder to be deployed. You can use the **Add File** or **Add Directory** option to select the deployment items.

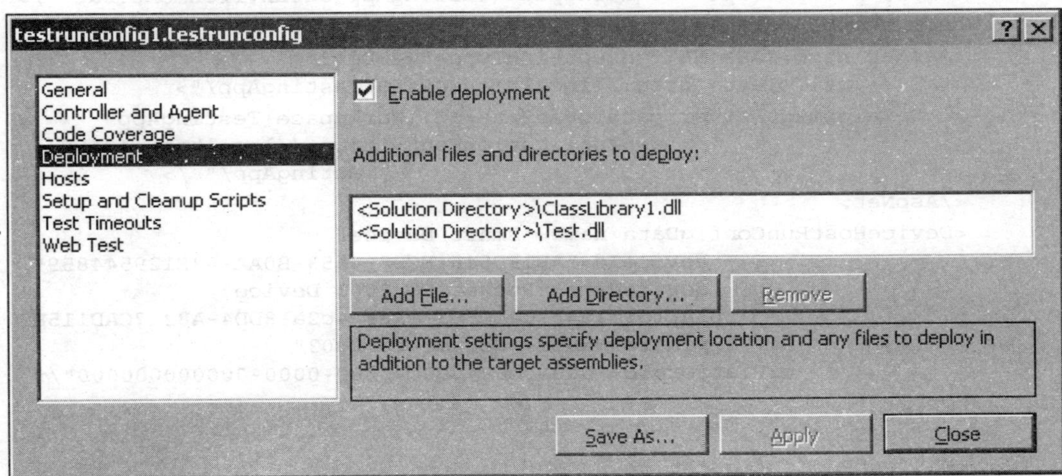

The other way of achieving the same is to edit the configuration XML file directly without using the tool. The XML file text below shows a sample test configuration file with a couple of additional deployment items, test timeouts, user defined naming scheme, and a setup script.

```
<?xml version="1.0" encoding="UTF-8"?>
<TestRunConfiguration name="TestRunConfig1"
                      id="fa788594-6ac2-495e-a484-2229faa94326"
                      xmlns="http://microsoft.com/schemas/VisualStudio
                             /TeamTest/2006">
  <Description>Test configuration file with the user defined
            scheme</Description>
  <CodeCoverage enabled="true">
    <Regular>
      <CodeCoverageItem binaryFile="C:\Workspace\CustomRules\bin\
                                    Debug\CustomRules.dll"
                        pdbFile="C:\Workspace\CustomRules\bin\Debug\
                                 CustomRules.pdb"
                        instrumentInPlace="true" />

    </Regular>
```

```
  </CodeCoverage>
  <Timeouts runTimeout="1800000" testTimeout="2700000" />
  <Remote controllerName="&lt;Local - No controller&gt;" />
  <Deployment>
    <DeploymentItem filename="Test.dll" />
    <DeploymentItem filename="ClassLibrary1.dll" />
  </Deployment>
  <NamingScheme baseName="User1@MyPC" useDefault="false" />
  <Scripts setupScript="C:\Workspace\TestingApp\SetEnvironment.bat" />
  <Hosts skipUnhostableTests="false">
   <AspNet name="ASP.NET" executionType="WebDev"
           urlToTest="http://localhost:49459/TestingApp/">
     <DevelopmentServer pathToWebSite="C:\Workspace\TestingApp"
                        webApplicationRoot="http://localhost:49459/
                                           TestingApp/" />
   </AspNet>
   <DeviceHostRunConfigData name="Smart Device"
                        deviceId="AE1FD546-ECB8-4553-B0AA-53E129544859"
                        deviceName="Pocket PC 2003 Device"
                       platformId="3C41C503-53EF-4c2a-8DD4-A8217CAD115E"
                        platformName="Pocket PC 2003"
                  uiPlatformId="00000000-0000-0000-0000-000000000000"/>
  </Hosts>
  <TestTypeSpecific>
   <WebTestRunConfiguration
       testTypeId="4e7599fa-5ecb-43e9-a887-cd63cf72d207">
     <Browser name="Internet Explorer 6.0">
       <Headers>
         <Header name="User-Agent" value="Mozilla/4.0
                    (compatible; MSIE 6.0; Windows NT 5.1)" />
         <Header name="Accept" value="*/*" />
         <Header name="Accept-Language"
                 value="{{$IEAcceptLanguage}}" />
         <Header name="Accept-Encoding" value="GZIP" />
       </Headers>
     </Browser>
     <Network Name="LAN" BandwidthInKbps="0" />
   </WebTestRunConfiguration>
  </TestTypeSpecific>
</TestRunConfiguration>
```

If we need more files to be added as part of deployment, we can update the **Deployment** section directly in the XML file and then add the files. Given here is the updated deployment section, which includes an additional file `CustomRules.dll` to be deployed:

```
<Deployment>
  <DeploymentItem filename="Test.dll" />
  <DeploymentItem filename="ClassLibrary1.dll" />
  <DeploymentItem filename="CustomeRules.dll" />
</Deployment>
```

We can edit any section of the XML file to change the configurations. This is similar to the configurations set using the IDE.

Using deploymentItem attribute

This attribute can be specified as part of the unit test methods to deploy additional items for a single test. To specify the attribute, open the unit test code and open the `TestMethod`. Add the `DeploymentItem` attribute to the method. Specify the file or folder as a parameter to the attribute. For example, the following code deploys the `test.dll` file as part of the test deployment.

```
  [TestMethod()]
[DeploymentItem("Test.dll")]
public void GetTotalPriceTest()
{
    Class1 target = new Class1();
    double expected = 0F;
    double actual;
    actual = target.GetTotalPrice();
    Assert.AreEqual(expected, actual);
}
```

This parameter can specify the file or folder with an absolute path or a relative path. Relative paths are relative to the path specified in the test configuration file.

Deploy items for individual test

The items specified in the test configuration setting are the default additional deployment items for the test project. Each test has its own properties, which includes the list of additional deployment items. These are specific to this test and not for the entire test project. To specify the items for a test, open the **Test List Editor** or the **Test View** window and select the test. Open the test **Properties** window and open the string collection editor for the deployment items and specify the list of deployment items. For example, the following screenshot shows the properties specified for a test with two additional deployment items, **Test.dll** and **Classlibrary2.dll**.

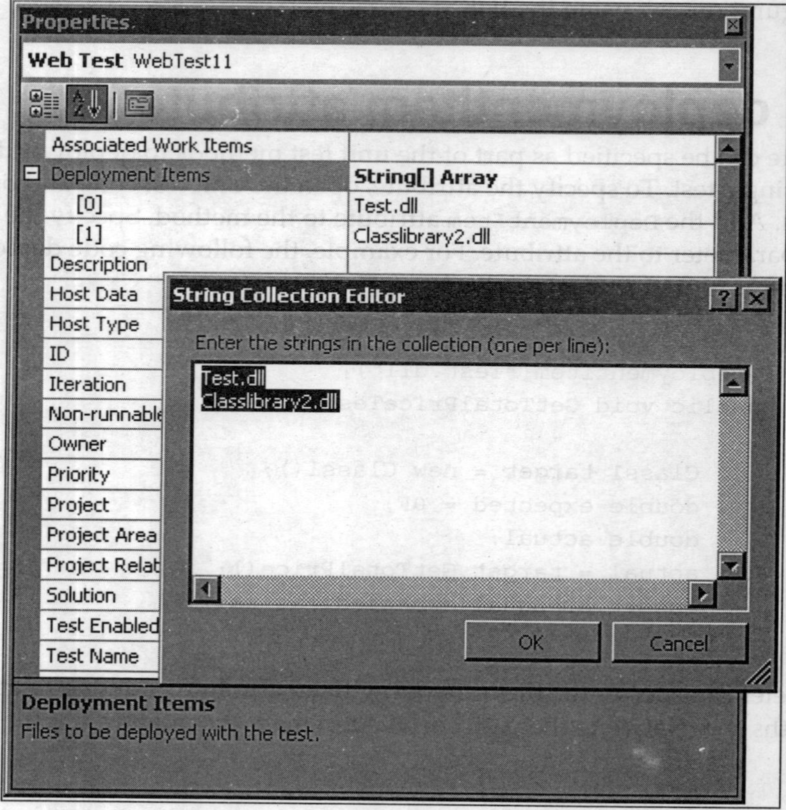

The deployment item is a collection property, which contains the list of all the deployment items specified for the test.

Deployment order

We have seen the different deployment configurations in the above sections. There are multiple places to specify the deployment items. We can specify on the project level, the individual test level, and on the method level. But what happens if we have files with the same name specified in different levels. The answer is that the file that gets copied later will override the existing file. There is an order for copying the deployment items. The order is listed as follows:

- Test assemblies and test files are copied first
- Instrumented binary files
- Items specified in the test run configuration file
- Dependent files and application configuration files
- Test deployment items for each test including the items specified for the test methods
- The deployment items specified for each test has higher precedence over the other files

Running tests

Running the test is very simple and easy in Visual Studio. All the options such as running, rerunning, stopping, and scheduling the test run are all possible in Visual Studio. The toolbars available in the **Test List Editor**, **Test View**, and the **Test Results** windows provide all these options.

Run and rerun a test

Running the test is done through the following different options provided in Visual Studio:

- Using **Test View** window
- Using **Test List Editor** window
- Using the **Test Results** window
- Using the **Source Code** editor

The following is an example for running the test from the Test List Editor. Select the checkboxes against the tests listed in the editor and then use the option in the toolbar to run the test. For the other windows, the toolbar option is very much similar to the Test List Editor.

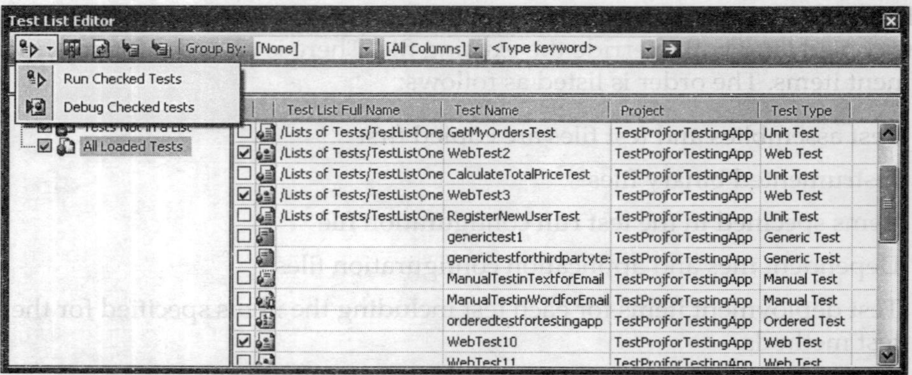

Whatever test is selected in the above list, it will start running one after the other with the result shown in the results window.

Pause, resume, and stop a test run

Pausing a test run is like holding the tests run in its current state until it is restarted again. The screenshot below shows the three tests under progress. The test is paused using the toolbar option. This will not affect the current test that is running, but will stop the next test from running.

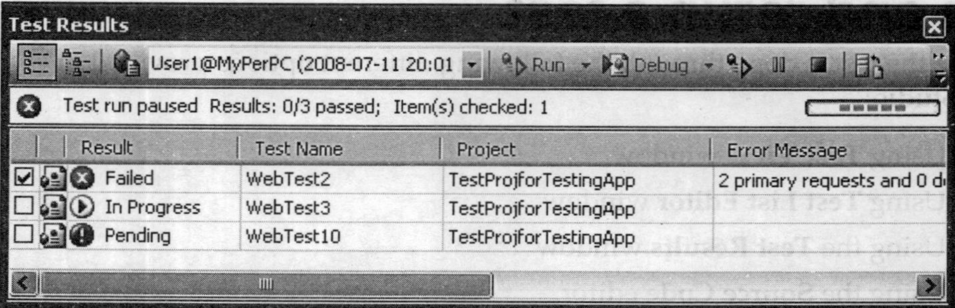

The screenshot above shows that the first test run is complete, but all the subsequent tests are paused. To restart the remaining tests, select the **Resume Test Run** option in the toolbar.

For stopping the test run, choose and click on the **Stop** option in the toolbar, which stops all the current test runs. If any test is running and not yet completed, it will get aborted.

Schedule test run

Scheduling a test run cannot be done through Visual Studio IDE as none of the windows have that option in the toolbar. This is only possible through the windows scheduler, which can run the batch program. The batch in turn can use the MSTest command line test run utility to run the tests. For more details about MSTest utility refer to the next chapter that explains the command line utility and options in detail.

Summary

This chapter discussed the different types of deployment and setting the configuration information for deployment. The additional files that are to be part of deployment, the editing of the configuration XML file, and addition of the attribute to the test code were also discussed. Finally, we saw the different ways of running and rerunning the tests, and also how to pause the tests. The next coming chapter will talk about the command line utility to run the test.

9
Command Line

We have seen different types of testing and running the test through Visual Studio 2008 IDE. It is very simple to run the test from Visual Studio user interface using the Test List Editor or Test View window as we have seen in the previous chapters. For creating or preparing the test project we need the Visual Studio IDE, but once the test is created we may not require the IDE. We may only want to run the test and collect the output.

This chapter explains the command line tool used for running the test instead of Visual Studio IDE. We can run the same tests with different options.

MSTest utility

This is the command line utility supported by Visual Studio. Using this **MSTest** tool, we can run the tests created in Visual Studio.

To access the **MSTest** tool, add the Visual Studio install directory to the path or access the Visual Studio command prompt from the **Tools** section of the Visual Studio group in the start menu.

After opening the command prompt, type **MSTest**.

```
Visual Studio 2008 Command Prompt
Setting environment for using Microsoft Visual Studio 2008 x86 tools.

C:\Program Files\Microsoft Visual Studio 9.0\VC>mstest
Microsoft (R) Test Execution Command Line Tool Version 9.0.21022.8
Copyright (c) Microsoft Corporation. All rights reserved.

Please specify tests to run, or specify the /publish switch to publish results.

For switch syntax, type "MSTest /help"

C:\Program Files\Microsoft Visual Studio 9.0\VC>
```

The `MSTest` command expects the parameter to be specified, which is the name of the test to be run. To know the options of MSTest, just type `MSTest/help` or `MSTest/?` in the command prompt.

The help option lists the different parameter options that can be used with the `MSTest` and the description of each parameter and its usage.

Option	**Description**
`/help`	Displays this usage message **<Short form: /? or /h>**
`/nologo`	Does not display the startup banner and the copyright message

`/testcontainer:[file name]`	Loads a file that contains tests; you can specify this option more than once to load multiple test files
	Examples:
	`/tescontainer:mytestproject.dll`
	`/testcontainer:loadtest1.loadtest`

`/testmetadata:[file name]`	Loads a metadata file Example: `/testmetadata:testproject1.vsmdi`
`/runconfig:[file name]`	Uses the specified run configuration file Example: `/runconfig:mysettings.testrunconfig`
`/resultsfile:[file name]`	Saves the test run results to the specified file Example: `/resultsfile:c:\temp\myresults.trx`
`/testlist:[test list path]`	The test list to run as specified in the metadata file; you can specify this option multiple times to run more than one test list Example: `/testlist:checkintests/clientteam`
`/test:[file name]`	The name of a test to be run; you can specify this option multiple times to run more than one test
`/unique`	Runs a test only if one unique match is found for any given `/test`.

Option	Description
`/noisolation`	Runs a test within the `MSTest.exe` process. This choice improves test run speed but increases risk to the MSTest process
`/noresults`	Does not save the test results in a TRX file; the choice improves test run speed but does not save the test run results
`/detail:[property id]`	The name of a property that you want to show values for, in addition to the test outcome; please examine a test results file to see the available properties. Example: `/detail:errormessage`

In addition to the above options, there are many other options which can be used with `MSTest` if team explorer is used.

Option	Description
`/publish:[server name]`	Publishes results to the TFS
`/publishbuild:[build name]`	The build identifier to be used to publish test results
`/publishresultsfile:[file name]`	The name of the test results file to be published; if none is specified, use the file produced by the current test run
`/teamproject:[team project name]`	The name of the team project to which the build belongs; specify this when publishing test results
`/platform:[platform]`	The platform of the build against which to publish the test results
`/flavor:[flavor]`	The flavor of the build against which to publish test results

We will run and see some test for the above options using the `MSTest` command line tool.

Running a test from the command line

Let us see some of the options for MSTest and see the results produced by these options. The MSTest utility does not work for manual tests. It is applicable only for the automated tests. Even if we apply the command for the manual test, the tool will remove the non-automated test from the test run. For example, if we run the test container command for the manual test, the reply would be similar to the one shown below:

```
C:\WINDOWS\system32\cmd.exe
C:\Program Files\Microsoft Visual Studio 9.0\Common7\IDE>mstest /testcontainer:C
:\Workspace\TestProjforTestingApp\ManualTestinTextforEmail.mtx
Microsoft (R) Test Execution Command Line Tool Version 9.0.21022.8
Copyright (c) Microsoft Corporation. All rights reserved.

Loading C:\Workspace\TestProjforTestingApp\ManualTestinTextforEmail.mtx...
Starting execution...
Warning: The non-automated test 'ManualTestinTextforEmail' was removed from the
test run.
No tests to execute.

C:\Program Files\Microsoft Visual Studio 9.0\Common7\IDE>_
```

/testcontainer

The testcontainer option requires the file that contains information about the tests that must be run. The test container file differs across tests. For example, the unit test information is contained in the unit test project assembly file. For the ordered test, it would be the <ordertestproject>.orderedtest file, which contains information about the ordered test.

If we have multiple test projects created under the solution, each of these projects has its own container for the tests within the project.

Let us consider an ordered test which contains four different tests such as generictest1.generictest, GetTotalPrice Unit test, and couple of manual tests. The name of the ordered test file is OrderedTest1.orderedtest. Now let us try using the MSTest for running the tests in the ordered test file. You can see the output of the test as shown in the following image. The automated tests removed the manual non-automated tests from the list and ran only the automated tests.

```
Visual Studio 2008 Command Prompt

C:\Program Files\Microsoft Visual Studio 9.0\VC>mstest /testcontainer:c:\workspace\testprojfortestin
gapp\orderedtest1.orderedtest.
Microsoft (R) Test Execution Command Line Tool Version 9.0.21022.8
Copyright (c) Microsoft Corporation. All rights reserved.

Loading c:\workspace\testprojfortestingapp\orderedtest1.orderedtest...
Starting execution...
Warning: The non-automated test 'ManualTestinTextforEmail' was removed from the test run.
Warning: The non-automated test 'ManualTestinWordforEmail' was removed from the test run.

Results               Top Level Tests
-------               ---------------
Failed                c:\workspace\testprojfortestingapp\orderedtest1.orderedtest
0/1 test(s) Passed, 1 Failed

Results               orderedtest1
-------               ------------
Aborted               c:\workspace\testprojfortestingapp\generictest1.generictest
Failed                TestProjforTestingApp.Class1Test.GetTotalPriceTest
0/2 test(s) Passed, 1 Aborted, 1 Failed

Summary
-------
Test Run Failed.
  Failed   2
  Aborted  1
  ----------
  Total    3
Results file:      C:\Program Files\Microsoft Visual Studio 9.0\VC\TestResults\User1_MyPerPC 2008-10
-28 16_44_39.trx
Run Configuration: Default Run Configuration

C:\Program Files\Microsoft Visual Studio 9.0\VC>
```

For Unit tests and Web tests, the test project file will be an assembly. For example, the following command will load the `TestProjforTestingApp.dll` assembly and run the test within that assembly.

```
Visual Studio 2008 Command Prompt
C:\Program Files\Microsoft Visual Studio 9.0\VC>mstest /testcontainer:C:\Workspace\TestProjforTestin
gApp\bin\Debug\TestProjforTestingApp.dll /nologo
Loading C:\Workspace\TestProjforTestingApp\bin\Debug\TestProjforTestingApp.dll...
Starting execution...

Results                 Top Level Tests
-------                 ---------------
Passed                  TestProjforTestingApp.Class1Test.CalculateTotalPriceTest
Failed                  TestProjforTestingApp.Class1Test.GetTotalPriceTest
Failed                  TestProjforTestingApp.ProgramTest.GenericMethodSampleTest
Inconclusive            TestProjforTestingApp.ProgramTest.MainTest
Inconclusive            TestProjforTestingApp.ProgramTest.ProgramConstructorTest
Failed                  TestProjforTestingApp.Service1Test.GetMyOrdersTest
Failed                  TestProjforTestingApp.Service1Test.RegisterNewUserTest
Failed                  TestProjforTestingApp.Service1Test.SendMailMessageTest
Failed                  TestProjforTestingApp.Service1Test.ValidateNewUserTest
Error                   TestProjforTestingApp.WebTest11Coded
Error                   TestProjforTestingApp.WebTest7Coded
1/11 test(s) Passed, 6 Failed, 2 Inconclusive, 2 Error

Summary
-------
Test Run Error.
  Passed        1
  Failed        6
  Inconclusive  2
  Error         2
  ----------------
  Total         11
Results file:      C:\Program Files\Microsoft Visual Studio 9.0\VC\TestResults\User1_MyPerPC 2008-06
-10 21_06_55.trx
Run Configuration: Default Run Configuration

Run has the following issue(s):
```

First, the `MSTest` will load all the tests within the ordered test and then start them executing one by one. The result of each test run is also shown. The results are not shown but the detailed test run is also stored in the test trace file. We can load the trace file and see the details of the test run.

/testmetadata

The `testmetadata` option is used for running the tests in multiple test projects under a solution. This is based on the metadata file created under the solution. The metadata file contains a list of all the tests added to the Test List Editor. Using this Test Editor, we can create a new list of tests from all the available tests under the solution irrespective of the projects.

The `testcontainer` option is specific to a test project whereas `testmetadata` is for multiple test containers with the flexibility of choosing tests from each container.

For example, the following image shows two different test lists which contain different tests added to the list from all the available tests in the solution:

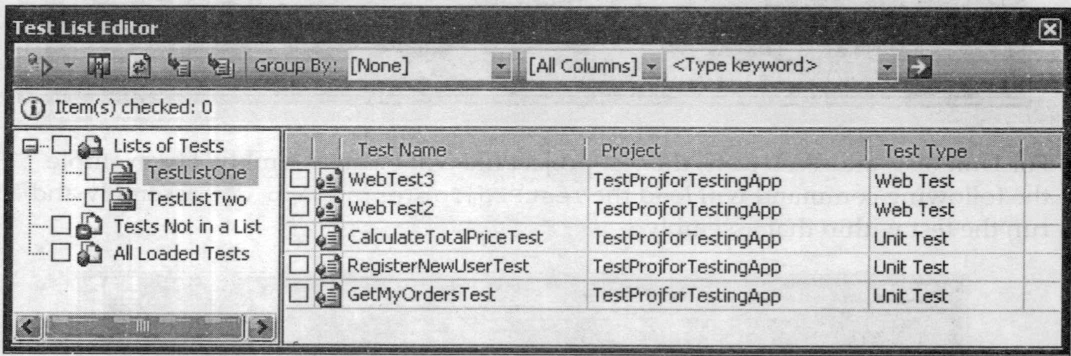

Any change or update made to the test list editor, will be saved in the metadata file. Now, to run only the tests added to the test lists in the editor, we use the option metadata. To run a specific test list, we should use the `/testlist` option along with the `testmetadata` option as shown:

```
mstest /testmetadata:[file name] /testlist:[test list name]
```

The following command runs all the tests added to the list, `TestListOne`:

```
Visual Studio 2008 Command Prompt

C:\Program Files\Microsoft Visual Studio 9.0\VC>mstest /testmetadata:C:\Workspace\TestingApp\TestingApp.vsmdi /t
estlist:TestListOne /nologo
Loading C:\Workspace\TestingApp\TestingApp.vsmdi...
Starting execution...

Results               Top Level Tests
-------               ---------------
Failed                <TestListOne/>TestProjforTestingApp.Service1Test.GetMyOrdersTest
Failed                <TestListOne/>c:\workspace\testprojfortestingapp\webtest2.webtest
Passed                <TestListOne/>TestProjforTestingApp.Class1Test.CalculateTotalPriceTest
Failed                <TestListOne/>c:\workspace\testprojfortestingapp\webtest3.webtest
Failed                <TestListOne/>TestProjforTestingApp.Service1Test.RegisterNewUserTest
1/5 test(s) Passed, 4 Failed

Summary
-------
Test Run Failed.
  Failed  4
  Passed  1
  ---------
  Total   5
Results file:      C:\Program Files\Microsoft Visual Studio 9.0\VC\TestResults\User1_MyPerPC 2008-06-09 14_15_4
1_.trx
Run Configuration: TestRunConfig1

C:\Program Files\Microsoft Visual Studio 9.0\VC>
```

If there are no tests added to the test list, and if it is an empty list, the `Mstest` command will clearly display a message saying there are no tests to be run in the list.

/test

There are situations where we might have to run a particular test from the available list of tests. In that case, we can use the `/test` option with the `testmetatadata` option or the `testcontainer` option. For example, the following command runs only the `CalculateTotalPriceTest` test from the list:

```
Visual Studio 2008 Command Prompt

C:\Program Files\Microsoft Visual Studio 9.0\VC>mstest /testmetadata:C:\Workspace\TestingApp\Testing
App.vsmdi /test:RegisterNewUserTest /nologo
Loading C:\Workspace\TestingApp\TestingApp.vsmdi...
Starting execution...

Results               Top Level Tests
-------               ---------------
Failed                <TestListOne/>TestProjforTestingApp.Service1Test.RegisterNewUserTest
0/1 test(s) Passed, 1 Failed

Summary
-------
Test Run Failed.
  Failed  1
  ---------
  Total   1
Results file:      C:\Program Files\Microsoft Visual Studio 9.0\VC\TestResults\User1_MyPerPC _2008-0
6-09 15_54_55_.trx
Run Configuration: TestRunConfig1

C:\Program Files\Microsoft Visual Studio 9.0\VC>
```

The `/test` option can be used along with `testmetadata` or `testcontainer`, but not both. There are different usages for the `/test` option:

1. We can specify any number of tests using the `/test` multiple times against `testmetadata` or `testcontainer` option.
2. The name used against the `/test` option is the search keyword of the fully qualified test names. For example, if there are test names with fully qualified names such as:

    ```
    TestProjforTestingApp.Class1Test.CalculateTotalPriceTest
    TestProjforTestingApp.Service1Test.RegisterNewUserTest
    TestProjforTestingApp.Service1Test.GetMyOrdersTest
    ```

    And if the command contains the option, `/test:TestingApp` then all the above three tests will run as the name contains the `Testingapp` string in it. Even though we specify only the name to the `/test` option, the result displays the fully qualified name of the tests run in the results window.

/unique

This option will make sure that only one test, which matches the given name, is run. In the above examples, we have three different tests with the string `TestingApp` in its fully qualified name. If we run the following command, all the above three tests will be executed:

```
mstest /testmetadata:c:\workspace\testingapp\TestingApp.vsmdi /test:
TestingApp
```

But if we specify the `/unique` option along with the above command, the `MSTest` will return the message saying more than one test was found in the same name. It means that the test will be successful only if a unique test name is found with the name given.

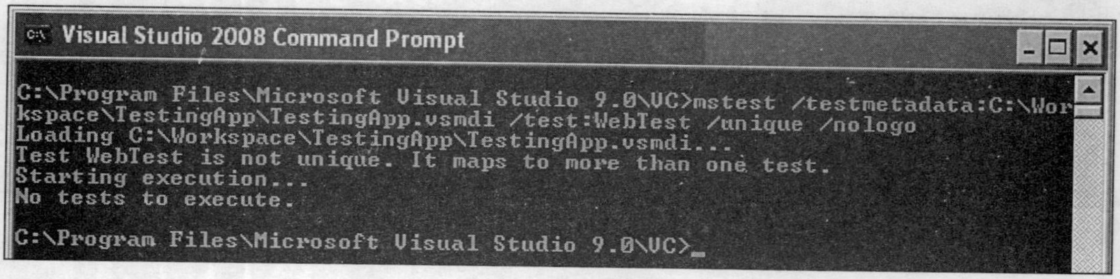

```
Visual Studio 2008 Command Prompt

C:\Program Files\Microsoft Visual Studio 9.0\VC>mstest /testmetadata:C:\Wor
kspace\TestingApp\TestingApp.vsmdi /test:WebTest /unique /nologo
Loading C:\Workspace\TestingApp\TestingApp.vsmdi...
Test WebTest is not unique. It maps to more than one test.
Starting execution...
No tests to execute.

C:\Program Files\Microsoft Visual Studio 9.0\VC>_
```

The following command will execute successfully as there is only one test with the name `Webtest3`:

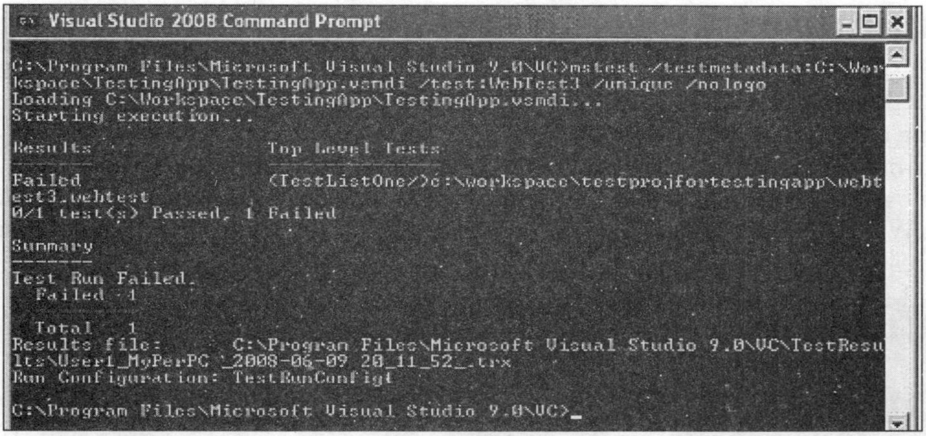

```
Visual Studio 2008 Command Prompt

C:\Program Files\Microsoft Visual Studio 9.0\VC>mstest /testmetadata:C:\Wor
kspace\TestingApp\TestingApp.vsmdi /test:WebTest3 /unique /nologo
Loading C:\Workspace\TestingApp\TestingApp.vsmdi...
Starting execution...

Results               Top Level Tests
-------               ---------------
Failed                <TestListOne/>c:\workspace\testprojfortestingapp\webt
est3.webtest
0/1 test(s) Passed, 1 Failed

Summary
-------
Test Run Failed.
  Failed  1
  --------
  Total   1
Results file:      C:\Program Files\Microsoft Visual Studio 9.0\VC\TestResu
lts\User1_MyPerPC 2008-06-09 20_11_52_.trx
Run Configuration: TestRunConfig1

C:\Program Files\Microsoft Visual Studio 9.0\VC>_
```

/noisolation

This option runs tests with the `MStest.exe` process. This choice improves test run speed, but increases risk to the `MSTest.exe` process.

Usually, the tests are run in a separate process which takes its own memory. If we launch the `MSTest.exe` with the `/noisolation` option, the tests are run in a process which avoids more memory usage.

/runconfig

This is to specify to the test run to use a specific configuration file. If the configuration file is not specified, the `MSTest` uses the default configuration file. The following example forces the test to use the `TestRunConfig2` configuration file:

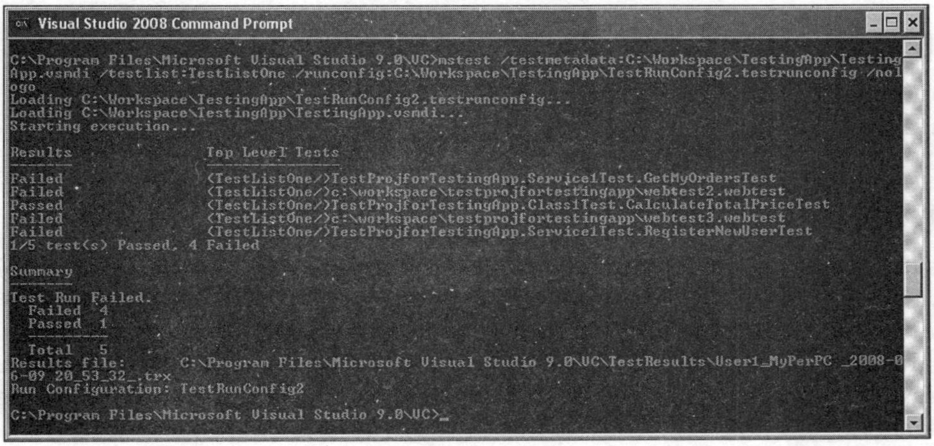

```
Visual Studio 2008 Command Prompt

C:\Program Files\Microsoft Visual Studio 9.0\VC>mstest /testmetadata:C:\Workspace\TestingApp\Testing
App.vsmdi /testlist:TestListOne /runconfig:C:\Workspace\TestingApp\TestRunConfig2.testrunconfig /nol
ogo
Loading C:\Workspace\TestingApp\TestRunConfig2.testrunconfig...
Loading C:\Workspace\TestingApp\TestingApp.vsmdi...
Starting execution...

Results               Top Level Tests
-------               ---------------
Failed                <TestListOne/>TestProjforTestingApp.Service1Test.GetMyOrdersTest
Failed                <TestListOne/>c:\workspace\testprojfortestingapp\webtest2.webtest
Passed                <TestListOne/>TestProjforTestingApp.Class1Test.CalculateTotalPriceTest
Failed                <TestListOne/>c:\workspace\testprojfortestingapp\webtest3.webtest
Failed                <TestListOne/>TestProjforTestingApp.Service1Test.RegisterNewUserTest
1/5 test(s) Passed, 4 Failed

Summary
-------
Test Run Failed.
  Failed  4
  Passed  1
  --------
  Total   5
Results file:      C:\Program Files\Microsoft Visual Studio 9.0\VC\TestResults\User1_MyPerPC 2008-0
6-09 20_53_32_.trx
Run Configuration: TestRunConfig2

C:\Program Files\Microsoft Visual Studio 9.0\VC>_
```

/resultsfile

In all the command executions, the MSTest stores the test results to a trace file. By default, the trace file name is assigned by the MSTest with the login user ID, the machine name and the current date and time. We can force the test tool to use a specific file to store the test results. For example, the above test result is stored in the file User1_MyPerPC_2008-06-09 20_53_32_.trx at the default Visual Studio folder. We can use the resultsfile option to change the location and the filename of the results file.

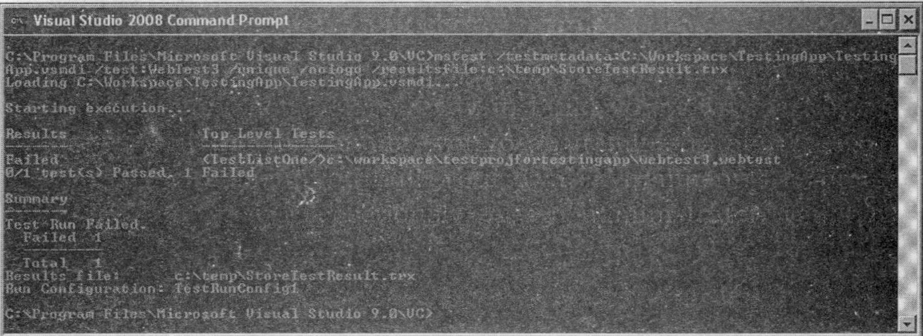

The previous image shows the test results stored at the c:\temp location in the results file, StoreTestResult.trx.

/noresults

This option is to inform the MSTest application to not store the test results to the TRX file. This choice does not store the results but increases the performance of the test execution.

/nologo

This option is to inform the MSTest tool to not display the copyright information which is shown at the beginning of the test run.

/detail

This is the option used for getting the values of the properties of each test run result. Each test result provides information about the test such as error messages, start time, end time, test name, description, test type and many more properties. Using this option we can get the property value after the test run. For example, the following command shows the start and end time of the test run and also the type of the test run.

```
Visual Studio 2008 Command Prompt
C:\Program Files\Microsoft Visual Studio 9.0\VC>mstest /testmetadata:C:\Workspace\TestingApp\Testing
App.vsmdi /test:WebTest3 /nologo /detail:starttime /detail:endtime /detail:testtype
Loading C:\Workspace\TestingApp\TestingApp.vsmdi...
Starting execution...

Results               Top Level Tests
-------               ---------------
Failed                <TestListOne/>c:\workspace\testprojfortestingapp\webtest3.webtest
[starttime] = 6/10/2008 2:39:45 AM
[testtype] = Web Test
[endtime] = 6/10/2008 2:39:48 AM
0/1 test(s) Passed, 1 Failed

Summary
-------
Test Run Failed.
  Failed  1
  ---------
  Total   1
Results file:      C:\Program Files\Microsoft Visual Studio 9.0\VC\TestResults\User1_MyPerPC 2008-0
6-09 21_39_43_.trx
Run Configuration: TestRunConfig1

C:\Program Files\Microsoft Visual Studio 9.0\VC>
```

The detailed option can be specified multiple times to get multiple properties value after the test run.

Publishing test results

This option is valid only if we have the Team explorer installed, and if the Visual Studio is connected to the Team Foundation Server (TFS). This publishes the test data and results to the TFS team project. Please refer to MSDN for more information on installing and configuring TFS and Team explorer.

Using the command line utility and the various options, we can publish the test run results. The publish option with `MSTest` will first run the test and then set the flavor and platform for the test before publishing the data to the TFS. Some of these options are mandatory for publishing the test run details.

We will see the examples of different publishing options available for the command line `MSTest` tool.

/publish

The `/publish` command should be followed by the URI of the TFS if the TFS is not registered in the client. If it is registered, we can use just the name of the server to which the test result has to be published.

`/publish:[server name]`

- Example 1: `/publish:http://MyTFSServer`

  (If the TFS Server is not registered in the client)

- Example 2: `/publish:MyTFSServer`

  (If the TFS Server is registered with the client)

/publishbuild

This option is used for specifying the build name for publishing. This is the unique name that identifies the build from the list of scheduled builds.

/flavor

This is a mandatory option for publishing the test results to the TFS. Flavor is a string value which should be used in combination with the platform name and should match with the completed build that can be identified by the `/publishbuild` option. Before publishing the test run results to the TFS, `MSTest` will run the test and then set the flavor and the platform properties.

```
/flavor:[flavor string value]
```

- Examples 1: `/flavor:Release`
- Example 2: `/flavor:Debug`

/platform

This is a mandatory string value used in combination with the `/flavor` option which should match the build option.

```
/platform:[string value]
```

- Example 1: `/platform:Mixed Platforms`
- Example 1: `/platform:.NET`
- Example 1: `/platform:Win32`

/publishresultsfile

`MSTest` stores all test results in default trace files with the extension `.trx`. Using this `/publishresultsfile` option we can publish the test results `output/trace` file to the TFS. The name of the file is the input to this option. If the value is not specified, `MSTest` will publish the current test run trace file to TFS.

```
/publishresultfile:[file name string]
```

- Example 1: `/publishresultfile`

  (current test run trace file will be published)

- Example 2: `/publishresultfile:`

Trace files

Before publishing the test result we have to store the test results in a trace file. Use the /tracefile option with the MSTest command line to store the test results. The default extension for the trace file is trx. It is better to use the same extension when we force the Visual Studio to use a specific trace file for the test results.

For example:

```
MSTest /testmetadata:TestProject.vsmdi /testfile:TestProject.trx
```

Publishing

To publish the test result, we can use a combination of the different options seen above, and the only option is /publishresultsfile.

Let us try creating a trace file and then create a build type for the project. Then we can publish the test result trace file to the build.

Step 1: Create test project

The following image contains the solution **ClassLibrary1**. The solution contains a simple class library project **ClassLibrary1**. Use the menu option, **Test | New Test** from the Visual Studio IDE and then choose the unit test type. Name the test and select the existing project or choose the option to create a new project to add the new test. The following image shows the test project named **ClassLibrary1TestProject**.

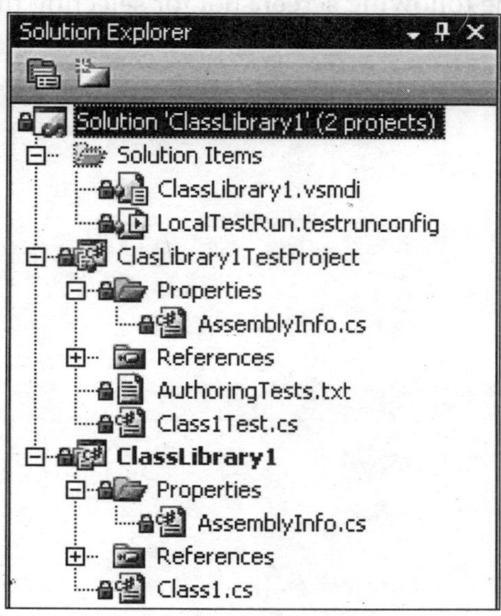

Step 2: Running the test

The test project **ClassLibrary1TestProject** contains two unit test methods. Run the test and by default, the test result is stored in the trace files `<file name>.trx`.

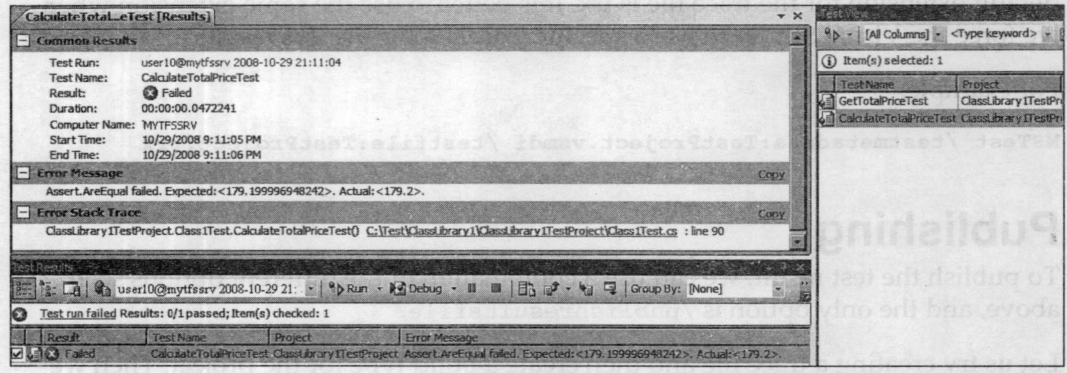

Step 3: Create Build

Now is the time to create the build type for the team project. The steps and the details behind creating the build types are out of the scope of this book. So let us do an overview on how to create the build type using the Team Explorer. Within the Team Explorer, select the **Build definitions** under the **Builds** option folder, which is under the team project. Right-click and choose a new build definition and configure the options by choosing the projects in TFS and the local folder. In one of the steps, you can see the following screenshot for selecting the project and setting the configuration information for the build.

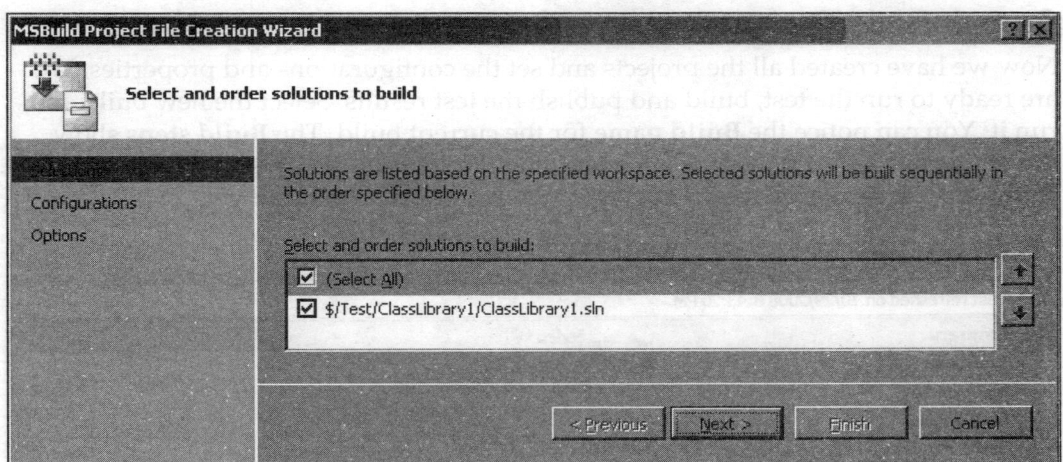

The following screenshot shows the important configuration setting required for build, which should match the test results publishing parameters: the platform and the flavor values:

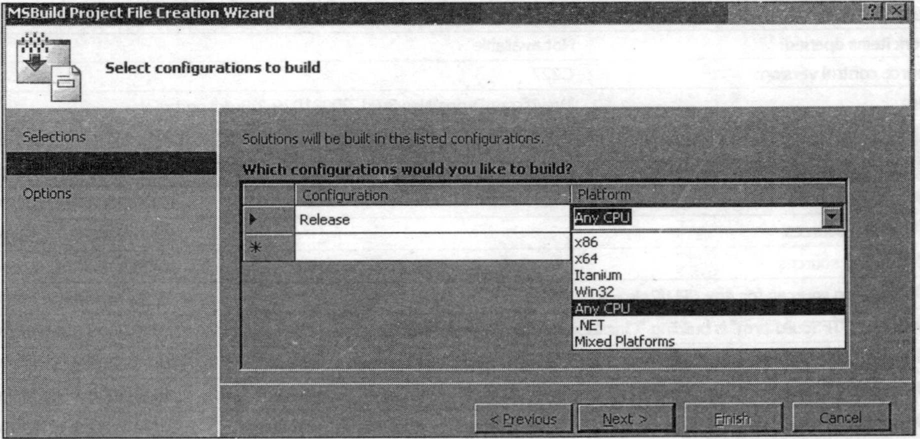

Step 4: Build Project

Now we have created all the projects and set the configurations and properties. We are ready to run the test, build and publish the test results. Select the new build and run it. You can notice the **Build name** for the current build. The **Build steps** show the platform and the flavor used for building the solution. The result details section shows no test results as we do not have any test results published yet.

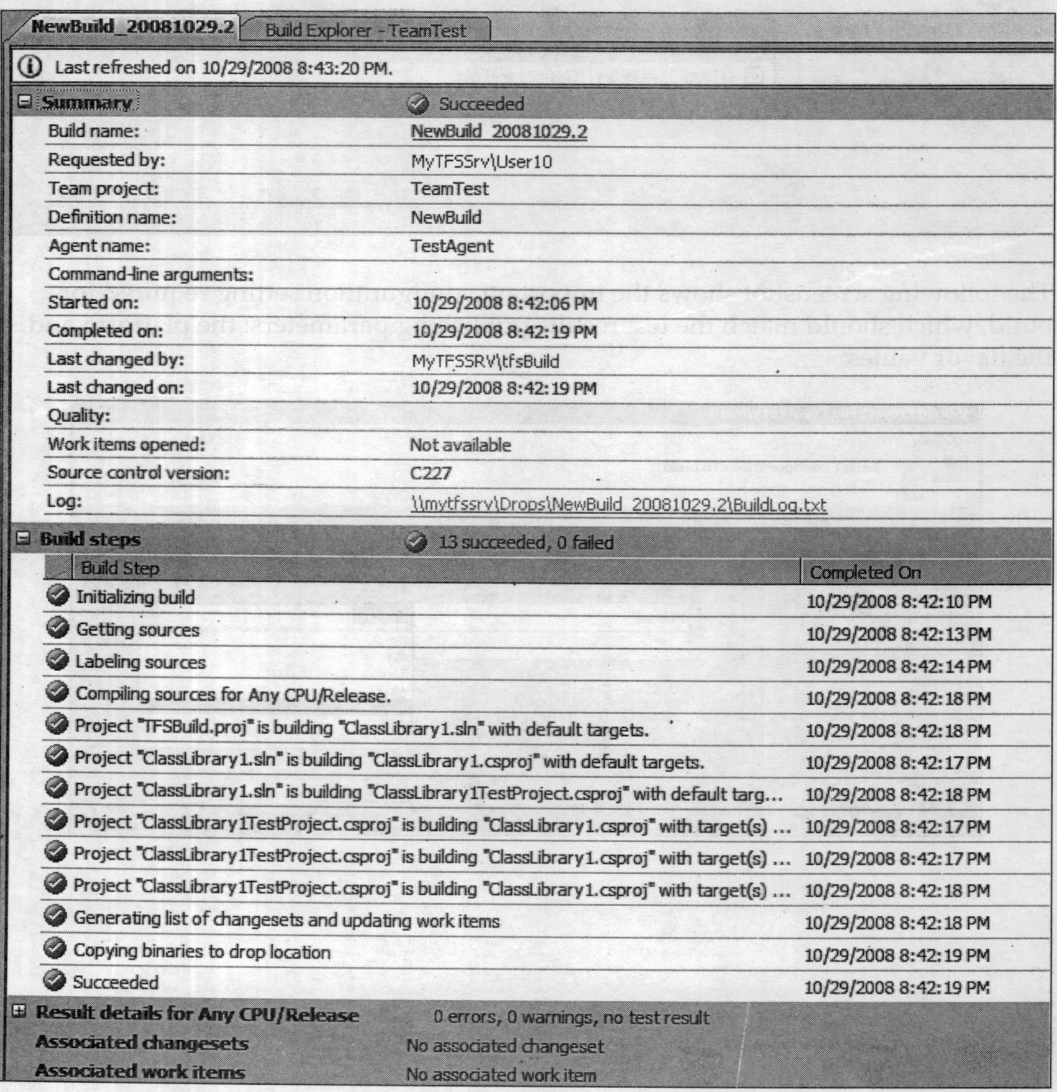

Step 5: Publish Result

So far we have created the test results file and also built the projects. All the test runs were successful in which the test failed. Now is the time to publish the test results to the build. We have seen the options used for publishing the test results using the MSTest command line. The following command publishes the two test results to the build specified:

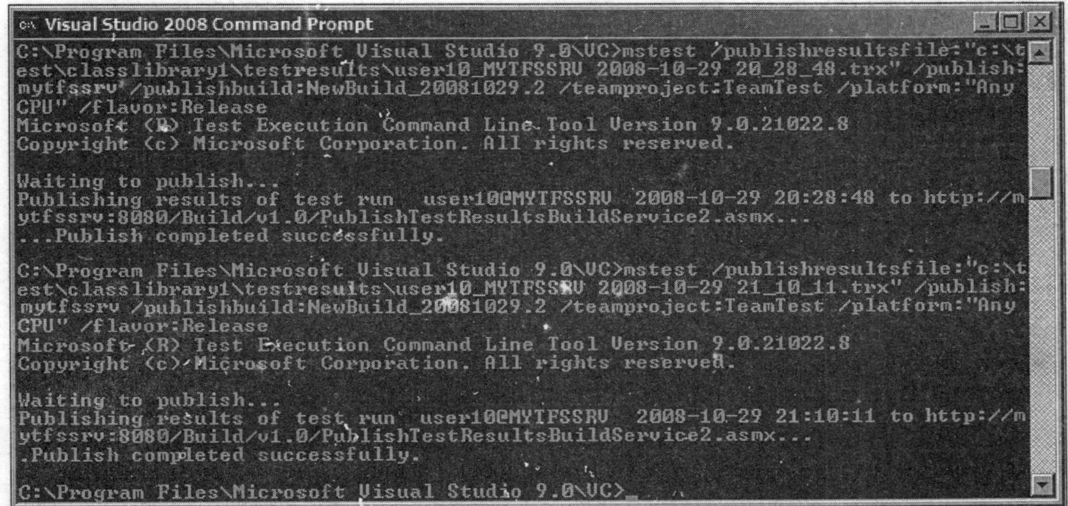

The command line options used in the above picture shows the test result trace file used for publishing. The command line also has the platform and the flavor values matching the build configurations set in step 3 above. The publishing is done using the web service shown previously. There are different methods exposed by the web service.

After publishing the test results, if you open the build **NewBuild_20081029.2**, you can see the test information as shown in the following image, which is nothing but information from the trace file.

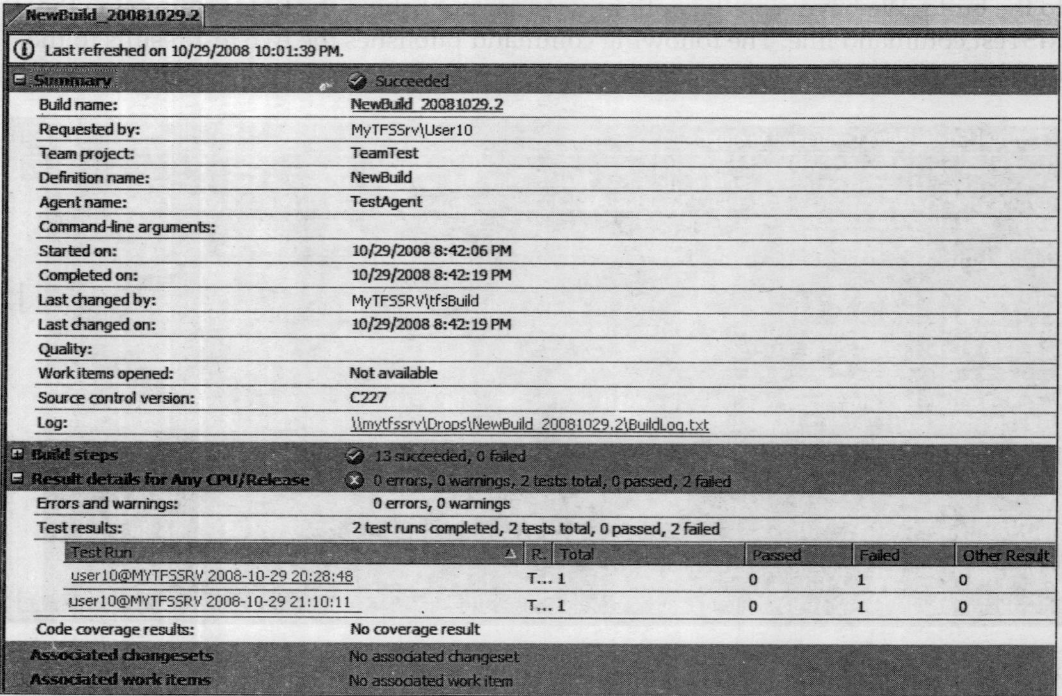

The test URL will open the page which shows all the details of the test run. You can publish any number of test results to the TFS and bind it to a particular build so that the test results correspond to that particular build.

Summary

This chapter explained the use of the command line utility, `MSTest`, used for running the test without using the UI. We have seen different command line options for running the test, and their usage. We have not only run the test but have also seen how to publish the test results using the command line options. The next chapter covers more on test results and on raising the defects directly using the Test Results window.

10
Working with Test Results

The test results are not only useful to see if the method and class are returning the expected result, but also to analyze the application and to verify the build. We can add the test as part of the Team Foundation Server automated build, so that we can verify the build and make sure the latest code checked in to the source control is working as expected. The build process produces the same results as we get when we run the test project and the results are stored in the Test Results folder. Whenever there is a test failure, we can directly create a defect from the test results window into the Team Foundation Server as a work item of type defect. Chapter 9 explained about publishing the test result to the corresponding build using the command line utility. The test result from the **Test Results** window can also be published directly to the Team Foundation Server build, which is explained in detail later in this chapter.

Test results

All the tests run through the Test List Editor or Test View window. Using the solution explorer will show the test results in the **Test Results** window. This window shows the status of the test and the link to the test result details. The test name is the same as the test result; `.trx` is the file created by the test run.

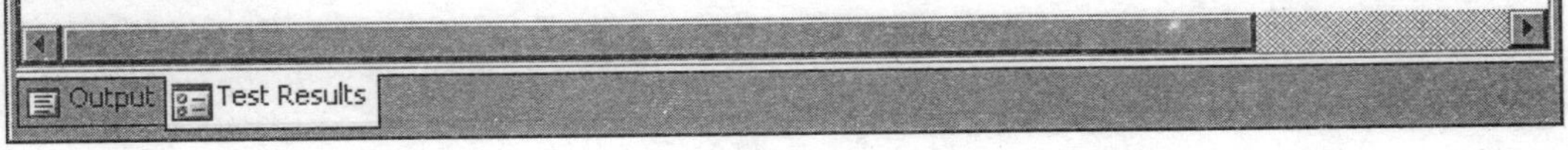

Test Results

TestProject@MyPC (2008-02-15 19:· Run Debug

Test run completed Results: 2/2 passed; Item(s) checked: 0

Result	Test Name	Project	Error Message
Passed	GetTotalPriceTest	ClasLibrary1TestProject	
Passed	CalculateTotalPriceTest	ClasLibrary1TestProject	

Output Test Results

Test as part of Team Foundation Server build

The TFS is the place to maintain the code for all the projects including the test projects. Let us assume that we have a **ClassLibrary** project and the unit test project for the class library, and both are checked into the Team Foundation Server. Whenever there is a change or fix in the code, the test project has to run and verify that the fix is producing the expected result.

Team Foundation Server provides the automated build utility to build the team projects. There is a set of procedures to be followed to create the build project in TFS. The screenshot below shows the build project, which contains the class library project and the test project for the **ClassLibrary**.

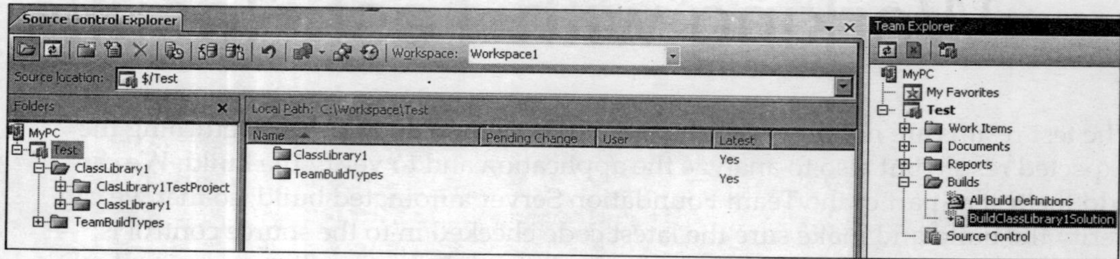

The build project automates the process of building the projects in the solution selected for the build and can also run the test project after compiling and building it, which would verify the code fix. There are some options to be set while creating the build project.

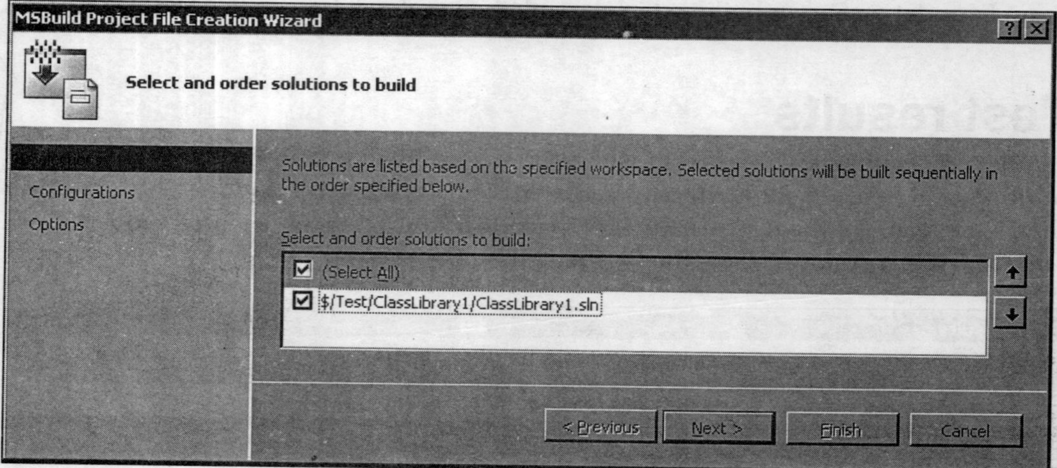

The **Selections** option shown in the above screenshot selects the solution to build. The solution can be single or many. When the build starts, the TFS will start building the solutions as selected in the above screenshot. Once the solution is selected, the system will display the test lists within the solution. We can select the test list from the list shown.

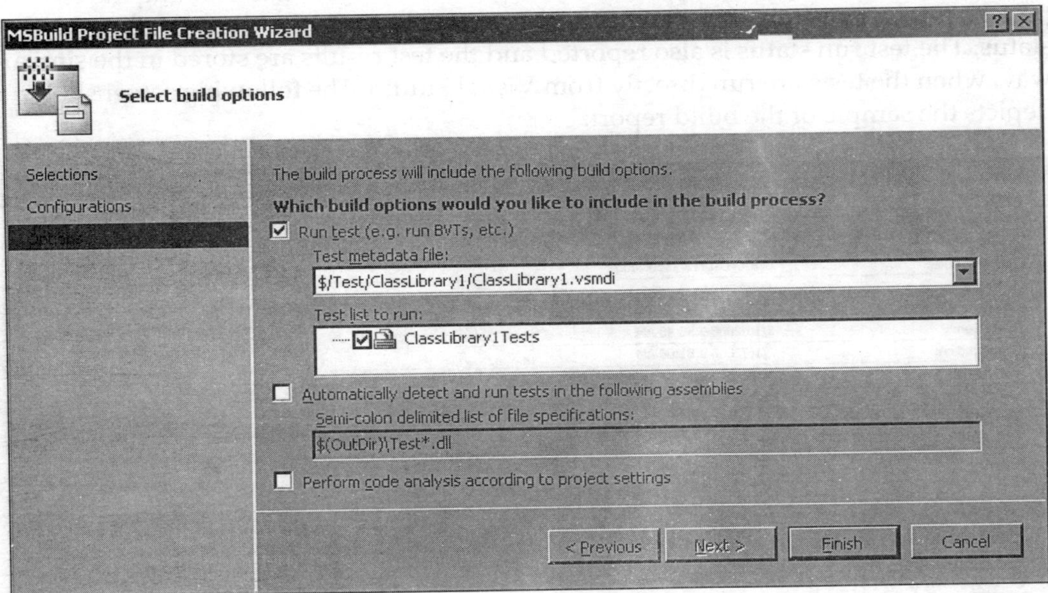

The test lists shown in the above screenshot are the test lists created using the Test List Editor for the solution. All the test lists belong to the solution we selected in the previous screen. Each test list may contain more than one test. The tests in the selected test lists above are run after building the project.

Build report and test result

The VSTS takes the source code from the solution of the TFS and builds the projects, and reports it immediately. The report is also saved in TFS for future reference. Each and every step is reported in the build report. It consists of getting the source for the project, compiling the projects, compiling the test project, and running the test project, if it is set to run after the build. The report also includes the overall build status. The test run status is also reported and the test results are stored in the similar way, when the tests are run directly from Visual Studio. The following screenshot depicts the sample of the build report:

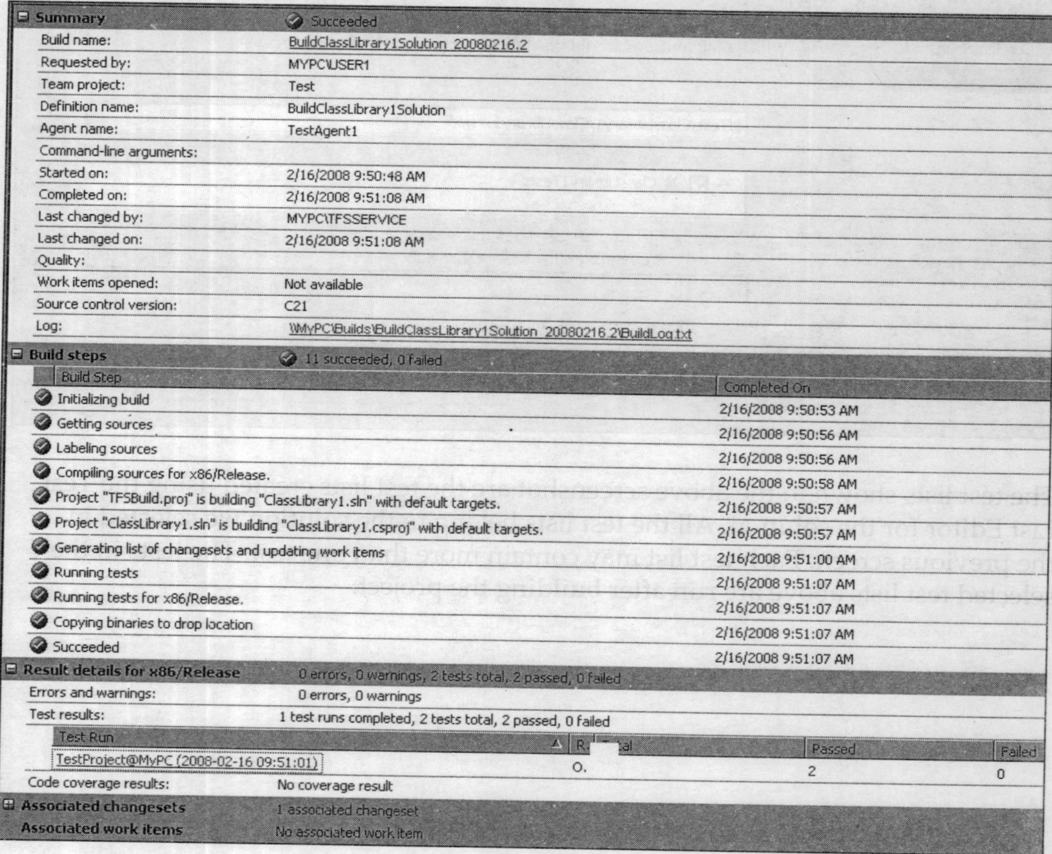

The above build succeeded without any errors in building the projects in the solution **ClassLibrary1** and running the test. The test result is also shown under the section **Result details for x86/Release**. This is the result of tests in the test list included in the build for the solution. This is the same result shown in the test results window, when the tests are run using Test View or Test List Editor. This section also has the URL link for the test result folder where the test result `.trx` file and the other binaries are stored. The URL opens the test results folder as shown here:

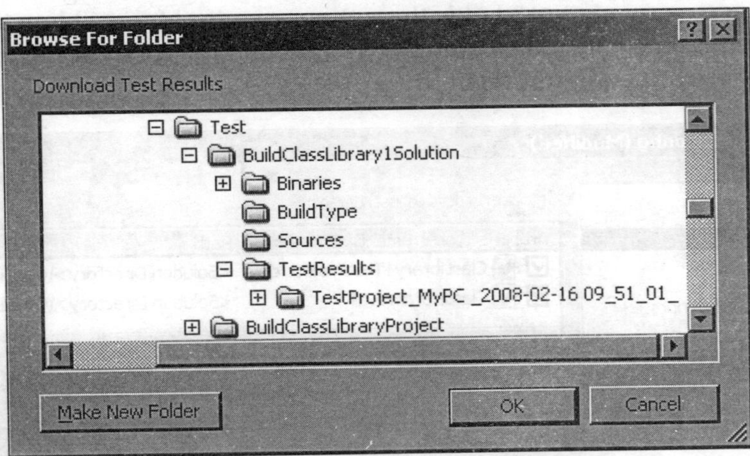

Select a particular folder of the current test by the build under the **TestResults** folder and then clicking on **OK**, the results are imported to the **Test Results** window and the window shows up with the tests and the status.

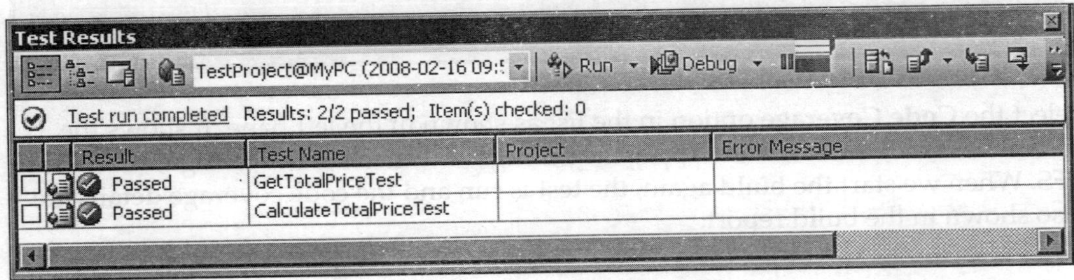

Code coverage

We are aware about code coverage as we have gone through some samples in Chapter 2, *Unit Testing*, but we will recall that and see as part of build process here. The test run step in the build process can also include the code coverage for the current test. Code coverage is the process of finding out the percentage of code that is covered by the unit test. This helps us know better how much of the code remains to be tested and what percentage of code has been tested. The configuration file `LocalTestRun.testrunconfig` holds the settings required for enabling the code coverage for unit tests. Open the Solution Explorer and the configuration file, which in turn opens up the configuration utility.

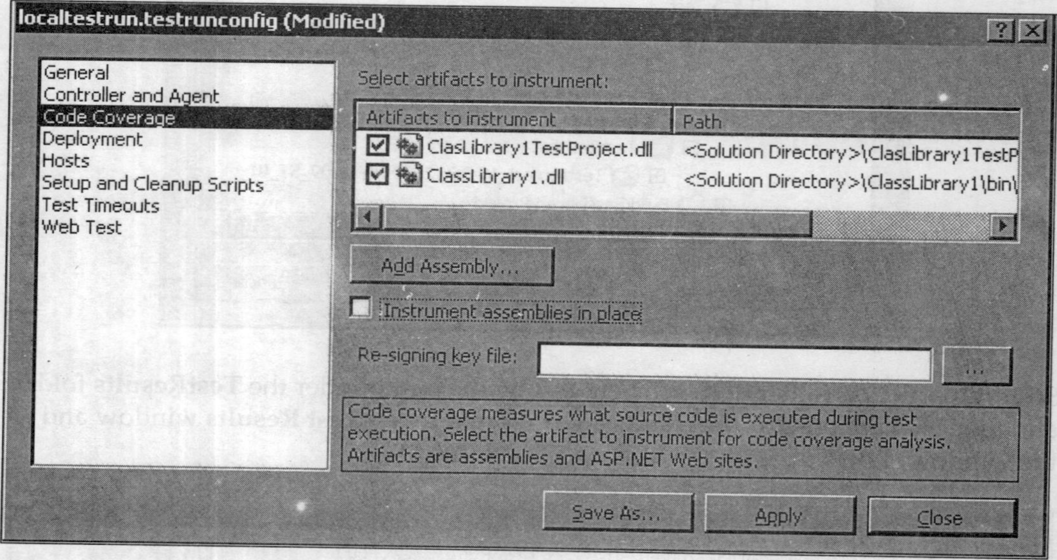

Select the **Code Coverage** option in the list as shown in the left pane. It shows the assemblies from the solution. Apply the settings and check in the configuration file to TFS. When we start the build again, the test is run and the code coverage details are also shown in the build report.

The code coverage results are shown after the test results under the section, **Result details for x86/Release**. The following report shows the code coverage section with the total percentage of blocks covered and the percentage of code covered in each assembly. The percentage of blocks not covered by the code is also shown in the report.

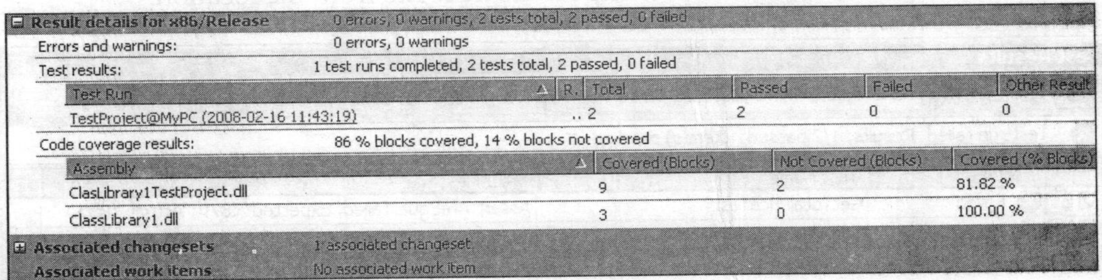

Result details for x86/Release	0 errors, 0 warnings, 2 tests total, 2 passed, 0 failed
Errors and warnings:	0 errors, 0 warnings
Test results:	1 test runs completed, 2 tests total, 2 passed, 0 failed

Test Run	R.	Total	Passed	Failed	Other Result
TestProject@MyPC (2008-02-16 11:43:19)	..	2	2	0	0

Code coverage results: 86 % blocks covered, 14 % blocks not covered

Assembly	Covered (Blocks)	Not Covered (Blocks)	Covered (% Blocks)
ClasLibrary1TestProject.dll	9	2	81.82 %
ClassLibrary1.dll	3	0	100.00 %

Associated changesets	1 associated changeset
Associated work items	No associated work item

Build report with failed test

Whatever we have seen so far is the positive side of testing. Now let us do some code changes to make the test fail. For example, one of the methods in the **ClassLibrary1TestProject** is modified with a different expected value from the test. Check the code and start the build process.

The TFS builds the solution and presents the build report with the status of each step during the build process. The following screenshot shows the build report:

Completed on:	2/16/2008 1:04:44 PM
Last changed by:	
Last changed on:	2/16/2008 1:04:44 PM
Quality:	
Work items opened:	Not available
Source control version:	C23
Log:	\\MyPC\Builds\BuildClassLibrary1Solution_20080216.4\BuildLog.txt

Build steps: 9 succeeded, 2 failed

Build Step	Completed On
Initializing build	2/16/2008 1:04:24 PM
Getting sources	2/16/2008 1:04:27 PM
Labeling sources	2/16/2008 1:04:27 PM
Compiling sources for x86/Release.	2/16/2008 1:04:29 PM
Project "TFSBuild.proj" is building "ClassLibrary1.sln" with default targets.	2/16/2008 1:04:29 PM
Project "ClassLibrary1.sln" is building "ClassLibrary1.csproj" with default tar...	2/16/2008 1:04:28 PM
Generating list of changesets and updating work items	2/16/2008 1:04:31 PM
Running tests	2/16/2008 1:04:43 PM
Running tests for x86/Release.	2/16/2008 1:04:42 PM
Copying binaries to drop location	2/16/2008 1:04:43 PM
Partially Succeeded	2/16/2008 1:04:44 PM

Result details for x86/Release	0 errors, 0 warnings, 2 tests total, 1 passed, 1 failed
Errors and warnings:	0 errors, 0 warnings
Test results:	1 test runs completed, 2 tests total, 1 passed, 1 failed

Test Run	R.	Total	Passed	Failed	Other Result
TestProject@MyPC (2008-02-16 13:04:32)	O..	2	1	1	0

Code coverage results: 79 % blocks covered, 21 % blocks not covered

Assembly	Covered (Blocks)	Not Covered (Blocks)	Covered (% Blocks)
ClasLibrary1TestProject.dll	8	3	72.73 %
ClassLibrary1.dll	3	0	100.00 %

Associated changesets	1 associated changeset
Associated work items	No associated work item

As we had expected, the test failed in the build process while running the test. So the status of the build is partially completed. This is because the compilation of all the projects was successful. Also running the test was successful, but the test failed because the result did not match up with the expected result. Let us now look at the test result. Click on the test result URL link and import the trace file from the location.

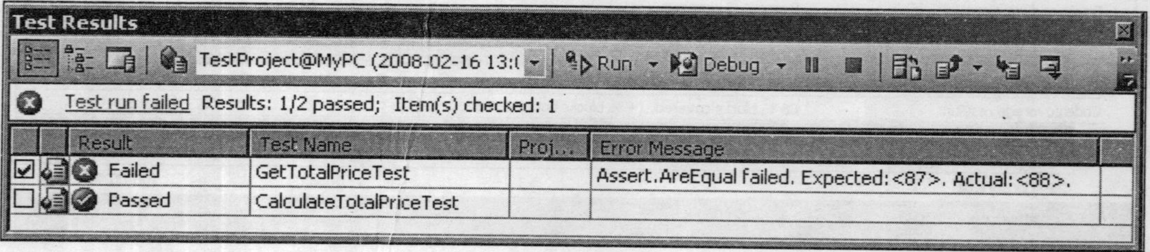

The result window shows the methods that passed the test and the ones which failed. The error message is also shown as the expected result is different from the actual.

Right-click on the failed test in the **Test Results** window, and select the **View Test Result Details** option, which shows more details about the failed test. The details window shows the summary of the test such as the time the test started and ended, the duration, and the test name. The second section shows the error message from the test.

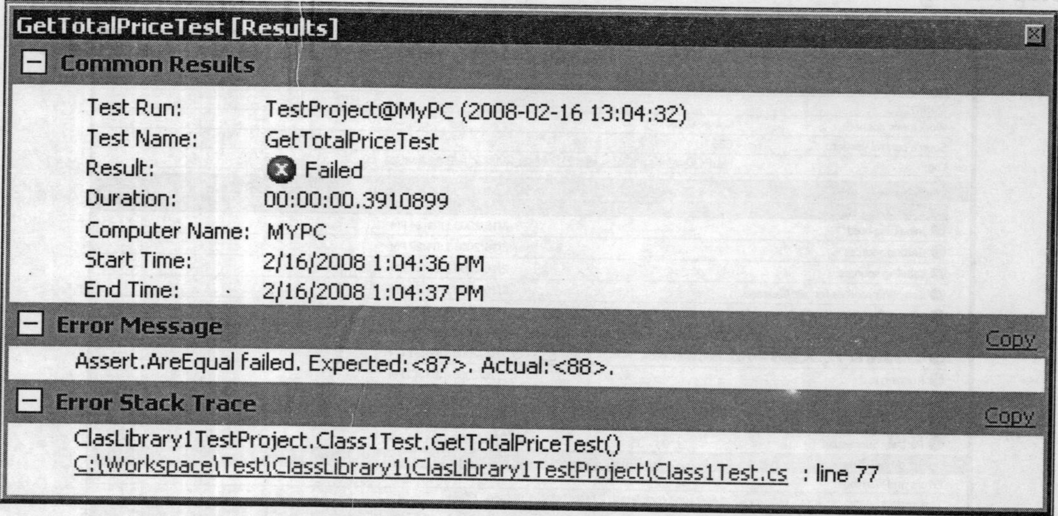

Stack trace

The **Test Results** window has the detailed section, which shows the **Error Stack Trace** of the failed test. This one clearly shows the line at which it failed in the class file. The section also has the URL link which will directly take us to the point where the test has failed. As shown in the above image, the URL opens the **Class1Test.cs** file and the cursor is placed on **line 77**.

Creating Work Item from the result

Work item is an item in the TFS, which refers to a unit of work. It could be just an item, which is a task or a defect or a work item of type Bug, or it could be an issue or a requirement item. The following screenshot shows the option to add a work item using the menu option in VSTS menu. The option lists the different types of work item.

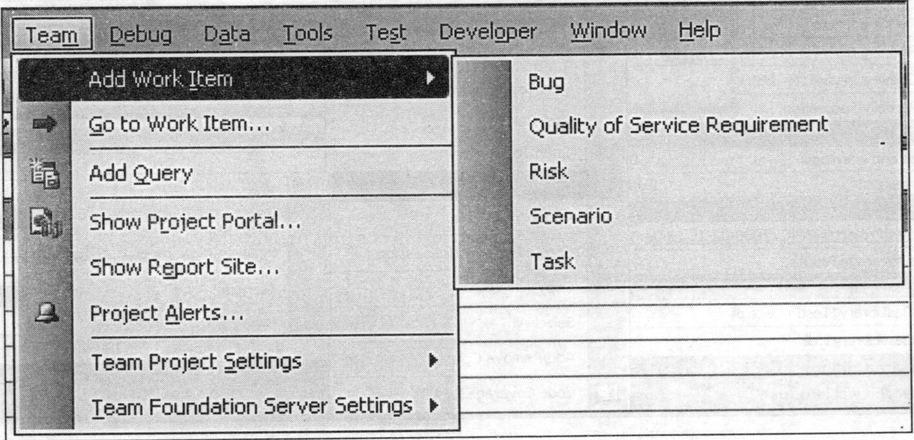

The work item of type **Bug** is a defect raised against a failure or error occurred from the application. Now in our example above, the test result throws an error from the code saying **the expected result does not match with the actual result**. This code has to be fixed by the developer who wrote the code. Now we can add the corresponding bug work item to TFS using the menu option, or we can directly add that from the **Test Results** window.

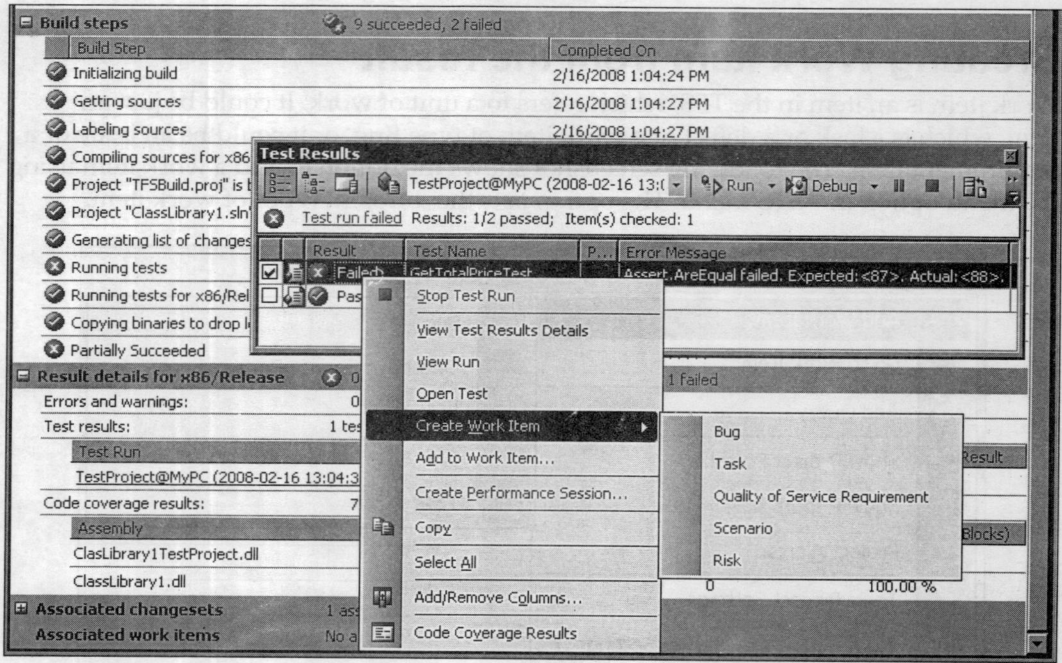

The error is added as a **Bug** to the TFS work item. It also fills the details required for the bug. We can overwrite the details as per our requirement if we want. The Bug has different sections to it. We can overwrite or fill additional details to the **Title** and **Description** field for the Bug.

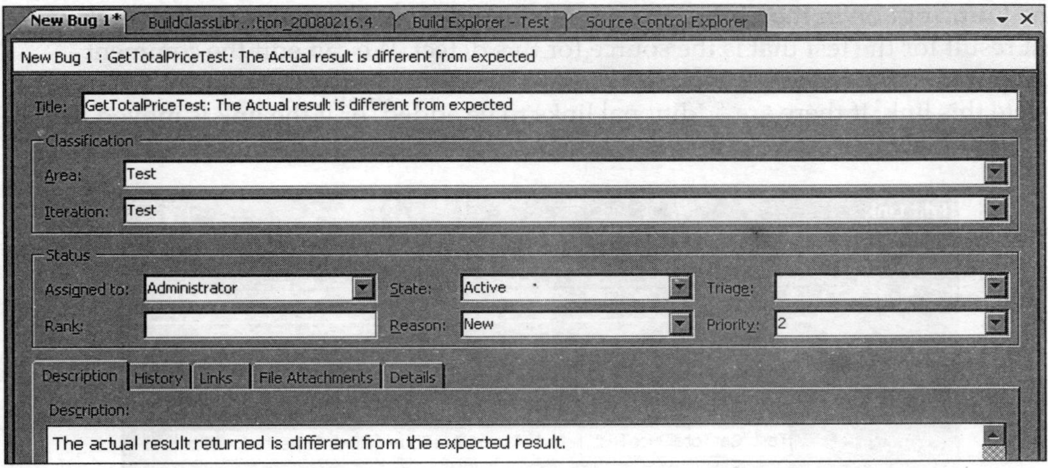

The second tab contains the history of the defect changes. Whenever we modify the properties of the Bug, it is tracked here in the **History** tab. The third one is the **Links** tab, which contains the link to the source from which this defect occurred. It is automatically filled by TFS when we create this defect. There are some options to the right of this **Links** tab. The **Open** option opens the **Test Result** and the Test Result details window.

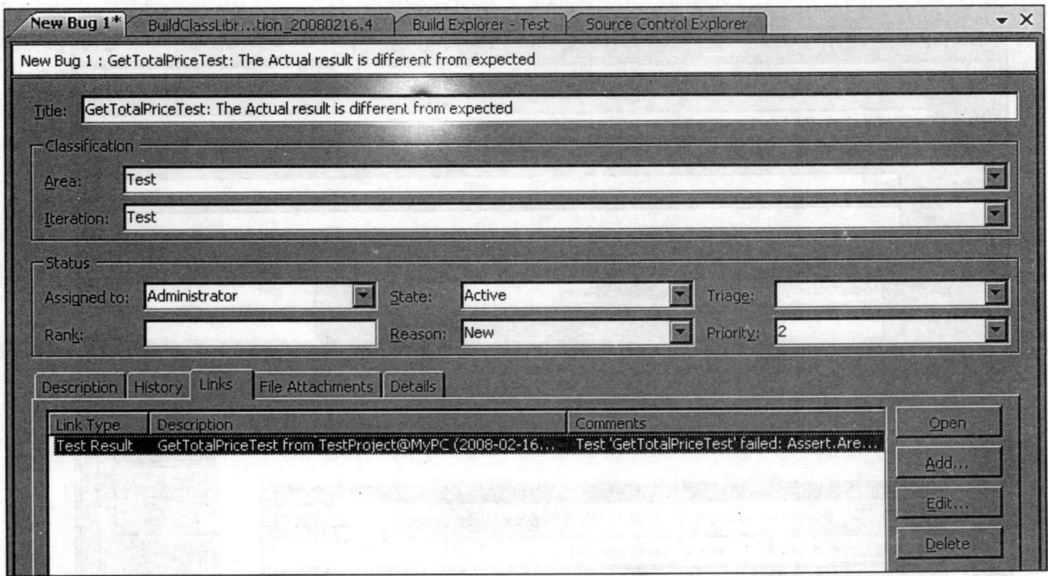

The **Edit...** option in the **Links** tab opens the window that contains the link to the test result for the test that is the source for this defect. We can edit the comment if required. If we still do not have the test result in the **TestResults** folder, we can delete this link. If there are additional links to be added, or if the link is moved to a different place, we can add it.

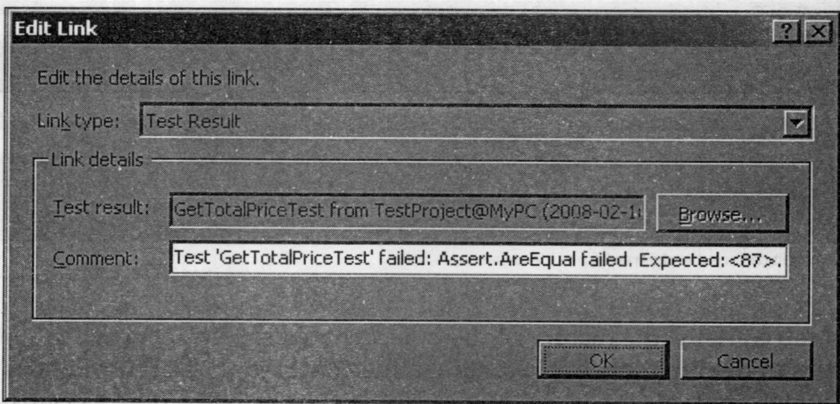

The next tab in the bug work item is that of **File Attachments**, which has the trace file for the test attached to it. Select the trace file and click on **Open** which opens the test result window with the results loaded in the window.

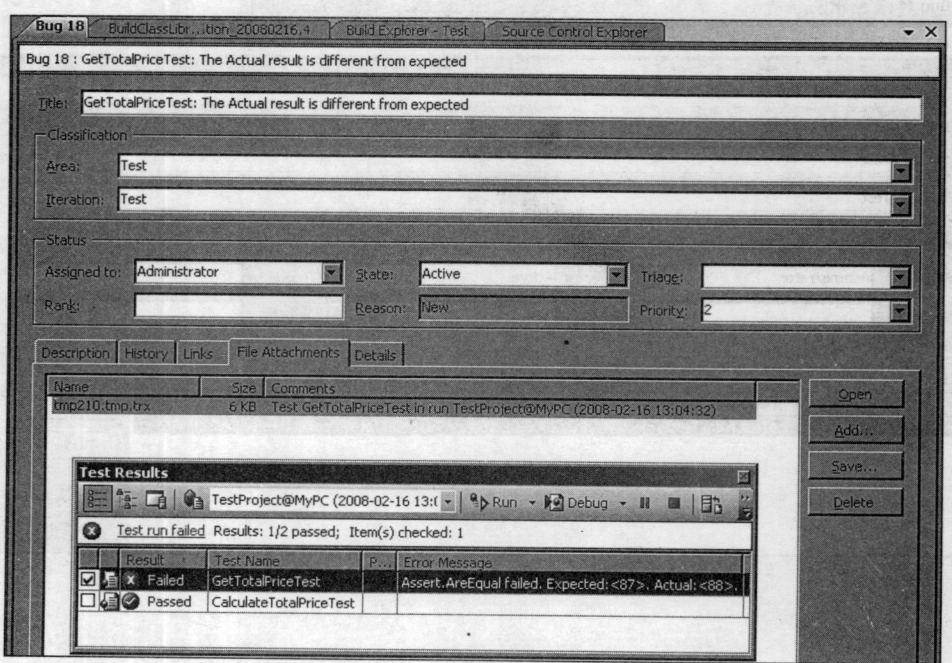

This tab also has different options to add another attachment, save the attachment to a different location or to delete it.

Publish test results

So far, what we have seen in this chapter is about running the tests and creating the work item for the test result and setting its properties. But we still have the test results stored in the local machine. Think about the different testers in different locations running the tests. Everyone will have the test results in his/her local machine. How do we consolidate and let other project teams or the other team members know about the test results? TFS maintains the operational store, which is a central database where all the details are stored for future use.

VSTS provides an option to publish the test results to the TFS operational store so that the other team at a different location can easily look at the test results that are published to a central location.

The **Test Results** window has the option to publish the results. Select the check box option against the test results in the window and click on the **Publish** button on the test results toolbar.

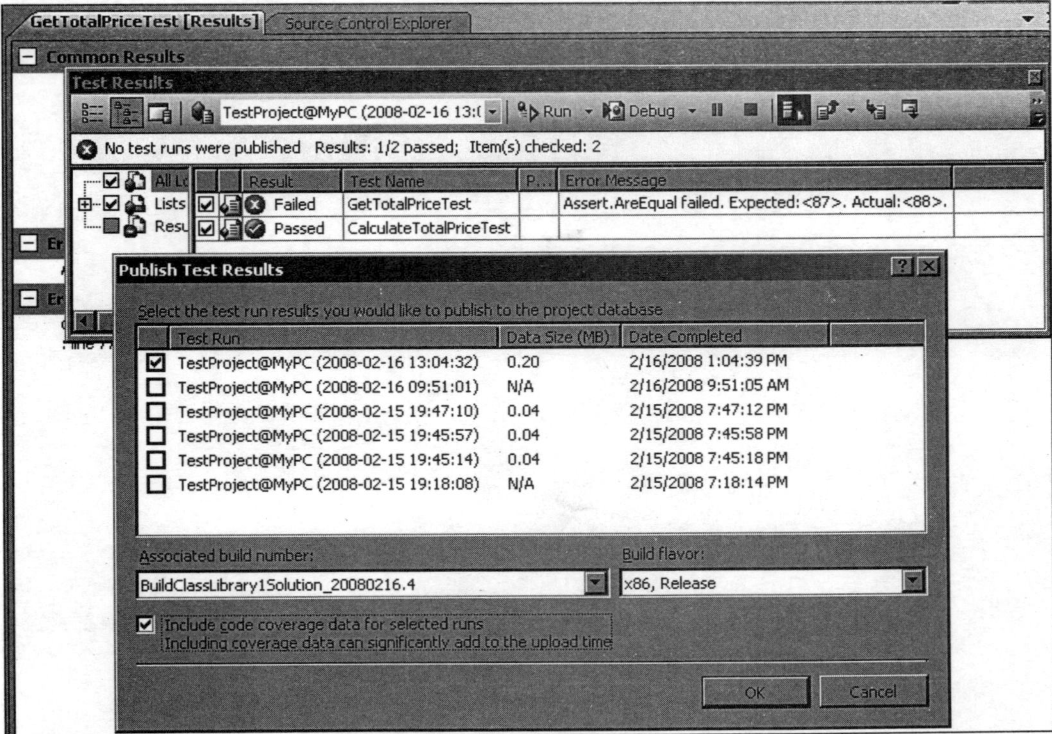

The publish option opens a new window, which lists all the test results in the current **TestResults** folder. Select the test to be published and select the **Associated build number** and the **Build flavor**. The code coverage data can be published along with the test result by selecting the option **Include code coverage data for selected runs**.

Summary

Whenever a test is run from solution explorer or the Test View window or the Test List Editor, the results of the tests run are shown in the test results window. It has different options to filter, import, export, and publish the test to TFS. The Test Results window also provides a detailed window which shows the error messages for the failed test and the stack trace for the failed unit test result to take us directly to the code where the error occurs. It is very easy for the development team to find out the cause for the test. The testers also do not have to spend time in logging the defect for the error. The VSTS provides the feature to directly log the defect in the TFS. The next chapter explains the different ways of presenting or viewing the defects and the work items that we created in TFS. The VSTS provides better reporting tools, which are used for grouping the details and presenting in graphical and grid formats. The chapter also explains how to customize the reports.

11
Reporting

We have seen different types of testing methods and diffrent ways of running the tests using VSTS 2008. The previous chapters explained the different ways of running the tests and looking at the test results through the **Test Results** and the **Test Run** window. The **Test View** window, **Test List Editor,** and the **Solution Explorer** window are used for maintaining the tests. The test result summary window provides the selected test result after the test run. But how do we get the collective information about all the tests run based on some specific parameters? VSTS 2008 Team Foundation server provides built-in reports to get collective information on all the tests run. There are several other reports to get information about the work items and builds. These reports are very useful in studying and analyzing the project quality and status at any point of time.

The TFS comes with different process templates that can be used for the team project. Each process template in TFS contains a number of predefined reports. The team project is the central data store for one or more projects. The data store maintains all the information about the project including the source code, build details, and tests. The **Team Explorer** is the user interface to get details about the work items, test results, and builds.

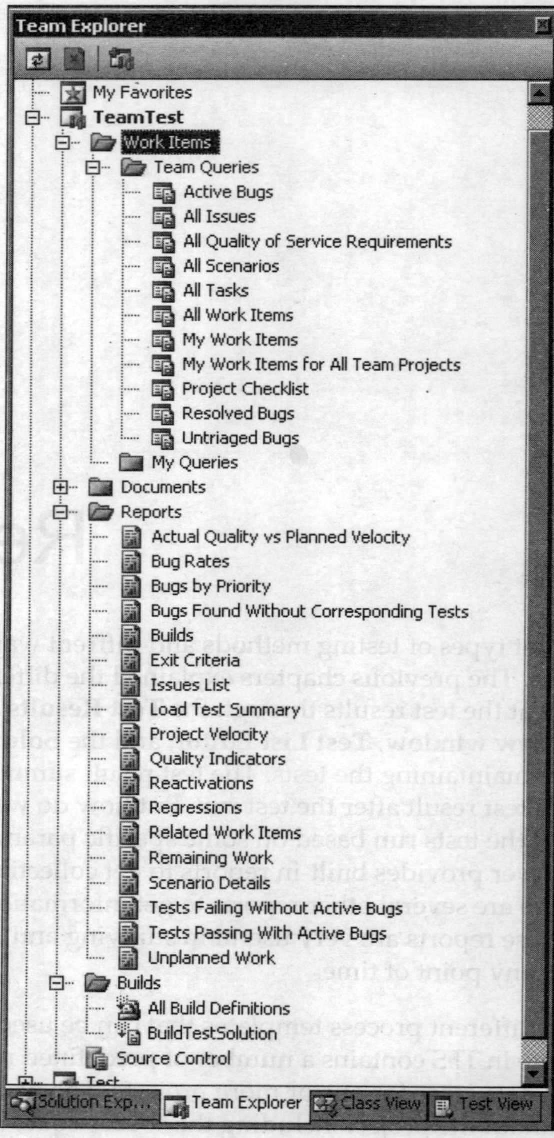

TFS uses the SQL Server 2005 Reporting/ Analysis Services to create and manage reports. SQL Server 2005 is the default data store used by TFS to maintain all information about the projects including the source code, tests, reports, documents, and build information. Whenever a new project is created, a set of predefined reports from the selected process template is created under the **Reports** folder of the project. All these reports can be customized based on the requirement. Alternatively, we can also create new reports so that the other teams can share the same reports.

Creating reports for VSTS can be done by using any tool that connects to a relational database or analysis database. It could be the Microsoft Excel or Visual Studio Report Designer. Excel is easier to use, but provides less functionality when compared to the Report Designer. Some of the important features provided by the Report Designer are:

- Detailed reporting
- Sharing the report using Team Explorer
- Updating the existing reports
- Getting the report faster and managing the reports

All these reports have the feature to export and print the current report. The report can be exported in different formats such as XML, CSV, TIFF, Acrobat (PDF), and Excel. There is a print option that comes along with the report to print the current report result for the selected parameters.

TFS reports for testing

TFS has several built-in reports readily available for the selected process template. Some of these reports are specific to defects, and some are specific to testing while some others are common to work items.

Bugs

Bugs are the list of defects found during the test run or code compilation, or during the build, or an exception during the test. All these defects can be added as work items of type **Bug** to the team project under the TFS. There are different parameters to the work item such as the iteration, area, priority, triage, description, title, and other additional details for the defect. Every time the defect is modified, a history is maintained. The first time the defect is added, the status would be **active**. Whenever the defect is fixed, the developer can change the status to resolve so that the tester can test the defect in the next deployment of the application and change it to **fixed**. All these activities are tracked, and history is maintained in the SQL Server 2005 Analysis Services by the TFS. The report fetches the information from the data maintained in the SQL Server and presents it in the expected format.

Bug rates

This report gives the overall bug count between the time period based on the selected priority, iteration, and area. The number of bugs that are active, new, reactivated, and resolved as fixed are all shown on this report. The graphical view shows the count per day basis. We can change the parameters and rerun the report. It provides the flexibility to export and print the current report. This report is available in both process templates in TFS. The following is the sample graph, which shows the number of bugs in the **TeamTest** team project in TFS.

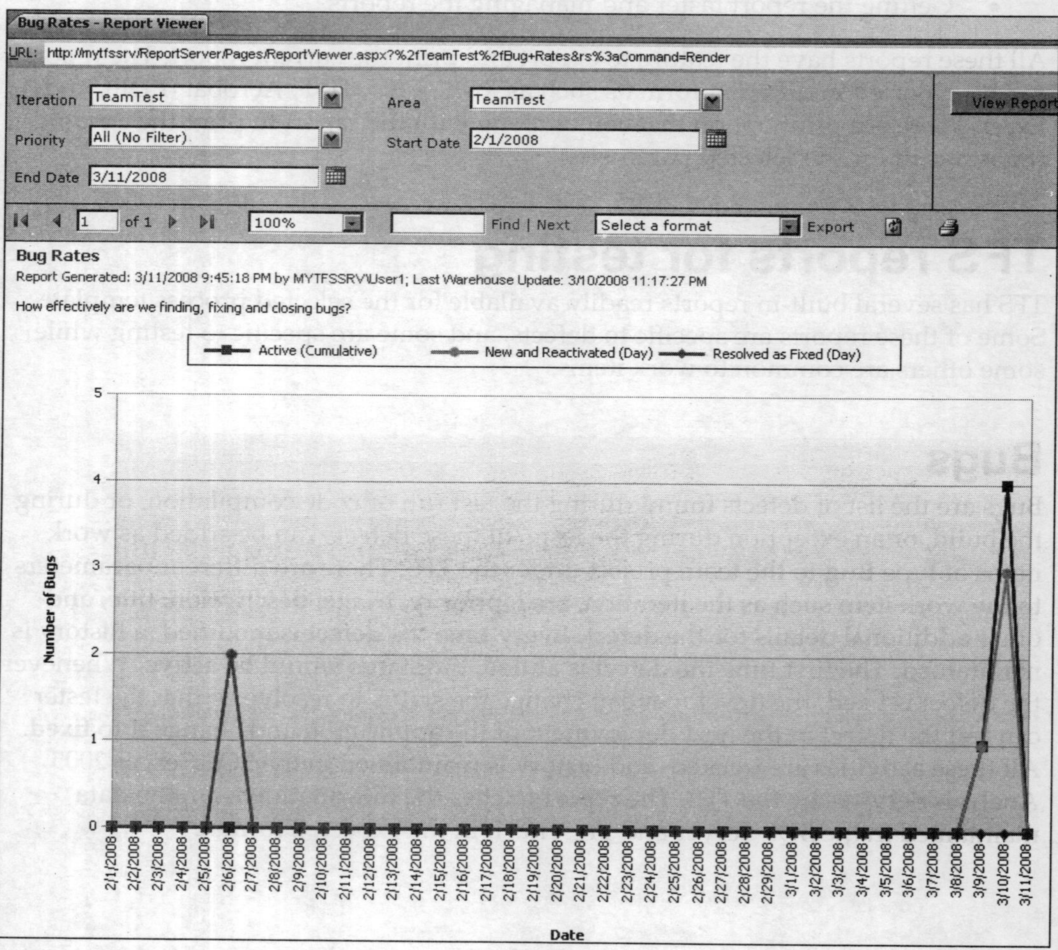

Bugs by priority

This report gives the number of bugs grouped based on the priority and status. The count is presented on a daily basis. This report can be generated based on a date range, iteration, and area. The following screenshot shows the sample of bugs with **Priority 2**. There are no defects with a different priority in the selected date range.

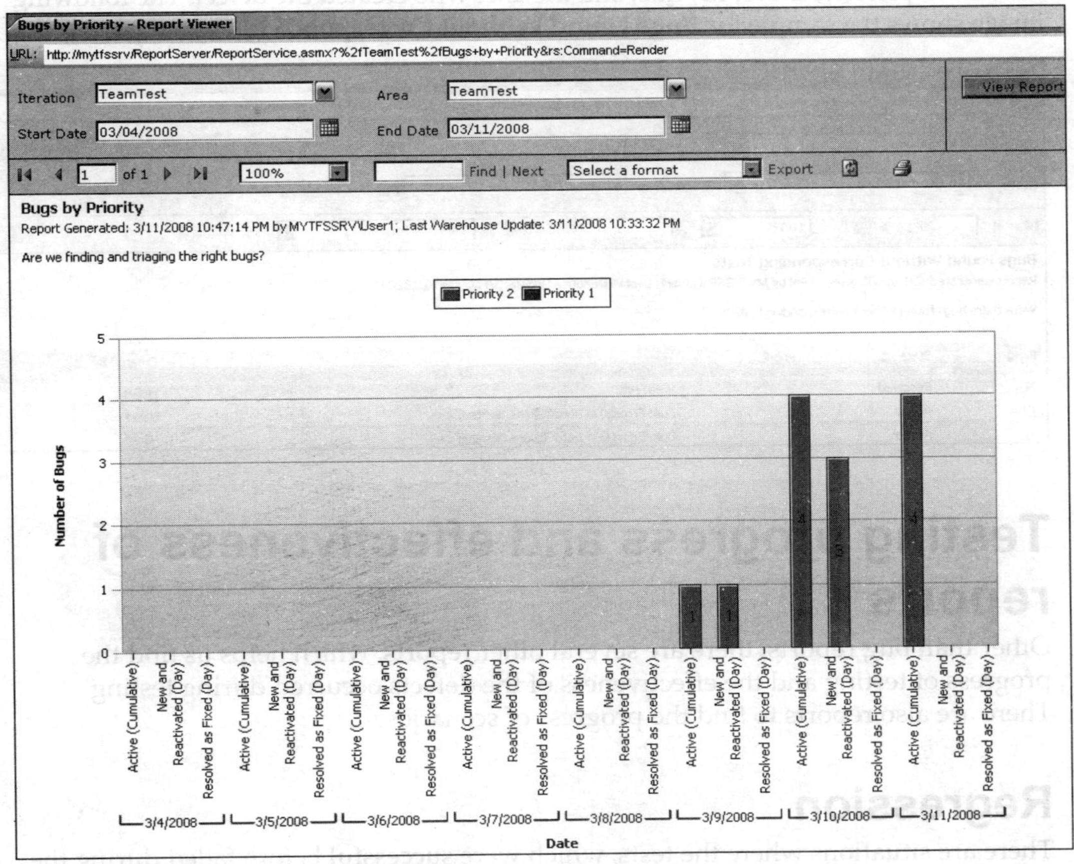

Bugs found without corresponding tests

This report shows the list of defects that were published to the team project but were not part of any test. These are the defects that could have occurred during the code compilation, or it could be an exception that is not part of running the test. We can log any type of error as defect to the team project. This report gives the current state of the defect, priority, defect ID, title, and the user who created the defect. The following image shows the sample for **Bugs Found Without Corresponding Tests** report:

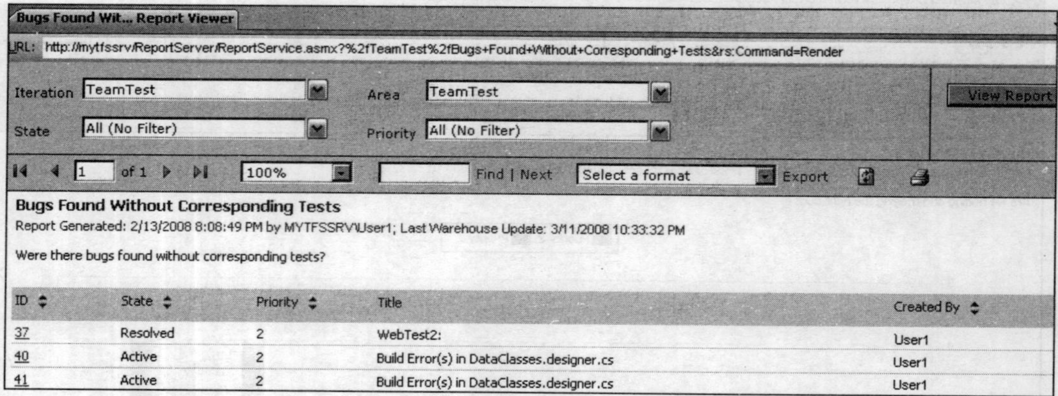

Bugs Found Wit... Report Viewer

URL: http://mytfssrv/ReportServer/ReportService.asmx?%2fTeamTest%2fBugs+Found+Without+Corresponding+Tests&rs:Command=Render

Iteration: TeamTest — Area: TeamTest — View Report

State: All (No Filter) — Priority: All (No Filter)

1 of 1 — 100% — Find | Next — Select a format — Export

Bugs Found Without Corresponding Tests

Report Generated: 2/13/2008 8:08:49 PM by MYTFSSRV\User1; Last Warehouse Update: 3/11/2008 10:33:32 PM

Were there bugs found without corresponding tests?

ID	State	Priority	Title	Created By
37	Resolved	2	WebTest2:	User1
40	Active	2	Build Error(s) in DataClasses.designer.cs	User1
41	Active	2	Build Error(s) in DataClasses.designer.cs	User1

Testing progress and effectiveness of reports

Other than bug reports, there are several other reports, which helps us find the progress of testing and the effectiveness of the defects occurred during testing. There are also reports to find the progress of scenarios.

Regression

There are situations where the tests, which were successful before failed during the rerun. It could be because of various factors such as the new changes to the code, or change in the data source, or any change to any of the environment. The following report shows the test name, category, and the machine name:

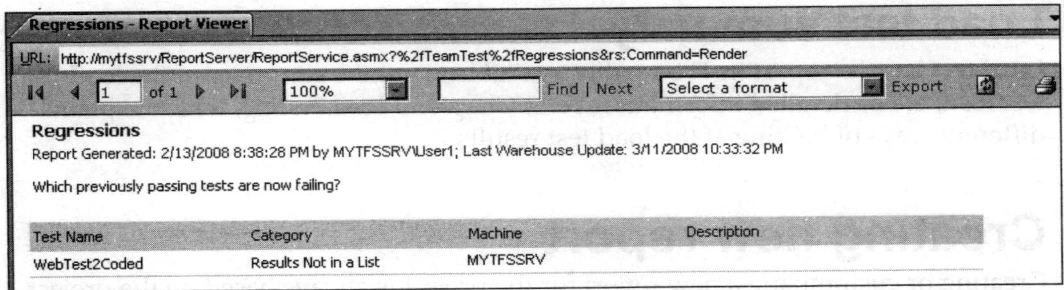

Tests passing with active bugs

This report shows all the active bugs from the tests that are passing. This could be because the bug is not affecting the test, or that the bug is fixed but the status is not changed. For example, there could be a bug during the test because the network connection was broken during the test and the bug is logged. Immediately after this the connection could come up and pass the test when it is rerun. The following screenshot shows the sample report which lists the passed tests with the active bugs. The list contains the **Bug ID** with the URL attached to it. This URL will open the bug details page to know more about the defect.

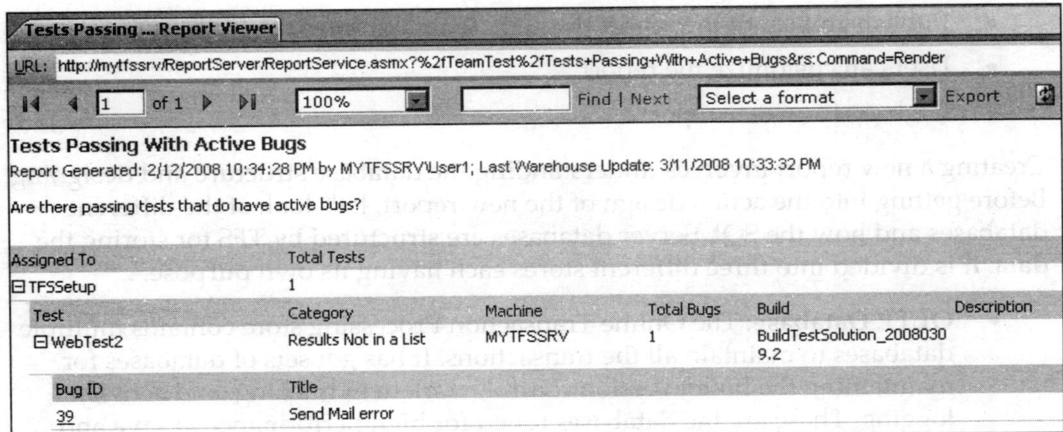

Tests failing without active bugs

This report is similar to the previous one, but this report lists the tests that are failing without any active bugs associated to it. If the test is failing and there is no defect to fix that means there is something missing. Either the defects are not logged in correctly or there is some issue with the test run itself. All these things would be covered with the use of this report.

Load test summary

Load test has the report in TFS readily available to get the summary of the load test results. For detailed information, refer Chapter 5 *Load Testing*, which explains different ways of looking at the load test results.

Creating new report

Creating or customizing a new report for the project is always based on the project reporting requirement. In some cases, the existing reports may not be suitable or will not provide enough information required for the project. In TFS, all the information is stored in MS SQL Server, and it uses the SQL Reporting Service and Analysis Services for reporting purposes. With the existing installation of Visual Studio, we cannot create a new report or customize the existing report. It requires an additional tool called the Business Intelligence Development Studio, which comes along with the SQL Server 2005. There is another option in MS EXCEL, which uses the **pivot** tables to get data from the SQL Server databases and present it in spreadsheet. However, the following are possible if we are planning to use Visual Studio for creating reports:

- Write your own SQL queries to get the data
- Publish and share the report through Team Explorer
- User can customize the report
- High performance report

Creating a new report involves understanding the database structure and designing. Before getting into the actual design of the new report, let's look at the different databases and how the SQL Server databases are structured by TFS for storing the data. It is divided into three different stores each having its own purpose:

- **OLTP Database**: The Online Transaction Processing store contains multiple databases to maintain all the transactions. It has got sets of databases for maintaining the build, version control, work item tracking, and activity logging. These are the databases tuned for high performance to save and retrieve the transactions online.
- **Relational Warehouse**: This store is built for queries instead of online transactions. This database is optimized for queries and reporting instead of transactions. Data is transferred into these databases periodically using adapters collecting data from the tools like work item tracking, build, and other tools.

- **OLAP Cube:** The third one is the Online Analysis Processing Database, which stores the historical data for future reference. It has its own query language. This can be maintained and accessed using the SQL Server Analysis Services.

We will be using the above database for building and designing our new report. The warehouse database is broken down into dimensions and facts, which is more important for the reports. The dimensions are the parameters, and facts are the actual values. Parameters are used for controlling the data to be fetched from the store while the facts are the actual values like the count of defects or build number or work item ID. You can explore more on these databases and tables using the SQL Server Management Studio. The `TfsWareHouse` is the name of the warehouse database in SQL Server.

We will start designing a new report, so let's not go into the details of the database. To get started with reports, we have to make sure we have the required tools. The following are the list of tools required:

- The TFS installed and is available for the clients
- SQL Server client tools containing the Business Intelligence Development Studio, which is mandatory
- VSTS

Report server project

After installing the required tools, Visual Studio will have the **Report Server Project** in the **Templates** of the **Project types** list. Otherwise, we can also launch the Visual Studio using the **SQL Server Business Intelligence Development Studio** menu option available under the Windows Programs menu.

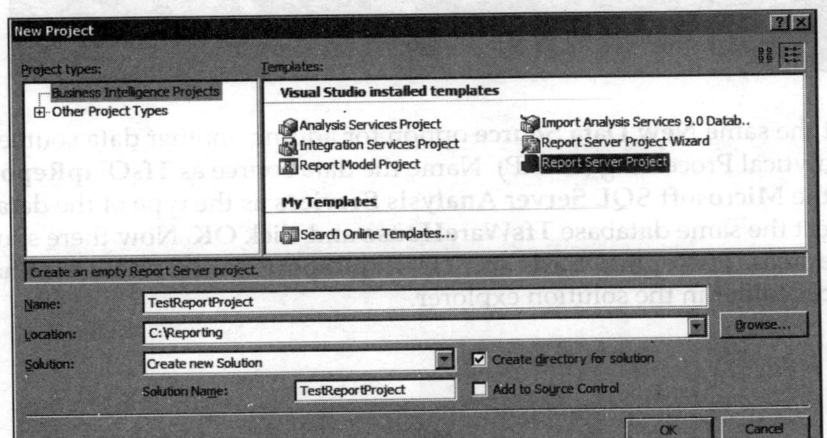

Select the **Report Server Project**, name it and select **OK**. The solution and project get created and the project contains two folders, **Shared Data Sources** and **Reports**. For creating the report, we need to connect to the OLTP and warehouse databases. Create or add the data sources by following these steps:

1. Select the option **Add New Data Source** by right-clicking the **Shared Data Sources**.
2. **Name** the data source as **TfsReportDS**. The name is important here as most of the reports in Team Foundation Server are using this data source name.
3. Select **Microsoft SQL Server** as the **Type** of the data source.
4. Click on the **Edit...** option next to the **Connection String** box and in the new window, select the server name from the list or enter the server name used by the TFS.
5. Select the **TfsWareHouse** database from the list and click on **OK**.

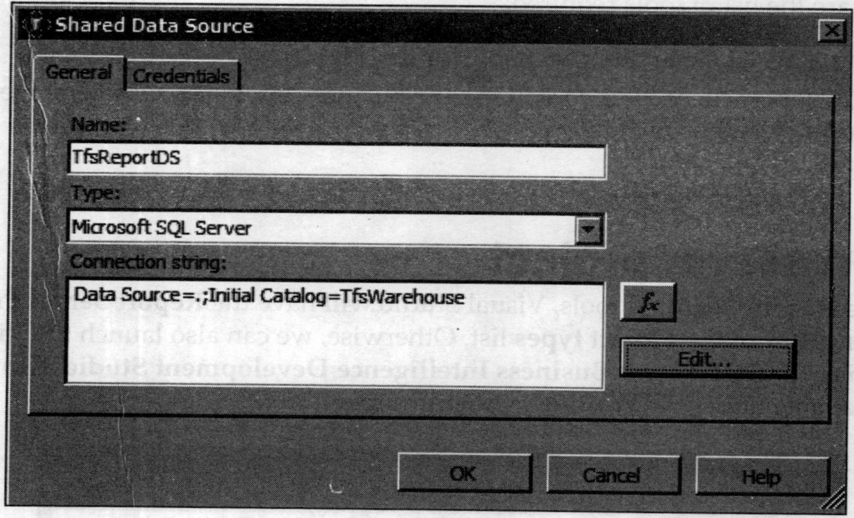

Now select the same **New Data Source** option for adding another data source for Online Analytical Processing (OLAP). Name the data source as **TfsOlapReportDS** and select the **Microsoft SQL Server Analysis Services** as the type of the data source. Select the same database **TfsWareHouse** and click **OK**. Now there should be two data sources, **TfsReportDS.rds** and **TfsOlapReportDS.rds**, under the **Shared Data Sources** folder in the solution explorer.

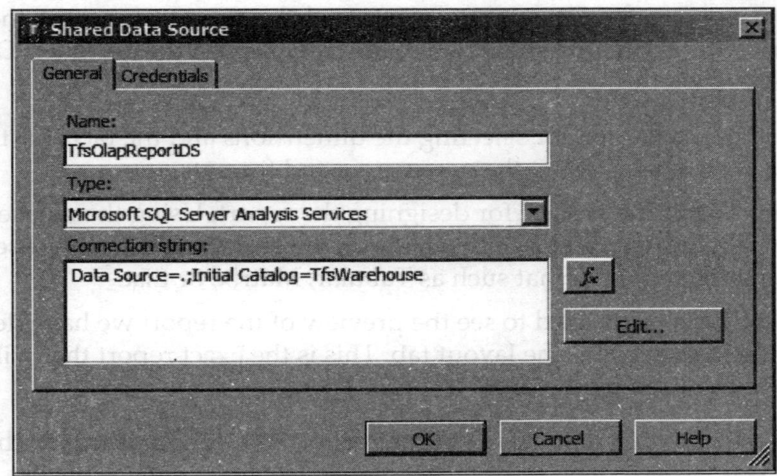

We have created the reporting project in Visual Studio and created the required data sources. Now we can proceed towards creating our report. Follow these steps below to create a new report:

1. Open the Solution Explorer if not opened.
2. Right-click the **Reports** folder and select **Add | New Item**.
3. Select the **Report** template from the available templates.
4. Enter the name for the report and click **OK**.

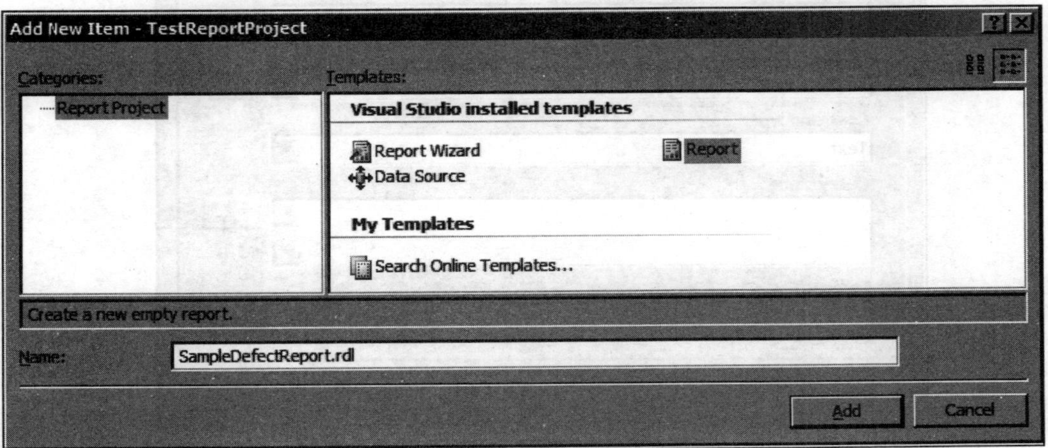

Now the template is ready in the designer, but we have to edit the report and redesign it based on our requirement. There are three tabs in the designer: Data, Layout, and Preview.

- **Data**: This tab is used for selecting the dimensions and the facts for the report. It also helps select the parameters and formats.
- **Layout**: This is the surface for designing the report. Using the dataset built in the data tab, we can place the fields on the surface. This is also used for selecting the report format such as Tabular, Matrix, or List.
- **Preview**: This tab is used to see the preview of the report we have designed using the data tab and the layout tab. This is the exact report that will be deployed or used by the user.

Let us see the steps involved in modifying the report to meet our needs in the Data tab:

1. Create a new dataset to get data from the OLAP cube. Select the **<New Dataset...>** option from the **Dataset** drop-down list.
2. Enter the name for the data set as **DataSet1.**
3. Select **tfsOlapReportDS (shared)** and then click **OK**.

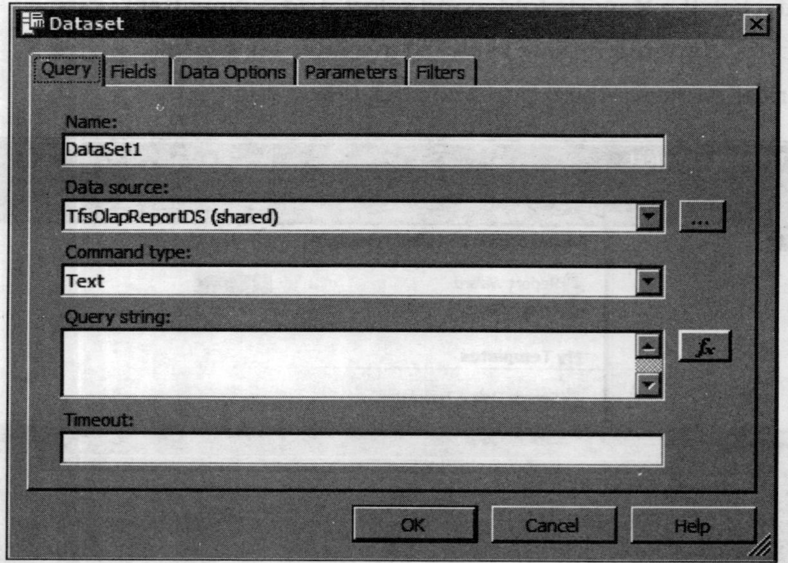

Under the Dataset selection option we can see the Build Cube selected by default. Select the option in the cube box to open the cube selection window and select the **Team System Cube**, which contains all the cubes. The cube is totally based on the type of data we need for the report design. Let us select the Team System cube.

The **Data** tab now contains four different sections—Metadata, Calculated members, Query Results, and Dimensions or filters. The **Metadata** section contains all the dimensions and facts from the cube, which we will select for the report.

Now let's try building a simple defect report, which contains only three or four fields to show the details such as the bug title, the bug current status, and the status change count for each defect. We will also add parameters for data range and bug status. Follow these steps to select the dimensions and facts for the query:

1. In the **Metadata** tab, under **Measures,** we can see all the dimensions from the Team System Cube. Scroll down in the list and select the **Work Item** dimension and select the **Work Item.Title** and drag that onto the query results surface. Do the same thing for **Work Item.State**.
2. Lets us also try to get the history of state change counts for the defects. To do this, Expand Work Item History under Measures and select **State Change Count** and then drag-and-drop that onto the query results surface. Keep selecting whatever data is needed for the report.
3. Now we have selected the data to be presented on the report but not the filters. Let us select the date filter and the work item state and type as filters and parameters for filtering the data:
    a. Select the **Team Project.Team Project** attribute in the **Team Project** dimension from the list in the **Metadata** and drag-and-drop that into the **Dimensions section**. In the **Filters** area, select the Team Project dimension from the grid and select and choose the team project in the **Filter Expressions** drop-down. This will filter the displayed results.
    b. Select the **Date.Date** attribute under the **Date** dimension and drop that into the **Dimension** area. In the **Hierarchy** drop-down, select the format for the date. To have the date range, select the option **Range(Inclusive)** option from the drop-down under the **Operator** column. To make the date to be parameterized, select the check boxes against the **Date** dimension under the column heading **Parameters**.
    c. Select the **Work Item.State** attribute from the **Work Item** dimension and drop that onto the **Dimension** area.

d. The next important thing is the Work Item Type. The above selections will display all the work items irrespective of their types. But we need only the bugs, not the all work items. To filter this, select the **Work Item.Work ItemType** from the **Work Item** dimension and drop that onto the Dimensions filter section. Under the **Filter Expression**, select the type as **Bug**.

4. On dropping the filters and dropping the attributes on the query results area, we can see that the query gets executed and displays the results. This is to verify whether the selection is providing the expected result.

The final **Data** tab of the report would look like the one shown here for the sample report:

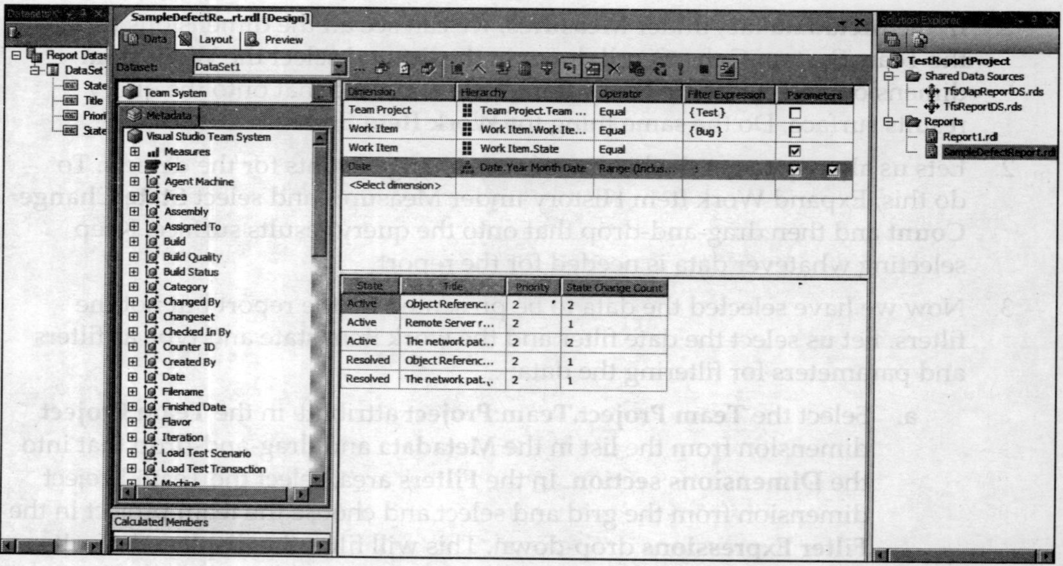

We have the dataset and parameters ready for the report. Now is the time to design the UI for the report and place the fields for the report. To begin this, select the **Layout** tab in the report designer. Keep the Datasets explorer and the Toolbox open. The layout shows the report surface to drop the fields from the dataset. To design the report:

1. Select the format from the **Toolbox** such as **Table**, **Matrix**, or **List** and drop it on the report surface. There are other options like **Subreport** or Chart.
2. Now drag-and-drop the fields from the **Datasets** onto the report. Place the controls from the toolbox and design the report as required. The report layout should be similar to the one shown as follows:

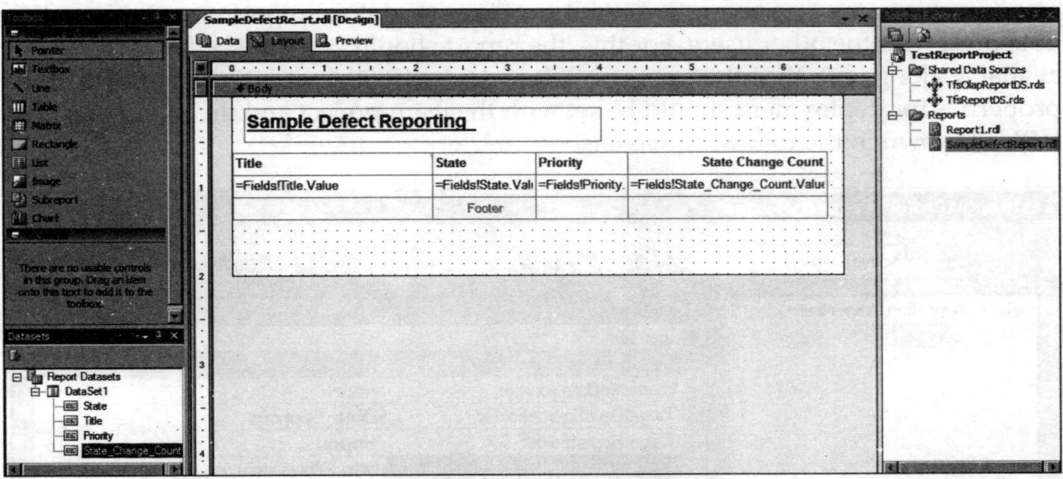

The dataset is ready and report layout is ready. Now, we can check the preview and finalize the report to see if it is as per expectations. We can go back to the layout or data tabs anytime and modify the report. The **Preview** tab shows the parameters for selection. This is based on the **Parameters** checkbox selection against the filter expression in the **Data** tab. Once you select the parameters and click on **View report,** you can see the actual report generated. The final report preview would be similar to the one shown next. The preview also has the option to print, export to a file in different formats, or refresh the report.

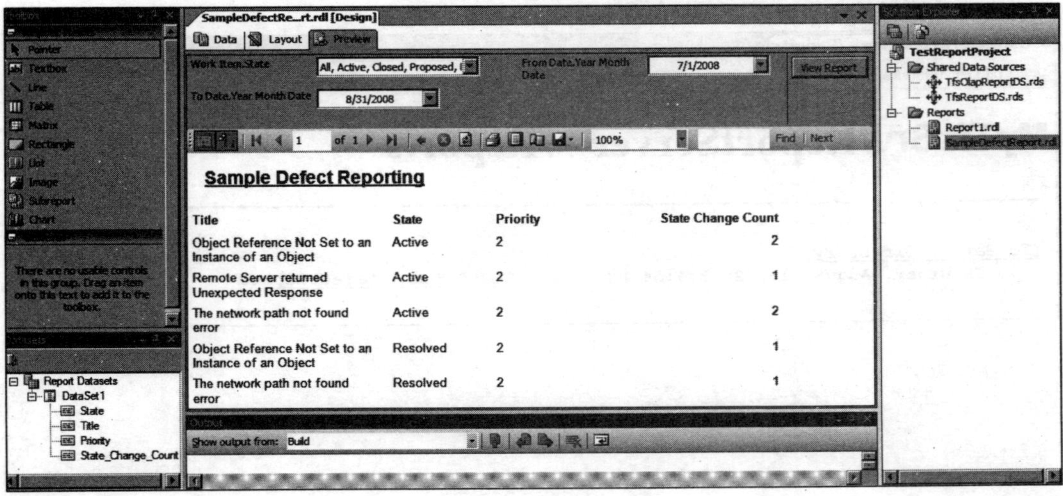

The report is now complete and verified, and is a standalone report now. It has to be shared with the other users. For this, the report should be published and made available along with the other reports. Before deploying the report, the report project properties for deployment should be set with the team project and the report server URL as shown in the following screenshot:

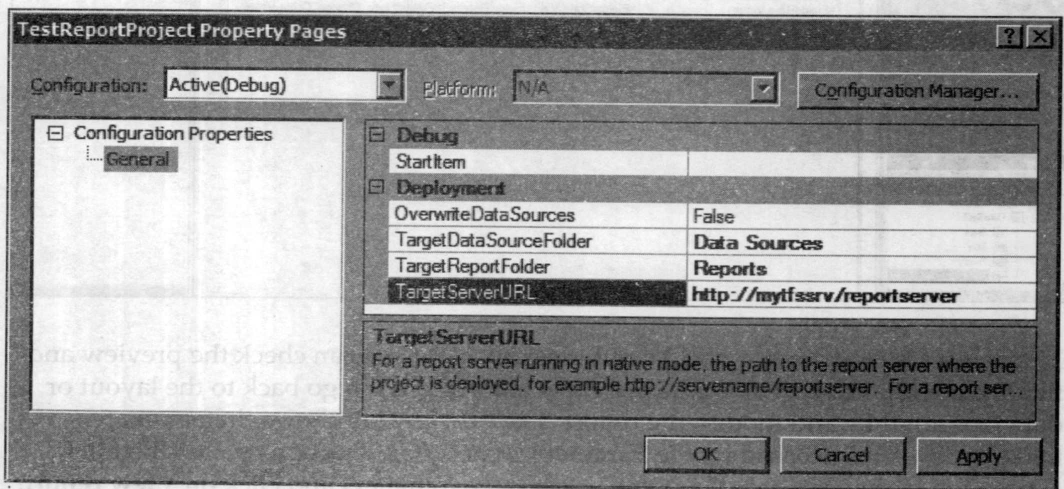

Build the report and deploy it using the **Deploy** option under the **Build** menu. Wait for the deployment succeeded message and then open the URL to which the report is deployed. As per the above example, it should be at the URL as follows:

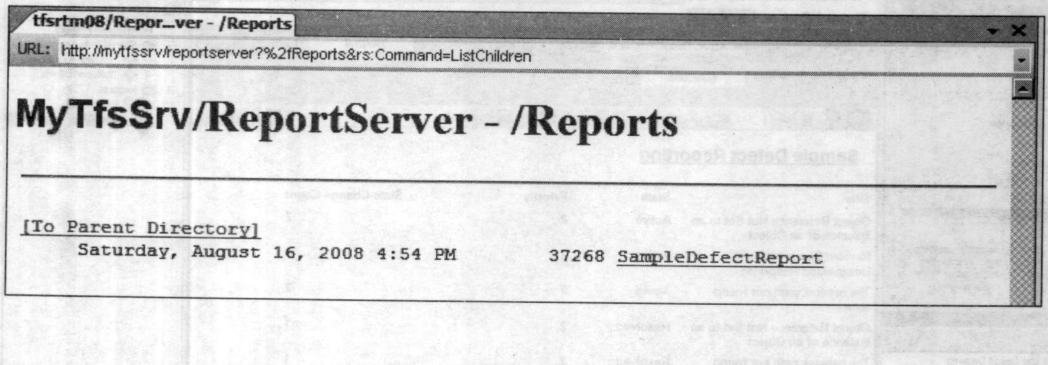

When you click the report name **SampleDefectReport**, it will open the report, which is the same as the one we saw in the **Preview** tab of the report designer.

We can add the report to the Team Foundation Process template so that the other team projects can make use of the new report. This can be done by following the steps as shown:

1. Select the menu option **Process Template Manager** under **Team | Team Foundation Server Settings** menu in Visual Studio and select the process you would like to add to the report. Download the process template to your local machine.
2. Open the downloaded process template file using Visual Studio menu option **Tools | Process Editor | Process Templates | Open Process Template** and select the **Reports** from the **Methodology** tree view. Upload the **SampleDefectReport.rdl** file that we created and save that file after providing the name and the data sources.

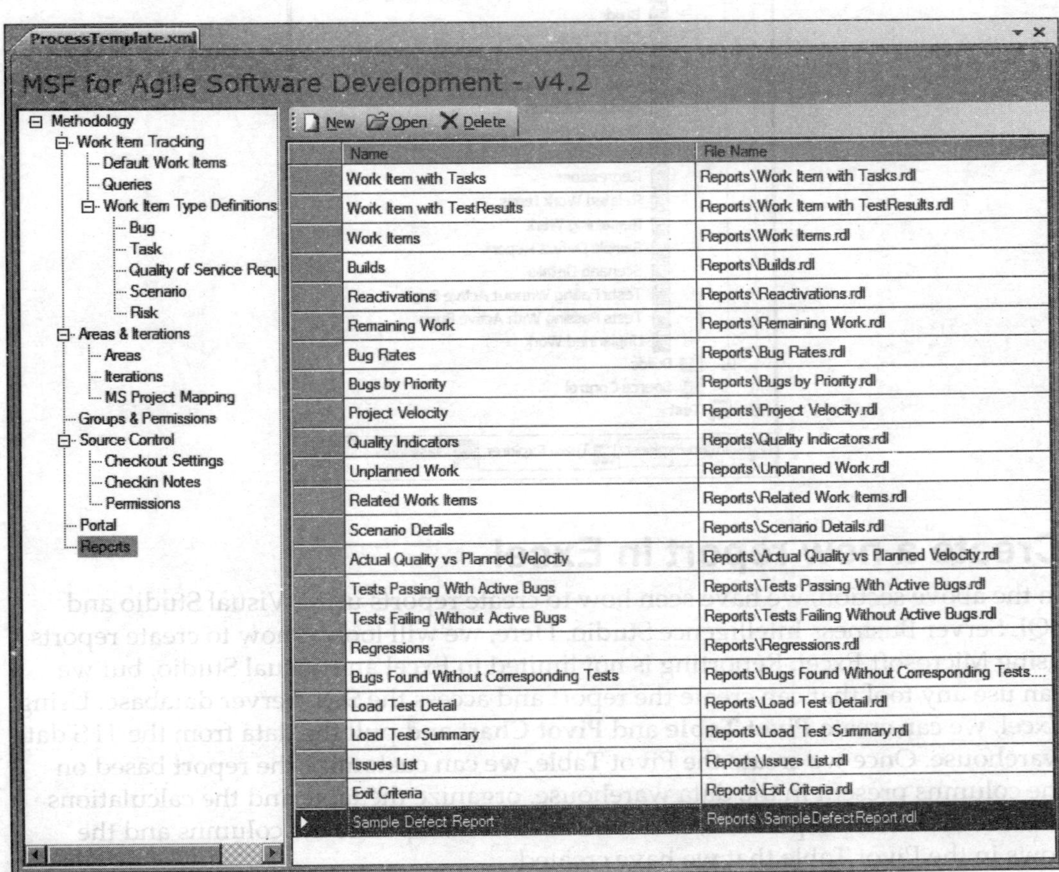

3. Open the **Process Template Manager** and upload the modified Process template file using the **Upload** option in the Process Template manager. Now the process template is uploaded to the TFS.

4. Create a new team project and check the reports. The list should have the new report **SampleDefectReport** in the list as shown here with the highlight report:

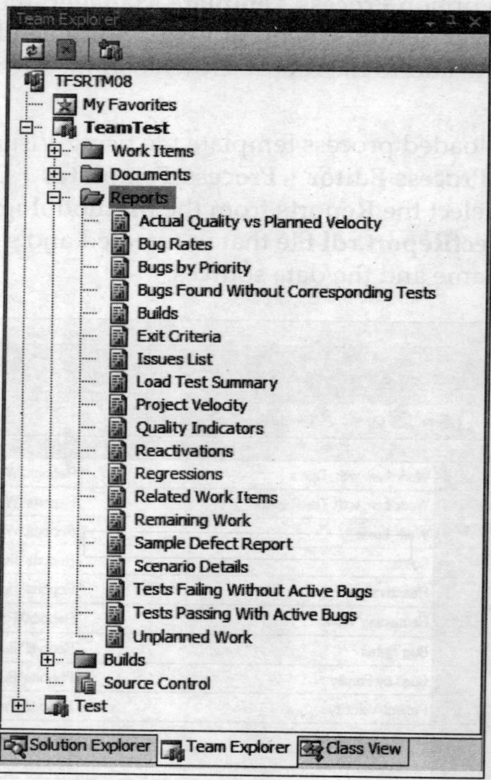

Create a new report in Excel

In the above section, we have seen how to create reports using Visual Studio and SQL Server Business Intelligence Studio. Here, we will look at how to create reports using Microsoft Excel. Reporting is not limited to Excel and Visual Studio, but we can use any tool that can create the report and access the SQL Server database. Using Excel, we can create **Pivot Table** and **Pivot Chart** and pull the data from the TFS data warehouse. Once we create the Pivot Table, we can customize the report based on the columns present in the data warehouse, organize the table and the calculations that the table should perform, and we can even manipulate the columns and the rows in the Pivot Table that we have created.

To get connected to the SQL Server database and the TFS data warehouse, the user must have enough access to read the data from the warehouse to use the Excel report. The user should be a member of the **TfsWarehouseDataReaders** security role in the Analysis Services, and the member will have server-wide privileges and can perform any task within the instance of the Analysis Services.

The prerequisites are:

- Microsoft Excel
- Microsoft SQL Server 2005 Analysis Services 9.0 OLE DB Provider
- User should be member of the TfsWareHouseDataReaders security role

Creating the Pivot Table and placing the field is very simple in Excel. The following are the steps to create report in MS Excel 2007:

1. Open the Excel workbook for creating the report and select the **Data** menu and select **Get External Data.**
2. Select **From Other Sources | From Analysis Services,** which will display the **Data Connection Wizard**. In the **Data Connection Wizard, Connect to Server,** enter the name of the SQL Server name used by the TFS in the **Server Name** text box.
3. Click **Next** to get the dialog **Data Connection Wizard, Select Database and Table.** Select the **TfsWareHouse** database from the drop-down and select the **Team System** cube from the list.

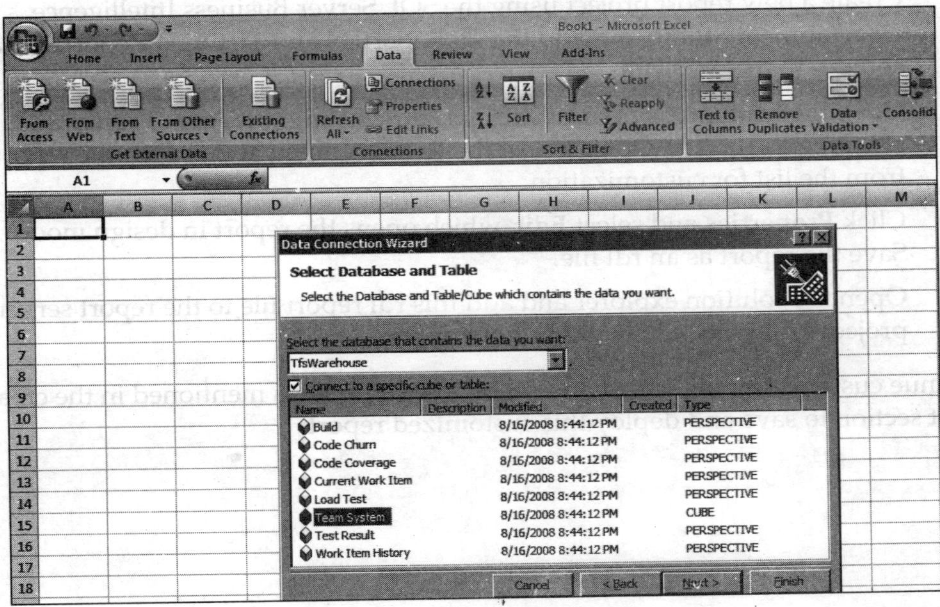

4. Click **Next** and select finish in the dialog window **Data Connection Wizard – Save Data Connection File and Finish**, which opens the **Import Data** dialog window. Select **Pivot Table Report** and click **OK**, which displays the Pivot Table fields list.
5. Select a measure group and then select a measure for that particular measure group. From the **Pivot Table** fields list pane, select necessary fields and drag it to the row labels box and column labels box. To filter the report, select the fields and drag it to the **Report Filter** box. Repeat this step until we have selected all the required fields in the corresponding columns and rows.

Now the report is ready in Excel. It can be saved in normal XLS, XML, or in any other supported file format.

Customizing report

In the previous sections, we have seen how to create a new report using the report designer and add the new report to the process template. There are chances that the existing report in Visual Studio can be reused with minimum changes, or can be modified to suit our needs. In this scenario, we might have to customize the existing report and use it. All the processes are the same as those for creating the new report except that we have to export the existing report, attach it to the new report server project, and then modify it. After updating the report we have to upload it again and use it. Follow these steps to customize a report:

1. Create a new report project using the SQL Server Business Intelligence Development Studio and add the TfsReportDS and TfsOLAPReportDS data sources to the project.
1. Open the team project portal site by right-clicking the **Team Project** and selecting the option **Open**. Select the **Reports** menu and choose the report from the list for customization.
2. Click **Properties** and select **Edit**, which opens the report in design mode. Save the report as an rdl file.
3. Open the solution explorer and add this rdl report file to the report server project using the **Add existing item** option.

Continue customizing the report and follow the same steps mentioned in the create report section to save and deploy this customized report.

Summary

This chapter explained the different ways of presenting what is available to the user so that they know the current progress and the quality of the project. There are lot of in-built reports and queries to get the details from the TFS data store. Using SQL Server reporting and Business Intelligence Development Studio and Visual Studio, it is very easy to create and customize reports. We have seen both these in this chapter. The deployment is the easiest among all the steps. The process template can also be updated very easily by including the new report and uploading it back to TFS. This will help the new team projects inherit the template and use the new report that is readily available now. Even if the user does not have Visual Studio or SQL Server client installed on the machine, the report can easily be created using Microsoft Excel and easily customized.

Index

A

B

C

Q

R

S

T

U

V

W

X

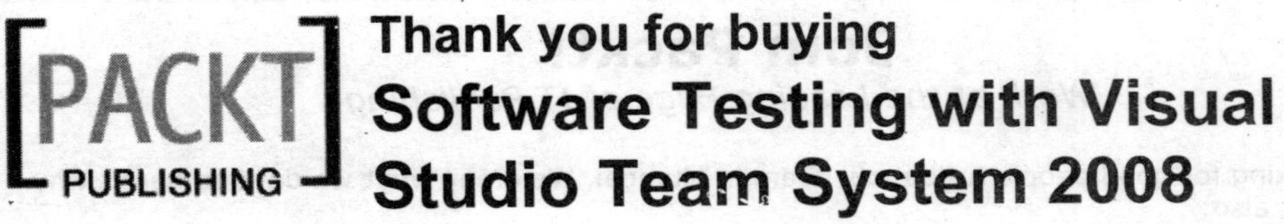

Thank you for buying Software Testing with Visual Studio Team System 2008

About Packt Publishing

Packt, pronounced 'packed', published its first book "*Mastering phpMyAdmin for Effective MySQL Management*" in April 2004 and subsequently continued to specialize in publishing highly focused books on specific technologies and solutions.

Our books and publications share the experiences of your fellow IT professionals in adapting and customizing today's systems, applications, and frameworks. Our solution based books give you the knowledge and power to customize the software and technologies you're using to get the job done. Packt books are more specific and less general than the IT books you have seen in the past. Our unique business model allows us to bring you more focused information, giving you more of what you need to know, and less of what you don't.

Packt is a modern, yet unique publishing company, which focuses on producing quality, cutting-edge books for communities of developers, administrators, and newbies alike. For more information, please visit our website: `www.packtpub.com`.

Writing for Packt

We welcome all inquiries from people who are interested in authoring. Book proposals should be sent to `author@packtpub.com`. If your book idea is still at an early stage and you would like to discuss it first before writing a formal book proposal, contact us; one of our commissioning editors will get in touch with you.

We're not just looking for published authors; if you have strong technical skills but no writing experience, our experienced editors can help you develop a writing career, or simply get some additional reward for your expertise.

Shroff / Packt Publishing Reprints

ISBN	Title	Author	Year	Price
9788184045802	**Active Directory Disaster Recovery, *256 Pages***	**Rommel**	**2008**	**325.00**
9788184045802	**Active Directory Disaster Recovery, *256 Pages***	**Rommel**	**2008**	**325.00**
9788184042436	Advanced Microsoft Content Management Server Development, *544 Pages*	Ying	2005	475.00
9788184042443	**Ajax and PHP: Building Responsive Web Applications, *288 Pages***	**Darie**	**2008**	**250.00**
9788184046700	**Alfresco Developer Guide: Customizing Alfresco with actions, web scripts, web forms, workflows, and more, *560 Pages***	**Potts**	**2009**	**525.00**
9788184046717	**Apache OFBiz Development: The Beginner's Tutorial, *476 Pages***	**Howell**	**2009**	**475.00**
9788184045772	**Apache JMeter, *144 Pages***	**Halili**	**2008**	**225.00**
8184046176175	**ASP.NET 3.5 Application Architecture and Design, 264 Pages**	**Thakur**	**2008**	**300.00**
9788184046724	**ASP.NET 3.5 Social Networking, *582 Pages***	**Siemer**	**2009**	**550.00**
9788184044621	**ASP.NET Data Presentation Controls Essentials, *258 Pages***	**Kanjilal**	**2007**	**325.00**
9788184042382	BPEL Cookbook, *186 Pages*	Blanvalet	2006	200.00
9788184046014	**Business Process Driven SOA using BPMN and BPEL, *334 Pages***	**Juric**	**2008**	**400.00**
8184046236236	**Building Powerful and Robust Websites with Drupal 6, *382 Pages***	**Mercer**	**2008**	**450.00**
9788184042412	Building Telephony Systems with Asterisk, *178 Pages*	Gomillion	2005	200.00
9788184042405	Building Websites with Joomla!, *342 Pages*	Graf	2006	350.00
9788184042467	Building Websites with Mambo: A Step by Step Tutorial, *250 Pages*	Graf	2005	275.00
9788184042474	Building Websites with Microsoft Content Management Server, *638 Pages*	Ying	2004	550.00
9788184042320	Building Websites with PHP - Nuke, *322 Pages*	Paterson	2005	350.00
9788184042399	Building Websites with VB.NET and DotNETNuke 4, *338 Pages*	Egan	2006	350.00
9788184042245	Business Process Execution Language for Web Services, 2/ed, *374 Pages*	Mathew	2004	375.00
9788184043907	**Business Process Management with JBoss jBPM, *220 Pgs***	**Cumberlidge**	**2007**	**250.00**
9788184044607	**Catalyst Accelerating Perl Web Application Development, *202 Pgs***	**Rockway**	**2007**	**275.00**
9788184045734	**CakePHP Application Development, *336 Pages***	**Bari**	**2008**	**425.00**
9788184046731	**CISSP in 21 Days: Boost your confidence and get a competitive edge to crack the exam, *324 Pages***	**Srinivasan**	**2009**	**350.00**
9788184043891	**CodeIgniter for Rapid PHP Application Development, *262 Pages***	**Upton**	**2007**	**325.00**
9788184045727	**ColdFusion 8 Developer Tutorial, *404 Pages***	**Farrar**	**2008**	**475.00**
9788184042368	Configuring IPCop Firewalls: Closing Borders with Open Source, *244 Pgs*	Dempster	2006	275.00
9788184042313	Creating your MySQL Database: Practical Design Tips and Techniques, *108 Pages*	Delisle	2006	125.00
9788184042290	Designing and Implementing Linux Firewalls and QoS Using Netfiler, Iproute, NAT and L7 - Filter, *288 Pages*	Gheorghe	2006	300.00
9788184046748	**Django 1.0 Template Development, *276 Pages***	**Newman**	**2009**	**325.00**
9788184042283	DNS in Action: A Detailed and Practical Guide to DNS Implementation, Configuration and Adminstration, *198 Pages*	Dostalek	2006	225.00
9788184043969	**Documentum Content Management Foundations: EMC Proven Professional Certification Exam E20-120 Study Guide, *284 Pages***	**Kumar**	**2007**	**350.00**

ISBN	Title	Author	Year	Price
9788[illegible]044706	Drupal 5 Themes, *262 Pages*	Shreves	2007	325.00
9788184046755	Drupal 6 Site Builder Solutions, *356 Pages*	Noble	2009	375.00
9788184046774	Drupal 6 Themes, *317 Pages*	Shreves	2009	350.00
9788184046762	Drupal for Education and E-Learning, *404 Pages*	Fitzgerald	2009	400.00
9788184046786	Drupal Multimedia, *268 Pages*	Winborn	2009	325.00
9788184046168	DWR Java AJAX Applications, *232 Pages*	Salkosuo	2008	300.00
9788184045307	EJB 3 Developer Guide, *276 Pages*	Sikora	2008	275.00
9788184042306	Enhancing Microsoft Content Management Server with ASP.NET 2.0, *226 Pages*	Harbar	2006	250.00
9788184046212	Entity Framework Tutorial, *232 Pages*	Kanjilal	2008	300.00
9788184046069	Expert Python Programming, *376 Pages*	Ziade	2008	450.00
9788184042429	GDI + Custom Controls with Visual C# 2005, *276 Pages*	Serban	2006	300.00
9788184043884	Google Web Toolkit: GWT Java Ajax Programming, *248 Pages*	Chaganti	2007	300.00
9788184044089	Java EE 5 Development using GlassFish Application Server, *426 Pages*	Heffelfinger	2007	450.00
8184046186182	Java EE 5 Development with NetBeans 6, *404 Pages*	Heffelfinger	2008	400.00
9788184045345	JDBC 4.0 and Oracle JDeveloper for J2EE Development, *446 Pages*	Vohra	2008	500.00
9788184044690	Joomla! Accessibility, *156 Pages*	Connor	2007	250.00
9788184044584	Joomla! Cash Money-making weapons for your Joomla! websiteBrandon, *182 Pages*	Dawson	2007	300.00
9788184046793	Joomla! Web Security, *268 Pages*	Canavan	2009	325.00
9788184043952	jQuery Reference Guide, 268 Pages	Swedberg	2007	325.00
9788184046809	Learning Dojo, *268 Pages*	Svensson	2009	300.00
9788184046816	Learning Ext JS, *328 Pages*	Frederick	2009	350.00
9788184045369	Learning Facebook Application Development, *240 Pages*	Hayder	2008	300.00
9788184042337	Learning Jakarta Struts 1.2, *222 Pages*	Wiesner	2005	225.00
9788184043921	Learning Joomla! 1.5 Extension Development: Creating Modules, Components, and Plugins with PHP, *178 Pages*	LeBlanc	2007	250.00
9788184046823	Learning Joomla! 1.5 Extension Development, *288 Pages*	LeBlanc	2009	325.00
9788184043976	Learning jQuery: Better Interaction Design and Web Development with Simple JavaScript Techniques, *380 Pages*	Swedberg	2007	425.00
9788184046830	Learning Nagios 3.0, *320 Pages*	Kocjan	2009	350.00
9788184043877	Learning PHP Data Objects, *188 Pages*	Poppel	2007	225.00
9788184046847	Lighttpd, *240 Pages*	Bogus	2009	275.00
9788184044638	LINQ Quickly A practical guide to programming Language Integrated Query with C#, *254 Pages*	Kumar	2007	325.00
9788184044737	Lotus Notes Domino 8 Upgrader's Guide, *278 Pages*	Speed	2007	325.00
9788184044713	Managing eZ Publish Web Content Management Projects, *322 Pages*	Bauer	2007	375.00
9788184044539	Managing Software Development with Trac and Subversion, *122 Pgs*	Murphy	2007	200.00
9788184044676	Mastering Joomla! 1.5 Extension and Framework Development, *490 Pgs*	Kennard	2007	500.00
9788184042252	Mastering Mambo E-Commerce, Templates, Module Development, SEO, Security and Performance, *306 Pages*	Hauser	2005	325.00
9788184044003	Mastering OpenLDAP: Configuring, Securing and Integrating Directory Services, *484 Pages*	Butcher	2007	450.00

ISBN	Title	Author	Year	Price
9788184042351	Mastering PHPMyAdmin 2.8 for Effective MySQL Management, *316 Pages*	Delisle	2004	350.00
9788184043853	Microsoft AJAX Library Essentials: Client-side ASP.NET AJAX 1.0 Explained, *300 Pages*	Darie	2007	300.00
9788184045604	Microsoft Visual C++ Windows Applications by Example, *438 Pgs*	Björnander	2008	400.00
9788184045710	Moodle 1.9 E-Learning Course Development, *388 Pages*	Rice	2008	450.00
9788184046854	Moodle Administration, *380 Pages*	Büchner	2009	425.00
9788184046861	Moodle Course Conversion: Beginner's Guide, *320 Pages*	Wild	2009	350.00
9788184045338	Mobile Web Development, 238 Pages	Mehta	2008	300.00
9788184044591	Moodle Teaching Techniques, *194 Pages*	Rice IV	2007	275.00
9788184045703	Object-Oriented JavaScript, *360 Pages*	Stefanov	2008	375.00
9788184044546	Object-Oriented Programming with PHP5, *274 Pages*	Hayder	2007	350.00
9788184044010	ODP.NET Developer's Guide: Oracle Database 10g Development with Visual Studio 2005 and the Oracle Data Provider for .NET, *328 Pages*	Pulakhandam	2007	425.00
9788184042238	Open VPN Building and Integrating Virtual Private Networks, *274 Pages*	Feilner	2006	300.00
9788184046076	Oracle Modernization Solutions, *436 Pages*	Laszewski	2008	475.00
9788184045796	Oracle Web Services Manager, *238 Pages*	Lakshminarayanan	2008	300.00
9788184044720	osCommerce Webmaster's Guide to Selling Online, *428 Pages*	Gurevych	2007	450.00
9788184043914	OSWorkflow: A guide for Java developers and architects to integrating open-source Business Process Management, *212 Pages*	Diego	2007	275.00
9788184043945	PHP Oracle Web Development: Data processing, Security, Caching, XML, Web Services, and Ajax, *396 Pages*	Vasiliev	2007	450.00
9788184044096	PHP Web 2.0 Mashup Projects, *306 Pages*	Chow	2007	325.00
9788184044645	Professional Plone Development, *422 Pages*	Aspeli	2007	425.00
9788184044652	Programming Microsoft® Dynamics™ NAV, *482 Pages*	Studebaker	2007	475.00
9788184045291	Programming Windows Workflow Foundation: Practical WF Techniques and Examples using XAML and C#, *256 pages*	Allen	2008	300.00
9788184043983	Project Management with dotProject: Implement, Configure, Customize, and Maintain your DotProject Installation, *232 Pages*	Jordan	2007	300.00
9788184043938	Qmail Quickstarter: Install, Set Up and Run your own Email Server, *152 Pages*	Wheeler	2007	225.00
9788184045352	Quality Assurance for Dyanmics AX-Bassed ERP Solutions, *182 Pages*	Gupta	2008	250.00
9788184046199	RESTful PHP Web Services, *224 Pages*	Abeysinghe	2008	300.00
9788184042269	RSS and Atom: Understanding and Implementing Content Feeds and Syndication, *282 Pages*	Wittenbrink	2005	325.00
9788184044577	Ruby on Rails Enterprise Application Development, *530 Pages*	Smith	2007	525.00
9788184045314	Ruby on Rails Web Mashup Projects, *280 Pages*	Sheong	2008	350.00
9788184045765	SharePoint Designer Tutorial: Working with SharePoint Websites, *190 Pages*	Poole	2008	250.00
9788184042375	Smarty PHP Template Programming and Applications, *256 Pages*	Maia	2006	275.00
9788184046045	SOA Cookbook: Design Recipes for Building Better SOA Processes, *274 Pages*	Havey	2008	350.00
9788184043860	SOA and WS-BPEL, *250 Pages*	Vasiliev	2007	350.00
9788184046205	SOA Governance, 232 Pages	Biske	2008	300.00
9788184045758	Service Oriented Architecture with Java, *196 Pages*	Caselli	2008	250.00

ISBN	Title	Author	Year	Price
9788184045376	**Service Orinted Java Business Integration, *438 Pages***	**Binildas**	**2008**	**500.00**
9788184044553	**SOA Approach to IntegrationXML, Web services, ESB, and BPEL in real-world SOA projects, *376 Pages***	**Juric**	**2007**	**400.00**
9788184046878	**Software Testing with Visual Studio Team System 2008, *360 Pages***	**Kumar**	**2009**	**375.00**
9788184044560	**SQL Server Integration Services Using Visual Studio 2005, *322 Pgs***	**Krishnaswamy**	**2007**	**375.00**
9788184045321	**Swing Extreme Testing, *328 Pages***	**Lavers**	**2008**	**375.00**
9788184044669	**Tapestry 5 Building Web Applications, *272 Pages***	**Kolesnikov**	**2008**	**325.00**
9788184042450	TYPO3: Enterprise Content Management, *626 Pages*	Altmann	2005	525.00
9788184046038	**TYPO3 Extension Development, *238 Pages***	**Dulepov**	**2008**	**300.00**
9788184042276	UML 2.0 in Action: A Project - Based Tutorial, *248 Pages*	Grassle	2005	200.00
9788184042344	Understanding TCP/IP, *482 Pages*	Dostalek	2006	350.00
9788184043990	**Visual SourceSafe 2005 Software Configuration Management in Practice, *406 Pages***	**Serban**	**2007**	**475.00**
9788184046885	**WCF Multi-tier Services Development with LINQ, *380 Pages***	**Liu**	**2009**	**425.00**
9788184046052	**WordPress for Business Bloggers, *360 Pages***	**Thewlis**	**2008**	**425.00**
9788184046021	**WordPress Theme Design: A complete guide to creating professional WordPress themes, 230 Pages**	**Silver**	**2008**	**300.00**
9788184044683	**Xen Virtualization, *148 Pages***	**Chaganti**	**2007**	**225.00**
9788184045741	**Zen Cart: E-commerce Application Development, *318 Pages***	**Sarkar**	**2008**	**375.00**
9788184045789	**Zenoss Core Network and System Monitoring, *282 Pages***	**Badger**	**2008**	**350.00**
9788184044614	**Zimbra Implement, Administer and Manage, *222 Pages***	**Resnick**	**2008**	**300.00**
US EDITION AVAILABLE AT INDIA SPECIAL PRICE:				
9781904811114	Alfresco Enterprise Content Management Implementation, *360 Pages*	Shariff	2006	US$ 59.99
9781904811251	Building and Integrating Virtual Private Networks with Openswan, *360 Pgs*	Wouters	2006	US$ 59.99
9781904811138	Building Online Communities with phpBB 2, *360 Pages*	Stefanov	2005	US$ 39.99
9781904811022	Building Websites with Plone, *416 Pages*	Cooper	2004	US$ 49.99
9781904811923	cPanel User Guide and Tutorial, *208 Pages*	Pedersen	2006	US$ 29.99
9781847190901	Deep Inside osCommerce: The Cookbook, *400 Pages*	Mathé	2006	US$ 49.99
9781904811060	**Domino 7 Lotus Notes Application Development, *228 Pages***	**Speed**	**2007**	**US$ 59.99**
9781847190932	**Hacking Vim: A Cookbook to get the Most out of the Latest Vim Editor, *228 Pages***	**Schulz**	**2007**	**US$ 39.99**
9781904811862	ImageMagick Tricks: Web Image Effects from the Command Line and PHP, *232 Pages*	Salehi	2006	US$ 34.99
9781904811909	JasperReports: Reporting for Java Developers, *344 Pages*	Heffelfinger	2006	US$ 44.99
9781904811015	Learning eZ publish 3: Building Content Management Solutions--Leaders of the eZ publish community guide you through this complex and powerful PHP-based Content Management System, *329 Pages*	Borgermans	2004	US$ 59.99
9781847192721	Liferay Portal Enterprise Intranets, *408 Pages*	Yuan	2008	US$ 59.99
9781904811374	Linux Email: Setup and Run a Small Office Email Server using PostFix, Courier, ProcMail, SquirrelMail, ClamAV and SpamAssassin, *316 Pages*	Taylor	2005	US$ 39.99

ISBN	Title	Author	Year	Price
9781904811299	Moodle E-Learning Course Development, *256 Pages*	Rice	2006	US$ 39.99
9781904811794	PHP Programming with PEAR, *292 Pages*	Stephan	2006	US$ 39.99
9781904811442	PHPEclipse: A User Guide, *228 Pages*	Chow	2006	US$ 29.99
9781904811213	Programming Windows Workflow Foundation: Practical WF Techniques and Examples using XAML and C#, *300 Pages*	Allen	2006	US$ 44.99
9781904811121	SpamAssassin: A Practical Guide to Integration and Configuration, *240 Pgs*	McDonald	2004	US$ 39.99
9781904811077	SSL VPN: Understanding, evaluating and planning secure, web-based remote access, *212 Pages*	Steinberg	2004	US$ 49.99
9781904811633	Upgrading to Lotus Notes and Domino 7, *340 Pages*	Speed	2006	US$ 59.99
9781904811459	User Training for Busy Programmers, *92 Pages*	Rice	2005	US$ 12.99

- **Dates & Prices of forthcoming titles are tentative and subject to change without notice.**
- **All Prices are in Indian Rupees**
- **TITLES RELEASED AFTER January 2007 ARE MARKED IN BOLD.**

For Wholesale enquiries contact:-

SHROFF PUBLISHERS & DISTRIBUTORS PVT. LTD.

C-103, TTC Industrial Area, MIDC, Pawane, Navi Mumbai - 400 705.
Tel: (91 22) 2763 4290 • Fax: (91 22) 2768 3337 • E-mail: spdorders@shroffpublishers.com

Branches:-

Bangalore
7, Sharada Colony, Basaveshwarnagar,
8th Main, Bangalore 560 079
Tel: (91 80) 4128 7393 • Fax: 4128 7392
E-mail: spdblr@shroffpublishers.com

Chennai
23, Damodharan Street, (Old No. 12)
T. Nagar, Chennai - 600 017
Tel: (91 44) 2431 5343 • Fax: 2431 5342
E-mail: spdchennai@shroffpublishers.com

Mumbai
6, M. A. Sarang Marg, (Tandel Street South) Dongri, Mumbai-400 009.
Tel.: (91-22) 6610 7594/95 • Telefax: 6610 7596 • e-mail:spddongri@shroffpublishers.com

Delhi
Basement, 2/11 Ansari Road,
Daryaganj, New Delhi - 110 002
Tel: (91 11) 2324 3337 / 8 • Fax: 2324 3339
E-mail: spddel@shroffpublishers.com

Kolkata
7B Haati Bagan Road,
CIT Paddapukur, Kolkata - 700 014
Tel: (91 33) 2284 9329 / 7954 • Fax: 2835 0795
E-mail: spdkol@shroffpublishers.com

RESIDENT REPRESENTATIVES

Hyderabad	K. Jayashanker	Mobile : 09885059050	E-mail: jayashanker@shroffpublishers.com
Kolhapur	Santosh Patil	Mobile : 09867228324	E-mail: santosh@shroffpublishers.com
Madurai	T. G. Jothikumar	Mobile : 09360653881	E-mail: jothikumar@shroffpublishers.com
Pune	Devendra Shinde	Mobile : 09823953174	E-mail: devendra@shroffpublishers.com

For retail enquiries contact:-

Mumbai

Computer Bookshop (I) Pvt. Ltd.
Kitab Mahal Bldg., Ground Floor, Next to Central Bank of India.
190, Dr. D. N. Road, Fort, Mumbai 400 001
Tel: (91 22) 6631 7922 / 23 / 24 • Fax: 2262 3551
E-mail: cbs@vsnl.com

Sterling Book House
181, Dr. D. N. Road, Fort, Mumbai - 400 001.
Tel. : (91-22) 2267 6046, 2265 9599 • Fax : 2262 3551
E-mail : sbh@vsnl.com • www.sterlingbookhouse.com

Shop #1, Cassinath Building, 172/174,
Dr. D. N. Road, Mumbai - 400 001.
Tel. : (91-22) 2205 4616/17 • Fax: 2205 4620
E-mail : customerservice@bookzone-india.com
www.bookzone-india.com